ROBERT SCHUMANN

THE BOOK OF SONGS

ROBERT SCHUMANN

THE BOOK OF SONGS

Jon W. Finson

HARVARD UNIVERSITY PRESS

Cambridge, Massachusetts

London, England

2007

Library of Congress Cataloging-in-Publication Data
Finson, Jon W.
Robert Schumann : the book of songs / Jon W. Finson.
p. cm.
Includes bibliographical references (p.) and index.
ISBN-13: 978-0-674-02629-2 (alk. paper)
ISBN-10: 0-674-02629-2 (alk. paper)
1. Schumann, Robert, 1810–1856. Songs.   2. Songs—Analysis,
appreciation.   3. Songs—History and criticism.   I. Title.
ML410.S4F59 2007
782.42168092—dc22   2007008166

To the memory of Dorothy Jane Finson

Contents

Preface

At the heart of this book lies a pragmatic aim to summarize and render available the latest research on Schumann's songs to singers, pianists, and the educated musical public. Scholars who are not Schumann specialists may also find its encapsulated descriptions of individual opuses and songs useful, but I do not provide comprehensive or exhaustive explications, analyses, or commentaries on any given song. And while I have researched this book using many original documents, I have also relied on the extensive work now under way for the new Schumann edition in which I will serve as an editor for some lieder. I mean to supplant here a book long since out of date, Eric Sams's *The Songs of Robert Schumann*, which appeared in its last edition over a decade ago and even then did not reflect the most recent state of scholarship. Singers, pianists, and writers of program notes often cite Sams, including some of his inaccuracies. And general aficionados of lieder also consult the volume, even though it has changed little since its original appearance in 1969, while the field of Schumann scholarship has altered greatly.

The information in the present study relies heavily on two extraordinary publications in the new complete edition of Schumann's works, Helmut Schanze and Krischan Schulte's *Literarische Vorlagen der ein- und mehrstimmigen Lieder, Gesänge und Deklamationen* and Margit McCorkle's *Thematisch-Bibliographisches Verzeichnis*. I have also availed myself of Schulte's ". . . *was Ihres Zaubergriffels würdig ware!" Die Textbasis für Robert Schumanns Lieder für Solostimmen*, a companion to *Vorlagen*. The first of these volumes gives all of the texts for Schumann's solo and part songs in parallel versions, the left column with the version that served as the composer's exemplar and the right column recording his departures from the original copy. Schanze and Schulte also provide biographical data for all the poets they could identify and details of how they reached their conclusion about which sources Schumann consulted for his texts (this information appears in parallel English translation). The book is indispensable for anybody working with Schumann's songs in any capacity, and while Schanze and Schulte have not tracked down every source or identified every author, they have come very close. McCorkle's thematic index provides not only incipits and dates of composition and publication but also a wealth of information about correspondence, reviews, extant manuscripts, and secondary bibliographical information. It exists only in German, and so transmitting its information in English has constituted an important task (and I have often looked at the first editions or copies of correspondence to augment McCorkle's already astonishing detail). I count the collation of information about the composition and publication of Schumann's songs as a major benefit of the present volume. It will now become available to those who do not read German or who do not specialize in Schumann scholarship.

The underlying premise of this book maintains that Schumann's songs should be treated by opus (unlike Sams's study, which proceeded chronologically by song). This may seem self-evident for the song cycles we have come to regard as indivisible "works," but it is much less obvious for the many collections that gather settings of one author's poetry but imply no narrative, or for so-called miscellanies that set loose collections of various poets. Schumann gave a good deal of thought to ordering songs for publication even in these last two types of song volumes, often grouping them by key and sometimes by a pattern of content, whether similar or contrasting. By proceeding in this way, I do not mean to suggest that singers and pianists cannot remove songs from their opus for individual performance. During his lifetime, Schumann published individual songs out of context, even removing them from narrative song cycles, not to mention miscellanies. And after the composer died, the widowed Clara Schumann continued to accompany songs detached in just this way from their opuses. In writing this book, I was concerned with what moved Schumann to publish collected songs together under one opus number, especially where no connection is readily apparent. But however he labored to create logical opuses for publication, the composer would have found a categorical ban on excerpting songs from their context for performance odd and perhaps unacceptable.

Within the framework of the basic premise, I have then proceeded in two large chronological groupings. I have addressed the opuses with songs written during Schumann's first efflorescence in song composition, 1840 to 1841, in the first section of the book, while the opuses largely containing songs from the second efflorescence, roughly 1849 to 1851, appear in the second section, devoted to the marked change in his style of setting text. This causes a few minor anomalies, to be sure: opp. 127 and 142, published respectively at the end of the composer's life and posthumously, consist largely or solely of songs written in 1840 and 1841, as do opp. 27 and 51, the first two in the series of *Lieder und Gesänge* published in the late 1840s. Op. 77, on the other hand, though it begins with one famous number from 1840, contains mostly later songs. Majority rule is not so bad a principle as it might first appear in such cases, since Schumann had to rationalize the inclusion of songs from disparate periods in one volume to his publishers and public to satisfy financial considerations and commercial habits. The correspondence with publishers about the various opus numbers reveals that a justification for the content of song volumes constantly occupied the composer's mind, as did other, more technical considerations such as overall length and the placement of page turns.

Within these larger chronological bounds, I have considered songs under various topics, especially for Schumann's first outpouring of lied composition. Collections strongly associated in subject matter to his marriage with Clara, the two parallel Heine cycles, the wayfaring cycles, and the various groups of romances and ballads all belong together logically enough. Within these chapters, central theses arise, about biographical connection, narrative or semantic content, genre, and structure. The composer's second burst of song writing lends itself much less well to this approach, partly because the distinction between "cycles" and "collections" becomes much less pronounced. But for the lieder Schumann composed between 1849 and 1852, the question of his new approach to setting text becomes more acute, and so the grouping of collections by content or genre recedes somewhat in importance at the same time that cultural context comes to the fore.

Since this volume presents a survey, the space devoted to any one opus or any one song is necessarily limited. I have offered a trenchant comment or two on each solo song included, and I have often spent some time on Schumann's changes to the texts that inspired his setting (he felt entitled in many instances to alter the verse even of classic authors). But most songs receive very brief consideration in the interest of wider coverage. One only needs to read an article such as Susan Youens's remarkable essay on "Die beiden Grenadiere" (op. 49, no. 1) to see how much textual and cultural enterprise and meaning attach to just one Schumann song. But applying this wonderful depth of exposition to every Schumann lied would have produced a study running to many, many volumes, impracticable and undesirable here. By the same token, those familiar with Schumann's output will see that I have focused relatively more attention on his later songs than on his earlier ones. With many excellent article- or book-length studies on cycles such as *Dichterliebe, Frauenliebe und Leben,* the Eichendorff *Liederkreis,* the Kerner *Liederreihe,* and other works from the composer's 1840 and 1841 oeuvre, it seemed best to point readers in the direction of the copious literature already at hand after outlining the basic facts and offering some insight. Neglected songs deserved more attention.

One important caveat exists in my selection of lieder: I have followed the organization of the first complete edition in determining which solo songs to include. Thus, in spite of some readers' urgings, I have omitted the *Spanisches Liederspiel,* op. 74, and the *Minnespiel,* op. 101, because they consist of part songs, trios, and duets as much as or more than solo songs. If we accept the integrity of the opus as a governing premise, then different principles determined Schumann's structuring of these collections from those primarily containing solo songs. By the same token, a few duets from works such as *Liebesfrühling,* op. 37, and even a trio (with two additional *ad libitum* voices) from *Lieder für die Jugend,* op. 79, sneak into this book. But Clara Schumann's and Brahms's rule of thumb for the first complete edition (the only one available as I write this) seems the best guide. This edition also served as the textual basis for musical examples.

As an analytical model and as a paradigm for the discussion of German lieder altogether, I have adopted the approach formulated by the editor of the solo songs for the new Schubert complete edition, Walther Dürr, in his incisive *Das deutsche Sololied im 19. Jahrhundert: Untersuchung zur Sprache und Musik.* No other book extant in either German or English today addresses either the aesthetic background of the German lied in the nineteenth century or the complex interactions of text and music in songs of the period as well as Dürr's. Any serious student of the lied from the late eighteenth to the early twentieth century must acquaint himself or herself with this study. I cannot pretend to a knowledge of German poetic form as thorough and profound as Dürr's, but I have relied on Otto Paul and Ingeborg Glier's classic *Deutsche Metrik* for basic guidance about versification. And Heinrich Schwab's *Sangbarkeit, Popularität und Kunstlied. Studien zu Lied und Liedästhetik der mittleren Goethezeit 1770–1814* has provided immensely useful background information about norms of genre leading up to the epoch of the "polyrhythmic lied" (Dürr's term, adapted from the nineteenth-century Swiss critic Nägeli).

The large number of studies specifically devoted to Schumann's songs, many of them in German, also informed much of my discussion. Aside from books devoted to particular opuses, the relatively recent series of *Schumann Forschungen* and *Schumann Studien* contain many helpful articles. I have cited the appropriate volumes generally in the bibliography, with specific references in the appropriate chapters to particular articles in the context of the works they discuss. But I have not duplicated entries for each article in the bibliography, and readers will need to turn to particular opuses to find the contributions of those authors.

A number of scholars have offered very helpful advice and support concerning this study. Chief among these are the musicologists at the Schumann Research Center in Düsseldorf, Bernhard Appel, Matthias Wendt, and particularly Kazuko Ozawa, who has an almost encyclopedic knowledge of Schumann's songs. Without their gracious hospitality and generously granted access to materials, I could not have written this book. I have also appreciated the help of Gerd Nauhaus (now retired) and Ute Bär at the Robert Schumann House in Zwickau, as well as the willingness of Otto Biba at the Gesellschaft der Musikfreunde in Vienna and Helmut Hell at the Music Division of the Staatsbibliothek zu Berlin to let me view autograph and printed material. Others have offered valuable comments on and evaluated parts of the book, including Rufus Hallmark, Susan Youens, Roe-min Kok, and the late John Daverio (whose insights are sorely missed).

Parts of this book originated in my previous studies listed in the bibliography. These include essays on *Lieder für die Jugend* (1990), the Eichendorff *Liederkreis,* op. 39 (1994), the Andersen *Lieder,* op. 40 (2002), the Reinick *Lieder* (2004), and the two sets of *Romanzen und Balladen,* opp. 45 and 49 (2005) in Helmut Loos's *Robert Schumann: Interpretationen seiner Werke.* In the natural course of events, some of the research and thought behind those essays appears in this book, sometimes reconsidered, sometimes reasserted. Support for the research on those articles and this book have come from the Research Council at the University of North Carolina, Chapel Hill, and also from the Faculty Partner's Fund in the College of Arts and Sciences at that same institution. My thanks to Dean (now Provost) Bernadette Gray-Little for her support of research for this project with monies from this last-named fund.

I should credit my lifelong interest in Schumann's songs specifically to Barbara Kinsey-Sable, a talented singer, instructor, and poet who had the ability to grasp the interaction of words and music in songs. Her interest in the lied brought Schumann songs to my attention in the first place, before I knew much about his other music.

Finally, I dedicate this book to my mother. While she lived, she encouraged its progress; I only wish she had not passed away before it appeared in print.

Schumann's Early Songs and the Lieder of His First Maturity

Introduction:
Schumann's Criticism and Early Lieder

Schumann's Aesthetic of Song

Part of our fascination with Robert Schumann's artistic career originates in his extensive activity as a founder of and music critic for a prominent music journal still flourishing today, the *Neue Zeitschrift für Musik*. He shared this journalistic proclivity with a number of nineteenth-century composers, Weber, Berlioz, and Wagner among them. But perhaps no other composer-critic wrote about so many other musicians or addressed such a broad range of topics as Schumann. We might think that his wide-ranging literary education (the family business published inexpensive editions of great authors) and the refined musical sensibilities exhibited in his criticism would incline him toward frequent commentary on the lieder of his day, but this proved not to be the case. Before he began issuing his own songs, he contributed only one substantial review of contemporary lieder to the *Neue Zeitschrift* in 1837,[1] and after his extraordinary output in the genre began to appear, he limited himself to just five further articles on the subject. In short, Schumann did not reveal much about his thinking on songs, and if we wish to learn something about his artistic criteria for lieder from his reviews, we must tease them out of rather slender evidence. Still, the exercise offers a glimpse of Schumann's aesthetic of song, and a brief examination yields some dividends.

Perhaps Schumann's most revealing single appraisal of the solo lied comes in a retrospective comment on more than a decade of criticism near the end of his tenure as editor of the *Neue Zeitschrift*. He recounts in an 1843 review of Robert Franz's *Gesänge*, op. 1:

One knows that in the years 1830–34 a reaction arose against the prevailing taste. The battle was not fundamentally difficult; it was one against ostentation in almost all genres, which manifested itself, with the admitted exception of Weber, Loewe, and others, mostly in the genre of piano music. The first attack also commenced in piano music; filigree compositions were replaced by more thoughtful creations, and the influence of two masters in particular made itself noticeable in the latter, that of Beethoven and Bach. The number of disciples grew; the new life forced its way into other venues. For the lied Franz Schubert prepared the way, but more in the Beethovenian manner, whereas the influence of Bach's spirit manifested itself in the achievements of the North Germans. Accelerating these developments, a new German poetic school evolved: Rückert and Eichendorff, although they had flourished earlier, became more familiar to musicians, who set mostly Uhland and Heine. Thus arose that more artistic and thoughtful kind of song, which former [composers] naturally could not have known, because the new poetic art was reflected back in music.[2]

This brief aside discloses a surprising number of important points about Schumann's view of German song. Underlying this passage, like the rest of his criticism, is the central theme of artistic progress. In Schumann's view, music and musical style should develop in an orderly way, and he always sought not only novelty but also "improvement" that lay in deeper means of expression, not in meretricious display. Schubert, a worthy master, nevertheless represented an artistic past superseded by advances in the genre, and this was only fitting. An overriding concern with the contributions of new song composers forms a salient feature of Schumann's articles on the field. Poetry, moreover, pointed the way to the future in the genre of the lied, something that reveals Schumann's literary training (which was much more extensive than his formal musical training) as well as offering an oblique glimpse of his approach to composing songs. Finally, the critic mentions two separate traditions of the lied as the basis for the artistic progress he expected, one stemming from what we might loosely characterize as the "southern" German school, the other from a "northern" German school. He does not specify the stylistic hallmarks of each school, but this separation had telling consequences for his own approach to setting texts.

We might be surprised that Schumann did not regard Schubert as the sole *fons et origo* of the nineteenth-century German solo lied, and the roots of this diffidence (quite unlike the critic's ecstatic reception of the C Major Symphony) lay in several areas. For one thing, Schubert's anteriority in Schumann's view entailed a certain uniformity in his piano parts, as we read in an 1840 review of posthumously released Schubert songs: "One encounters again here in these songs Schubert's familiar manner of holding fast to one rhythm, one accompanimental figure from beginning to end. One can well believe that they are written beautifully for the voice, and they are nowhere difficult to sing."[3] This theme surfaces again in a review of Theodor Kirchner's *Zehn Lieder für eine Singstimme mit Pianoforte,* which cautions against taking matters too far in the other direction:

> In connection with the developing art of poetry, the Franz Schubertian epoch has already been followed by a new one, which has availed itself particularly of progress in an accompanying instrument further improved in the meantime. The composer calls his songs "Lieder with Pianoforte," and this must not be overlooked. The singing voice alone cannot do everything, cannot render everything. Apart from the expression of the whole, the finer traits of a poem should also emerge, and so it is fitting that melody should not suffer from [this burden]. The young composer has certainly attended to this. His lieder frequently appear to be independent instrumental pieces, which often scarcely seem to require the voice part to achieve their full effect. They are frequently little more than translations of poems for the piano, songs without words as it were, but motivated by text. The voice part in them therefore often appears like a quiet murmuring of words, and the main expression lies mostly in the accompaniment. Nobody will be able to claim that the composer lacks melodic prowess, but it still relies too much on harmony, the behavior of the voice still bears too much of an instrumental character.[4]

Time and again Schumann sought to steer a middle course in the relationship between word and tone, and here lay another slight reservation about Schubert. In a review of several volumes of ballads by Bernhard Klein, the critic observes, "Where the verse [in "Gott und die Bajadere"] becomes more sensuous, more painterly, more Indian, the music remains brusquely remote; one wishes more here: soft, plump sounds. To the same degree that Franz Schubert, Loewe, and many of the moderns often paint too realistically, Klein does too little, and, even where he would affect [realism], without freedom or passion."[5] Much depended on the poetry: ballads (which combine epic, lyric, and dramatic modes of poetry) required a more varied and demonstrative melody and accompaniment. Folkish verse, however, made other demands, as we learn in this review of the youthful Hugh Pearson's songs to texts by Robert Burns: "Almost all of these songs suffer from a certain overabundance often engendered in younger composers partly by technical insecurity, partly by the desire to make good immediately. In short, it appears to us that too much display has been expended on these particular texts; there are too many notes for the simple words."[6] Though we might think, then, that Schumann's constant search for "progress" would result in more grandiose means of expression, the composer's actual concern revolved around more sensitive and refined settings of poetry.

All the preceding excerpts contain a notion that we might expect from a composer grounded firmly in a literary background: that songs proceed first and foremost from the verse they set. This certainly included the simple mechanics of accurate declamation. "Good vocal writing is to be found in each of the songs," Schumann wrote of W. H. Beit's lieder. "The accompaniment too does not miss each small turn, neither are small mistakes in declamation lacking, so small that we would overlook them in students, but in a more cultured man of talent they are sufficiently large not to point them out benevolently."[7] Schumann assumed much more than proper declamation, though. In the same review, he comes as close as he ever does to setting out his vision of the composer's task in a passage lauding a promising talent who had died young:

> I do not want discussion of what [makes] a beautiful lied. That is as difficult and easy as [what makes] a beautiful poem. "It's but a breath," says Goethe. *Norbert Burgmüller,* of the three mentioned [here], knew this best. He considered it his highest [goal], as all should, to recreate the aftereffect of the poem down to its smallest features in the finest musical material. Rarely does a feature escape him, or where he has grasped it, does he go astray.[8]

Schumann's brief praise of Burgmüller envisions a much more subtle and complex interaction between composer and poem than the simple notion of song "reflecting the meaning" of verse. Rather, the composer should seek to recreate the effect that reading a poem had on him or her. Inherent in this thought lie inevitable notions of subjective interpretation, artistic license, cognitive distance, and even dissonance, all of which involve much more than fidelity to the words. Schumann embraced a version of what Walther Dürr calls (following Nägeli's lead) the "polyrhythmic lied," in which the sound and sense of the verse, of the melody, and of the accompaniment run sometimes congruently, sometimes separately but in parallel, sometimes divergently.[9] The interaction of these several elements in a song produced an artwork that amounted to more than the sum of its parts, eliciting continually intensifying levels of reflection from the listener. Schumann asked composers to do more than interpret poetry; they were to intimate in music their reaction to a poem, a multilayered psychological process.

The modest means Schumann advocates to accomplish this psychologically challenging task must intrigue us. For the most part he disparaged the "overly realistic" devices that had become associated largely with the "southern" (read Viennese) Germans such as Schubert, whose songs sometimes presented miniature opera arias or cantatas with piano accompaniment. Lieder remained largely "Hausmusik" for Schumann. By the same token, the pious, sober approach of northern Germans such as Reichardt and Zelter could be too inexpressive (thus the objection to Klein quoted earlier), though Schumann's crusade against empty bravura steered him more in this direction. The trick lay in fashioning intellectually complex, expressive works of art without resorting on the one hand to flamboyant display for either voice or piano or descending into artless impassivity on the other. Schumann's experience with concise, piquant musical characterization in his piano miniatures of the 1830s fitted him perfectly to produce lieder possessing exquisitely subtle but intense poignance.

We must always bear in mind, finally, that Schumann considered the lied, like the symphony, to be a nationalistic enterprise displaying the literary and musical art of Germans to their finest effect. In his first article devoted to lieder in 1837, the critic wrote of Ferdinand Stegmayer's op. 16:

> To drive foreign singing from the field and to conserve our love of the people—that is, to revive again the music that expresses natural, profound and clear feelings artistically—requires above all the care and protection of our good German lied. Anybody knows how little in general we lack by way of lieder; one could paper over all of Germany with them every year. Who is capable, however, of overlooking nothing among this immense number, and how many of the modest ones may remain hidden here! The songs of Stegmayer may be imagined among these, which come from a sincere heart, a source that can never conceal its influence. Only a German can fashion such private, intimate songs. Moreover, they sing themselves, so to speak; nothing here detains or seeks to occasion learned astonishment. Thoughts of a fortunate lover, the happiness of a kiss, a song in the night, one in

springtime, that of a woman spinning, finally a delicious serenade, all in pretty words animated and adorned by the music.[10]

In the end, this passage may summarize best Schumann's expectations for his and other composers' lieder. Proceeding from a German poetic form with roots in folkloric practice, art song should remain a discreet genre that eschewed empty display. The new style of German poetry conducted Schumann deeper into this private realm rather than into the extroverted arena of the theatrical or virtuosic. While he welcomed increasing sophistication of means, artistic progress here served intimate ends that could impart the composer's innermost reaction to the verse at hand. Songs entailed a literary as well as musical experience meant primarily for the privacy of the home, and as such they had to suit the technical abilities of talented amateur singers and pianists of discerning taste. The moderation, delicacy, subtlety of gesture that win praise in Schumann's reviews of lieder compose the same qualities he would seek in his own output.

Schumann's Early Songs

In an autobiographical sketch dating from around 1840, Schumann gives an overview of his earliest artistic activity:

I had no instruction in composition until my twentieth year. I began to compose early, among other things in my twelfth year Psalm 150 with orchestra, a few numbers of an opera, many pieces for voice, many things for piano. . . . Many poetic attempts fall right at this time (before my twenties). The most significant poets of all countries were familiar to me. In my eighteenth year I developed an enthusiasm for Jean Paul; I also heard of Franz Schubert for the first time. . . .

Amid continuous production (musical and literary) I became 18 years old, when I went to Leipzig to study law per my mother's wishes, though my own, not yet clear, [were] to devote myself entirely to music.

New life from then on. Industrious study of the piano. Heard good music. Franz Schubert and Beethoven dawned on me; Bach flickered. Compositions [included] a large quartet for piano with strings, 8 four-hand polonaises, a bunch of songs by Lord Byron.[11]

Recollected a decade after the fact, Schumann lapsed just slightly in this last assertion: only one text by Byron appears among the surviving songs from his teenage years. By far his favorite poet from this period was Justinius Kerner, represented in five settings, followed by Schumann himself (sometimes under the pseudonym "Ekert"), represented in three settings, Johann Georg Jacobi in two settings, and finally Goethe in just one.[12]

All of these compositions come from the years 1827 and 1828, and scholars usually cite various adolescent crushes on Nanni Petsch, Liddy Hempel, Ida Stölzel, and Agnes Carus as the impetus for most of them. Chief among these was Agnes Carus, eight years older than Schumann, the wife of Dr. Ernst August Carus, and an amateur singer.[13] Schumann probably encountered her in 1827 at the home of her brother-in-law, Karl Erdmann Carus, a well-to-do merchant and manufacturer who lived in Zwickau. From November 1827, Agnes and her husband lived in Leipzig, where Schumann encountered them again in 1828 as a law student. Madame Carus dots the pages of the composer's diaries from this period, where he records such things as "I will go to bed and dream of her, of her. Good night, Agnes."[14] But there is no record that she returned the young composer's affections, and he broods with adolescent petulance in August 1828, "*My songs.* They are devoted to the true impression of my [very] self; but no human being can show what genius itself created; even *she* sang the most beautiful passages badly and did not understand me."[15] Amid dreams of other women and girls (including Clara Wieck), Schumann finally had musical satisfaction, at least: "*Agnes and the songs;* she learned to understand them better; they mostly recount all my feelings in tones."[16] Eventually this infatuation died away, leaving eleven complete songs and two fragments, from which Schumann saw fit to cull a fair copy that he considered publishing as "op. 2" sometime later, perhaps during 1829 or 1830.[17] He did not execute this plan, however. The songs appeared posthumously, three edited by Brahms in the 1893 supplement to the first Schumann edition, six more in a 1933 edition published by Karl Geiringer, and one in a supplement that same year to the *Zeitschrift für Musik,* commemorating the hundredth anniversary of its founding (the eleventh song for the projected "op. 2" remained unfinished). These ten songs will give some inkling of Schumann's initial foray into the lied.

The Early Songs: "Hirtenknabe" ("Ekert"), "Sehnsucht" ("Ekert"), "Die Weinende" (Byron), "Erinnerung" (Jacobi), "An Anna" ("Lange harrt' ich," Kerner), "An Anna" ("Nicht im Thale," Kerner), "Kurzes Erwachen" (Kerner), "Gesanges Erwachen" (Kerner), "Im Herbste" (Kerner), "Der Fischer" (Goethe)

We will be disappointed if we seek among Schumann's early songs masterpieces such as those the teenage Schubert fashioned a decade before.

From an early age, Schubert studied in a major city at an institution dedicated to training professional musicians, with Salieri as his teacher of vocal writing. Schumann came to his first songs as an amateur from a small town, instructed mostly in keyboard by the local organist (whose limitations he recognized). His early songs evince unmistakable talent and ambition, and they set their texts better than many of the lieder circulating at the time, but they remain student works. Redolent of adolescent melancholy in many cases, the songs intimate a potential for harmonic deftness and melodic lyricism not yet fully realized.

Schumann tried out the many options available to him in setting text, the most basic of which featured minimal accompaniment, limited melodic range, and strophic form. The most obvious poetic candidate for this treatment was his own "Hirtenknabe," which falls in the genre of "Lieder für die Jugend," to which he would return in the late 1840s. The iambic regularity of the poetry, the narrow range of the voice (spanning less than a octave), the limited harmonic palette, and the extremely simple accompaniment (largely block chords) all place this number in the realm of the folkish. Missing here are the subtle turns of phrase, poetic and musical, that made Schumann's later songs for children cleverly appealing to the adults who would play them. Nonetheless, we must recognize "Hirtenknabe" as a member of a genre harking back to the folkloric roots of the lied rather than regarding it as something unsophisticated by reason of inexperience (the song dates from 16 August 1828, toward the end of this early period).[18]

The other completed song with a text by the composer, "Sehnsucht," is slightly more ambitious but equally straightforward. Schumann's poetry has a predictable regularity in both sentiment and meter:

Sterne der blauen	Stars in the blue
Himmlischen Auen	Heavenly pastures,
Grüßt sie mir,	Greet her for me,
die ich geliebt!	She whom I loved!
Weit in die Ferne	To that far place
Möcht' ich so gerne,	Would I go gladly,
Wo das geliebte	Where the beloved
Mädchen mir weilt.	Maid awaits me.

The composer translates the steady alternation of dactyls with trochees into a cut time that should really be common time (with the quarter note rather than the half note receiving the beat). Aside from the brief instrumental prelude, Schumann provides sextuplet arpeggiations à la Schubert throughout, articulating harmonies that go no further than secondary dominants. In his melody Schumann exhibits a proclivity for expressive leaps upward of a sixth (on the word "himmlischen," for instance), and he also inserts a number of vocal turns by way of embellishment. Written in June 1827, this song displays graceful competence but little more.

Schumann responded more thoughtfully to the verse of other (and frankly better) poets in the remaining songs from this period. His setting from Byron's "Hebrew Melodies," "Die Weinende" ("I saw thee weep"), from July 1827, just a month after "Sehnsucht," has a much more harmonically daring accompaniment and is more varied in its rhythmic motion, even though Schumann relies mostly on block chords and doubles the voice part in the right hand. The young composer found the verse translated by Julius Körner in one of his father's pocket editions, and the setting's through-composed melody and rhythmic variety address in part the scansion of the German rendition:[19]

I saw thee weep—the big bright tear	Ich sah dich weinen! ach, die Zähre
Came o'er that eye of blue;	Schwamm auf des Auges blau;
And then, methought, it did appear	Und dieses Auge, dacht' ich, wäre
A violet dropping dew.	Ein Veilchen, nass vom Thau.

Schumann tends to respect the syntax of the verse rather than its divisions into lines, and though he reuses motivic cells in his vocal line, it avoids obvious periodicity, affording more declamatory freedom than the two songs discussed previously. Of course, the imagery of the text is more sophisticated than that in the composer's own poetry, prompting a melody and accompaniment that diverge more fancifully from the structure and meter of the verse.

Schumann's setting of Jacobi's "Erinnerung" has this same variety of accompaniment but, unlike "Die Weinende," avoids invariably doubling the voice in the right hand. This song, composed on 16 August 1828 along with "Hirtenknabe,"[20] takes varied strophic form and gives a fleeting premonition of Schumann's lyric gift. The frequent leaps upward of a sixth (which can sound like yodeling in some of his other early songs, when repeated too often) do not intrude here, and the composer carefully places emphasized words of text on higher pitches. The melody is gracefully restrained in range, easy to sing yet expressive (see ex. I.1). The fact that Schumann chose varied strophic setting for this poem while treat-

Example I.1.   Schumann's setting of Georg Jacobi's "Erinnerung" from 16 August 1828.

ing "Die Weinende" to through-composition should not lead us to view "Erinnerung" as less sophisticated or progressive. When a composer selects strophic setting (as many did throughout the nineteenth century), he or she embarks on the difficult task "to capture as if in one focal point" the overall sense of the poem, according to E.T.A. Hoffmann.[21] Through-composition requires more scrivening, but it allows the composer the convenience of declaiming each word separately and addressing each thought individually. A strophic setting must accommodate the structure of each stanza and distill meaning into one melody. A varied strophic setting like the short one for "Erinnerung" seeks the best of both worlds, but it may be more artistically challenging in the end than through-composition.

Schumann's best efforts at composing lieder during these early years came in response to German poets whom he would revisit in later years. His favorite as a lovesick adolescent, at least for musical treatment, was Justinius Kerner, a Swabian author of somewhat sentimental inclinations. Though Kerner earned his living as a medical doctor, he had an extensive literary career that included historical monographs, short stories, and a good deal of verse.[22] Schumann would later devote one song cycle solely to Kerner (op. 35) as well as writing two additional settings during 1840 that found their way into later miscellanies. The young composer selected five texts in June and July of 1828, writing to Gottlob Wiedebein, a Braunschweig song composer whom he admired, "Kerner's poems, which attracted me the most through that mysterious, supernatural power which one often finds in the verse of Goethe and Jean Paul, first gave me the idea of testing my weak abilities, because in every word of them is a world of sounds that can only be defined in notes."[23]

Two of the early Kerner texts feature blank verse as part of an epistolary conceit, "Andreas an Anna," providing an excuse for fanciful settings in which Schumann overreaches. He sets "Lange harrt' ich" as a through-composed, declamatory lied marked "Schwärmerisch," with many small segments in changing tempi, sudden modulations, and little motivic coherence. This is Schumann's weakest effort from 1828, because he strives too hard for effect. The second letter "An Anna," "Nicht im Thale," also comes across as rather affected, modulating suddenly in its middle section from F major to D-flat major, but it evinces more lyricism than its cousin and achieves more coherence by repeating the opening strophe with varied music (a formal device the composer used often in his mature works). The poetry has a suitably melancholy and somewhat melodramatic tinge:

Nicht im Thale der süßen Heimat,	Not in the valley of the sweet homeland,
Beim Gemurmel der Silberquelle—	By the murmur of the silvery spring—
Bleich getragen aus dem Schlachtfeld,	Carried wan from the battlefield,
Denk' ich dein, du süßes Leben!	I think of your sweet life!

The soldier lies dying (he expires during the course of the poem) amid many of his comrades, which prompts the distant modulation for the second stanza. But at least the vocal part exhibits some graceful turns.

Schumann fared much better with the three remaining, more conventional Kerner texts, all of them cast in regular, cross-rhymed verse that lends itself to strophic setting. Schumann adopts this approach for "Kurzes Erwachen" and "Gesanges Erwachen" with a twist: he sets the last strophe of each as a coda, using some motives from the previous stanzas but recombining them to create different conclusions. In each poem the last quatrain conveys the same moral: no matter how lovely nature might be, a disappointed lover cannot appreciate its beauty. Strophic or varied strophic form with a coda demarking the message in the final stanza would later become one of Schumann's favorite compositional devices for lieder. When the original poem consists of only three stanzas, David Ferris understandably views such settings as "bar forms" ("Stollen, Stollen, Abgesang," to cite the old formula), though Schumann does not follow the traditional rule in which the *Abgesang* usually has the length of the first two stanzas combined.[24]

"Im Herbste" is the gem of the Kerner group, offering a sample of what Schumann could accomplish in little space with limited means. The voice begins on the bittersweet top pitch of a diminished triad, moves directly to an expressively flatted third on the word "eilend," and then repeats the beautifully enjambed "einzig von mir, von mir, einzig von mir" on a rising scale, making a regular two-bar phrase that places the final "einzig" on the highest pitch (see ex. I.2). This last phrase exudes an effortlessness that would later constitute a hallmark of Schumann's mature vocal style. The uncertainty of mode, the harmonic simplicity with which the composer achieves it, and finally the delicate postlude ending in a plagal cadence all produce the ease of expression Schumann hoped to find in other composers' songs. Only a few ungainly vocal leaps and the incessant block chords in the accompaniment remind us that this lovely miniature is a student work.

The last complete song of this group, "Der Fischer," sets a well-known text by Germany's greatest poet, Goethe. He relates a wonderfully maca-

Example I.2. Excerpt from Justinius Kerner's "Im Herbste," in Schumann's setting from summer 1828.

bre tale of a fisherman lured to a watery grave by a beautiful woman who rises up out of the waves, a metaphor that probably appealed to Schumann around the time of his many amorous misadventures. The last lines of Goethe's poem must have spoken particularly to the adolescent's frustrations with women who seemed inviting yet caused him (if his diaries are any indication) constant unhappiness:

Sie sprach zu ihm, sie sang zu ihm;	She spoke to him, she sang to him;
Da war's um ihn geschehn:	Then this did come to pass:
Halb zog sie ihn, halb sank er hin,	She partly pulled, he partly sank,
Und ward nicht mehr gesehn.	And never more was seen.

We do not know whether Schumann, composing in June 1828, knew Schubert's wonderful setting of this ballad, penned in 1815 and published in 1821 as op. 5, number 3, but it seems unlikely.[25] The eighteen-year-old Viennese composer fashioned a masterful strophic rendition, whereas Schumann took an overly dramatized, ternary approach to the text, replete with rising glissandi for the waves in the outer stanzas (see ex. I.3), incessant tremolo chords, vocal leaps descending in sequence to depict the ocean's depths, and a pretentious fermata on "sank er *hin*" to set off the final line. All of this, especially the theatrical pause at the end, takes its cue quite obviously from Schubert's "Erlkönig," which Schumann could hardly have avoided during this period in German concert halls as well as in private homes.[26] "Der Fischer," however, does not feature an extensive cast or any dialogue and therefore supports dramatic treatment less convincingly. Schumann's song not only "paints too realistically" but also paints too obviously, and this may suggest why he sent his Kerner settings, but not the Goethe song composed at the same time, for evaluation to an experienced composer such as Wiedebein.

The evidence of the *Elf Jugendlieder* certainly speaks to Schumann's promise as a composer of songs, but not to a consistently accomplished technique or to discernment in gauging accurately which melodic and accompanimental devices applied in a given situation. The young amateur makes no overt blunders of declamation, though his sense of appropriate vocal motion still leaves much to be desired. And some of this music seems rough around the edges, although it can also reveal more polish; these two contradictory elements often intermingle in one and the same song. Schumann later mined these early songs for material: a variant of "An Anne" ("Nicht im Thale") found its way into the sec-

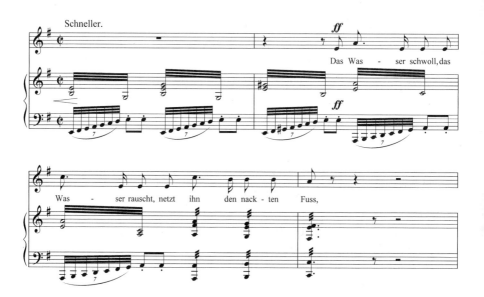

Example I.3. Beginning of the last section from Schumann's setting of "Der Fischer," summer 1828.

ond movement of the Piano Sonata, op. 11, a version of "Im Herbste" became a theme in the Piano Sonata, op. 22, and material from "Hirtenknabe" begins the Intermezzo, op. 4, no. 4.[27] But the songs themselves were hardly ready to play on the national stage to which the composer aspired.

Schumann's musical inexperience may explain at least part of the reason he stopped composing lieder for the next decade. He writes in his autobiographical note, "Finally in 1831 I began regular study of composition under Heinrich Dorn, the current kapellmeister in Riga, a highly shrewd, awe-inspiring, ingenious man. Around this time my first compositions also appeared in print; they are too small and rhapsodic to make a great deal of."[28] In the same paragraph the composer also recounts his intense study of piano, which ended in physical disaster. Nevertheless he required both pursuits—instruction in composition and piano—to realize his ambitions as a composer of songs. The "small and rhapsodic" piano pieces of the 1830s helped Schumann perfect the precision of idiom and trenchant characterization that enabled him to address lyrical poetry effectively in the 1840s. Without groups of piano miniatures such as *Papillons, Die Davidsbündlertänze,* and *Carnaval,* cycles such as *Dichterliebe,*

Frauenliebe und Leben, and *Myrthen* would have been unthinkable. Formal study of piano helped Schumann gauge the level and efficacy of his accompaniments, just as study of composition (mostly counterpoint) developed the more imaginative (and correct) voice leading that would enable him to negotiate the "polyrhythm" of the nineteenth-century German lied. Schumann understood that he needed experience, and his additional activity as critic sharpened his musical acumen as well as exposing him to a wider repertory.

Schumann's composition of lieder also had some connection, direct or indirect, to his various romantic entanglements and pursuits. Not only can we read the cautionary tale of "Der Fischer" quite easily in this way, but many other texts he selected during his teenage years concerned separated lovers or revealed adolescent yearnings left mostly unfulfilled. Moreover, at least one song from the period bears the title "Lied für XXX," leaving several possible candidates as dedicatee.[29] By the evidence cited above from the composer's diaries, his infatuation with the singer Agnes Carus during 1828 directly inspired some of his lieder. But having claimed that a young man's fancy turns to song during courtship, we must exercise caution in assuming too simplistic a connection. Schumann had infatuations during the 1830s that did not result in lieder. And if we seek romantic motivations only, we will be hard-pressed to understand later why a composer in the midst of a happy, requited relationship with his future wife might contemplate such bitter, scornful denunciations of love as we find in op. 24 and op. 48. We shall discover a connection between Schumann's courtship of Clara Wieck and his 1840 "year of song," but the relationship of his composing to his courtship has many facets, not all of which involve expression of affection or anxiety. We must take seriously the conviction stated in Schumann's criticism that lieder served above all to display and intensify a composer's reaction to poetry, especially in that wonderful era of German literature that motivated not only many of his songs but his instrumental works as well.

1

Songs of Marriage

In her study of Schumann's "conversion" to vocal composition, Barbara Turchin cautions that "a broad view of the period preceding Schumann's outburst of song [in 1840] reveals a complex of circumstances and pressures which, taken together, eventually forced him to strike out on a new path."[1] Of course, the path was not entirely new: we have seen that Schumann had dabbled in song during his adolescent years, partly as a manifestation of his erotic frustrations. Admitting this, Turchin seeks nonetheless to undermine the myth that Schumann began composing songs in later years simply out of romantic infatuation. While Schumann's "year of song" exhibits an undeniable component of his enthusiasm for Clara Wieck, his marriage was just one manifestation of his life's ambitions. Robert's love for Clara *and* the promotion of his career, both aspects of achieving adult respectability, combined to form the framework for his renewed interest in the lied.

By 1839 Schumann's personal life and career had come to an intertwined crisis. He exerted growing influence as a music critic and journal editor in select artistic circles, but his compositions for piano had failed to gain wide acceptance. Shortly before this time he decided to marry his former Leipzig piano teacher's young daughter, whom he had first encountered a decade previously. His prospective father-in-law, Friedrich Wieck—divorced and possessive of his daughter, both personally and financially—opposed this match. He decried Schumann's financial insecurity, citing the readiest objection at hand: Robert's lack of success as a composer (later charges also included an unsubstantiated history of alcoholism). Schumann did everything he could to counter the older man's objections, not realizing at first that no amount of persuasion would avail. His desires for Clara and for success in his career naturally became intensely interwoven, and eventually he schemed with his future bride (also completely smitten) in a lawsuit to circumvent the necessity of her father's consent. The task was twofold: to demonstrate public recognition of Robert's compositional efforts and in doing so to prove his ability to support a family.

Robert, with Clara's help, made various efforts to bolster his reputation, including relocation of the *Neue Zeitschrift* permanently to Vienna (unsuccessful) and a quest for an honorary doctorate (granted by the University of Jena in February 1840). Of the various projects he entertained to gain fame as a composer (quartets, a possible opera), the one that held the most promise for a quick and remunerative outcome involved songs. To this end, in 1839 Robert and Clara began collecting verse in a manuscript labeled "Copies of Poems for Composition," which the couple maintained over the course of their marriage.[2] Clara recorded most of the 169 entries representing 34 authors (only 61 texts appear in Robert's hand), and between the two of them they set roughly two thirds of the selections. The collection reveals how the couple's passion for each other and for Robert's success became interdependent. In one sense the book presents a partial blueprint for their vocal projects (though in the event Robert set 94 of the poems to Clara's 7). In another sense it presents a monument to a romance, including as it does a good deal of endearing poetry but eschewing Heine's more cynical verse and the macabre and violent poetry ultimately used for Robert's collections of ballads.

Having deliberately prepared a project designed to further his career and also to win the legal battle for Clara's hand, Robert began to compose solo songs with a vengeance in 1840. He produced more than 125 (half his output in the genre) over the course of ten months, and he published a number rather quickly for relatively lucrative fees. Two cycles (op. 24, with 9 songs, and op. 25, comprising 26 songs) and a collection (op. 30, including 3 songs) had appeared by the end of 1840, and his publishers paid 212 taler for solo lieder alone in that year (fully one quarter of Schumann's annual income).[3] But this was only the tip of the iceberg. The year 1841 saw the publication of another four works containing a total of 30 songs, 23 more appeared in 1842, and this pace continued into the mid-1840s, when the vein finally played out and new songs had to be produced.

All this marked a significant change in Schumann's compositional fortunes, and he celebrated the success of the strategy with his future wife in a letter from May 1840: "It is also not insignificant how much I earn by my compositions, and it is becoming better and better. . . . In this half year I earned close to 400 Taler by my compositions—it is amazing; I produce no songbook of five sheets for less than six louis d'or."[4] So many songs appeared that Breitkopf, one of his publishers, sniffed in a backhanded rebuke to the composer dated 18 December 1841, "We have learned . . . that the rapid appearance of two works by one and the same composer in the same genre injures both. And we ourselves believe this must already be the case with the many volumes of your beautiful songs, which coincidentally appeared at the same time more by happenstance, [and] negligence of publishers, than by your wishes."[5] But Schumann could shrug off the complaints of the publisher who had issued his first volume of songs because he had another object in mind. He hoped to triumph with songs where avant-garde pieces for piano had failed, as he explained to the Flensburg organist W. H. Rieffel on 11 June 1840: "Your remarks about my piano works have delighted me again. If only I could find more people who understood my meaning. With song compositions I hope I shall succeed more easily."[6] And succeed he did: the Leipzig court ruled in July 1840 that Robert and Clara could marry, giving Friedrich Wieck until 11 August to offer further objections (he declined). On 12 September, just one day before Clara attained her majority, she and Robert wed.[7]

Schumann's return to the composition of songs expressed more than his love for Clara alone; it entailed everything that accompanied it: his hopes for a family, for recognition of his artistic talent, for success. He sought all the trappings of an artistically enlightened, *bürgerliche* respectability—that is to say, a validation of his own worth. And though Schumann loved his wife dearly, on one level she became an emblem of his status, just as the lied represented one path to professional recognition. From the outset Clara was much more than a wife and mother: she was an artistic collaborator, a famous, indispensable breadwinner, and her husband's champion, initially enjoying far wider renown than he.

While recognizing the oversimplification involved in attributing Robert's "year of song" solely to romantic involvement or viewing all his music from that year through the lens of his courtship, we can still find it appropriate to begin the examination of his mature lieder with the cycles bound closely to his marriage.

Myrthen. Liederkreis . . . für Gesang und Pianoforte . . . Opus 25 (for dates of composition see below; published August 1840 by Fr. Kistner)

Dedicated to "his beloved bride," *Myrthen* constitutes a sumptuous wedding gift. Its title, *Myrtle*, originates in the traditional flower of bridal bouquets, and this in turn connects the twenty-six numbers to a venerable artistic tradition reaching back into the eighteenth century. Heinrich Schwab lists countless collections of lieder by Reichardt, Schnoor, Himmel, and others with titles such as "Musikalischer Blumenstrauß" beginning in the 1770s, and he defines the genre "as a gift *for* specific people and groups of people *addressing* specifically designated occasions and purposes."[8] Schumann assembled and published op. 25 as just such a "musical bouquet," enlisting the publisher Friedrich Kistner in March 1840: "For some time I have cherished a pet scheme, in which you will perhaps agree to participate. It is intended as a bridal gift, which will require the kind of adornment that you particularly know how to provide so thoughtfully and tenderly."[9] Having composed the songs over a two-month period between early February and early April,[10] Schumann presented Clara with an elaborately bound copy of *Myrthen* on 7 September, just five days before their wedding.[11] Clara already knew many of the individual numbers in op. 25, but the assembled collection must have come as something of a surprise. Robert hinted coyly at it only once, in a letter of 28 February: "I want to dedicate some things to Emilie and Elise [List], perhaps to Pauline [Garcia], too, if it's really good. I also have something in mind for you."[12]

By invoking the tradition of the "musical bouquet," Schumann ties his lieder to the intimate genre designed for the home, but the role of personal *donum* (gift) by no means contradicts the notion of public artistic *opus* (work). The composer explicitly included "Liederkreis" in the subtitle of *Myrthen*, and he conformed its structure precisely to the manner in which consumers would encounter it in print.[13] Mid-nineteenth-century collections of lieder delighted not only the ear and intellect but also the eye. Published in loose gatherings easily handled by an accompanist and in a large format legible to the singer standing behind, elaborate song cycles initially appeared in paper-covered "volumes" (*Hefte*) comprising groups of no more than six or seven numbers.[14] Consumers could purchase these separately, and therefore composers often arranged each volume as a coherent entity, as if it were a chapter in a book. The book as a whole then assumed a larger integrity when assembled. Schumann's op. 25 therefore offers a primer to the construction of printed nineteenth-century song cycles in addition to revealing Schumann's conjoined artistic and marital hopes.

Heft I: "Widmung" (Rückert, n.d.), "Freisinn" (Goethe, 3 February), "Der Nussbaum" (Mosen, 16 February), "Jemand" (Burns, 25 February), "Lieder aus dem Schenkenbuch im Divan" I–II (Goethe, 4 February)

The dates of the various numbers in this and the remaining volumes of *Myrthen* make it clear that the songs do not appear in the order in which Schumann composed them, excluding tightly knit musical organization. Similarly, the disparate selection of poets would tend to limit a narrative framework. Instead, the volumes of this cycle, and the cycle as a whole, gain coherence sometimes through musical pairing of adjacent songs, sometimes through dramatic contrast, sometimes by means of a central idea around which the songs rotate likes spokes in a wheel. The first volume of op. 25 makes free use of all these devices. The declaration of "Dedication" in the first song contrasts diametrically with the celebration of independence in "Free Spirit"; the wishful, romantic dreaming under "The Walnut Tree" and about "Somebody" seems to contradict the cheerful solitude in the two selections from Goethe's *West-östlicher Divan* (roughly, *Middle Eastern Anthology*). Both Robert and Clara entertained ambivalent feelings about the loss of their personal and professional freedom in the bonds of matrimony,[15] and volume one of *Myrthen* treats the prelude to marriage, with all its enthusiasms and misgivings, its fantasies and apprehensions, its eagerness and reluctance. Added to these contradictions comes uncertainty about the identity of the persona. If the composer speaks directly through any of his songs, it must be through "Widmung"; though narrowly construed, the gender of the persona is unspecified. Are we meant to assume next that the dreaming maid in "Der Nussbaum" speaks in "Jemand," the persona of which is also neutral? "Freisinn" and the remaining Goethe selections *may* feature a male speaker (but in this event, are we to detect homoeroticism in the last song?). The composer leaves us to exercise our own imaginations.

Rather than resolving these uncertainties of message and focus, Schumann intensifies them through the tonal arrangement of the volume. He deliberately pairs "Widmung" and "Freisinn" by placing them in related flat keys, moving backward significantly around the circle of fifths (A-flat major–E-flat major), as if the promise of dedication were renounced for the spirit of freedom. "Widmung," with its prominent central section in distant E major, also opens the tonal space that allows for "Der Nussbaum" (G major), with *its* central section ("Sie flüstern von einem Mägdlein") in A minor dwelling often on its E major dominant. The parallel E minor beginning of "Jemand" fits right into the plan by ending in E major. Schumann then concludes with the E major-to-A major progression in the pair from the *West-östlicher Divan*. We encounter tonal connections here that go well beyond the arbitrary but fall short of the tightly knit.

Some of these tensions extend into the individual songs themselves. "Widmung" is the most elaborate of this first group, a preface for both the volume and the larger cycle. The untitled verse originated in the "first bouquet" (no. 3) of Friedrich Rückert's *Liebesfrühling*. Schumann's accompaniment features arpeggiations running symbolically in parallel motion—two voices acting as one—and the internal dotted figuration in almost every measure adds exuberance (see ex. 1.1). The pattern also embodies the marking "heartfelt, lively." But what intrigues the ear most is the composer's willful manipulation of the poem's meter. Rückert cast his

Example 1.1.   Beginning of "Widmung," with two accompanimental voices in parallel.

verse in an iambic tetrameter that plays on a dichotomy between "du" and "mein":

> Du méine Séele, dú mein Hérz,
> Du méine Wónn', o dú mein Schmérz

Schumann has it otherwise, emphasizing "du" at every turn while deemphasizing "mein." He also shifts the poem's lines at will within the triple meter, a technique that serves him particularly well when he runs two and a half lines together in one ecstatic rush, ending midline on "Grab." But the composer saves his most arresting gesture for the poem's final quatrain: the augmented note values involuntarily slow the rhythmic motion to half speed, and this combines with an abrupt common-tone modulation from A-flat major to E major supported by chordal triplets in the accompaniment. The dramatic emphasis responds movingly to the semantic level of the text: "You are repose, you are peace / you are the heaven bestowed on me." Here we have the composer's most personal reaction to a poem of explicitly biographical import.

"Freisinn" carries forward the energetically uneven rhythms of "Widmung" in the service of what seems a diametrically opposed message. Here the ostensibly male speaker can think of nothing but his freedom, especially from things domestic. But we could read this selection differently, as a cheerful excursion into the unknown under the watchful eye of divine Providence, and thus the text captures something of the ambivalence with which one might enter into marriage. In any event, this song marks a subtheme of *Myrthen* as a whole: settings from Goethe's *West-östlicher Divan*. Schumann selected relatively little Goethe for his lieder, and then mostly in the latter part of his life (the youthful essay "Der Fischer," discussed in the introduction, established no pattern). The composer would return only one more time to this exotically flavored part of the poet's output after op. 25, in late 1849 (see the discussion of op. 51 in Chapter 5). These early settings do not accord the master particular deference, either: Schumann uses Goethe's verse freely, repeating his first stanza to create the song's ternary form. But this freedom may find its justification in the irregularity of the original, which appears in a subsection of the *Divan* called "The Singer's Book."[16] Goethe's first stanza falls in trochaic pentameter, the second in an irregular tetrameter. This occasions quite a different declamation in the song's internal section, which would

not have made a very satisfying conclusion to a song that begins so energetically and carries the marking "sprightly."

In contrast to "Freisinn," "Der Nussbaum" stands out for its soporific
lassitude. Here we find Schumann's only solo setting of Julius Mosen, an
acquaintance from the composer's earlier years in Leipzig.[17] The irregularity of the verse belies the dreamy mood of the treatment it receives:

Es grünet ein Nußbaum vor dem Haus,	A walnut blooms outside the house,
Duftig,	Fragrantly,
Luftig	Airily
Breitet er blättrig die Aeste aus.	It spreads its leafy boughs.

Schumann tends to deemphasize the urgency of the rhymed single words
that repeat in each of Mosen's stanzas by absorbing them into one line
(the exception for syntactic reasons occurs in the third stanza). The composer floats the whole over gently undulating, mimetic arpeggiations rip-
pling from hand to hand, but we are always left with an ambiguity. Does
the prelude form the first two measures of the phrase then completed by
the voice, or does the accompaniment complete the phrase after the voice
has sung? Probably the latter, though Schumann takes great pleasure in
leaving this riddle unsolved. His settings from 1840 are mostly quadratic:
they presume that a line of text will fit a four-bar phrase. Where the poetry frustrates this assumption, the composer can manipulate the melody or accompaniment to fulfill the convention, and deviations from the
norm draw our attention.[18] We can easily understand what prompted
Schumann to choose this verse by a very obscure poet of no great stature:
its picture of the walnut tree's rustling branches whispering of a maiden,
of her longing, and of the bridegroom in her future seems to be made for
Myrthen.

The immediate juxtaposition of "Jemand" with "Der Nussbaum" im-
plies a limited narrative progression (the prophecy in the first number
now makes a conscious entrance, though the heart has not identified the
object of its affection). "Jemand" presents the exception to the rule in
op. 25 concerning lyrical quadratic style. This translation by Wilhelm
Gerhard of Robert Burns's "For the sake o' Somebody" takes the form of
irregular octaves, but Schumann could have smoothed these out. He
makes a small nod toward the folkloric in his initial use of E minor, but
eventually the setting becomes declamatory: unpredictable in its phrase
structure, often flat in its melodic shape, and hinting distantly at parallel

strophes (one minor, one major). With halting, uneven declamation, constantly shifting accompaniment and melody, the composer responds to the querulous sentiments of the persona.

Schumann returns to the *West-östlicher Divan* for the paired numbers "From the Cupbearer's Book" ("Aus dem Schenkenbuch") to summarize the contradictory sentiments found in the rest of op. 25's first volume. Goethe's modest sestet for the first number, with its short rhyming couplets, bespeaks the joys of the single life, and the composer sets this whimsically, repeating the first couplet to create his ternary form. The second number of the pair in a juxtaposition arranged by Schumann consists of two parts in Goethe's original, with subtitles omitted from *Myrthen*. The poet's first part addresses "the landlord" in a declamatory style that warns against his rudeness as host, but when "the cupbearer," a handsome youth, arrives on the scene, the speaker welcomes his company. The composer sets this episode lyrically, as if to say that beauty is always welcome, a fitting moral for the end of this grouping.

Heft II: "Die Lotosblume" (Heine, 12 February), "Talismane" (Goethe, February), "Lied der Suleika" (Willemer, n.d.), "Die Hochländer-Wittwe" (Burns, 24 February), "Lieder der Braut" I–II (Rückert, 1, 4 March)

Whereas volume one entertains shifting, conflicting sentiments, volume two displays firm commitment, with all it entails. "Die Lotosblume" receives an utterly simple accompaniment that belies Schumann's complex and subtle treatment of Heine's verse. We might think that this poem from the "Lyrisches Intermezzo" (immediately preceding "Im Rhein, im heiligen Strome") falls into a fairly regular iambic trimeter, but in fact it proceeds in a special kind of iambic tetrameter called *Langzeilenvers*, particularly favored by nineteenth-century German poets.[19] In this conventional form of verse, which we encounter again and again, the last two syllables of the first line both receive an accent, while a silent foot follows the syllable with an accented ending in the second line of each couplet:

> Die Lótosblúme áeng-stígt
> Sich vór der Sónne Prácht ['],
> Und mít gesénktem Háup-té
> Erwártet sie tráeumend die Nácht ['].

Schumann accords word accent primacy in this case (otherwise he would set "ängstigt" over two dotted half notes), accommodating the silent foot in a typical way by a half measure of rest in the voice. And where it suits his emphasis, he also ignores the iambic pattern by placing the first syllable of a line on an accented beat instead of an upbeat ("sich" and "und"). This plasticity of declamation lends his mature songs their natural expressiveness, facilitated in part by the flexible and unobtrusive accompaniment. The composer leaves no room for doubt about the symbolic lotus's faith in her unearthly lover, cost what it may ("She yields fragrance and weeps and trembles for love and love's pangs"). "Lotosblume" shares the same intense message as the lead song in volume one, though this may not strike us at first glance, and it also features a transcendent common-tone modulation to a flatted mediant key ("Der Mond der ist ihr Buhle").

Schumann may have meant the next two songs as a pair. "Talismane" bows to the inevitability of God's will from a male point of view (the persona is the poet), while its counterpart, the feminine "Lied der Suleika," also appears in Goethe's *Middle Eastern Anthology*. The key relationship of the two songs, however, is indirect ("Talismane" features E minor in its middle section, minor dominant of the A major in "Suleika"). And the pairing poses another irregularity: Schumann assumed that Goethe had written "Suleika," but in fact it originated from the pen of Marianne von Willemer, Goethe's mistress.[20] Charming though we might find this number, the verse does not lend itself to the same clarity of declamation as Goethe's poetry. Still, the pair plays well together, with the forceful accompaniment and exclamations of the former casting the arpeggiations and lyricism of the latter in relief.

The last three songs may also form a group, by virtue of key as well as content. All circle around the nexus of E minor and the relative G major. "The Highland Widow" might strike us as an inappropriate choice for a bridal bouquet, but in it a wife binds herself to the disastrous fortunes of her spouse. This song adds retrospective poignance to Suleika's consecration of her life to her husband and also to his prayer in "Talismane," "As I barter, as I write / Guidest thou my path aright!" The accompaniment in "Hochländer-Wittwe" offers frantic repetition of an uneven rhythmic figure, with the parlando vocal line reaching its highest pitch for the final distressed outburst, "Oh weh, oh weh, oh weh!" ("Och-on, och-on, och-rie! / Nae woman in the warld wide / Sae wretched now as me.") In the ensuing songs love transfigures the female persona's affection for others and emboldens her to risk the uncertain future with determination. Schumann employs two notable conceits in his music for these texts from Rückert's *Liebesfrühling* (the "fourth bouquet"). In the first "Bride's Song" a vocal turn from "Lied der Suleika" appears on the word "also" and then throughout the song, reemphasizing commitment to the beloved (compare exx. 1.2a and 1.2b). Whether Schumann deliberately carried this motive over in composition (we cannot date "Lied der Suleika") or this simply represents stylistic habit, the similarity forms one of those hooks of memory that prompts the listener to think of the earlier song when the latter is heard. For the second "Bride's Song" the composer closes with the same simplicity that opened the volume, this time a chorale texture that connotes sacred overtones. But Schumann plays with our expectations of a strophic hymn, halting progress in the midst of the phrase "Enden? [pause] enden soll sich's nie." ("End? . . . end it never shall.") The conclusion then trails off into a postlude that gives the singer the last word, "lass mich!" Schumann had learned by 1840 that he could wield simple means with understated sophistication to achieve a rhetorical poignance that constituted the intimate essence of the lied.

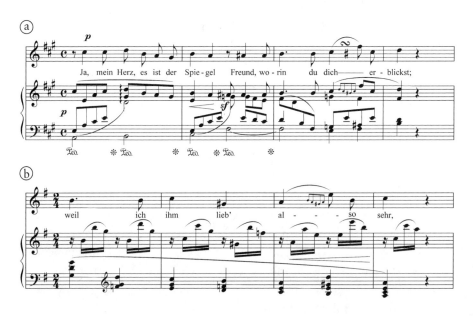

Examples 1.2a–b.   Vocal turns from "Lied der Suleika" and "Lied der Braut I."

Heft III: "Hochländers Abschied" (Burns, 12 February), "Hochländisches Wiegenlied" (Burns, n.d.), "Aus den hebräischen Gesängen" (Byron, 9 February), "Räthsel" (Fanshawe, end of February), "Zwei Venetianische Lieder" (Moore, 13–14 March)

This third volume of *Myrthen* might well bear the title "the British collection," featuring as it does poetry by Robert Burns, Lord Byron, Catherine Fanshawe, and Thomas Moore in translations from various sources. The presence of so much foreign verse concentrated in a single volume of a German song cycle is intriguing. In one sense Robert displays for Clara his wide acquaintance with poetry, and in another he inserts exotic blooms in the bridal bouquet, suggesting journeys of the imagination the couple might share. This may account particularly for the significant presence in *Myrthen* of Robert Burns, from whom the composer drew almost a third of his texts (eight) in Wilhelm Gerhard's recent translations.[21] Schumann had encountered Gerhard socially in Leipzig at the salon of Richard and Livia Frege, a university law professor and his wife, a professional singer who played an important role in the musical life of the city (see the discussion of op. 125 in Chapter 8).[22] The progressive political elements as well as the folkloric quality of Burns's poetry might well have piqued the composer's interest amid this intellectual atmosphere.[23]

The fabled allure of northern Scotland, which fascinated so many of Schumann's contemporaries,[24] combined with the increasing idealization of rural climes in the nineteenth century accounts for the lead song in the third volume, "My Heart's in the Highlands." This poem was one of Burns's most famous during this period, and a number of composers fashioned settings, most notably the popular Henry Russell. While a number of scholars look askance at Gerhard's repeated failure to render the Lallans dialect that plays such an important role in Burns's poetry, the original of "My Heart's in the Highlands" ("Hochländers Abschied") features none. Schumann responds to this verse with a mildly folkloric style: minor mode, heavy accents (in the sixteenth-note figure emphasizing downbeats, cleverly traded between accompaniment and voice), uneven "hunting" rhythms, and the varied strophic form all portend "Scottish" traits.

The ensuing "Highland Lullaby" appears more gently folkloric in its deeply moving simplicity. But Schumann employs a motivic economy in this setting that he could not have achieved without a formal study of composition in the preceding decade. The melody unfolds as a set of "continually developing variations," with the first measure presenting a cell that the composer varies and ornaments in each subsequent measure (see ex. 1.3). Finally in measure 7 Schumann detaches the coaxing, folkloric syncopation and develops it in sequence. The gently rocking unevenness, underlain by a persistent drone, soothes in this case, exuding an undeniable tenderness from a man who cherished hopes of becoming a father.

The vocal waywardness of the Byron setting "Aus den hebräischen Gesängen" stands in stark contrast to the soothing regularity of the preceding "Lullaby." This number offers the most unusual musical treatment of any song in *Myrthen*. Its prelude invokes a topos (that is, a combination of stylistic features that assumes a stereotypical, extramusical association) we encounter again in the opening bars of "Zwielicht" (op. 39/10) and "Muttertraum" (op. 40/2), both of which preface foreboding with a chromatically tortured, contrapuntal figuration. Over this uneasy accompaniment the voice moves disjunctly, occasionally in nonperiodic phrases. Still, Byron's message has its consolation, which must have touched a bride and groom particularly attuned to music:

My soul is dark!—Oh! quickly string	Mein Herz ist schwer! auf! von der Wand
The harp I yet can brook to hear;	die Laute, sie mag ich noch hören;
And let thy gentle fingers fling	Entlockte mir geschickter Hand
Its melting murmurs o'er mine ear.[25]	ihr Töne, die den Schmerz bethören!

Schumann makes quite free with Körner's translation, inserting words that further undermine the regularity of the verse, and for all the soothing qualities attributed to music in the verse, this setting strikes the most melancholy note in the whole cycle.

The remaining songs in volume three seek to avert the gloomy omen of "Mein Herz ist schwer!," and nothing could do this better than the ensuing "Riddle [on the letter H]." Schumann labored under the misapprehension that this text came from the pen of Byron; it appeared in several nineteenth-century anthologies of his poetry, whence it made its way into a pocket edition published by the Schumanns' publishing firm.[26] Catherine Fanshawe, an obscure British poet, was the real author, and Karl Kannegießer made the clever translation of the well-known verse. Schumann goes Kannegießer one better by leaving the text blank under the last vocal pitch, adding a note in the sheet music: "The musician

Example 1.3.   Continually developing variation in "Hochländisches Wiegenlied."

trusts he has expressed himself clearly enough in remaining silent." This is a clue: the composer supplies the answer by entering B natural (H according to the German system) as the unvoiced pitch, a witticism that falls in well with the patter of the setting.

Schumann also indulges a sense of whimsy in the final two songs, settings of poems by Thomas Moore in translations by Ferdinand Freiligrath. The first would seem to be a conventional "gondola song" at first, with the stereotypical rocking motion we can hear in other such compositions from the period by Chopin, Mendelssohn, or Liszt. But Schumann interrupts this gently undulating texture with parlando style for the second couplet of each stanza, which offers a wry contrast to the conventional romantic pining in the initial couplets. The moral, for instance, in the two concluding lines of the second stanza runs, "Ah! did we take for Heaven above but half such pains as we / Take day and night for woman's love, what angels we should be." The composer's setting for the second Venetian song might come right out of *Papillons* or *Carnaval*. Prefaced by a spirited prelude, this romantic vignette from Shrovetide seems less than serious, and even the tenderness of the minor mode in the second half of each stanza is dispelled by the lighthearted postlude.

Heft IV: "Hauptmann's Weib" (Burns, 12 February), "Weit, weit!" (Burns, n.d.), "Was will die einsame Thräne?" (Heine, 11 February), "Niemand" (Burns, n.d.), "Im Westen" (Burns, mid-February), "Du bist wie eine Blume" (Heine, n.d.), "Aus den östlichen Rosen" (Rückert, beginning of April), "Zum Schluss" (Rückert, 1 or 2 March)

Having dwelled in related sharp keys for most of volume two and all of volume three, Schumann now wends his way back in volume four to the flat keys of the cycle's opening amid tales of separation familiar to him and Clara in their long struggle. But the setbacks detailed in the texts of this volume only serve to demonstrate that the bond has been made fast in the end and will continue eternally. The two Burns settings not only supply a link to the previous volume; they also form a pair that introduces the subject of the last one. Both concern the distant beloved, and both invoke the minor mode (E minor and A minor, respectively) that often accompanies "Scottish" subjects. Gerhard alters Burns slightly at the end of "Hauptmann's Weib" in a way that may have prompted Schumann's selection:

Burns	*Gerhard*
When the vanquished foe	Should we beat your foe,
Sues for peace and quiet,	Then go kiss your husband,
To the shades we'll go,	Dwell with him together
And in love enjoy it.	In peace's shadow.

Schumann accords the warrior (battling Friedrich Wieck?) an aggressive accompaniment in the two outer A sections, while the interlude ("Tönet Trommelschlag") features a brooding motive that returns constantly in the left hand of the piano. He does not rearrange Gerhard's translation to achieve the ternary form of this song. The composer simply attends to the fact that the last four lines of the second stanza repeat the poem's opening four lines. This setting assumes a more dramatic aspect than the lyrical strophic setting of the ensuing "Weit, weit!" ("The Bonnie Lad that's far awa'" in the original), which receives a gentler compound meter for the female persona speaking in iambic tetrameter. In this song, outwardly so straightforward, Schumann actually took considerable liberties with Gerhard's original verse, which falls into sestets, with the last two lines always repeating the third and fourth lines. The composer apparently thought this much reiteration excessive, and he reduced the stanzas to quintains that repeat just the final line. Schumann also omitted the third stanza of the original, possibly because it was too reminiscent of recent events: "My father threw me from the house, / And nobody was prepared to console me: / Only one man took my part, / But this one is far, far away!" "Weit, weit!" reminds us that *Myrthen* has more autobiographical import than any other song cycle from 1840.

"Was will die einsame Thräne?," cast in the parallel major mode to "Weit, weit!," now begins to turn the tide by introducing the notion of a final lone tear from disappointed love. In Heine's poem from a subsection of the *Buch der Lieder* entitled "Die Heimkehr," love itself flees. But Schumann pointedly ignores Heine's irony, seizing instead on the thought that grief has flown. The composer therefore sets the poem to a lyrical melody supported by a very placid accompaniment of block chords. These, in conjunction with the slow tempo, lend the effect of arioso to this otherwise conventional treatment of *Langzeilenvers*. The effect is bittersweet, not bitter, with strong overtones of pensive consolation.

Melancholy over misfortune having passed, Schumann moves toward a conclusion to round *Myrthen*, first with an explicit reference to the opening volume in a pair of Burns poems cast in F major. For "Niemand" he leaves the explicit instruction "Companion piece to 'Jemand,' no. 4." But where the female persona in "Somebody" contemplated the unknown, the male persona in "Nobody" knows just what he wants. This celebration receives a dancelike accompaniment, especially in its spry postlude, which contrasts markedly with the gentler compound meter of "Im Westen" from the female point of view (mirroring the gendered opposition that opens volume four). While marked "simply," the chordal accompaniment does not merely persist throughout. To emphasize the optimism of Burns's second stanza, Schumann adopts an arpeggiated pattern, supplies the voice with a new melody (retaining only a rhythmic motive from the first phrase), and marks the passage "more lively."

The concluding group belongs together tonally (A-flat major–E-flat major–A-flat major), serving to close the cycle as a whole in the key in which it began. And if *Myrthen* speaks generally to marriage, "Du bist wie eine Blume," "Aus den östlichen Rosen," and "Zum Schluss" (recalling the second person of "Widmung") form a peroration that addresses Clara most directly. The pulsing block chords of "Du bist wie eine Blume" recall "Die Lotosblume"; the pattern often marks strong emotion in Schumann's catalog of accompanimental devices (we might think, for instance, of "Ich grolle nicht" in *Dichterliebe*). "Du bist" and "Die Lotosblume" also share the same flexible treatment of *Langzeilenvers,* as if it were iambic trimeter. We cannot say exactly why Schumann altered the text of Heine's second line ("so hold und schön und rein" in *Die Heimkehr;* "so schön, so rein und hold" in op. 25). The composer may repeat "so" for emphasis, but the missed rhyme is more puzzling and may have resulted simply from transposing the related last line of the

poem ("So rein und schön und hold" in Heine's original). Some performers correct the passage, and this certainly seems justified where we can
find no apparent reason for Schumann's alteration and where the correc-
tion does not change a meaning he may have had in mind.[27]

Rückert's "Ein Gruss an die Entfernte," from the *Oestliche Rosen,*
presents a different challenge for setting and occasions arguably the most
graceful and loveliest song of the triptych that closes op. 25. Schumann
floats the poet's iambic pentameter over an arpeggiated accompaniment
with an interlude between each line. This allows the five feet to expand
and contract in the space of two and a half to three measures, with the
accompanimental interludes unobtrusively completing the expected four-
measure phrases (see ex. 1.4). Because the poem consists of a single octave with cross-rhymed couplets, the composer is free to choose any form
he will—ternary in this case, like so many settings in *Myrthen.* The first
two couplets run in parallel, the third offers a harmonic diversion, and
the fourth supplies the rounding A′ section. But here Schumann cannot
help embellishing Rückert's apothegm—"If you but think on this joyless
man, / Then my nocturnal heavens become bright"—by repeating the
last line. The setting reveals the depth and sophistication of the composer's early talent for accommodating more intricate meters within a
seemingly artless framework, creating a fluidity that enables the depth of
feeling indicated in its initial marking, "calmly and tenderly."

"Zum Schluss" returns to the "first bouquet" (no. 46) of *Liebesfrühling* and to a chorale texture proceeding from its sacred reference. Schumann heeds Rückert's syntax by fashioning four-measure phrases that
bridge the poet's exquisite enjambments in the first, second, and fourth
couplets:

Example 1.4.   Opening of "Aus den Östlichen Rosen."

Hier in diesen erdbeklommnen	Here amid these earthly anguished
Lüften, wo die Wehmuth thaut,	Breezes, in which sadness wafts,
Hab' ich dir den unvollkommnen	Have I for you this imperfect
Kranz geflochten, Schwester Braut!	Wreath plaited, sister bride!
Wenn uns droben aufgenommnen	When we are received above
Gottes Sonn' entgegen schaut,	And God's sun shines all around,
Wird die Liebe den vollkommnen	Love will plait the perfected
Kranz uns flechten, Schwester Braut!	Wreath for us, sister bride!

The solemnity of the topos gives way in the setting of the last couplet, however, to a slightly more inflected melody. The composer obviously wanted to emphasize the phrases "Wird die Liebe" and "den vollkommnen" by delaying their entrance until the second beat of their respective measures, a gesture he repeats without the voice in the accompanimental postlude.

Myrthen offers the wide array of styles available to Schumann in creating the polyrhythm between poetry (structure, syntax, and meaning), vocal line, and accompaniment. Because of its loosely knit construction, the cycle extends many options to performers. Singers and pianists can and do excerpt individual songs with a clear conscience, they can present individual volumes as coherent units, or they can tackle the whole *Liederkreis,* though this taxes endurance. One successful strategy to combat the last difficulty involves dividing the songs between two singers, one male and one female. In this way a rendition can capitalize on the multiple points of view entailed in this lavish gift and opus.

Frauenliebe und Leben von Adelbert Chamisso. Acht Lieder für eine Singstimme mit Begleitung des Pianoforte, op. 42 (sketched 11–12 July 1840; ostensibly realized August 1840; revised April–May 1843; published July 1843 by Fr. Kistner)

Frauenliebe, one of Schumann's canonic cycles (the others include *Dichterliebe* and the Eichendorff *Liederkreis*), has the distinction of being the first group of lieder to have its dates of composition entered in the household accounts (we must glean information about earlier songs from letters, sketches, or the autograph realizations bound in the *Liederbücher*). Over the ensuing days, following a habit of dwelling on a collection by a favorite author, the composer went on to set other selections from Chamisso's *Lieder und Lyrisch Epische Gedichte,* which begins with "Frauen-Liebe" (as the title appears in its literary source). The original nine poems were conceived as a cycle per se, and Schumann set the first eight in order, omitting the ninth poem and segments from the remaining eight as well.[28]

Because of its subject matter and because it still receives many performances, op. 42 has become the focus of continuing debate about the portrayal of women by nineteenth-century male authors and composers. Some feminist readings find the cycle highly problematic,[29] but Kristina Muxfeldt observes that such approaches do not "reach far beyond asserting the superiority of modern social values."[30] She continues with a perceptive assessment of both Chamisso's stature during his lifetime and the contemporary significance of the exercise entailed in his (and then Schumann's) attempt to speak in a female voice. Born in France of parents who fled the revolution in 1790, Louis Charles Adelaide de Chamisso (1781–1838) lived the greater part of his life in Berlin, eventually becoming a distinguished scientist in charge of the botanical gardens there. He published scientific studies as well as fiction, and he was known particularly for his translations of foreign poetry as well as for his own verse. Such distinguished contemporaries as E.T.A. Hoffmann, August Wilhelm Schlegel, and even the acerbic Heine thought highly of Chamisso's writings, and later Thomas Mann devoted an admiring essay to his poetry.[31] Chamisso's progressive sympathies led him "to portray neglected segments of culture and to champion the lives of the ordinary people within them," a context in which we can profitably view *Frauenliebe*.[32] It certainly records the values of an earlier period in a more blatantly sentimental manner than we would find suitable for art literature today, partly because we have consigned sentimentality and nostalgia to the realm of popular culture, where they flourish unabashedly.

We have already seen in *Myrthen* that Schumann could indulge sentimentality and that op. 25 also contains a good deal of poetry written by male authors in the voice of female personae, including "Lied der Suleika" (which Schumann attributed incorrectly to Goethe), "Hochländer-Wittwe," "Lied der Braut," and "Weit, weit!" In his correspondence with Clara before their marriage, Schumann sometimes switched gendered places in a playful counterpoint: "Adieu, dear girl of my heart, dear brother of my heart, my dear spouse; adieu, I love you with all my heart; give my regards to your dear friends—I'll write to Emilie with the next letter. Now we must part. Robert Wieck."[33] Robert and Clara's marriage developed into a partnership unusual for its day (especially given the nine-year difference in the couple's ages), though Clara initially had to fight for her career. It is altogether fitting that Schumann composed *Frauenliebe,* though it sometimes sits oddly with our mores.

Op. 42 does not present so much a connected narrative as a chronological series of vignettes in a woman's courtship and marriage, though Schumann omitted Chamisso's epilogue disclosing these as reminiscences imparted by a widow to her granddaughter. Because a lied (as opposed to a ballad) reveals the internal thoughts of a fictional persona, cycles devoted to the reflections of a single speaker yield a series of psychological snapshots. And in the case of *Frauenliebe,* Schumann accords the individual pictures an unusually dramatic treatment, as if he had a *"Liederspiel"* (a play made from songs) in mind. Muxfeldt suggests that "the woman of the *Frauenliebe* poems maintains an extremely active life of the imagination," and this may also account for the composer's somewhat operatic approach.[34] Op. 42 demands a singing actor of considerable talent, providing another reason for its persistence in the repertory. During the nineteenth century even a baritone such as Julius Stockhausen included this piece in his repertory, and it remains a favorite of female opera singers today.[35]

The operatic overtones of *Frauenliebe* may inhere in Chamisso's texts, which tend to treat subject matter in groups. The first two poems map initial infatuation, the second three address engagement leading to marriage, the sixth and seventh concern childbirth, and the last song speaks of the husband's death. This seems to have suggested to Schumann that he set the numbers in declamatory-lyrical complexes bearing some resemblance to cantabile-cabaletta or sometimes arioso-aria.

The detached, punctuated chords in "Seit ich ihm gesehen" map a halting progress that underpins a somewhat irregular phrase structure and shifting metrical placement, as if both singer and accompanist have been thrown off-balance. True, the phrases appear in pairs. But in this case Schumann folds the trochaic tetrameter of Chamisso's two initial couplets into three-measure phrases that displace the beginning of the second line to a weak beat, a shift accentuated by piano interjections at the end of each line (see ex. 1.5). Eventually the composer returns to quadratic phrasing ("Wie im wachen Traume"), and toward the end of each stanza the voice reaches its highest point before pronounced disjunct motion emphasizes the word "tiefsten" ("deepest"). The melody, parts of which unfold in more parlando style, encompasses one stanza in fourteen mea-

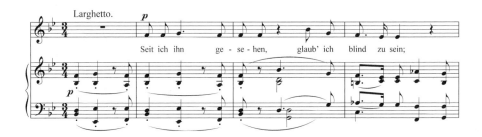

Example. 1.5.   Shifting accentuation between voice and piano in "Seit ich ihm gesehen."

sures. Here Schumann intermingles declamatory and lyrical style to introduce the basic situation.

"Er, der Herrlichste von Allen" features more regularity than the first number; its vocal display intimates aria more than song. Though bel canto lay very far from Schumann's aesthetic, the vaulting arpeggiations, large leaps, and frequent ornaments here lend themselves to glorious display by an agile voice. The hammered block chords in the accompaniment take on an almost orchestral fullness that serves to underscore the vehemence of passion in the singer's vocal exhibition. Schumann builds cunningly to the central point of this number, beginning calmly with the persona's resignation ("Wandle, wandle deine Bahnen") and rising at her noble self-abnegation to an operatic G-flat ("Nur die Würdigste von Allen / darf beglücken deine *Wahl*"). We might almost expect a cadenza at the dramatic ritardando that marks the singer's final utterance, but in fact Schumann assigns this function to the piano postlude. In a distant sense, the initial two songs, the first, in B-flat, serving as dominant to the second, in E-flat, form a pair akin to the cantabile and cabaletta of contemporary opera arias, though we could carry this characterization too far if we took it literally.

The next two songs form a pair as well, again with some theatrical resonance. The persona's realization that her feelings of affection are requited leads to the marking "with passion" and an exceptionally sparse texture of widely spaced chords supporting a predominantly repeated-note melody. The phrases assume more of a quadratic structure (again Schumann sets *Langzeilenvers* as trimeter in the service of natural word accent), but the melodic contour could not be called lyrical. The composer underscores this parlando quality by inserting instructions for many tempo modifications, and thus "Ich kann's nicht fassen" dwells in a realm between recitative and aria, really a kind of arioso. This setting particularly fits utterances such as "It seemed to me as if he had said: I'll be forever thine" ("Mir war's, er habe gesprochen: Ich bin auf ewig dein"). The C minor arioso prepares the aria in the relative E-flat major, "Du Ring an meinem Finger." Marked "heartfelt," this song offers classic lyricism emphasized by the regularity of the accompanimental arpeggiations and a conventional setting of *Langzeilenvers* as tetrameter ("Du Ríng an méinem Fíng-ér, / da hást du mich érst beléhrt ['] "). The more dramatic contrasting section ("Ich will ihm dienen"), with its repeated block chords, adds just enough variety to emphasize the return of lyrical style with the opening phrase. And the B section also coincides well with the persona's declaration of complete devotion, something that runs as a theme through much of Chamisso's cycle as a whole. The courtship ends in betrothal; the persona takes stock of her feelings using the lyrical style traditionally associated with internal reflection.

The bridal song "Helft mir, ihr Schwestern" begins with an accompanimental pattern we have seen before in "Widmung," the first number of *Myrthen* (in fact, myrtle is specifically mentioned in the text of "Helft mir," possibly prompting a musical allusion). The vaulting arpeggios featuring dotted rhythms have the same athletic energy here, betraying the same passion (see ex. 1.6), but there are important differences as well. First, and most important, Schumann casts this trochaic verse in duple meter, and though the arpeggiations disguise the fact, through much of the song the vocal line actually offers a wedding march. Not until the postlude does this become blatantly evident in the piano, when the procession to the altar emerges from the arpeggiations and then recedes deli-

Example 1.6. Accompanimental pattern in "Helft mir, ihr Schwester" similar to that in "Widmung."

cately in horn fifths. The vocal part in "Helft mir" assays a fairly wide range, ultimately an octave and a half, and though it does not feature much ornamentation, the second varied strophe does end on a high, demonstrative pitch for the voice. Alone among all the numbers in *Frauenliebe*, however, "Helft mir" finds its roots in instrumental style, and we should not be surprised to see that the piano tends to play a more important role in providing energy.

"Süsser Freund" and "An meinem Herzen," arguably the most intimate of numbers in the cycle, continue the pairing of a more declamatory and a more lyrical number joined by a tonal relationship (G major moving to its dominant, D major). These two songs are also the most empathetic to the viewpoint of a woman, focused as they are on the speaker's role as mother rather than on her admiration for her husband, which has such patriarchal overtones in *Frauenliebe*. "Süsser Freund" is the most erotically charged poem in Chamisso's cycle, and it seems fitting, therefore, that Schumann effaces the poetic meter in the interest of free and vivid expression. We lose almost all sense of musical meter in the outer sections as well, though "Weisst du die Thränen" briefly ushers in a pronounced beat, as the wife bids the husband to press his head closer to her heart. Schumann abridged this poem, omitting its third stanza:

Hab' ob manchen Zeichen	About the many signs I've
Mutter schon gefragt,	Already asked Mother,
Hat die gute Mutter	My good mother
Alles mir gesagt,	Has told me everything,
Hat mich unterwiesen,	Has instructed me
Wie, nach allem Schein,	That, by all appearances,
Bald für eine Wiege	Soon for a cradle
Muß gesorget sein.	Provision must be made.

The composer's version avoids shifting focus away from the couple in their passion, and it saves the mention of pregnancy for the end of the number, directing the action more forcefully to that disclosure. Though the voice part does move in even, periodic phrases throughout this song, the melody itself features parlando style that permits the full dramatic latitude of arioso.

The paired "aria" of this small episode finds the female persona right after childbirth, where the man becomes entirely superfluous in the presence of the nursing mother and her child: "Oh how I pity a husband, / who cannot feel a mother's happiness!" This song has no break in the vocal line, unusual in a cycle filled with dramatic pauses and silences; the arpeggiations reinforce the headlong rush with a jubilant background. Only when the new mother addresses her child does Schumann reduce the accompaniment to a sparser texture, at the same time introducing more inflections of tempo. This song arguably constitutes the dramatic apogee of the cycle, the text defining the role a man can never remotely share or fathom. We may think cynically that Chamisso, and Schumann with him, relegates the persona to a domestic part, immures her in her motherhood. But the effervescent accompaniment and the nonstop vocal line seek to communicate an undeniable, almost militant pride. The male role in procreation is, in the end, transitory and shallow compared to the sacrifice of women, something both poet and composer hoped to relate.

The contrast between "An meinem Herzen" and "Nun hast du" could not be greater, yet another instance of the theatricality Schumann invoked for *Frauenliebe*. Again we are presented with an oddity of structure that pervades various selections in the cycle: on the surface we have paired, repeated phrases, but the lack of rhythmic pattern in the accompaniment and the relatively flat vocal shaping suggest something more like recitative than lied. The many strikingly dissonant harmonies, which emphasize individual words rather than poetic structure, add to this affective manner of setting. Again, we could view this song as a self-serving product of the male ego, but is this fair? Aside from the loss of a child, life holds no heavier emotional blow than the loss of a spouse, here viewed from the standpoint of a woman.

The postlude of "Nun hast du" performs the important tonal task of moving back to the opening key of the cycle, but we could hardly call this a subtle modulation. In fact, the composer seems to pursue a deliberate disjunction, raising the question of why he chooses such a disturbing transition. We have noted that Schumann omitted the epilogue of Chamisso's cycle, in which the female persona casts the previous poems as memories related to her granddaughter. Some writers view the coda to the last song, which quotes extensively from the cycle's first number, as an attempt to provide an instrumental analogue of the missing poem:

Schumann's postlude may be thought to represent a memory, and not merely a symbolic or formal return, precisely because the past is brought back through the filter of present emotion and experience. The very inaccuracy of the repetition, its muted passion, intimates the perceptual mechanisms of a memory that has no hope of being revitalized by physical proximity.[36]

This view, articulated by Muxfeldt, hits upon the question of whether music can "intimate the perceptual mechanisms of memory," and here Karol Berger, writing on poetic modes in art and music, offers insight:

> Composers have at their disposal a whole range of punctuating devices, such as cadences of various strengths, with which to articulate their musical discourses. . . . In Liszt's piano transcription of Schubert's setting of the "Erlkönig," the final recitative contrasts so strongly with the preceding gallop that, even without Goethe's text in our ears, we are likely to read it as an appearance of a new world suddenly pushing the old one into the distance.[37]

What appears to be a clumsy modulation between the body of "Nun hast du" and the piano postlude presents just the kind of interruption to which Berger refers, a jarring event that heralds the "appearance of a new world . . . pushing the old one into the distance." And Schumann's ensuing instrumental postlude to *Frauenliebe* serves effectively as an analogue to the recollection of past events in Chamisso's epilogue to *his* cycle of lieder.

We are left, then, with the persistent question of whether *Frauenliebe und Leben* gives little more than an "elegant view of how the more authoritarian paterfamilias hoped to be regarded by his wife, and particularly how he assumed she would greet his death."[38] Chamisso's poems aspire to something beyond this, cover a wider range of feminine experience, and are remarkable for the endeavor. Perhaps this verse is not as unsuccessful as modern critics would have us believe: we need only compare them to, say, Elizabeth Barrett Browning's less explicit, loftier, but equally effusive *Sonnets from the Portuguese* (1850), written for Robert Browning, to realize that Chamisso did not miss his mark completely. Certainly a female poet speaks more authentically in this arena; the value for a male author lies in the exercise. Schumann treated these poems in a singular way, much more theatrically than any of his other 1840 cycles taken as a whole. This may testify to the insight he derived from trying to assume a woman's point of view, just as the persistence of the cycle in the repertory of singers bears witness at least to his artistic success.

Zwölf Gedichte aus F. Rückerts Liebesfrühling für Gesang und Pianoforte von Robert und Clara Schumann, op. 37/12 (nos. 1, 3, 5–10, 12 composed by Robert 4–11, 16 January 1841; nos. 2, 4, 11 composed by Clara by 6 June 1841; published September 1841 by Breitkopf & Härtel)

"The week of Christmas has just come upon me," wrote Robert in the Schumanns' common "Marriage Diary." "How gladly would I describe it, and how much my heart's brightness [*Kläre*] has thrilled me and bestowed on me. I was particularly delighted by 3 songs in which she still has a girl's enthusiasm and composes much more clearly [*klarere*] than before. We have a lovely idea about interweaving them with some by me and then have them printed. This would produce a volume truly warmed by love."[39] The honeymoon persisted, evidently: Robert's endearing plays on Clara's name marked the first months of the couple's marriage (they both kept the diary and used it, among other things, to pass notes to each other). Even before their marriage, Robert dreamed in a letter to Clara on 13 June 1839 that "we will publish many things *in both our names;* posterity will think of us as one heart and one soul and won't find out what's yours and what's mine."[40] Finally in 1841 the singular idea of a common opus of songs combining the talents of the newly married couple came to fruition in *Zwölf Gedichte aus F. Rückerts Liebesfrühling,* presented to Clara on 13 September, her birthday.[41]

The Schumanns led a widely collaborative artistic life, although much of it appears only in circumstantial evidence. Even before their wedding Clara championed Robert's works for piano; after their marriage all his symphonies (with the exception of the Third) received their premieres on programs featuring Clara as soloist, and she frequently served as accompanist either for performances of his songs and chamber works in salon or, later, for his activities as a choral director in Dresden and then Düsseldorf. It is hard to believe, moreover, that Clara did not somehow participate in Robert's compositional process, serving as she did on a number of occasions as his copyist.[42] The *Liebesfrühling* collection, however, is the couple's only explicitly documented collaboration. After Robert composed his contributions in early January 1841, he urged his wife to follow his example: "Clara should also set now a few from *Liebesfrühling.* O, do it, Clari!"[43] Clara developed writer's block but kept trying through most of May and into early June, finally presenting her husband on his birthday with four settings of Rückert's poetry.[44]

Schumann had already tried to interest Kistner in publishing a joint opus of lieder (settings of Rückert by him, settings of Burns by Clara), but this failed. A collection solely of Rückert settings had more appeal when Robert suggested it to Breitkopf in June 1841: "I would like to delight my wife a bit on her birthday, which falls in the middle of September, with the following: we have composed a number of Rückert songs that relate to one another like questions and answers, and so forth. I would like to bestow on her this collection in print on that day."[45]

Rückert's poetry is well represented among Robert's solo lieder and duets,[46] and *Liebesfrühling* had special significance for the Schumanns throughout in their marriage. Rückert (1788–1866) had studied philology and later became a professor of oriental languages, but not before marrying his landlord's daughter, Luise Wiethaus, and writing the more than four hundred poems organized into *Liebesfrühling*. The Schumanns must have noticed the parallels to their own romance, and this in turn may have prompted Robert to mine the collection so frequently in 1840–41. As we have seen in *Myrthen,* Rückert sometimes assumes a feminine as well as a masculine voice. The mellifluousness of his poetry, with its many sonorous repetitions and refrains as well as its deep sentiment, made it a favorite of composers. The Schumanns' choice to set Rückert jointly and Breitkopf's rapid publication of their efforts should come as no surprise.

Heft I: "Der Himmel hat eine Thräne geweint" (Robert), "Er ist gekommen" (Clara), "O ihr Herren" (Robert), "Liebst du um Schönheit" (Clara), "Ich hab' in mich gesogen" (Robert), "Liebste was kann denn uns scheiden?" (Robert), "Schön ist das Fest des Lenzes" (Robert)

Rufus Hallmark makes a case for *Liebesfrühling* as a cycle,[47] and in the sense that the Schumanns experimented with different orderings of the songs and also organized them into somewhat coherent volumes, op. 37 deserves this designation as much as *Myrthen.* The structure proceeds by volume, Hallmark argues, each containing a dialogue between lovers and closing with a duet celebrating love. The songs also group by key, the first volume revolving clearly around A-flat major. Clara quite probably had heard Robert's contributions when she started writing, and either she made an attempt to pick up some of Robert's melodic ideas for the sake of consistency or the couple arranged the opus to highlight similarities. Though quite different in mood and their accompaniments, numbers one and two, for instance, begin with head motives bearing some resemblance (featuring alternations of two adjacent pitches). This subgroup also has consistency of tonic in the end (A-flat major–F minor–A-flat major). And though the text of the first song nowhere specifies gender, the second song clearly speaks in a female voice. Numbers three and four, which stand in the relationship of tonic to dominant, both emphasize an initial leap upward of a fourth, as does number five. If the songs follow an alternating pattern, this group begins and ends with the poet speaking, while the beloved addresses him in between (she advises him to love "a mermaid" if he desires wealth). The sixth song comes from a male point of view (addressed to "Liebste"), but playful interjections involve both singers, and Schumann changes the lyrics for the refrain ("wollen wir, o Liebster / Liebste sein"), an indication that he concerned himself specifically with gendered content. The last two songs in volume one obviously form a pair, sharing the same key and the same head motive inverted, and requiring both singers acting as one in the canonic march "Schön ist das Fest des Lenzes."

If the songs in the volume, whether by Robert or Clara, intertwine convincingly, they also exhibit the proclivities of their respective composers. Robert takes far more harmonic risks and indulges more rhetorical variation in his songs as a rule. He is willing to alter the accompanimental rhythm, to minimize the piano, to tinker with the metrical placement of the text (as we have seen earlier), and to experiment with form. Clara keeps her eye more firmly on the tonic and tends to hold accompaniments steadier, partly because she tends toward strophic design (at least in this volume). Her writing for the piano flows more, she is not afraid to demand a wider range from the voice, and she too reverses iambic and trochaic accentuation where expression requires it. Robert trades more modest demands on the pianist and singer for unpredictability; Clara offers more predictability of pattern in exchange for more virtuosity. The superiority of hindsight allows us to pinpoint these differences, but distinguishing one composer from the other without foreknowledge would take some doing—precisely what Robert had in mind ("Posterity will think of us as one heart and one soul and won't find out what's yours and what's mine").

To take specific examples of the differences in the composers' approaches, we might contrast "Er ist gekommen" with "Liebste was kann

uns denn scheiden?" Both texts present metrical problems for a composer. If one reads "Er ist gekommen" iambically (Er íst gekóm-mén), the
trimeter must somehow fit into the basic quadratic assumptions of the
style, while trochees would involve duel accents (Ér íst gekóm-mén), an
option Clara takes for the fifth line of the first two stanzas. Quite aside
from this problem are the seven lines in each strophe, another item to be
reconciled with quadratic tradition. To create the proper mood of unrest, she chooses iambic trimeter for most of this song, subsuming the
poem's metrical irregularities in a virtuosic, arpeggiated accompaniment
that surely responds to "in Sturm und Regen" (see ex. 1.7). This then allows her to address the semantic level of the last verse with a much
calmer patter in the piano, highlighting the delightful ambiguity of the
text: he ("er" in German) refers both to the male beloved and to spring
(the masculine "*der* Frühling"), for the message of the coda, setting the
last verse, relates that "he" (the beloved and love's spring) moves on, but
the promise of his affection or warming has been fulfilled and continues.

   Robert chooses quite an opposite course for "Liebste," deliberately ex-
hibiting its playfully odd changes in length of line by means of a minimal-

Example 1.7.   Entry of the voice and piano figuration in Clara's "Er ist
gekommen."

Example 1.8.   Beginning of Robert's "Liebste, was kann denn uns scheiden?"

ist accompaniment that stops and starts erratically. Even then he must re-peat some words to fulfill quadratic expectations:

Rückert	*Schumann*
Ob wir uns zu sehn vermeiden,	Ob wir uns zu sehn vermeiden,
Ungescheiden	Ungescheiden, Ungescheiden
Wollen wir im Herzen seyn.	Wollen wir im Herzen sein.
Mein und dein,	Mein und dein, dein und mein,
Dein und mein,	Wollen wir, o Liebste, sein.
Wollen wir, o Liebste, seyn.	Wollen wir, o Liebster / Liebste, sein.

Robert tends to manipulate the text to his ends, disclosing its irregularity at the beginning of his setting but reforming it toward the end (which of course initially highlights its playfulness by way of contrast; see ex. 1.8). He uses the vocal line and word repetition to his structural and expressive ends where Clara uses the accompaniment. We could not claim, of course, that Robert never uses accompaniments in this way or that Clara considered only the piano; merely that their proclivities, the one literary, the other pianistically virtuosic, tended to manifest themselves.

Heft II: "Flügel! Flügel!" (Robert), "Rose, Meer und Sonne" (Robert), "O Sonn', o Meer, o, Rose!" (Robert), "Warum willst du And're fragen" (Clara), "So wahr die Sonne scheinet" (Robert)

The songs in the second volume form two subgroups, the first revolving around B major, the second around the concluding E-flat major. Not surprisingly "Flügel," "Rose, Meer," and "O Sonn', o Meer" directly follow one another in an "interlude" during the "third bouquet" of Rückert's *Liebesfrühling,* and so the group's related keys and the motivic link between numbers two and three follow from the order in which Robert encountered them. "Flügel! Flügel!" must be the most theatrical setting in *Liebesfrühling,* expressing Rückert's wide-ranging sentiments of elation, and in it Robert indulges an internal section of quasi-recitative between the two related outer sections, which rise and fall, as it were, on the wind. This dramatic, through-composed approach stands in stark relief to the gentle lyricism of the ensuing two strophic songs, which unfold almost as a set of vocal variations paralleling Rückert's poetic recastings (compare exx. 1.9a and 1.9b). One particularly lovely touch binding the two songs together comes in their shared postlude. These three songs form one of Robert's most interesting attempts to build larger structures from shorter units by means of both dramatic contrast and motivic commonality.

The concluding group in the second volume of *Liebesfrühling* assumes a tone of elegant simplicity, with Clara's "Warum willst du" in A-flat major and Robert's duet, "So wahr die Sonne," in E-flat major. Clara's song displays all the subtle expressive power a composer could derive from a varied strophic setting. She connects Rückert's first two stanzas without pause, initially leading us to expect straightforward repetition of the mel-

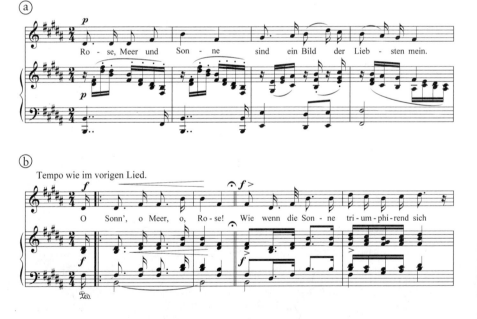

Examples 1.9a–b.   Melodic transfer from "Rose, Meer und Sonne" (a) to "O Sonn', o Meer, o, Rose!" (b).

ody for each verse. But the music for the second stanza has a very slightly different ending, and the separated third stanza varies the conclusion again to emphasize its point: "No matter what my lips may say, look in my eyes—I love you." The composer accords "you" ("dich") the highest pitch and then reinforces the whole thought by repeating it, beginning on the same F and bringing the melody down to its conclusion. Each reiteration save for the last, then, becomes more intense, focusing our attention on the parallel imagery that concludes each of Rückert's stanzas. A casual glance at Robert's final duet might lead us at first to think of chorale texture, but this setting clearly stems from the tradition of the part song, with the accompaniment providing the inner voices. The horn fifths in the beginning phrase and sprinkled strategically throughout the rest of the number transport us to a pastoral, not a sacred, realm. And the conceit of the part song permits a lovely touch: voice exchange beginning with "Die Sonne mag verscheinen," a fitting end to the Schumanns' intertwined opus.

Hallmark asserts that *Liebesfrühling* deserves far more attention than it has generally garnered from the academic and performing communities. At the very least, it provides both a case to test issues of gender in composition and a vehicle for combined presentation by a male-and-female pair.

Liebesfrühling also has a remarkable epilogue: on 24 May 1842 Robert dispatched a copy of op. 37 to the poet at his summer home near Coburg, and three weeks later Rückert replied with a dedicatory poem. It concludes:

Meine Lieder singt ihr wieder,	You sing my songs again,
Mein Empfinden klingt ihr wieder,	You intone my sentiments again,
Mein Gefühl beschwingt ihr wieder,	You brandish my feelings again,
Meinen Frühling bringt ihr wieder,	You bring my springtime back,
Mich, wie schön verjüngt ihr wieder:	Rejuvenating me as handsome as before:
Nehmt meinen Dank, wenn euch die Welt,	Take my thanks, if the world,
Wie mir einst, ihren vorenthält!	As it did from me once, withholds its.
(Und wendet ihr den Dank erlangen,	(And should you receive thanks,
So hab' ich meinen mit empfangen.)	I receive mine along with yours.)[48]

Liebesfrühling in its turn provides a fitting epilogue to this section on the "songs of marriage," simply because no matter how much credit redounds to Robert for his extraordinary songs, we must suspect that Clara influenced many of them. It stretches credulity to suppose that the artist who presided at the keyboard for many first performances and remained intimately connected to her husband's career all her life did not offer him informal reaction and advice. And so Clara must count as an implicit as well as explicit collaborator in his collections of lieder, just as she served as both direct and indirect motivator for the more successful and mature phase of his career.

2

Irony and the Heine Cycles

If the song cycles connected to Schumann's marriage found him in a sentimental mood, his two Heine cycles from 1840 provided the antithesis in their depictions of thwarted relationships that use the stereotypical conventions of lyrical poetry to draw more cynical portraits. Some writers have considered Schumann's Heine cycles in the context of his romance with Clara Wieck,[1] but this has engendered puzzlement on the one hand and willful interpretations on the other, because of the disparity between the strength of the couple's bond and the bitter rejection described in the poetry.

Warranted though it might be to draw biographical connections for cycles such as *Myrthen* and *Liebesfrühling* (tied specifically by the composer to his marriage), such an approach to the Heine *Liederkreis* or *Dichterliebe* emphasizes the problems inherent in using biographical tools unreflectively for artistic interpretation. For one thing, the impetus to create does not always find its roots in an artist's current situation. For another, the bitterness and cynicism in Heine's poetry result from more than romance alone, as Christiane Westphal reminds us: "Heine could connect only conditionally to the romantic lyrics of his predecessors. For unlike them, the topic of love in Heine includes social and political themes. Unhappy love relationships in Heine also become metaphors for similar experiences of being foreign, excluded, and socially isolated."[2] Schumann considered Heine one of Germany's finest poets because he captured the alienation of a generation disillusioned by the political and social retrogression promulgated at the Congress of Vienna. Sociopolitical disaffection in the context of Schumann's inherently nationalistic view of the lied may explain why he produced more solo settings of Heine's verse (which often employs pointedly German symbolism) than of any other single poet's.

Heine's writing also must have appealed to Schumann's long-standing proclivity for the ironic. The composer writes in his student diaries of the playwright Christian Grabbe: "He is often reminiscent of the bizarre-rie in the Heine lieder, that burning sarcasm, that *enormous* despair, all the caricatures of majesty and dignity that he holds in common with Heine."[3] We encounter an analogously sarcastic and witty tone in some of Schumann's early piano music and in his criticism.[4] The composer would also have appreciated Heine on the more profound and philosoph-ical level of Romantic irony, which entailed "an eternal longing for a world never truly believed to come within reach"[5] and a view of existence as not merely chaotic but fundamentally contradictory. "Irony is the form taken by the paradoxical," Friedrich Schlegel once wrote. "Every-thing that is at once good and great is paradoxical."[6] Given Schumann's deep admiration for Schlegel and authors such as Jean Paul, he could hardly have forgone setting Heine, whose verse summoned some of the composer's finest moments.

The root of "irony" lies in the Greek *eiron*, literally a "dissembler in speech," somebody who intends the opposite of or something different from what his utterance means on its surface. The problem with irony comes in its detection: either we must know the context of a passage in advance in order to perceive the disparity between thought and word, or something about the speech must arouse our suspicion. At all events, whether ironic speech mocks or offers a more detached view of an indif-ferently conflicted universe, it always presents a paradox. By this token, we also interpret situations as "ironic" if they produce a result opposite to what we expect.

Since we mean the term "irony" in several different ways and since this device can be difficult to detect in literature, the relationship of Schu-mann's music to irony has occasioned a great deal of varied opinion.[7] Some authors ask whether the composer created an analogue to poetic irony in setting a particular text, some wonder whether a setting offers a context that aids in detecting submerged meaning, some suggest that the music of a setting can itself be ironic, and some question whether a set-ting needs to reinforce or react to irony in verse at all (does the poetry itself not suffice?). Schumann's lieder avail themselves of several options in treating Heine's irony, which we can explore in the context of the *Liederkreis* and *Dichterliebe*.

Liederkreis von H. Heine für eine Singstimme und Pianoforte . . . op. 24 (composed February 1840?; published May 1840 by Breitkopf & Härtel)

"Allow me to send a collection [op. 24] enclosed, on which I have worked long with enthusiasm and love," Schumann wrote to the music publisher Breitkopf & Härtel on 23 Feburary 1840, adding wryly, "Since people know me only as a piano composer, I imagine it will excite interest here and there."[8] If we are to believe this letter, the composer was hard at work writing lieder well before 1 February 1840, usually considered the beginning of the "year of song." The autograph gives us little help in dating op. 24: it was inserted into *Liederbuch I* in a particularly clean fair copy that served as the exemplar for engraving. Schumann may well have worked on the cycle for some time before the songs that now appear in the *Liederbuch* were engraved as op. 24.[9] But whatever the chronology of op. 24's genesis, we must attach significance to the fact that he chose as his first published vocal work a preexisting *Liederkreis* from a section of Heine's *Buch der Lieder* (1827) cleverly titled "Junge Leiden. Lieder." ("Early Sorrows. Songs.").[10] Schumann accorded this author pride of place much like an editor positioning a lead article in the first issue of a new volume of a journal. Though it is often overshadowed by *Dichterliebe,* op. 24 ranks as one of Schumann's greatest song cycles, a fact just now being recognized in the increasing number of recordings accorded to it. Indeed, Schumann modeled *Dichterliebe* directly on op. 24, in both its implied narrative and its shape. In other ways op. 24 holds more in common with *Frauenliebe,* sharing its dramatic tone and the variety of its musical style. Positioned in this way, op. 24 contains some of the composer's most lyrical moments combined with some of his most dramatic vocabulary, rewarding singer-actors and listeners alike.

Heine took great pains over a considerable period to craft the cycle of nine poems, some of which appeared singly in various literary journals during the second decade of the nineteenth century. Originally the poet gathered fourteen selections together under the title *Minnelieder* in his first book of *Gedichte* (1822). But for the first edition of his *Buch der Lieder,* published in 1827, he removed five songs and supplanted the titles of individual poems with numbers. Heine revised the language once more for the third edition of the *Buch der Lieder* (1839), but Schumann did not consult this particular edition.[11] In the 1827 version set by the composer, the cycle traces a narrative that begins with the persona's anticipation of his beloved's arrival (nos. 1 and 2), hopes for her affection (nos. 3 and 4), rejection (no. 5), rage and flight (nos. 6 and 7), resignation (no. 8), and a reflexive account of healing that enshrines the story in verse (no. 9). Though the narrative describes "an old story" (to borrow a phrase from another Heine poem), its imagery is vivid to the point of exaggeration, running the gamut from subtle irony to intense sarcasm. This provided Schumann with the impetus to deploy his full range of musical idiom in setting the songs, each in a distinctive style that nevertheless integrates well into the whole.

We can tell from the manuscript for op. 24 that Schumann originally conceived the cycle in two volumes, each ending with a showpiece, respectively "Schöne Wiege meiner Leiden" (no. 5) and "Mit Myrthen und Rosen" (no. 9). In casting the music (we can see the actual markings in the autograph), Breitkopf's engraver managed to fit the cycle into one long volume of twenty-three pages, but it is still profitable to consider the composer's original plan.[12] In tonal shape volume one would have progressed from D major to B minor to B major to E minor to E major, with volume two moving around the circle of fifths back to the starting point, from E major to A major to D minor to D major. Thus arranged, a sarcastic miniature in parallel minor sets up the magisterial concluding song of each volume, rather in the manner that a slow introduction prepares the body of a longer instrumental movement. Even in its final published form, the fulcrum of the cycle falls on "Schöne Wiege," with four songs leading up to it and then four songs leading away. In this way Schumann reflected Heine's meticulously considered structure, which places the longest poem and turning point at the center while treating the final poem as valediction.

The first two songs, revolving around anticipation, connect by key signature and incessant tempo changes that reflect Schumann's reading of the persona's uncertainty. In other ways the poetry and settings contrast markedly, however. Westphal observes that the ironic essence of "Morgens steh' ich auf" lies in its constant juxtaposition of antitheses: arrival and absence, expectant mornings and disappointed evenings, nights spent sleepless and days spent slumbering.[13] To this the composer adds a further level of "polyrhythmic" contradiction outlined by Berthold Hoeckner, in which the melody traces an ever-increasing agitation by reaching successively higher pitches in each phrase (a progression continued by the piano in its penultimate measure).[14] The piano, at least until the final measures of the postlude, contradicts the growing agitation on a different level by means of a most unassuming pattern of alternating bass notes and replying right-hand chords, an accompanimental cliché. This steadfast nonchalance on the part of the accompanist, played against the rising pitch of a melody at odds yet further with the repeated contradictions in the poetry, creates the irony of this song, revealing that, at least in Schumann's reading, the persona's mounting anxiety belies his superficial vacillation and paralysis.

In "Es treibt mich hin" the persona's impatience erupts with full force. The accompanimental pattern now vacillates wildly, while the melody paradoxically traces a varied strophic form (Heine's quatrains begin with the same phrase but end differently). For this song the composer adopts a far more dramatic idiom, replete with a miniature cadenza, theatrical pauses, and the piano's thundering commentary on the persona's parting shot, "Secretly plotting in gruesome alliance, [the seasons] maliciously spite lovers' haste." The speed of the postlude, however, displays the ironic distance between time's recalcitrance and the speaker's impatience. This further emphasizes Schumann's dramatic response to the bizarre exclamations in this text, where the persona addresses not just inanimate objects but anthropomorphizes abstract concepts: "The hours are a lazy folk! . . . 'Move it, you lazy people!'" Here we encounter the first of several overwrought, one-sided dialogues with improbable or imaginary respondents, disclosing the mentally disturbed state to which the speaker's paranoid frustration has brought him.

Heine combines improbable respondents with another of his favorite devices, the question left mysteriously unanswered, to motivate his next entry in the cycle, "Ich wandelte unter den Bäumen." What is the "little word" taught to the "little birds" by the maiden passing by, the "golden word" that should comfort the persona but occasions only mistrust? Schumann leaves this riddle hanging. He responds instead to the oddity of improbable dialogue: this song would be strophic if not for the quotation marks around the third stanza, which elicits the striking modulation to G major, repeated-note declamation, and the flat melodic shape of recitative. In contrast to this uncanny birdsong, the speaker's melody assumes a tone that is not wildly lyrical but at least exhibits some melodic range, which the sighing postlude in the piano then extends. Westphal solves the unanswered riddle in this poem for us by supplying Heine's original title for this text in the *Gedichte* of 1822, "Das Wörtlein Liebe."[15]

As prelude to the central climax of the cycle, both Heine and Schumann craft a sarcastic and highly amusing miniature. The poet's language depends for its sarcasm on redundant devices, especially synonyms ("schlimm und arg," "hämmert und klopfet"), pleonasm ("Todtensarg"), and polyptoton ("Lieb Liebchen," "Zimmermann/zimmert," "Schlaf/ schlafen").[16] He adds to this a large number of diminutives that would be comical if the subject matter were not so grim. Of course the metaphoric carpenter fashions his "death coffin" not for the persona but for his romantic aspirations. A lesser composer might be tempted to overdo his musical response, but Schumann stays out of the text's way. He creates a minimal accompaniment (often right hand only), allowing himself only one mocking comment at the end of both parallel stanzas, in the disjunction of the cadence between piano and voice. The composer hangs the speaker's preposterous self-pity out to dry, as it were.

Schumann's minimal treatment in E minor of "Lieb Liebchen" renders "Schöne Wiege" in E major all the more striking for its magnificent excess. It must be one of Schumann's most exquisite and inspired settings, limning by means of a rondo the text's diametrical contradictions between stanzas. Withdrawal offers one of the main refuges for the wounded ego, and as Westphal observes, this song invokes a long tradition of folk songs about melancholy departure ("Bremen, ich muß dich nun lassen," "Innsbruck, ich muß dich lassen," "Nun leb' wohl du kleine Gasse," and so forth).[17] Anaphora particularly dominates Heine's initial stanzas—

Schöne Wiege meiner Leiden,	Fair cradle of my sorrows,
Schönes Grabmal meiner Ruh',	Fair tombstone of my peace,
Schöne Stadt, wir müssen Scheiden,	Fair city, we must part,
Lebe wohl! ruf' ich dir zu.	Farewell! I call to you.
Lebe wohl! du heilge Schwelle,	Farewell! you holy threshold,
Wo da wandelt Liebchen traut;	Where my dear darling strolled;
Lebe wohl! du heilge Stelle,	Farewell! you holy place,
Wo ich sie zuerst geschaut.	Where I first beheld her.

—to which Schumann responds lyrically with successively rising phrases (see ex. 2.1) that finally debouche in a reiterated cadential tag ("Fare-

Example 2.1.   Successive variations in "Schöne Wiege meiner Leiden."

well! I call to you. Farewell! Farewell!"). When the speaker reverses himself in the third stanza (rejecting his nostalgia), the composer changes
abruptly from major to parallel minor, from lyrical melody to emphatic declamation that demarks the first episode of the rondo. Schumann reads the fourth stanza as an attempt to regain composure, occa-
sioning a return of the rondo theme, but this proves even less truthful
("Never did I wish to touch your heart; never did I plead for love"). The
second episode in the rondo casts off both the bonds of stable tonality and, gradually, melodic coherence itself for a hysterical assent that
contradicts the actual text ("And with weary, sluggish limbs I hobble
away"). After a bit of text painting (descent into a "cool grave"), Schumann rewrites Heine by repeating the opening stanza, emphasizing yet
more pointedly the disparity between the persona's ostensible affection

for his beloved and his intense hostility. The piano postlude recalls this suppressed enmity in one last stifled upwelling of discontent. In this brilliant song Schumann affords us a display of how manipulation of text and creative use of musical style and form can intensify irony to stunning effect.

What Schumann had originally projected to be the second volume of his cycle moves from flight and rage to resignation. The exaggerated rhetoric of "Warte, warte, wilder Schiffsmann," misogynistic in associating the beloved with both biblical and classical disaster (the loss of paradise, the downfall of Troy), strikes a bitterly sarcastic tone. Schumann's setting indulges overstatement in its octave scales, in its sudden changes of tempo, in its melodic leaps of an augmented fourth ("Ei, mein Lieb"), in its high-pitched exclamation on "Flamm' und Tod," and in its pell-mell tempo. The scalar imitation between accompaniment and voice (see ex. 2.2), while far from true counterpoint, represents an allusion to fughetta, the "fleeing" of the persona. The block-chordal texture of the slower sections (such as "Kennst du doch das alte Liedchen") creates such contrast that the falsely diminutive vocabulary seems to drip with venom. The lengthy sections devoted to the "fleeing" motive in the solo piano then reemphasize the speaker's frantic state.

The headlong frenzy of embarkation in "Warte, warte" finds its antithesis in "Berg und Burgen," the actual journey down a deceptively placid Rhine. If the accompaniment of the former reinforces the overstatement of Heine's text, the listless "wave" figures of the latter offer a prosaic approach to setting. The only ripples on the "mirror bright" surface occur in a vocal part that could articulate the trochaic verse with complete reg-

Example 2.2.   Imitative voices in "Warte, warte, wilder Schiffsmann."

ularity but instead begins some lines with double anacruses (for instance, "*in den* spiegelhellen"). Schumann goes out of his way, by means of conventional accompaniment, lyricism, periodicity, and strophic form, to construct an apparently normal framework, only to insert sporadic idiosyncrasies in declamation, a hint of the danger that lurks beneath the beloved's superficial attraction.

"Anfangs wollt' ich" and "Mit Myrthen und Rosen" form a pair in which the half-cadence of the first, in D minor, prepares the ensuing D major of the second. For "Anfangs" Schumann hit on a brilliant allusion, assigning the piano the block chords and four-square rhythms of Georg Neumark's well-known chorale, "Wer nur den lieben Gott läßt walten," to the voice part (compare exx. 2.3a and 2.3b). To the irony *within* Heine's text ("At first I almost wanted to despair, and thought I could never bear it, but I bore it; just do not ask how") Schumann's allusion adds a second level of subversive commentary, possibly referring to the second stanza in Neumark: "What good is deep sorrow, what good are doleful cries? What good does it do to bemoan our troubles every morning? We only make our cross and suffering heavier through melancholy."

Examples 2.3a–b. Allusion to "Wer nur den Lieben Gott läßt walten" (a) in "Anfangs wollt' ich" (b).

This deceptively prepares "Mit Myrthen und Rosen," where the speaker exaggerates his lament to epic proportions.

Heine loads the valediction of his cycle with particularly vivid imagery combining intimations of life ("myrtle and roses") and death ("cypress" and "mausoleums"), celebration and mourning, natural upheaval ("Aetna") and inner peace ("the spirit of love"), anger and forgiveness, sorrow and happiness. In a reflexive gesture he lets the mask fall to reveal the persona as a fictional poet of the preceding songs, a stereotype recalling the epilogue of many previous cycles ("Nimm sie hin denn diese Lieder" from *An die ferne Geliebte* comes to mind). The final irony proceeds from this reflexive disclosure: poetic creativity results from romantic failure ("I shall decorate this book like a mausoleum and entomb all my songs in it"). To this exaggerated imagery Heine adds a thoroughgoing metric irregularity, mixing dactyls, trochees, iambs, and occasional anapests, as if the fictional poet's hyperbole perturbs his rhythm. The irregularity poses a challenge for Schumann, who must mix triple with duple subdivisions of the quarter note in both voice and piano to accommodate highly variable syllable counts for a given line.

We can perceive just a hint of derision in Schumann's initial treatment of the persona's utterances. The composer fashions a "rondo theme" that rises and falls in almost comical fashion, mounting to a high point for "lieblich und *hold*," falling back down, climbing just a bit higher up the scale for "Todten*schrein*," then retracing its steps. The detached first line of the second verse ushers in a calmer episode, while the rondo theme returns for the third stanza and its images of Aetna pouring forth poetic lava in a shower of sparks. The music for the first episode returns for the fourth stanza, and a varied, much subdued version of the rondo theme's habitual rise and fall closes the song (and the cycle) with the thought that the beloved will read the poems (and presumably hear the music).

This formal description can scarcely capture the drama of "Mit Myrthen," which in its constant alternation of mood and variation of tempo has almost the same admixture of lyrical and dramatic contrast as "Schöne Wiege." Schumann renders the distant allusion in the poetry to the last number in *An die ferne Geliebte* all the more poignant with a quiet ending, reversing Beethoven's more assertive (and naive) conclusion. The Heine *Liederkreis* presents arguably Schumann's most meticulously crafted cycle.

Dichterliebe. Liedercyklus aus dem Buch der Lieder von H. Heine für eine
Singstimme mit Begleitung des Pianoforte . . . Op. 48 (composed 24 May–1 June
1840; published August 1844 by C. F. Peters)

As one of Schumann's three "canonical" cycles, *Dichterliebe* has received
much scholarly attention and very thorough study, in book length by
Hallmark and Perrey.[18] Hallmark observes that the "warm response" to
op. 24 may have prompted the composer to fashion op. 48,[19] and *Dichterliebe* does have several points in common with its older cousin, even
though Heine did not group the poems as a cycle in the *Buch der Lieder.*
Rather, Schumann personally selected and arranged the verse for op. 48
from a subsection of the poet's collection, the "Lyrisches Intermezzo,"
making it likely that he wanted to repeat his earlier success through emu-
lation as well as staking his own authorial claim.[20] In its initial conception *Dichterliebe* contained twenty songs, but publishers repeatedly rejected this version of the cycle: first Bote & Bock in Berlin on 22 July
1840, then Jan Hofmann in Prague on 22 May 1843, and finally Breitkopf on 5 September 1843.[21] On 6 October 1843 Schumann offered the
cycle to Ferdinand Böhme at C. F. Peters, who promptly accepted it. But
Schumann continued to revise the piece in press, where it assumed its
present form, encompassing just sixteen songs.[22] A number of writers
compare the composer's original conception to the final version,[23] but
here I will limit my discussion to the version Schumann published (see
opp. 127 and 142 in Chapter 5 for a discussion of the remaindered
songs).

The title *Dichterliebe* invokes Heine's prologue to the "Lyrisches Intermezzo," which portrays an absurdly oafish cavalier, a parody of the heroic knights who dotted the Romantic novels of such popular writers as
Sir Walter Scott. This poor, unattractive clod falls asleep late one night
and dreams of an alluring water nymph, by whom he is completely smitten. But as his revels climax in her water palace,

Der Ritter, der will sich zu Tode freu'n,	The knight enjoys himself to death,
Und fester umschlingt er sein Liebchen—	And embraces his darling more tightly—
Da löschen auf einmal die Lichter aus,	But all at once the lights go out,
Der Ritter sitzt wieder ganz einsam zu Haus,	The knight again sits alone at home,
In dem dustern Poetenstübchen.	In his gloomy poet's chamber.

Educated consumers who performed or listened to the cycle at home may well have been familiar with this prologue from reading the *Buch der Lieder*. They would know from the outset, reminded by Schumann's title, that all of the poetry in the "Lyrisches Intermezzo" rings fundamentally untrue: here love is a sham, a hopeless delusion. "Everything I am about to relate," Heine might have written, "consists of shameless lies." For those unaware of this context, however, the composer could provide musical clues through the polyrhythm between text, melody, and accompaniment, creating more irony in the process.

In their published form, *Dichterliebe*'s two volumes each encompassed eight songs. Schumann often maintained tonal continuity between contiguous numbers, sometimes moving around the circle of fifths over the course of several songs or switching between relative and parallel minor and major keys. The cycle also features tonal rounding at its conclusion, if we accept the oft-cited correlation between the C-sharp major-minor seventh chord at the end of "Im wunderschönen Monat Mai" and the C-sharp major triad (enharmonically spelled in D-flat major) concluding the final postlude.[24] But attempts to see the cycle unfolding in some organic tonal scheme remain unconvincing,[25] and Perrey argues that part of the cycle's ironic effect lies in its fragmentary nature.[26] We can nevertheless find a more loosely knit tonal and narrative order in the cycle. Roughly speaking, the first volume of the cycle traces its way from sharp keys (F-sharp minor–A major) to the C major and A minor of numbers seven and eight, while the second volume returns eventually from D minor back to the C-sharp minor-major of number sixteen. The trajectory of the unsuccessful relationship, suggested by psychological snapshots, runs the same course, taking approximately the same shape as an extended op. 24. The speaker entertains hopes of love that are finally dashed at midpoint ("Ich grolle nicht" and "Und wüssten's die Blumen"). On being jilted, he runs through stages of rage, grief, and resignation that lead him to a deeper philosophical understanding of love's irony ("Aus alten Märchen winkt es"). Finally, the persona delivers a reflexive valediction very like that in "Mit Myrthen und Rosen" from op. 24, identifying himself as a poet who "buries" his songs in bitter mockery ("Die alten bösen Lieder") of the conventional gesture that ends *An die ferne Geliebte* ("Take these songs, then").

To signal the essential irony of *Dichterliebe* from the beginning, Schumann uses disparity between accompaniment and text or accompaniment and melody in the first two numbers of the cycle. Heine's texts might arouse our suspicions—the anaphora between the two stanzas of "Im wunderschönen Monat Mai" (the speaker repeats himself effusively), the synonyms ("Sehnen und Verlangen"), or the droll impossibilia in "Aus meinen Thränen"—but in the absence of the prologue these devices might be overlooked. Therefore Schumann employs tonal instability in the first number to suggest that all is not what it seems. The accompaniment begins disoriented, as if in F-sharp minor, but the voice part always enters in the relative A major. Just when the tonality seems secure at the end of each stanza, Schumann retreats into the vacillation between the subdominant and dominant seventh in F-sharp minor, and he finally ends inconclusively on a half-cadence (see ex. 2.4). The tonal basis of the first song, and by implication the foundation of the whole cycle, is a sham: the home key, like love itself, does not exist. "Aus meinen Thränen" presents a different variety of unsatisfactory cadence, in which the voice constantly ends on a half-cadence that the accompanist must then complete. It were as if the pianist mocked the singer/speaker with a disparaging affirmation (the musical equivalent of "oh, sure"). This reverses the cadential irony between voice and piano encountered in "Lieb Liebchen" (op. 24).

Example 2.4.   Half-cadence at the end of "Im wunderschönen Monat Mai."

Schumann treats the ensuing three poems quite differently, reinforcing the irony in the first while letting the texts speak largely for themselves in the second two. Heine uses assonance ("Die Kleine, die Feine, die Reine, die Eine") and polyptoton ("liebt / Liebeswonne / Liebe Bronne")[27] for overemphasis in "Die Rose, die Lilie," to which Schumann adds a motoric, almost zany accompaniment, clichéd in its alternation between single left-hand bass notes and answering offbeat chords in the right. In case we miss Heine's overemphasis, the composer repeats a portion of lines 3 and 4 from Heine's original to produce the balanced eight-bar phrase denied by Heine's six-line stanza. In contrast, Schumann's setting of "Wenn ich in deine Augen seh'" is almost too flat, with the repeated-note melodic declamation opening every line (save the last) echoed in the piano ritornelli. Hallmark relates that the composer was tempted to treat the word "bitterlich" chromatically, but he apparently concluded that Heine's paradox needed no highlighting.[28] This superficial normalcy persists in "Ich will meine Seele tauchen." Heine's imagery in this poem is highly suggestive, mixing symbols of death and resurrection (the lily) with eroticism (plunging the soul into the calyx, that is, the cup or "throat" of the flower, and the trembling and quivering of the beloved's kiss). Schumann surrounds this ecstatic description with a diaphanously arpeggiated accompaniment that barely perturbs the rhythm of the strophically varied melody. It almost seems as if the composer hesitated to disturb the erotic vision, though the song's minor mode might seem discordant.

"Im Rhein, im heiligen Strome" counts among Schumann's most inspired settings of a remarkable Heine poem. The text must have appealed to the composer for several reasons. It draws heavily on the nationalistic imagery of the Cologne cathedral, begun in 1248 but left unfinished until an outpouring of patriotism finally prompted the Prussian government to fund the resumption of construction in the 1840s. And the text, as Westphal might put it, "caricatures majesty and dignity" amid this awesome setting in a singular way by turning the persona's religious adoration of the Virgin Mary unexpectedly into a bizarrely lubricious event ("The eyes, the lips, the lips, the cheeks, the same as my darling's exactly"). The poet's disturbingly errant image leads nowhere, but Schumann knows that disaster lies dead ahead. Hallmark connects the song's *alla breve* time signature with a solemn chorale,[29] but the equally salient topos of the funeral march attaches to these traits (relatively low range, duple meter, dotted rhythms, minor mode). The composer suspends the vocal melody like a cantus firmus over the instrumental dirge (see ex. 2.5), suggesting that the speaker's ardent (and inappropriate) longing is doomed. Just to make sure we recognize the disjunction between vocal ardor and bleak accompanimental destiny, the march continues relentlessly, long after the voice has ceased.

We discover just how far the distance between desire and realty lies in the last two songs of *Dichterliebe*'s first volume. The sarcastic polyrhythm between text, melody, and accompaniment in "Ich grolle nicht" hardly requires explanation, even to the unsophisticated listener. Heine rarely uses pentameter in the *Buch der Lieder,* and therefore Schumann must work to reconcile each line of "Ich grolle nicht" with quadratic expectations. He does this by breaking most lines into their component parts, which he then repeats over the even phrases of a piano pounding obsessively away with its own vehement musical logic. Even as the speaker abjures reproach over and over again, the piano remonstrates. To intensify the reiteration even further, Schumann appends the first phrase of Heine's second stanza to the first, then inserts a pseudo-strophic gesture by repeating the opening line of the first stanza before setting the rest of the second. This approach lacks subtlety, but the resulting potboiler

Example 2.5.   Topos of the funeral dirge in "Im Rhein, im heiligen Strome."

(with its flamboyant, optional high A) has become a favorite of both performers and audiences.

Where Schumann takes extraordinary liberty with the verse of "Ich grolle nicht," the poetry, melody, and accompaniment of "Und wüssten's die Blumen" run congruently in the relative minor with Heine's verse. The initially strophic setting with its invariable accompanimental tremolo parallels the anaphora at the beginning of each short stanza ("Und wüßten's die Blumen," "Und wüßten's die Nachtigallen, "Und wüßten's sie"). When Heine drops anaphora in the last stanza, the composer responds with a harmonic excursion, but he nevertheless maintains the same pattern of declamation and holds the piano tremolo steady in recognition of the parallelism in meaning that gives the poetry its impact. Then repeating Heine's last phrase, Schumann recasts the apothegm ("She herself has ripped asunder my heart") as quasi-recitative. The vehement piano postlude, featuring an entirely new pattern, highlights the concluding ironic reversal so typical of the poet. Thus ends the first volume of the cycle tracing the progression from expectation to consummation to betrayal and disintegration.

The second volume of *Dichterliebe* traces the way back, both tonally, from the flat keys to the sharp (in a very loosely knit fashion), and psychologically, from grief to resignation. "Das ist ein Flöten und Geigen" finds the persona at his beloved's wedding, wryly joined in his mourning by sympathetic cherubs. Its setting reverses Schumann's customary polyrhythmic balance between text, voice, and accompaniment. This song takes Heine's two quatrains as a pretext for a piano miniature, a demented reel or waltz in minor mode, over which the composer repeats phrases of poetry and even changes words to help fill out the prevailing eight-measure phrases articulated by the dance. Hallmark relates that Schumann made a much more elaborate sketch of the piano part than of the voice, revising the vocal melody several times to arrive at a final version while leaving the accompaniment relatively unchanged.[30] The impetus for the instrumental pattern here derives from the poetic imagery, which serves much as a program for a song without words. And while it would be an exaggeration to say that "Das ist ein Flöten" could exist without its melody, the accompaniment certainly predominates over the poetic structure and vocal line. Whether Schumann originally conceived it as heading the second volume or not, this song does provide a rather elaborate beginning to this "chapter" in the cycle.

The ensuing two songs, both plaints in their own ways, demonstrate that through-composed songs can still articulate the strophic form of the original poetry and comment trenchantly within the traditional style of the lied. The arpeggiated accompaniment of "Hör' ich ein Liedchen" recedes in the presence of the voice, whose melody follows the mostly iambic tetrameter, aside from a slight perturbation in accentual pattern for the first line of text. The piano becomes remarkable only in a lengthy postlude that comments snidely on the speaker's "overwhelming [literally: overly large] woe." Schumann's melody for "Ein Jüngling liebt ein Mädchen" imposes equally little on the mostly iambic verse, and its quadratic phrases fit nicely to a polkalike rhythm. The cheerful mood of the traditional dance runs congruently with the poetry's age-old story, intensifying the paradox between the nonchalance of Heine's verse and the grief that lurks beneath.

"Am leuchtenden Sommermorgen" stands a bit by itself, not because of its varied strophic form or its declamation of the largely iambic text but because of the way Schumann treats the final couplet and its crucial message. Heine's text indulges the conceit of imaginary respondents seen earlier, in op. 24. Here we find anthropomorphized flowers that speak, not just figuratively but literally. In the last couplet they implore the persona, "Do not be cross with our sister, you sad, pale man!" Schumann fleetingly touches on G major, which casts the flowers' dialogue in a special tonal light that raises the normal initiation of each phrase on B-flat up to a B-natural (ex. 2.6). While the description of the jilted lover may strike us as wry (its snide characterization of his wan complexion refers to the first stanza of the prologue), the composer takes the admonishment to forgive seriously in an especially extended postlude. It postpones its final cadence several times, like a long, cathartic denouement.

Numbers thirteen through fifteen in *Dichterliebe* bring us to the heart of the paradox in the "Lyrisches Intermezzo," revolving around the illusory nature of romance. All three poems involve transient dreams that recall the oafish cavalier of the prologue, and all three feature the kind of reversal in the last stanza that Heine used so often to create irony. "Ich hab' im Traum geweinet" elicits a singular approach to the relationship between voice and piano from Schumann, elements of which we find in some of his other songs, but nowhere so pronounced. The voice begins this setting without keyboard support, and only after a line of verse does the piano enter with punctuation. At first this may seem like recitative,

Example 2.6.   Heightened dialogue in "Am leuchtenden Sommermorgen."

especially in light of the melody's many repeated notes. But the first couplet unfolds in four-square groups, and the low range of the piano interjections, with their dotted rhythms in E-flat minor, invokes the topos of a
halting funeral march. The last couplet of each stanza elicits more plastic
rhythms, and in a variation on the final stanza the composer provides a
rising melodic line to underscore the paradox between the imagined fidelity of the beloved and the grief it occasions.

The E-flat tonic of "Ich hab' im Traum" serves as a tonal fulcrum, prepared by the B-flat dominant of "Am leuchtenden Sommermorgen" and
moving by enharmonic common tone (E-flat respelled as D-sharp) to
the B major of "Allnächtlich im Traume." Schumann changes meter to
emphasize the comical turns of phrase that conclude Heine's first two
stanzas: "and loudly weeping I cast myself at your sweet feet" ("süßen
Füßen"; "Perlenthränentröpfchen" at the end of the second stanza
sounds equally odd in German because of its alliteration). The last stanza
achieves its effect differently, not through peculiar phonetic juxtapositions but through the beloved's presentation to the persona of a funeral
bouquet (symbolized by cypress) and the words that vanish upon wak-
ing. The composer delays acceleration in this case until the last line to
emphasize the transitory nature of the dream.

The previous two numbers' movement from slow to moderate tempo leads to the last in the dream sequence, one of Schumann's most glorious songs, providing the moral of the cycle. The vocal melody for "Aus alten Märchen winkt es" declaims the text in a relatively straightforward manner, supported by a largely homorhythmic accompaniment that often doubles the melody in the top voice of the right hand (see ex. 2.7). Schumann refers in this relationship to an older epoch of the lied, the era of Reichardt, in which the accompaniment often followed the voice's simple declamation in lockstep, offering just a few interludes. This old-fashioned style, together with the compound meter, invokes the topos of the *romanza*, a reference to Heine's "old fairy tale" cast in folklike *Langzeilenvers*. Both poetry and music unfold ironically, however. Heine's imagery, with its singing trees, its phantasmagoric reels, its psychedelic sparks, freshets, and glistening brooks, sounds far too fabulous. The poet relates a sham fairy tale, much as Schumann offers a faux-naive setting, which modulates with sudden violence from strophe to strophe, ending in a tonal excursion that leads us finally to F-sharp major (the secondary dominant key at "Und blaue Funken brennen"). The closing stanzas reveal the imposture: the unattainable land disappears like "mere foam," recalling the illusory water nymph of the prologue. The composer sets these lines by repeating the opening melody of the song with the erudite simplicity of augmentation. When the accompanimental postlude mockingly attempts to revive the *romanza*'s tempo primo, it must cede ultimately to quotidian moderato, the crux of *Dichterliebe*.

Like the final song in the op. 24 *Liederkreis*, "Die alten bösen Lieder" serves as valediction. But in creating this reflexive parallel, Schumann goes Heine one better, for it rejects the whole preceding cycle. "Mit

Example 2.7. Romanza topos in "Aus alten Märchen winkt es."

Myrthen und Rosen" finds the poet-persona entombing his songs in a book, hoping that it will move the beloved to fond memories at some future date. Not so the poet-persona of "Die alten bösen Lieder": he would bury both grief and love beyond any chance of exhumation (the land of happy illusion ironically occasions real sorrow and anger). Heine's verse evokes one German nationalist image after another to make this exaggerated point, from the barrel in the Heidelberg tavern to the lengthy span at Mainz to the massive statuary in the Cologne cathedral. Schumann responds with an implacably motoric funeral march, ending in a bathetic recitative that mocks even Heine's sarcasm. Only in the lengthy postlude does the composer seem to relent, borrowing a passage from the conclusion of "Am leuchtenden Sommermorgen," as if to say, "Do not be cross with our sister, you sad, pale man." But this too dissembles. If we attach any meaning to the tonality of this coda, then the cycle concludes not on a satisfying tonic resolution but suspended still on a C-sharp (D-flat) major chord, the dominant triad of the first song's inconclusive final cadence. We have engaged musically in an empty exercise: futile movement with no resolution. It is the tale of a pathetic dolt, full of sound and fury, signifying nothing.

Dichterliebe has found its central place in the repertory of Schumann's lieder because of its scope, because of its thoroughgoing lyricism, and because the composer acted as author. It may lack the tightly knit structure of op. 24, and its songs may not rise to the dramatic heights of its older cousin, but it shows the composer in one of his most imaginative moments. Most of op. 48's lieder dwell, nevertheless, within the traditional boundaries Schumann set for the genre. Talented amateurs could perform *Dichterliebe* in their homes to great effect. The artful piano parts are not too difficult, the vocal lines are not too operatic, the formal designs recall the strophic origins of the genre, and rarely do the accompaniments render the voice superfluous. Above all, op. 48 shows that the polyrhythm between text, melody, and accompaniment can engender Romantic irony and, just possibly, that music can *be* ironic (in features such as the tonal misdirection of the first song left unresolved at the end of the last). The cycle, both text and music, leaves us with "an eternal longing for a world never truly believed to come within reach."

3

Cycles of Wandering

Among all the many varieties of cycle that Schumann essayed during his "year of song," perhaps the most widely popular was the wanderer's cycle, and accordingly he devoted three separate opus numbers to the genre among his early published output. The Kerner *Liederreihe,* op. 35 (appearing in May 1841), *Sechs Gedichte,* op. 36, to texts by Reinick (July 1842), and the Eichendorff *Liederkreis,* op. 39 (August 1842), were all composed in 1840, though in reverse order (op. 39 in May and June, op. 36 in July, op. 35 in November and December). Each of them underwent notable reprintings or second editions during the composer's lifetime, often within the space of a few years, an indication of the market for the genre.

Several elements contributed to the popularity of wanderer's song cycles, not the least of which was the familiarity of the type. Barbara Turchin produces a substantial list of the best-known in Schumann's time, which includes (in addition to Müller's *Schöne Müllerin* and *Winterreise,* set by Schubert and others) poetry by Uhland, Grüneisen, Marsano, Schwarz, and Vogt set by Kreutzer, Dessauer, Marschner, Schindler, and Skraup.[1] These entries represent merely the tip of the iceberg. Two central Romantic threads converge in wanderer's cycles. One prized wayfaring as a salutary activity, an immersion in a diverse world full of delightful, miraculous, or terrifying but always fascinating phenomena. The other proceeds from coming-of-age narratives, or *Bildungsgeschichten,* such as we find in Goethe's *Wilhelm Meister,* Tieck's *Franz Sternbald,* Novalis's *Heinrich von Ofterdingen,* Eichendorff's *Aus dem Leben eines Tauge-*

nichts, Dickens's *David Copperfield,* and countless others. Summarizing Meyer Abrahms on coming-of-age wayfaring in Romantic literature, Turchin writes that the journey

> is both an education and a psychological process, which begins with man's fall from unity in self-division, self-conflict, and self-contradiction. The dynamic of this process is to move towards a balance, an integration, a closure of these divisions and contraries. The goal of the inner quest is to achieve a higher state of unity, a greater wholeness through increased self-awareness. The beginning and end of the journey is man's ancestral home which is often linked with a female counterpart from whom the wanderer departs when setting out.[2]

Travel itself educates the wayfarer, of course, and his experience may lead him back to his beloved or may end in disastrous loss. The outcomes are as various as the authors and the characters who set out, but some of these elements recur in all such works. In the event, none of Schumann's cycles originated with their three authors: the composer created them in the spirit of the genre out of poetry he selected from anthologies of their respective writers. As such, these cycles display the whole range of available motivations, experiences, and outcomes, without generating (or requiring) close-knit narrative coherence.

Zwölf Gedichte von Justinus Kerner. Eine Liedereihe für eine Singstimme mit Begleitung des Pianoforte . . . Op. 35 (composed November–December 1840; published May 1841 by C. A. Klemm)

All through the last part of November and into December of 1840, Schumann immersed himself in the poetry of Justinius Kerner (1786–1862), aiming to fashion what became an ever more ambitious cycle of songs. After setting three texts, he announced on 22 November that "a small cycle of Kerner poems is finished," but he persisted with four more in the next two days. He kept adding, three settings from 10 to 12 December and another four from 17 to 29 December. On 3 January 1841, Clara wrote in the marriage diary, "Robert has composed yet another very beautiful *Wanderlied* by Kerner and has now completed a volume of twelve songs by Kerner."[3] In fact Schumann had set fourteen of the poet's texts by this time, but "Trost im Gesang" and "Sängers Trost" were relegated to miscellanies, one published later in the composer's life and one posthumously (see the discussion of opp. 127 and 142 in Chapter 5).

Kerner had been a favorite of Schumann's in his student days, and his verse is well represented in Robert and Clara's collection of texts for setting.[4] The Swabian poet practiced medicine for a living and spiritualism as a consuming hobby, but his fascination with the occult and somnambulism did not attract the Schumanns as much as his sentimentalism. As Heinz Rölleke observes, "The composer did not choose to set even one of Kerner's many macabre poems. . . . What appealed to him in Kerner (aside from the genuinely folk-like, *Wunderhorn* resonance), apparently even really captivated him, was a tone in [the poet's] lyrics one might characterize in best Goethean fashion as 'the rapture of melancholy.'"[5]

Among the several elements available to the genre of the wanderer's cycle, the Kerner *Liederreihe* emphasizes nostalgia, the "fall from unity" and departure from "man's ancestral home" of which Turchin speaks. She makes a compelling case for an implied narrative in op. 35:

> "Lust der Sturmnacht" (song 1) presents a young man blissfully lost in love, at peace in the arms of his beloved while a storm rages outside their room. His ardent feelings are crushed in "Stirb Lieb' und Freud!" (song 2) where we learn that his beloved has renounced worldly love in favor of the more powerful calling of God. Rejected in love, denied the emotional bond that links the individual to society, the young man becomes one of the solitary wanderers he pitied in the opening song. His journey is the subject of the following ten poems.[6]

Rather than a sequential travelogue like *Die schöne Müllerin,* however, the rest of the *Zwölf Gedichte* offers snapshots of the journey in the manner of *Winterreise,* and for this reason Hans Joachim Köhler writes, "Schumann created neither cycle nor collection, but a series of songs [*Liederreihe*]."[7] Op. 35 presents a related series, nonetheless, not only thematically but also tonally and sometimes motivically; individual glimpses of wayfaring rather than tightly knit progressions of episodes constitute the norm in Schumann's wanderer's cycles.

To open the first volume of the Kerner *Liedereihe* (which included the first five numbers of op. 35), Schumann fashioned a pair of songs establishing the basic premise. Whereas the task of setting Heine or Rückert or any number of other German poets sometimes consisted of accommodating irregular feet within otherwise regular musical meter, Kerner's verse tends toward a uniformity that Schumann apparently sought to enliven. For the picture of the two lovers housed snugly amid the raging storm in

"Lust der Sturmnacht," the composer employs compound meter to set Kerner's trochaic tetrameter, but he starts the voice mid-measure. For this reason the primary accent of every second measure in the music's quadratic scheme falls on the penultimate syllable of each line (italicized below):

> Wenn[8] durch Berg' und Thale *drau*-ssen
> Regen schauert, Stürme *brau*-sen,
> Schild und Fenster hell er*klir*-ren,
> Und in Nacht die Wandrer *ir*-ren.

This displacement produces a singular emphasis on important verbs in the first stanza, and it also creates a disturbed cross-rhythm appropriate to the tempestuous scene. Schumann additionally changes mode from minor to major and inserts interludes irregularly between lines of verse to capture the poem's varying moods.

The E-flat minor-major of "Sturmnacht" leads directly to the A-flat of "Stirb, Lieb' und Freud'!," one of the most striking and affective settings in the *Liederreihe*. Kerner's text, combining narrative about a young woman taking the veil with dialogue, falls more in the subgenre of a ballad than of a lied narrowly defined. Schumann responds first on a generic level with an accompanimental pattern akin to that in "Abends am Strand," a Heine text probably set in April 1840 and published in *Romanzen und Balladen, Heft I,* op. 45. On a second level the composer treats the ecclesiastical scene with an antique meter necessitating archaically augmented note values (see ex. 3.1) and with inner voices in the accompaniment moving like counterpoint between slower outer voices in a chorale prelude. In the first edition Schumann also went to the unusual length of marking the voice part "preferably for tenor," because the speaker reveals himself specifically as the woman's heartbroken admirer. As in the previous song, the composer breaks the regularity of the poetic meter by spacing couplets and individual lines of verse (cast remarkably in septains) with interludes of varying lengths. While the same motives pervade the whole song, Schumann transposes them to various pitch levels according to the sentiment expressed, especially the beloved's high-pitched final declaration in C minor, "This poor maid consecrates herself as nun; die love and joy!" The harmonic excursus here moves the song toward a conclusion on a mediant chord with a Picardy third and intima-

Example 3.1.   Archaic time signature and chorale prelude texture in "Stirb, Lieb' und Freud'!"

tions of a plagal cadence. This triad then serves as secondary dominant for the beginning of the next song.`

The remaining three songs of volume one in op. 35 record the persona's decision to leave the scene of his unhappiness and submerge his woe in a consoling nature. "Wanderlied" assumes a topos much favored by Schumann for such songs, that of a jaunty march replete with G-flat major trio in accordance with its optimistic text. In this case the composer emphasizes rather than disguises the regularity of Kerner's meter. The dactylic dimeter of the verse (with anacrusis at the beginning of each octave) fits common time in relatively uncomplicated fashion, with the longer, accented syllables of each line falling on the first and third beat of each measure, while the unaccented syllables fall on the second and fourth beats subdivided in various ways (two eighths or a dotted eighth and a sixteenth). The clearest example comes in the "trio": "Da grúessen ihn Vóe-gel / be-kánnt überm Méer [´], / Sie fló-gen von Flú-ren / der Héi-math hie-hér [´]," and so forth. By means of straightforward declamation, major mode, and frequently homorhythmic accompaniment, Schumann plays on the folkloric tone in Kerner's verse.

The second two numbers in the group, however, return to the realm of

Kunstlied. Both share the key signature of "Wanderlied" but unfold in the relative G minor, a fact that Schumann emphasizes pointedly by closing his march on a second inversion chord while opening "Erstes Grün"[9] on a held G-minor chord juxtaposed in the same register. Not only does the composer break the regularity of iambic declamation for the second couplet of each strophe, but he changes mode to the parallel G major for the interludes between stanzas. The setting for "Sehnsucht nach der Waldgegend" also plays freely with the text's quite regular trochaic pattern (see ex. 3.2) and features a notable excursion to major mode, initially to F major serving as dominant preparation for a B-flat tonic never quite confirmed.[10] The intrusion of major mode in both these songs and especially the redolent lyricism of "Sehnsucht" create a mood of "soothing thoughts that spring out of human suffering," which concludes the first volume of the Kerner *Liederreihe.*

Volume two of op. 35, comprising its last seven songs, begins like volume one, as Köhler points out (nos. 1 and 2 of volume two parallel nos. 2 and 3 of volume one in both sentiment and theme).[11] This could have resulted from the fact that Schumann added to the cycle episodically over a month before determining its final shape, but in any event this retracing discourages construction of a strictly sequential narrative running from start to finish. If "Auf das Trinkglas eines verstorbenes Freundes" in the second volume stands in an analogous position to "Stirb, Lieb' und Freud'!," it obviously has a different subject, a *memento mori.* In nineteenth-century European and American culture intense sentimental attachment to the possessions of the loved and lost formed a regular part of everyday life (consider, for instance, Henry Russell's "Old Arm Chair" in just a slightly more popular vein). What may strike us, therefore, as morbid obsession was simply commonplace in Kerner's and Schumann's

Example 3.2.   Free declamation and lyricism in "Sehnsucht nach der Waldgegend."

day. It comes as no surprise, then, to hear the persona's reaction to drinking from a deceased friend's goblet:

Was ich erschau' in deinem Grund,	What I behold within your depths
Ist nicht Gewöhnlichen zu nennen,	Cannot be ordinarily expressed,
Doch wird mir klar zu dieser Stund',	But at this moment I know well
Wie nichts das Freund von Freund	That nothing can part friend from
kann trennen.	friend.

Schumann mostly employs chorale texture to impart solemn feeling to
this text, but one can hardly call it gloomy, for the cup summons consoling memories.

The loss described in "Auf das Trinkglas" prompts more traveling in
the first lines of "Wanderung": "Up and fresh away / to unknown lands!
Severed, yes, severed are many cherished ties." This song falls in the same
position as "Wanderlied" in op. 35's first volume, and, marked "Spirited,
with light and tender accompaniment," it assumes a similarly buoyant
tone but employs a different topos. The compound meter invokes a
"riding" figure, replete with horn fifths and staccato dotted eighth- and
sixteenth-note figures (see ex. 3.3) that disclose a cheerful sally into the
wider world. Kerner casts this jovial confidence in folkish *Langzeilenvers*, "Wohl-áuf und frísch ge-wán-dért / In's ún-be-kánn-te Lánd ['],"
and the composer responds with a melody that conforms quite closely to
the poetic meter and a minimal accompaniment that does not exactly
proceed step for step with the voice but rarely counters it either.

"Stille Liebe" and "Frage" together disclose the memories of a beloved
still cherished by the persona in his peregrinations. Despite its rather
moody ritornello, the first song in this E-flat major group comes fairly
close in poetic sentiment and musical tone to Beethoven's *An die ferne*

Example 3.3.   Riding figures and horn fifths in "Wanderung."

Geliebte (without actual allusion). Beethoven adopted instrumentally motivated strophic variation as his favorite device in that wanderer's cycle, usually changing the accompanimental pattern from stanza to stanza. In "Stille Liebe" Schumann modulates to flat mediant for the middle strophe, and he returns with an arpeggiated accompaniment in the home key for the last stanza à la Beethoven, with its conceit of song prompted by the pain of separation. "Frage" takes a more declamatory tack for a message of consolation found in nature, much like "Erstes Grün" in the first volume of the *Liederreihe*. This song serves more like a recitative, modulating from E-flat major to a conclusion in C minor on a half-cadence preparing the next song.

"Stille Thränen" alone among the songs in op. 35 deliberately courts the melodramatic, and for this reason it stands out as the oddest song in the *Liederreihe*. Though its key of C major would initially seem to separate it from the second volume's concentration on E-flat, B-flat, and ultimately A-flat major, "Stille Thränen" quickly and rather abruptly modulates by means of common tone to A-flat major ("So lang du ohne Sorgen"), moves again by common tone to C-flat major, and then finds its way back by means of E-flat major to the C tonic. In this sense it mediates indirectly between "Stille Liebe" on the one hand and "Wer machte dich so krank?" on the other. But the most peculiar thing about the song stems from its setting of Kerner's text, not because the melody or accompaniment runs contrary to the poetry's iambic meter but because they pay the text out very deliberately over a pattern of repeated block chords in a slow 6/4 time signature. The slow underlying pulse blunts the inherent lyricism of the melody, rendering this song emphatically theatrical and just a trifle bathetic.

Schumann may have thought that the overstatement of "Stille Thränen" would highlight the subdued twin lieder that end the cycle, for sadly the persona concludes in "Alte Laute" ("Old Strains") that he will find peace only in death:

Die Tage sind vergangen,	Those days have passed away,
Mich heilt kein Kraut der Flur;	No meadow's herbs can heal;
Und aus dem Traum, dem bangen,	And from my dream, so anxious,
Weckt mich ein Engel nur.	Only an angel will wake me.

The composer designates the first song (and presumably the second, therefore) "preferably for baritone," marking "Wer machte dich so krank?" and "Alte Laute" ("to the same tune") "slowly, softly" and "still more

Examples 3.4a–b. "The same melody" in "Wer machte dich so krank?" (a) and "Alte Laute" (b).

slowly and softly." Schumann clearly manufactured their interrelation: in Kerner's 1834 *Dichtungen,* which served as exemplar, the poems appear respectively on pages 35 and 61.[12] The text of "Wer machte dich so krank?" exhibits elements of the same intense melancholy as its cousin ("If I bear mortal wounds, that is the doing of man"), and for this reason the same melody, varied here and there, fits both well (see exx. 3.4a and 3.4b).[13] Both settings override the iambic meter of their texts, a device that renders them almost like arioso at this slow tempo.

The Kerner *Liederreihe* has not captured the modern fancy as much as some other cycles, perhaps because of its sentimentality. Many songs from this period are sentimental, of course, including a large number by Schumann, and for that matter we encounter sentiment regularly today in popular culture. Overt sentiment in present-day "classical" music is another matter altogether. A song such as "Stille Thränen" may strike us as melodramatic, but it must have seemed normal or even understated in the context of contemporary compositions in Schumann's time. However we regard it, op. 35 struck a real chord with the nineteenth-century public: Klemm reprinted it in 1844 (just three years after it first appeared) and later had to engrave new plates when the originals wore out.[14]

Sechs Gedichte aus dem Liederbuch [sic] eines Malers von Reinick für eine Sopran- oder Tenorstimme mit Begleitung des Pianoforte . . . op. 36 (nos. 1–3, 5 composed 22–23 July 1840, nos. 4 and 6 composed 22–23 August 1840; published by J. Schuberth in July 1842)

Robert Reinick (1805–1852), a somewhat obscure poet today, was well known to Schumann and later to his family. Born in Danzig, Reinick initially chose painting as a profession, which led him to study in Berlin. There he encountered Chamisso, Eichendorff, Kugler, and others who awakened an enthusiasm for verse. Reinick later moved to Düsseldorf, spent several years in Italy, and in 1844 settled permanently in Dresden, where he became acquainted with Schumann. For a time he worked on adapting *Genoveva* from dramas by Hebbel and Tieck for the composer's use as a libretto, but this collaboration fell through. In 1848 the poet became godfather to Ludwig Schumann, and he socialized frequently with the family while they lived in Dresden. Reinick specialized, understandably, in the confluence of graphic art and poetry, publishing *Drei Umrisse nach Holzschnitten von A. Dürer* in 1830, a *Liederbuch für deutsche Künstler* with Kugler in 1833, and three books of *Lieder eines Malers* beginning in 1837.[15]

Much of Reinick's poetry has a distinctly nationalistic bent, the theme that proved particularly attractive to Schumann in fashioning op. 36. Though it contains only six songs, it falls squarely into the composer's family of loosely knit wanderer's cycles. Accordingly, the *Sechs Gedichte* feature an initial song about wayfaring, numbers about wooing a beloved, and snapshots of various remarkable foreign locales. Tonal coherence proves more problematic. The first number begins in D major, the next two songs progress around the circle of fifths, and numbers four and five return to the area of sharp keys (A major, E minor-major). But the last song closes in a distant F major, perhaps less disturbing because the text offers a valediction. Schumann selected more cheerful poetry featuring more colorful scenes for this grouping than he did for the Kerner *Liederreihe,* and although op. 36 has received scant attention from scholars and infrequent recordings, its charming songs are worth exploring.

To begin this wanderer's cycle, Schumann chose "Sonntags am Rhein," a Reinick text that describes the beauty of various scenes along the river and that suggests a delightful journey by boat: "A skiff slides by on azure stream, / They sing and celebrate on board; / My little ship, is it not good / To sail amid such joy?" Considering Schumann's criticism of Schubert's unchanging accompanimental patterns in his songs, the constant repetition of a single pitch in the middle voice of the piano here and the tendency at many points for the right hand to double the vocal line might strike us as rather slack. But the composer obviously wanted to create an artificially folkloric atmosphere for a song that has distinctly patriotic overtones. The repeated eighth notes sounding a pedal point, the harmonic excursion underlining Romantic scenes of church processions and castles in the B section, and the frequent horn fifths in the left hand (see ex. 3.5) all respond to Reinick's concluding lines, "The fatherland, true and devout, / In its magnificence, / With joy and song all round about, / Held in our dear God's thoughts."

Having implied a wayfaring narrative and established the folkloric context of the cycle, Schumann then chose two poems to introduce a quest for a beloved, first a serenade and then what Wagner called in *Meistersinger* a *Werbelied* or "courtship song." "Ständchen" features a standard conceit for the first half of the nineteenth century, a lover singing beneath the window of his beloved at night, urging her to reveal herself as a sign of her interest. Schumann's piano may distantly suggest accompaniment by a lute or guitar in its alternation of a simple left-hand line and answering rolled chord on the last eighth note of each measure. The initial G pedal also offers a token of folkishness, and we can regard the song as falling in traditional German bar form (AAB, or "stanza, stanza, aftersong," though technically the aftersong should be twice the length of an individual stanza). The courtship song, "Nichts Schöneres," also offers a series of pedal points, this time supporting strophic variations. But here Schumann's declamation of text belies unreflecting simplicity. Reinick's regular iambic tetrameter would begin naturally on the upbeat of each measure in compound meter, but the composer starts each line of text on the downbeat, stressing the urgency of the persona's adoration. *Werbelieder* traditionally praise the attributes of the beloved, and in this case Reinick's text then continues on to betrothal and marriage. Schumann's choice of this text introduces a charming twist to the wanderer's cycle, which often focuses only on a quest for love rather than on fulfillment.

Example 3.5.   Interior eighth-note pedal and horn fifths in the last section of "Sonntags am Rhein."

"An den Sonnenschein" complicates the experience of traveling. Fair weather prompts exploration of the natural world, but wayfaring in this case entails separation from the beloved. Schumann marks this song "Im Volkston": the initial heavy-footed pedals, the somewhat marchlike rhythms, the relatively diatonic tonal language, and the predominantly homorhythmic texture all serve as emblems of popular style. Though the music maintains a cheerful mood throughout, the text relates bittersweet longing, which "Dichters Genesung" ("Poet's Convalescence") promptly seeks to redress. This poem fulfills the seemingly obligatory gesture by Schumann of placing at least one ballad in each of his 1840 *Wanderlieder* cycles. But where its counterpart in the Kerner *Liederreihe,* "Stirb, Lieb' und Freud'!," motivated the "narrative" of the remaining songs, "Dichters Genesung" concludes the "action." Prompted by disturbing dreams of his beloved, the wayfarer ventures into the forest, where he encounters an elfin queen presiding over a celebration (a variation on the unset prologue to *Dichterliebe*). But unlike the gauche cavalier in Heine's "Lyrisches Intermezzo," Reinick's persona resolves to seek his real beloved rather than pursue this supernatural one. Schumann's music, in keeping with the folkloric theme of op. 36, tends to repeat one simple phrase over and over again, except for the alluring speech of the elfin queen, which modulates to a different pitch level and receives its own declamatory melody. The accompaniment forgoes ornament or suggestive figuration, confining itself mostly to block or tremolo chords, with some doubling of the voice in the left hand. It is as if the composer wants us to focus on the unfolding events rather than on word painting or instrumental virtuosity, a restrained approach to a poem with inherently dramatic potential.

The *Sechs Gedichte* finish inconclusively, not only as hypothetical narrative but also tonally. "Liebesbotschaft" ("Message of Love"), in a distant F major, expresses a fairly conventional sentiment for wanderer's cycles, with the persona admonishing nature to carry his thoughts to a distant beloved:

Wolken, die ihr nach Osten eilt,	Clouds, thou that hasten toward the east,
Wo die Eine, die Meine weilt,	To where my own one dwells,
All meine Wünsche, mein Hoffen und Singen	All my desires, my hopes and singing
Sollen auf eure Flügel sich schwingen,	Shall soar on your wings,
Sollen euch Flüchtige	Shall, thou fleet ones,

Zu ihr lenken,	Guide thee to her,
Daß die Züchtige	That the chaste one
Meiner in Treuen mag gedenken.	May faithfully think on me.

As much as the conceit might remind us of the last number in *An die ferne Geliebte*, Reinick's verse is considerably more sophisticated in its irregular scansion and length of line. Schumann must have concluded, moreover, that the mask of a simple journeyman slips enough here to reveal the sophisticated poet. For though the composer adopts a varied strophic approach and some emblems hinting at folkishness (occasional pedal tones and right-hand doubling of the voice), the harmonic digression with lyrical appoggiaturas in the second quatrain of each octave belies folkloric gestures (see ex. 3.6).

"Liebesbotschaft" is a little-known gem from a collection replete with such exquisite settings, and it concludes with a refrain imploring remembrance—advice that we today might apply generally to op. 36. In Schumann's time, the collection was sufficiently popular for J. Schuberth to publish the songs as individual numbers and for Fritz Schuberth to print an English translation of number four at the firm's New York branch. Shortly before the composer's death, Simon Richault in Paris even brought out a French edition of op. 36 under the subtitle *Six mélodies chantées par Jenny Lind*.[16]

Liederkreis von Joseph Freyherrn von Eichendorff für eine Singstimme mit Begleitung des Pianoforte, op. 39 (composed in May 1840—first edition no. 1 on 22 June 1840; first edition of two volumes published in Vienna by Tobias Haslinger, August 1842; revised edition with different first number published in Leipzig by F. Whistling, April 1850)

In an oft-quoted letter of 22 May 1840 to Clara Wieck, who was performing in Berlin, Robert Schumann boasts, "By the way, I've heard that

Example 3.6.   Harmonic digression in "Liebesbotschaft."

people are talking a lot about the Heine song cycle [op. 24], and I'm very glad about that. I can promise you, fiancée, that the Eichendorff ones are even more melancholy and happy than the short ones you know. I reveled in these poems—and in your handwriting too." He adds elsewhere, "The Eichendorff song cycle is probably my most Romantic work, and there's a lot of you in there, my dear, sweet fiancée."[17] The connection between the Eichendorff *Liederkreis* and Clara stemmed from the fact that she had entered all of op. 39's poetry into the couple's joint copybook of verse (and perhaps helped to select it as well).[18] She and Robert obviously treasured these texts, and later performers, listeners, and critics have agreed: op. 39 completes the tally of Schumann's "canonic" cycles; performed often, it has attracted a longer list of scholarly monographs and articles than even *Dichterliebe*.[19] The *Liederkreis* represents the composer's most distinguished wanderer's cycle, a collection of evocative lyrics set with unfailing instinct for mystery and Romantic irony at every turn.

Op. 39 also has a fascinating history of publication. It proved sufficiently popular in Schumann's day to command a second edition, and in the process of republishing it with Whistling in Leipzig (the first edition appeared in Vienna with Haslinger), the composer substituted "In der Fremde [I]" for the first edition's "Der frohe Wandersmann."[20] Different authors advance several possible reasons for the revision, but perhaps the most interesting question remains why Schumann initially published the cycle with "Wandersmann" at its head (the song was composed as a distinct afterthought on 22 June 1840, a month after the rest of the cycle).[21] Schumann may have intended the number as an allusion to Schubert's *Schöne Müllerin*, which begins with the same sort of confident march in praise of wandering. And in fact "Der frohe Wandersmann" originally appeared at the very beginning of Eichendorff's novella *Aus dem Leben eines Taugenichts*, about a lazy miller's son expelled from the family business to make his way in the world.[22] The text was the first Eichendorff selection Clara entered in the copybook of verse. "Wandersmann" also fits the relatively cheerful frame of op. 39's first volume rather better than the gloomier "In der Fremde [I]," while generating more cognitive dissonance with the remainder of the cycle. In the first edition, headed by this cheerful, straightforward, D major march relating the joys of travel (see ex. 3.7), the ominous sense of loss that permeates the second volume comes as something of a surprise. Finally, the redolent *Volkston* of such a

Example 3.7.   Folkloric march in "Der frohe Wandersmann," the first number in op. 39's first edition.

beginning in the context of op. 39 as a whole parallels the tension be-tween folkloric structure and erudite imagery in Eichendorff's verse. This was precisely the kind of Romantic irony so dear to Schumann's heart in many of his other lieder from 1840.

The arguments for replacing "Der frohe Wandersmann" with "In der Fremde [I]" in the second edition seem clear enough. A number of au-thors observe that the F-sharp minor of "In der Fremde" meshes better with the key scheme of the cycle as a whole. The first volume in its second edition proceeds F-sharp minor–A major–E major–G major–E major–B major, while the second volume runs A minor–A minor–E major–E minor–A major–F-sharp major. The framing provided by F-sharp minor and F-sharp major invokes a certain abstract rounding, even though there can be no question of a tightly knit, overarching key scheme, no matter how closely Schumann might have tied pairs of songs together. He did not order the overall cycle strictly by key, nor did he compose the songs in the order in which they finally appeared.[23] Many writers also comment that the somber tone of "In der Fremde [I]" better fits the gen-eral mood of the cycle, because it shows the persona leaving his home-land literally under a cloud. But this argument has its problems in the context of the six numbers in volume one, and Reinhold Brinkmann finally concludes, after carefully weighing all the various considerations, that the matter "remains a puzzle."[24] In any event, performances of op. 39 headed by either "Der frohe Wandersmann" or "In der Fremde" remain viable options.[25]

If Schumann vacillated about the best way to establish the premise of the Eichendorff *Liederkreis,* he had no problem articulating the second component of a wayfarer's cycle—seeking the beloved—by means of "Intermezzo." This short song displays the tension between the folklike structure of Eichendorff's verse and Schumann's artful treatment. Much of the verse in op. 39 takes the form of so-called *Volksliedstrophe*, which appears at first to consist of iambic trimeter but is treated as the stylized tetrameter I have designated as *Langzeilenvers*. The cross-rhymed quatrains consist of couplets in which the last word of the odd lines receives an accent on both syllables while the even lines end with a silent foot. We have seen this pattern before, for instance in "Aus alten Märchen winkt es":

Wo búnten Blúmen blúe-hén	Where colorful flowers bloom
Im góldnen Ábendlícht, [´]	In golden evening light,
Und líeblich dúftend glúe-hén	And, sweetly scented, glow
Mit bráeutlichém Gesícht. [´]	With bridelike visage.

The first stanza of "Intermezzo" reads:

Dein Bíldniß wúndersé-líg	Your wonderfully blessed image
Hab' ích im Hérzensgrúnd, [´]	I hold in the depths of my heart,
Das síeht so frísch und fróeh-lích	It gazes so pertly and cheerfully
Mich án zu jéder Stúnd'. [´]	On me at all times.

Though the second stanza invokes "a lovely old lied" (the counterpart of the "old fable" in Heine's verse), Schumann treats Eichendorff artfully rather than folklorically. His setting of "Aus alten Märchen" stresses the two concluding syllables of odd lines and doubles the voice in the piano homorhythmically. Not so "Intermezzo," where the piano proceeds independently of the voice, with intermittent counterpoint and pulsing offbeats. The melody deemphasizes the final accented syllable of lines one and three in each couplet while ignoring the iambic meter at will. Finally, Schumann feels free to manipulate the text by repeating the initial stanza to create a ternary form. In effect, the music blunts the folkloric tone of the poetry.

An artful approach also marks "Waldesgespräch," the ballad selected by the composer for the first volume of op. 39. The presence of verse abandoning the "lyrical first person" in a Schumann wayfarer's cycle should surprise us no longer, and the settings of such miniature dramas had a tradition of elaborate musical characterization. Eichendorff bases his wayfaring vignette on the legend of the Loreley.[26] In this case a luckless hunter (replete with horn fifths over ostinato alternation of E and B bass notes) tries to seduce a beautiful maiden riding alone in the forest. He should have listened more carefully, for at the siren's dialogue Schumann modulates without preparation to an uncanny flat submediant (C major) and the accompaniment switches to a stereotypical wave figure. The Loreley warns him, "Oh flee, flee, you know not who I am!" But the suitor's ardor unseats common sense ("your young figure is so wonderfully beautiful") until he recognizes her—too late. She reveals herself over wave figures now in "his" key of E major and mocks him with his own words: "It's late, it's cold, you'll never leave this forest again." The hunter has become the prey, and as *she* abducts *him*, the composer allows the hunting figure (opening horn fifths over ostinato) to die away in a gruesomely cheerful E major that underlines the irony of the reversed roles.

Schumann incongruously juxtaposes this tale about the pitfalls of traveling with a lyrical song of utter contentment in "Die Stille." Eichendorff's verse falls mostly in dactyls, with an anacrusis for each line, but the syllable count is not quite regular, and so the variability of compound meter suits the composer's purposes well. The minimal, chordal punctuations in the accompaniment focus attention on the melodic line and also impart the appropriately lighthearted atmosphere to this interlude between more serious songs. Schumann took great liberties with Eichendorff's verse, which originated in the fourteenth chapter of *Ahnung und Gegenwart*, sung by a female character disguising herself in male costume on a winter's night. The composer omitted her third stanza:

Ich wünscht', es wäre schon Morgen,	I wish it were already morning,
Da fliegen zwey Lerchen auf,	When two larks will arise,
Die überfliegen einander,	They will overfly each other,
Mein Herze folgt ihrem Lauf.	My heart will follow their course.

Instead, Schumann sets Eichendorff's concluding stanza and then repeats the opening to create a ternary form with attached postlude. Concision may have prompted this change, both because the original's last stanza repeats the imagery of the third and because the musical form chosen supplies an extra stanza. In any case, we find again the tension between simple, folkloric tone and artful manipulation.

David Ferris observes that the last two numbers in the first volume of op. 39 form a pair, by virtue of both their subject matter and their musical material.[27] Perhaps more has been written about "Mondnacht" than any other lied, and many authors consider it one of the finest settings of one of the German language's greatest poems. In theory, the verse unfolds in *Volksliedstrophe*, reinforced by allusion to a formulaic beginning ("es war [einmal]"—"once upon a time") conjoined with the subjunctive mood ("als hätt' der Himmel"—"It was as if heaven had . . ."). Thus, in describing a brightly moonlit landscape on a clear night, Eichendorff transports the reader into the realm of dream, where ordinary events occasion extraordinary results (illumination impelling wind across field and forest and decoupling soul from body). Schumann's setting attains the epitome of understated elegance and mystery. He rejects the possibility of scanning the text as *Langzeilenvers* ("Es wár als háett' der Hím-mél") in favor of simple trimeter, and he tonicizes the dominant in such as way as to create the illusion that each couplet ends on a plagal cadence in B major. In this way the composer suspends the listener within Eichendorff's ethereal vision. Each couplet, moreover, receives the same melody, except for the penultimate one, which finally introduces the subdominant ("aus") to prepare the arrival "home" in the repeated cadences on the E major tonic in the long postlude.

"Schöne Fremde" continues exploration of the dreamlike realm first glimpsed in "Mondnacht," now intimating "great good fortune to come" ("künftigem großen Glück"). The second song of twin nightscapes lands in the key temporarily tonicized by the first, B major, and its opening varies the melodic phrase that repeats throughout the "Mondnacht" (compare exx. 3.8a and 3.8b). But here the similarities end, for "Schöne Fremde" is through-composed (in spite of the false strophic reference at

Examples 3.8a–b.   Melodic parallels between the openings of "Mondnacht" (a) and "Schöne Fremde" (b).

"was sprichst du wirr, wie in Träumen" in the middle of the second stanza). This song eventually becomes as unsettled in its wide-ranging vocal ambitus as "Mondnacht" is static in its placid reiteration, and it leaves no doubt as to its tonic. Schumann meant the contradictory pair to conclude the first volume, even as its last number urges us forward on a hopeful note.

Just as the first volume of the Eichendorff *Liederkreis* ends with an interrelated pair, so the second volume begins with two songs conjoined even more closely. "Auf einer Burg" and "In der Fremde [II]" not only share the same head motive and key, but the first song ends on a half-cadence that leads directly to the second. Together they present a melancholy picture of loss. Karen Hindenlang makes a convincing case for the underlying political symbolism in "Auf einer Burg," on its surface a description of a ruined castle like those one sees frequently on hillsides overlooking the Rhine. The fortress's crumbling statue of a knight, its empty window frames, and its general decay represent lost glory for which the German nation—represented by a bride—weeps as life follows its daily course (the wedding's cheerfully playing musicians).[28] To represent the faded past musically, Schumann begins with a brief reference to sixteenth-century counterpoint in artificially long note values, just enough to invoke the topos of *style antico*. "In der Fremde [II]" abandons this style for more agile harmonic motion, punctuating each line of text with a sixteenth-note ritornello figure. In spite of its different accompanimental texture, however, the second song's shared head motive and key invite us to recast the events of the preceding song. We find a castle here too, now glimpsed from above and afar, and another woman, a beloved who has long since died. Curiously, *Liederbuch II*, the manuscript in which Schumann first realized these songs, assigns no date to "Auf einer Burg," and some writers have assumed without any evidence that it was composed after "In der Fremde [II]."[29] The most we can claim is that all of the songs in the second volume originated in the period between 17 and 20 May 1840.[30]

"Wehmuth" stands rather by itself in op. 39's second volume, despite the fact that it shares the tonic of E with the ensuing "Zwielicht." It plays rather like a slow cantabile amid the more active surrounding numbers, a resting point of pure inner reflection. Reacting to its intimate revelation (it originally appeared in *Ahnung und Gegenwart* as a song performed by a female character pining for her beloved), Schumann simplifies the texture somewhat, doubling the voice in the right hand at almost all points and distributing the three stanzas evenly over each part of the ternary form. The composer has also adopted conventional declamation, clearly distributing the two accented syllables that conclude the odd lines of each iambic couplet ("Ich kánn wohl mánchmal sín-gén, / Als ób ich fróehlich séi [´]) over two full beats. But this generalization disguises a lovely subtlety within the basic framework: Schumann manages by means of rhythmic length or height of pitch, or both, to emphasize the important penultimate word of most lines ("manchmal," "fröhlich," "Thränen," "Herz," and so forth). As much as anything, this lends the setting its "emotionally reinforcing" qualities.[31]

"Zwielicht" and "Im Walde" form a pair not only by means of poetico-musical leading (the first song's open-ended text closes on a chord that serves as dominant for the next song) but by means of the shared aura of mystery and Romantic irony moving beneath their dissimilar surfaces. Brinkmann observes about the "extraordinary beginning" of "Zwielicht" that it invokes "*alter Styl* . . . Romantic historicism,"[32] two- and ultimately three-voiced Bach-like counterpoint in minor mode serving as emblem here of the Gothic (see ex. 3.9). Twilight obscures the reality of distant memory, confuses the senses, and conducts the persona into a realm of ominous foreboding: "The trees bestir themselves eerily, / Clouds drift by like still dreams—What does this dread mean?" In the half-light of Eichendorff's poem, a series of anxious visions unfolds—hunters stalking innocent animals (second stanza), disembodied voices wandering through the forest (third stanza), betrayal by friends (fourth stanza). And as the dreary world disappearing into the gloom awaits rebirth at dawn, the persona (or reader?) is admonished to "take heed and be alert." With its sequence of vignettes concluding in a shift to second-person imperative, "Zwielicht" alludes to the genre of the ballad, but

Example 3.9.   Bach-like counterpoint in the prelude to "Zwielicht."

it lacks a coherent narrative. Oddly, Schumann's strophic melody reinforces the poem's episodic disjunction by impelling the listener to seek the paranoid logic of the twilit world. The "Gothic," contrapuntal accompaniment creates an underlying mood of dread until the last stanza, where block chords underscore the drama of the final warning.[33]

The musical topos of "Im Walde," with its *romanza* meter, also intimates a ballad. But while each of Eichendorff's paratactic lines (self-contained thoughts isolated by Schumann's lengthy interludes) initiates a different narrative, the stories do not continue. Instead we encounter disconnected scenes of a wedding procession, a merry hunt, and then nightfall accompanied by unexpected dread. This list of events served the composer well in recalling themes from other numbers in the cycle, such as the wedding celebration in "Auf einer Burg," the hunt in "Waldesgespräch," nightscapes in "Mondnacht" and "Schöne Fremde," and uneasy nightfall in "Zwielicht." The lack of related images mirrors the paradox of the cycle as a whole, which in its various pairings and juxtapositions constantly invites a wanderer's narrative that does not exist, a coherence that never materializes, an implied causality without effect. When Schumann withdraws the pervasive *romanza* rhythm for the persona's last line, "I shudder in the depths of my heart," he evokes the ironic ending of another pseudo-ballad, "Aus alten Märchen winkt es," with its illusory phantasms.

If the apparent dread concluding "Im Walde" were not puzzling enough, the persona unexpectedly finds happiness at journey's end in an ecstatic finale. "Frühlingsnacht" also takes place in darkness, now neither mysterious nor threatening but joyful. Schumann creates the expectant mood of this ternary song (again, each section sets a stanza) by beginning the sixteenth-note accompanimental triplets in almost every measure just after the downbeat in the right hand. This rhythmic tick combines with scales cascading downward to lend a breathless quality against which the melody plays ascending scales in the outer sections of the song. The composer's other device for engendering excitement comes in his treatment of double anacruses in the verse, which he places sometimes on pick-ups, sometimes on the downbeat of the measure. Though Knaus makes much of the poem's original context in Eichendorff's collection "Frühling und Liebe,"[34] its new context in Schumann's cycle must take precedence. Given the reference to "Wandervögel" (stanza 1), the reappearance of wonders (stanza 2), and references to moon, stars, dreams, and rustling heather in the final strophe—all themes from earlier songs in op. 39—we are led to believe that the persona gains hope of winning his beloved. If op. 35 ends in loss and op. 36 ends inconclusively, then we can join Turchin in saying that the wayfarer in the Eichendorff *Liederkreis* has achieved "a higher state of unity, a greater wholeness through increased self-awareness," and perhaps even regained the "ancestral home which is often linked with a female counterpart from whom [he] departs when setting out."[35]

The whole magical journey in op. 39 unfolds to some of Schumann's most piquant music. During January 1847, Eichendorff called on the composer twice in Vienna, just after Schumann had conducted his First Symphony at the New Year's concert there.[36] And in appreciation for his settings of lieder, Eichendorff tendered the composer a poem inscribed on an album leaf:

Es träumt ein jedes Herz	Each and every heart doth dream
Vom fernen Land des Schönen;	Of a distant beauteous land;
Dorthin durch Lust und Schmerz	Thither amid joy and sorrow
Schwingt wunderbar aus Tönen	A sprite with tones wondrously
Manch' Brücke eine Fey—	Spans many a bridge—
O holde Zauberei![37]	O fair enchantment!

4

Romances, Ballads,
and the *Via Media*

"The ballad has something mysterious about it, without being mystic," Goethe writes in his classic characterization of the genre. "The latter attribute of a poem lies in its material, the former in its treatment." Speaking of its improvisational roots, he continues:

> The mysterious quality of a ballad derives from its manner of presentation. The singer has his pregnant material, his characters, their deeds and actions, so deeply ingrained, that he does not know how he will bring them to light. He employs, therefore, all three basic poetic modes to express that which excites the power of imagination and engages the intellect. He can begin in a lyric, epic, or dramatic [manner], continuing to change mode at will, hurrying to the end or long delaying it. . . . A selection of such verse, moreover, can display the whole range of poetry, because here the elements have not yet separated but are still united, as in a living, primeval egg *(Ur-Ei)* that need only be hatched to launch the most magnificent phenomenon into the air on wings of gold.[1]

Quite aside from noting the features of the genre itself (mystery; free combination of lyric, epic, and dramatic modes; generation of all other literary genres), Goethe details a manner of production with origins in an oral tradition where poet and musician were originally one and the same person. In the nineteenth-century German art ballad (*Kunstballade*) these roles separated, with the poet providing the lyrics that a composer then "sang" (or at least provided with a set of increasingly specific instructions for performance). Whether Goethe approved of the composer's intrusion into the process or not, his own forays into the genre ("Erlkönig" and "Der Fischer," for instance) undoubtedly gained their greatest fame in elaborate settings by composers such as Schubert and Loewe. And because the art ballad elicited from composer and performer alike a wide range of expression (to suit the lyric, epic, and dramatic modes), this special subgenre of lied appeared in public concerts far more often than purely lyrical songs during the first half of the nineteenth century.

Schumann lavished great care on the genre of the art ballad and apparently set great store by it. From the pieces composed during his first blooming of solo songs he culled four sets of *Romanzen und Balladen* (opp. 45, 49, 53, and 64), two early sets of ballads in translation (opp. 31 and 40), and one ballad with its own opus number (*Belsatzar,* op. 57). This last song actually appears as the first entry in *Liederbuch I* (although it does not bear the earliest date in this collection of realizations).[2] We have already seen that ballads also formed a regular part of Schumann's song cycles about wayfaring. If today his strictly lyrical songs vastly overshadow his ballads, this may result from his lack of enduring success as a dramatic composer (though his contemporaries esteemed his oratorio-like works highly). In any event, Schumann's romances are well worth performers' efforts, both for their relatively wide range of vocal display and for their particularly evocative writing for piano.

The Chamisso Ballads

After Schumann set Charmisso's *Frauenliebe und Leben* on 11–12 July 1840, he indulged his usual habit of leafing through the author's collected poetry further,[3] and he hit first on three ballads set on 13–14 July (published as op. 31), then on five more semiballads composed on 16–18 July (published as op. 40). With the exception of one text ("Die Löwenbraut" in op. 31), all of these ballad or balladlike texts represent Chamisso's translations of other authors' poetry: that of Pierre Jean de Béranger in op. 31 and that of Hans Christian Andersen (with the last poem "from modern Greek") in op. 40. These initial essays in the world of the ballad set a certain standard for the rest of Schumann's collections in this vein: they constitute more than miscellanies, and we can usually detect both musical and poetic threads underlying their various numbers.

Die Löwenbraut, Ballade. Die Kartenlegerin nach Beranger [sic]. Die rothe Hanne nach Beranger. von Adalbert von Chamisso. für eine Singstimme mit Begleitung des Pianoforte . . . Op. 31. (composed 11–12 July 1840; published March 1841 by A. Cranz)

If Schumann's collections of ballads and romances usually possess some sort of rough coherence, then op. 31 serves as a good initial case study. Though far from being a cycle in any real sense, this publication gathers three Chamisso poems about betrothal, fidelity, and marriage from a woman's point of view.[4] Women are the featured (if not always exclusive) characters in each tale, and the composer casts the individual numbers in closely related keys (G minor and major, E-flat major, B-flat major). Moreover, Schumann set the respective texts of all the songs using a relatively consistent approach, one that avoids the "modern" proclivity toward inflecting each word (which Schumann criticized in Schubert and Loewe)[5] while offering accompaniments that took selective advantage of contemporary developments in the range of the piano.

There can be no better example of Schumann's restrained approach to ballads than "Die Löwenbraut," the first song in op. 31. Ballads often relate tales of love, lust, and grisly death, and this poem about a woman mauled by her childhood pet when she bids it farewell on the eve of her arranged marriage displays all the conventional elements. A narrator begins Chamisso's tale in epic mode, much of the middle part of the ballad consists of dialogue from the bride-to-be lamenting her arranged match (dramatic mode), the bridegroom also speaks before he kills the enraged beast (too late), and the whole exhibits lyric mode in its metrically regular, cross-rhymed quatrains. Like almost all such tales, this one suggests several morals about the pitfalls of loveless matches and about jealousy (Collin's "Der Zwerg" presents a variation on this story, through we do not know whether Schumann had encountered Schubert's setting of the ballad published in 1823, D. 771). We could even project a biographical subtext onto the song, with Friedrich Wieck as the beast unwilling to part with his companion and Schumann as the youth who eventually slays the vengeful animal, but this would constitute little more than fanciful conjecture.

Schumann was well aware of operatic settings that assigned different melodies and voice ranges to each character ("Erlkönig" would have been his prime example), and he avails himself of dramatic options, but only to a limited extent. His treatment of "Löwenbraut" adopts a ternary form, with the outer two sections using the same archaic double common-time signature as "Stirb, Lieb' und Freud'!" (see ex. 3.1, above) to set third-person narration. The inner section of the ballad falls in 3/2 time, responding to the address of the unhappy maiden to the lion. Within these two contrasting sections, however, the melody unfolds strophically by and large, with a somewhat flat shape and almost exclusively syllabic declamation. The composer limits accompanimental activity in both sections as well: briefly punctuating chords with ritornelli between stanzas support the voice in the first A section, while a constantly recurring legato phrase in chorale texture marks the B section (see ex. 4.1). Eventually Schumann indulges more chromaticism and a more active piano part in the final A section, where the enraged lion commits its ghastly deed. But even this texture reverts to the unobtrusive initial pattern when the lion sinks meekly down to be slain in its turn. In short, the composer has relied largely on an older model for setting ballads, in which a minimal accompaniment allows the singer-actor considerable interpretive room. Schumann supplies the kind of melodrama that marks other "modern" art ballads only at the most theatrical juncture and then briefly. He tends to establish and consistently follow a *via media* between the demonstrative "Viennese" tradition on the one hand and the impassive "northern German" tradition on the other, just as his criticism would suggest.

"Die Kartenlegerin" offers the much more lighthearted story of a young girl reading her fortune in cards until her disapproving mother finds out. Initially the cards predict love and romance, but later they reveal the approach of a "wheezing old woman," the mother, which leads to the con-

Example. 4.1.   Repeated accompanimental figure for the middle section of "Die Löwenbraut."

clusion that "the cards never lie." This ballad adopts a reflexive approach to its narration: that is to say, the main character in the tale also relates the action, a conceit found in such well-known examples as Goethe's "Sorcerer's Apprentice." Schumann reacts not so much to this feature as to the odd structure of Chamisso's translation. The meter of the verse is regular enough (trochaic tetrameter, with few exceptions), lending itself to relatively straightforward two-measure subphrases. But the stanzas present more of a challenge, because the lines group into septains that fit poorly into the standard eight-measure units assumed by quadratic style. The composer solves this problem guilelessly (in keeping with the character of his young narrator) simply by repeating a line in each strophe, often the last. As in "Löwenbraut," the accompaniment here tends for the most part to punctuate the melody with supporting chords, intruding only with a delightful thirty-second-note ritornello that suggests the playfulness of the game at hand.

Schumann employs rondo form to give overall shape to "Kartenlegerin," with the first two stanzas using the rondo theme, an episode for the third stanza, and so forth by strophe (AA' BA'' CA'''). This sectional alternation lends the story a sense of progression that a simple strophic setting could not. At the same time it preserves the integrity of each stanza, something that a more operatic approach outlining every different scene or character in the narrative would obscure.

The last song in op. 31 views an unfortunate outcome of marriage rather than arranged betrothal or fantasies about a mate, and it sounds themes of social inequity that we hear again in other Schumann songs. "Die rothe Hanne" ("Red-haired Hanna") must turn away one suitor after another for lack of a dowry and falls prey to a ne'er-do-well, who is caught poaching to support his family. He lands in jail, and she languishes with her starving, freezing children, a monument to the deplorable condition of the poor (especially at the hands of the aristocracy) and the lowly status of women in society. In his day Chamisso was known for his interest in "neglected segments of culture and [championed] the lives of the ordinary people within them,"[6] an interest the composer shared.

Of the three numbers in op. 31 this text receives the most unadorned treatment. It has a minimal accompaniment consisting mostly of simple chords without figuration, and the ritornello that separates each stanza, serving as both prelude and postlude, reiterates a plain, unchanging measure-long figure repeated three successive times in various registers, ending with a held chord. The only embellishment (if we can call it that) arises from an optional four-part chorus for the refrain of each verse, "God preserve red-haired Hanna! The poacher sits under guard!" Schumann sets Chamisso's regular octaves largely in strophic form, with only two notable exceptions for the fourth stanza, where the poacher himself speaks, and then for the last stanza by way of coda (but even here the two-line refrain and postlude simply repeat). The composer clearly wants performers and listeners to focus on the plight of Hanna, not on fanciful music for either voice or piano. In short, Schumann gives notice in this song and in op. 31 as a whole that while he possesses the technique to reflect every nuance of a ballad, he chooses restraint instead.

Märzveilchen, Muttertraum, der Soldat, der Spielmann aus dem Dänischen von H. C. Andersen und Verrathene Liebe aus dem Neugriechischen übersetzt von A. v. Chamisso . . . Op. 40 (composed 16–18 July 1840; published September 1842 by C. C. Lose & Olsen in Copenhagen and Fr. Kistner in Leipzig)

Just after Schumann had chosen to set the ballads in op. 31, he paged through his Chamisso anthology further and hit upon a group of five poems in translation. Where the verse in op. 31 presents fairly conventional ballads that emphasize epic and dramatic modes, the much shorter texts in op. 40 consist of thumbnail sketches in lyric mode that seem more like semiballads.[7] They relate miniature vignettes, most of them by Hans Christian Andersen, whose talents in this vein Chamisso particularly esteemed: "Endowed with wit, caprice, humor, and folklike naiveté, [Andersen] also has within his power deeper notes capable of awakening resonance. He especially knows how to bring miniature portraits and landscapes easily to life with a few casually tossed-off strokes."[8] Schumann formed Chamisso's five translations into a coherent set linked by subject (love gone awry) and also by key, with what Ozawa calls two "framing songs" in G major and three interior numbers in D minor.[9] Indeed, internal tonal references and contiguity in the middle songs and the fact that "Spielmann" actually ends in G major lead Daverio to characterize op. 40 as a cycle.[10]

Because they condense vivid stories into very little space, the texts of op. 40 elicited a particularly intense reaction from Schumann, as he wrote to Andersen in an October 1842 letter accompanying a presentation copy of the songs: "[My music] will probably appear rather odd to you at first glance, but your poems seemed equally so to me at first. As I immersed myself more in them, my music assumed an ever stranger character. The fault, then, is yours alone."[11] Andersen seems to have agreed, for he sent a warm note of thanks for the "interesting and *characteristic* compositions [my emphasis],"[12] a catchword for pieces that carried overtones of the folkloric. In contrast to the less demonstrative treatment Schumann accorded to the epic ballads in op. 31, the "miniature portraits" of op. 40 elicited some especially piquant music.

The two outer songs in op. 40 provide a lighthearted frame for the grimmer numbers within. "Märzveilchen" relates the story of a maiden who catches a young man's eye through a frosted windowpane, and while the scene portends hope, the narrator ends with a hint of warning: "The icy flowers begin to melt—God be gracious to that young man!" Schumann's setting appears unremarkable at first—a conventional alternation of bass note and answering right-hand chord in support of a lyrical tune—but it has something amiss rhythmically. The composer displaces the accompanimental pattern in such a way that what should be a sixteenth-note upbeat to each measure actually comes as an upbeat to the second eighth note after the bar line. The listener does not discover this displacement until the singer enters with an anacrusis that emphasizes the true downbeat, and from then on the voice and the piano always seem slightly at odds (until the closing postlude finally places the accompaniment on firmer rhythmic ground). In "Verrathene Liebe" ("Love Revealed"), the ardent suitor makes ever more preposterous claims to his sweetheart about how their courtship has been disclosed "in all the streets and markets" to all the boys and girls in town. This is Schumann's most normal setting in this collection, except for its dynamic shape. The young man's protests grow louder, until a busy piano postlude intimates that the accompanist does not believe the excuse (that a private kiss on shipboard was espied by the stars, who told the sea, which informed the rudder, which communicated it to a sailor, who told *his* girlfriend). The outer two songs display a touch of wit in the language of art song.

The inner three songs of op. 40 present a gloomier catalog of frustrated passions: motherly love in "Muttertraum," brotherly love in "Der Soldat," and obsessive love in "Der Spielmann." The texts for these songs tend more toward the genre of the *Moritat* or *Bänkelsang*. Such songs usually related gruesome events—crime and punishment, romance ending in death, and reports of accidents or natural disasters. They were declaimed in earlier times from benches (or *Bänke*) in marketplaces by itinerant minstrels, who often illustrated their woeful tales by holding up cartoons on plac-ards.[13] The dismaying events in *Bänkelsänge* usually offered cautionary lessons for the edification of the listeners.

Chamisso's "Muttertraum" ("A Mother's Dream") obscures its story by translating both title and content in a misleading way. Andersen's original Danish heading for the poem reads "Tyveknægten" ("The Thiev-ing Knave"), and it relates the chilling prophecy imparted to a woman doting on her slumbering infant in its last stanza:

Men Ravnen kommer med al sin Slægt,	But a raven came with all his kin,
Og synger bag Ruden sin Vise:	And sang at the window his tune:
„Din Engel bliver en Tyveknægt,	"Your angel will become a thieving knave,
Og vi skal Engelen spise."	And we shall dine on the cherub."

The version published in Chamisso's *Gedichte* of 1834 renders the reason for the ill omen somewhat less clearly:

Der Rab indeß mit der Sippenschaft sein	At this a raven with all his kin
Kreischt draussen am Fenster die Weise:	Croaked at the window this tune:
Dein Engel, dein Engel wird unser sein!	Your angel, your angel shall be ours!
Der Räuber dient uns zur Speise!	The thief shall serve as our meal!

If Chamisso had left Andersen's title intact, the listener might divine the meaning more easily, but in this case the task of intimating the dark mood of the poem from the outset fell to Schumann. He creates a sense of foreboding by means of a minor-mode prelude, postlude, and accompa-niment similar in both contrapuntal texture and melodic content to the "Gothic" style used for the dreamlike setting of "Zwielicht" in op. 39 (as several authors note; see ex. 3.8, above).[14] Though we lack Andersen's leading title, we can hear the ominous portent in the piano.

"Der Soldat" communicates its grisly story—narrated reflexively by a young man who must execute his comrade—much more directly. Schu-mann employs a funeral-march topos for this tragic vignette, one so raw in its imitation of heavy-footed drum cadences that it would have done Gustav Mahler proud in one of his *Wunderhorn* songs two generations later. This short poem, only four quatrains, elicits more theatricality from Schumann than many longer ballads, first in the sonic effect of a proces-sion approaching softly from a distance, growing louder as it passes in front of the listener, and then receding for the third stanza. At the execu-tion itself the composer cannot resist breaking into right-hand triplets, perhaps in imitation of a drum roll. We can imagine the shot striking with a loud eighth-note chord on the emphasized word "*Ich*—aber, ich traf, ich traf ihn mitten in das Herz!*" ("*I*—but I hit him in the middle of the heart!"). The composer sets the rest of the line as an explicitly marked recitative over tremolo harmonies, and the piano postlude of half-note chords suggests the body slumping down, its life ebbing away. Schumann rarely indulged in such graphic writing, but here he was moved to augment the brief text with vivid musical imagery.

"Der Spielmann," the story of a musician playing at the wedding of his beloved to another man, takes the form of a demented waltz in the manner of "Das ist ein Flöten und Geigen." The bereft fiddler's madness in op. 40 manifests itself first in tonal instability. The accompaniment begins on a doubly diminished secondary seventh chord that leads toward D minor, but the first phrase lurches suddenly to G minor, and the music continues to modulate erratically from B-flat major to D major to C minor to A-flat major, changing for almost every couplet. The song ends, moreover, in a different key from its nominal beginning, G instead of D (an impression blunted somewhat by a cadence on an unstable second-inversion tonic). Some commentators also observe manifestations of derangement in a motivic similarity between the vocal melody of "Spielmann" and the slightly sinister wedding procession in op. 39's "Im Walde" (compare exx. 4.2a and 4.2b).[15] But "Spielmann" adds an extra twist to this phrase, a kind of quaver in the narrator's voice that carries

Examples 4.2a–b. Beginning melodic figure from op. 39, "Im Walde" (a), and vocal entrance of the wedding dance in "Der Spielmann," op. 40 (b).

over into the fiddler's playing (if we assume the accompaniment to be a wedding dance). The final Andersen text in Chamisso's ordering answers the promise of "Märzveilchen" with a chilling prayer: "O God, preserve us graciously / from being by madness overcome; / I am myself a poor musician." It was this evil omen that Schumann sought to avert in appending "Verrathene Liebe" to the end of the set.

Andersen's description of Schumann's op. 40 as "characteristic" hits the mark directly, if by "characteristic" we mean more "idiosyncratic rather than general or typical, the exception rather than the rule, 'interesting' and 'striking' rather than 'nobly simple,' coloristic rather than statuesque," as Carl Dahlhaus put it.[16] This aura was enhanced, perhaps unintentionally, by the fact that Schumann had the songs published simultaneously in Leipzig and Copenhagen, with parallel German and Danish texts (except for "Verrathene Liebe," of course).[17] And we know of at least one early performance of the complete set for a highly select audience from an account of a Leipzig sojourn in Andersen's diary:

> . . . a lovely, quite poetic evening awaited me at Robert Schumann's. The highly gifted composer had surprised me two years before with the honor of dedicating to me his music to four of my poems that Chamisso had translated into German. These were performed on that evening by Mrs. [Livia] Frege, whose tender singing has delighted and inspired many thousands. Clara Schumann accompanied, and the listeners consisted solely of composer and poet. A small, festive meal and a mutual exchange of ideas made for all too brief an evening.[18]

Sets of Romances and Ballads

In the summer of 1843 Schumann approached Friedrich Kistner with a proposal for several volumes of ballads and romances, to which the publisher replied tantalizingly in a letter on 24 July 1843: "I would be inclined to publish your cycle of *Romanzen und Balladen* with pleasure, only I could not take them on before the beginning of the coming year in any event." Just a month later, Friedrich Whistling accepted the offer,[19] and four volumes eventually appeared (opp. 45, 49, 53, and 64). But they make for much less than we would usually consider a cycle, especially in light of the fact that Schumann had not even selected the texts for the first two numbers in op. 64. Nor is it likely that the composer was projecting anything even so loosely knit as *Myrthen* in the summer of 1843, given the disparate ballads he had on hand at the time. But we are led by Kistner's letter to look at least for the internal consistency in each volume of *Romanzen und Balladen* and to revisit the question of what Schumann and his publishers might have considered cyclic in such a far-flung assemblage.

Romanzen und Balladen für eine Singstimme mit Begleitung des Pianoforte . . .
Heft I, Op. 45 ("Der Schatzgräber" and "Frühlingsfahrt" by Eichendorff, composed respectively 5 November and 31 October 1840; "Abends am Strand" by Heine, composed spring [?] 1840; published December 1843 by F. Whistling)

If op. 31 addresses marriage and op. 40 the vicissitudes of affection, op. 45 takes as its theme seeking one's fortune, with the subtext of wayfaring. The collection entails a satisfying coherence in spite of its two disparate poets, Eichendorff and Heine. "The Treasure Hunter" relates the misfortunes of those motivated purely by greed, "Spring Voyage" depicts the various fates of young men making their way in the world, and "Evenings on the Strand" delivers an ironically detached moral about those who seek their fortunes from the standpoint of those who remain at home. While Schumann does not connect this sequence melodically, he does create a strong tonal progression among the songs from G minor to D major to G major.

"Der Schatzgräber," the tale of a miner buried while digging for gold, constitutes an exception that proves the rule, one of the composer's few thoroughly "operatic" settings of a ballad (in this case more recitative than aria). As in selections from the op. 39 *Liederkreis*, this song displays the tension between folkloric elements in Eichendorff's poetry and Schumann's artful treatment. Taken by itself, the verse falls into an almost perfectly regular *Langzeilenvers*:

> Wenn álle Wáelder schlíe-fén,
> Er án zu gráben húb, [´]
> Rastlós in Bérges Tíe-fén
> Nach éinem Schátz er grub. [´]

Though it would sound absurd given the subject, this text would easily fit the same melodic phrases as "Aus alten Märchen winkt es." Schumann takes great pains in the first stanza, however, to suppress the poetic meter of "Schatzgräber" by playing with the length of syllables (especially for the second line of each couplet) and by running both lines together (see ex. 4.3). He also isolates the couplets from one another. The composer respects Heine's scansion more in the second stanza, but he reduces the voice almost to a monotone. In the third strophe, Schumann seizes on the sole line of dialogue in this poem ("'Und wirst doch mein!'") to interject a great deal of internal repetition. He also breaks this stanza in two, setting the second couplet to the music of the opening, as if a new strophe began here. The final stanza then receives more of the melodic monotone we heard earlier. All of this liberty with the text unfolds over an erratically modulating, chromatic accompaniment punctuated by dramatic flourishes that emphasize specific phrases. In this song Schumann allowed himself the rare luxury of "painting too realistically" in the manner of Schubert or Loewe, something he obviously enjoyed as an isolated display of his theatrical command.

"Frühlingsfahrt" returns to Schumann's regular manner of setting ballads, a predominantly strophic approach to the tale of two wayfarers. We can hear immediately that it adopts the musical topos of a wanderer's confident march that we have seen earlier in "Der frohe Wandersmann" (another Eichendorff setting written in 1840) and in Reinick's "An den Sonnenschein" (composed in August 1840). The form of a march, moreover, fits the varied fate of the two lads well. Narrated mostly in third person, the two initial stanzas, setting the scene, and the third, relating the happy marriage and familial life of the first young man, all unfold to the same D major music. The intermediary "trio" diverts to D minor, setting the harder fate of the man lured by the call of the sea (his ship founders, and it remains unclear whether he has drowned) to new material also

Example 4.3.   Irregular scansion of the "Schatzgräber" opening couplet.

deployed strophically. The march proper then returns for Eichendorff's moral, ending with an address by the narrator in first person:

Es singen und klingen die Wellen	The waves sing and resound
Des Frühlings wohl über mir;	In spring soothingly over me;
Und seh' ich so kecke Gesellen,	And when I see such bold fellows,
Die Thränen im Auge mir schwellen,	The tears well up in my eyes,
Ach Gott, führ' uns liebreich zu Dir!	Oh, God guide us kindly to Thee!

One of the striking features of Eichendorff's verse lies in its five-line stanzas, which Schumann usually conforms to quadratic style by fitting the first couplet into four measures and the next three lines into six measures, and then supplying a two-measure tag for the piano (though he evens the score for the last verse by repeating the final line to reemphasize the author's point). This also highlights the marchlike nature of the accompaniment.[20]

"Abends am Strand," a beautiful song in its own right, also demonstrates the importance of considering individual numbers in the context of their opus by providing a wry comment on the two previous ballads. Whereas "The Treasure Hunter" comes to no good in his quest and the two young men in "Spring Voyage" encounter mixed fates, the group on the beach watches a departing ship and speculates idly about fabled distant lands. Thus Heine mocks the wanderlust that forms a cliché in all songs about wayfaring. This ironic detachment qualifies "Abends" almost as an antiballad, a story *about* tales of travel. Its inversion extends to an odd mode of narration in second-person plural, aloof even in its dialogue reported at second hand: "We spoke of storm and shipwreck, / Of the sailor and how he lives, / floating between sky and sea, / between fear and joy. / We spoke of distant coasts, / Of South and North, / And of the strange people / And strange customs there." For this group of people contemplating exotic journeys rather than experiencing them, Schumann hits initially on an accompanimental figure of extraordinary lassitude, a calmly meandering eighth-note pattern setting the scene. The middle discursive stanzas witness increasing animation and an ever more declamatory melodic line, until the fantastic realms along the Ganges and the rude noises of Laplanders unfold at an apogee of velocity and pitch ("They squat over fires, roast fish, and squeak and scream"). But the last stanza sees a return to the initial lackadaisical accompaniment for Heine's point about tales of armchair wayfarers: "The girls listened earnestly, / and finally nobody spoke; / The ship was no more to be sighted, / It had grown far too dark." This sly moral might just as well apply to op. 45 as a whole, for art ballads about seeking one's fortune allow the listener to experience the vicarious thrill of wayfaring in the safety of the parlor.

Romanzen und Balladen für eine Singstimme mit Begleitung des Pianoforte . . . Heft II, Op. 49 ("Die beiden Grenadiere" and "Die feindlichen Brüder" by Heine, dated respectively 12–13 May and 24 April 1840; "Die Nonne" by Fröhlich, composed 7 November 1840; published July 1844 by F. Whistling)

Schumann's second volume of ballads takes its central cue from two subtexts, the main one dealing with faded memories and old passions, the other with comradely affinities (whether for good or ill), including fellowship, brotherhood, and sisterhood. The collection possesses less tonal coherence than volume one, though it is not quite so diffuse as it might seem at first glance. "Die beiden Grenadiere" falls unambiguously in G minor-major, and the B minor-D major duality of "Die feindlichen Brüder" does not seem such a departure (especially through the dominant relationship between G and D), but how might we regard "Die Nonne"? Here Schumann provides us a hint in the apparently odd key signature of the central section, ostensibly C-sharp minor (enharmonically parallel to the D-flat major tonic) but with heavy overtones of E major—not so distant from the B tonic of the preceding number. We must certainly stretch to make this connection, but not past the point of all plausibility.

If listeners recognize any Schumann ballad, they will generally know his setting of Heine's "Die beiden Grenadiere," and this may have held true in the composer's day as well. Napoleon remained—oddly for the Germans, whom he had defeated—a symbol of European political egalitarianism and progress: "He will be . . . admired by all, deified by all, if he is not already," the eighteen-year-old Schumann wrote to one of his fellow students.[21] The song offers a study in how differing linguistic features conditioned his ballads on multiple levels. To capture the general subject matter (imprisoned French soldiers returning home from Russia after Napoleon's defeat), the composer selects an apposite and widely understood topos, the funeral march, replete with drum cadences, minor mode, and relatively low-lying tessitura for both voice and accompaniment. Adoption of this stylistic complex renders the "essence of the poem in one focal point" (if we recall E.T.A. Hoffmann's well-known dictum), and it does so in this case by responding to the semantic level of the text (both martial and tragic). When Schumann famously quotes the "Marseillaise" to set Heine's final stanzas, this too addresses content: the defiant vision of the buried soldier rising to his country's call at the return of his emperor.

Within the two basic march topoi, Schumann tends to proceed conservatively, respecting the stanzaic structure of "Grenadiere," though he molds the original quatrains into double strophes. The newly minted octaves then form the basis for varied strophic settings, each "stanza" beginning in parallel but deflecting musical content after the second or third couplet. Only Heine's seventh quatrain receives isolated treatment, mainly to accomplish the psychological modulation from a dejected mood to a triumphant one, paralleled by the tonal modulation from the minor mode of the funeral march to the major mode of the "Marseillaise." In choosing an essentially strophic design, Schumann indicatively rejected other possibilities. He indulges relatively little text repetition, he does not assign the narrator and each of the two speakers their own music (as Schubert does in his setting of "Erlkönig," for instance), and even the famous musical quotation at the end of "Grenadiere" respects the structure of its reference. Again we find Schumann poised between overtly theatrical gestures on the one hand and unadorned formalism on the other. His setting does not lack drama, but it maintains the integrity of Heine's verse.

Heine's "Die feindlichen Brüder" receives a much more conventional treatment than "Die beiden Grenadiere," but one that makes ingenious use of tradition. Schumann provides a minimal accompaniment for this poem, little more than a bass line of supporting chords and, in the major-mode setting of stanzas 3 and 4, piano writing that tends to double the voice homorhythmically (something fairly rare in his songs and striking in its simplicity). Initially it is tempting to hear this section in the relative major as fundamentally different from the surrounding strophes (the composer again combines quatrains into octaves), responding to the narrator's account of the reason for the brothers' strife over the favors of the beautiful Countess Laura. But when we listen more carefully, we can hear that the tune of this section uses the same basic melodic shape and even the same pitches as the other strophes. Schumann has smoothed the line and its uneven rhythms a bit, but he has maintained enough resemblance to create a distant but still recognizable variation. Just as he tampers minimally with the verse, he declaims the trochaic tetrameter with little interference.

We must ask why Schumann took what seems to be such a straightforward, one might almost say unimaginative approach to this ballad, and to answer this question we must think a bit about Heine's point (since ballads aim to provide moral edification). The answer comes in the poet's last two stanzas, amplified subtly by Schumann's melodic treatment of the last couplet. Heine's "twist" deals with the fact that many generations after their epic contest ends in a mutual slaying, the brothers eternally reenact their enmity in ghostly form. The poet tells us that hatred, like love, is undying, which prompts Schumann to react with an obsessive accompaniment, strophic form changing and modulating little, and a phrase that repeats lamely (see ex. 4.4) for the last two lines rather than finding a satisfactory conclusion in the lower octave. Even the pianist cannot be dissuaded from persisting in his unrelenting figuration *a tempo* for the postlude. Both voice and accompaniment respond to unchanging characters locked in endless strife.

To these tales about men mingling past glory with regret, Schumann added a short, poignant song along the same lines devoted to women.

Example 4.4.   Repetitious closing of "Die feindlichen Brüder."

"Die Nonne" would be Schumann's only setting of the Swiss cleric and professor Abraham Emanuel Fröhlich (1796–1865). We do not know how the composer encountered the poet's verse in 1840, since the only source extant today appears as part of his *Gesammelte Schriften* from 1853.[22] In any event, nobody would credit Fröhlich's small vignette of a nun enviously regarding a bride as an enlightened view of women (the message would seem to be that a religious vocation cannot equal the more traditional role of wife and mother). Schumann responds with delicate lyricism in a ternary form that appears to take a very odd turn away from its D-flat major signature, until we realize that the composer has cast the B section in C-sharp minor (much easier to decipher than the enharmonic parallel minor of D-flat). The other oddity in this short song appears in its last stanza, where third-person narration yields to a first-person utterance by the nun ("How she [the bride] glows like a rose beneath her white veil, while I, [sitting] beneath a red rose, pale joylessly"). Schumann responds to this dialogue with a somewhat more declamatory line, a continually slowing tempo, and a conclusion on the dominant of C-sharp (that is, D-flat) minor for the repeated last phrase ("ich Freudenlose"). Thwarted sexuality apparently deserved an arrested cadence.

Romanzen und Balladen für eine Singstimme mit Begleitung des Pianoforte . . .
Heft III, Op. 53 ("Blondel's Lied" by Johann Gabriel Seidl, composed 26 October 1840; "Loreley" by Auguste Wilhelmine Lorenz, composed in early April 1840; "Der arme Peter" by Heine, sketched fall [?] 1840 and realized spring [?] 1843; published September 1845 by F. Whistling)

The third volume in Schumann's "cycle" of romances and ballads explores the rewards and snares of loyalty in the mediant key relationships of G major and E minor-major. Like volume two, this assemblage traces a negative trajectory, beginning with the virtues of the minstrel Blondel's quest to find Richard the Lionhearted but ending with the Loreley's treacherous siren call and the brokenhearted obsession of "poor" Peter. Lest we believe Schumann ghoulish in such a progression, we should remember that romances and ballads tended toward grisly accounts, the reflection of a common public predilection for uncanny and even gruesome stories.

"Blondel's Lied," Schumann's only setting of the Austrian poet and imperial court treasurer Johann Gabriel Seidl (1804–1875), offers an uncharacteristically sunny tale (amid this grouping) of a faithful minstrel. He locates Richard the Lionhearted, held captive from 1192 to 1194 by the Austrian duke Leopold at the behest of Holy Roman Emperor Henry VI. The appeal of this text in the nineteenth century lay in the exoticism of its medieval setting, and its story of a heroic deed on the part of a musician would have been especially attractive to a composer. In fact, Schumann encountered the verse while reading the second volume of the Viennese *Orpheus. Musikalisches Taschenbuch für das Jahr 1841* (which actually appeared in 1840); he published his setting in the ensuing volume of the yearbook before including it in op. 53.[23]

We might suppose that the regular octaves in trochaic tetrameter and refrain ("Seek faithfully, and ye shall find!") would elicit one of Schumann's more conventional settings as an instance of formal reflexivity in a song about a song. But the composer avoids the obvious treatment. He eschews imitation of a strummed zither, selecting instead a chorale-like accompaniment that responds to Blondel's pious fidelity to his liege. And while the music for the refrain almost always returns verbatim, Schumann rejects a strophic approach, contenting himself merely with repetition of the first stanza's music for the seventh and last stanza (he omitted Seidl's third strophe to tighten the narrative). The intervening stanzas respond to the action without indulging heavy-handed theatricality: when the prisoner is discovered echoing Blondel's serenade from within his fortress-prison, the music modulates very briefly to A major (secondary dominant in G), the dynamic drops to pianissimo, and the accompaniment temporarily dwindles to sparse chords. The regular pattern and key of G quickly return, however, accelerating ("Nach und nach schneller und stärker") for the confirmation that the minstrel has discovered the monarch. This episode is spirited but not blatantly operatic, recalling the traditional limits of the ballad while not fettering expression unreasonably.

Schumann accords "Loreley" a more routine setting, with comfortably familiar elements that seem ironically at odds with its irregularly formed text. The source of the verse and the manner in which the composer may have encountered it find Schanze and Schulte uncharacteristically at a loss. They make an educated guess that the "Wilhelmine Lorenz" indicated in Schumann's first edition might be identical with the Saxon author of novels, stories, and travelogues Auguste Wilhelmine Lorenz (1784–1861), or that she may have been the wife of Schumann's friend

Oswald Lorenz.[24] Whether she was related to Emilie Lorenz, the composer's sister-in-law, remains an open question.

The position of "Loreley" in *Liederbuch I* places it significantly in almost immediate juxtaposition to "Waldesgespräch," Schumann's other setting about the fabled siren.[25] The two songs have much in common, including the key of E major, compound meter, and a wave figure for the characterization of the water nymph. But where Eichendorff's text has a strong dramatic conflict in its dialogue between hunter and seductress, Lorenz's verse exhibits mainly lyrical features (although we do find a narrator, and the siren does speak):

Es flüstern und rauschen die Wogen	The waves whisper and murmur
Wohl über ihr stilles Haus.	Soothingly over her silent home.
Es ruft eine Stimme, "Gedenke mein!	A voice calls, "Remember me!
Bei stiller Nacht im Vollmondschein."	Mid quiet night in full moonlight."

It is not clear that Lorenz cast her original in verse, but if she did, her second stanza must have been incomplete, for Schumann repeated the main point of the song, "Gedenke mein!" in the second stanza three times to fulfill his varied strophic setting. His music speaks more to atmosphere than to action, and this may explain why the song opens on a doubly diminished seventh chord over a dominant pedal. It evokes the mysterious wonderfully in this miniature portrait, mediating between the serene confidence of "Blondel's Lied" and the irony of "Der arme Peter."

The text for op. 53's last number comes immediately after that for "Zwei Brüder" (aka "Die feindlichen Brüder", op. 49, no. 2) in Schumann's copy of the *Buch der Lieder,* and the composer may well have conceived them in close proximity during April 1840. But he appears not to have realized "Der arme Peter" until he contemplated publishing several contiguous volumes of romances and ballads, for he notes of the fair copy toward the end of *Liederbuch III,* "1840 componirt, 1843 aufgeschrieben." "Peter" represents one of two multipartite Heine ballads Schumann set (the other being "Tragödie," op. 64, no. 3, from 1841), and both feature sly, one might almost say sneering narratives. Op. 53, no. 3 relates the tale of a fellow who loses his sweetheart "Gretel" (German: Grethe), not to just anybody but to the fabled Hansel, who inhabits so many German folktales.

The first clichéd section about Hans and Grethe at their wedding occasions a stereotypical *Tanzlied,* a kind of *Ländler* that Schumann begins

Example 4.5.   Beginning of the last quartrain in "Der arme Peter."

with folkish drones and continues in a music-box G major. But against this deliberately hackneyed background "poor Peter" declines to follow the suicidal course mapped by the young Werther or by Schubert's miller lad, maintaining instead, "Ah, were I not so sensible, I would do myself harm." Thus ends Heine's first part, with the second entirely in first person relating the persona's desolation (he does not have the sense to move on). Schumann provides this section with an exaggeratedly melodramatic setting that features a good deal of recitative-like ebb and flow and ironic touches such as descending voice parts for lines like "I climb up to the mountaintop," a kind of reverse word painting. While the tonic migrates frequently in this section, the song circles mostly around E minor.

In the third section of Heine's poem, we discover that Peter has assumed the pallor of the grave and would be better off dead in spite of his initial resolve. To exaggerate Heine's bitter mockery of a pitiable fool, Schumann chooses the topos of an E-minor funeral march in triple meter. Its dotted rhythms respond to Heine's first line ("Poor Peter staggers by"), and the trudging cadences of the odd *marcia funebre* become most redundantly apparent in the last quatrain (see ex. 4.5). The finishing touch for this sarcastic concluding *Tanzlied* comes in the composer's protracted final cadence, which makes a feint toward a plagal progression before winking just slightly at the hero's protracted tribulations ("until Judgment Day") with a Picardy third.

Romanzen und Balladen für eine Singstimme mit Begleitung des Pianoforte . . .
Heft IV, Op. 64 ("Die Soldatenbraut" and "Das verlassene Mägdelein" by Eduard Mörike, composed 29–30 May 1847; "Tragödie" by Heine, composed 27 October 1841; published August 1847 by F. Whistling)

In February 1846, some months after the publication of op. 53, Whistling wrote to Schumann, "The submission of your last ballad volume, with which the cycle concludes, would please me." The composer replied in mid-March, "I still lack one number for the fourth volume of ballads, which I still hope to finish this year, heaven willing. I have a sufficient number of lovely texts; perhaps I can have new volumes follow the fourth one from time to time."[26] In fact, Schumann prevaricated slightly in his claim that he had the fourth volume almost ready, for he had composed only the third number by March 1846. He did not fashion the remaining two songs until more than a year later. When Whistling prompted him again for the promised collection in June 1847, the composer finally responded with a manuscript at the end of the month.[27] This exchange recalls the question of just what kind of "cycle" opuses 45, 49, 53, and 64 comprise (and what the composer and Whistling understood by that term in general).

The particulars of op. 64 reveal that Schumann had again selected a theme linking its three numbers together, in this case the vicissitudes of women. Since he had already composed the last number, "Tragödie," in late 1841, he probably selected the two Mörike texts to complement the Heine. "Die Soldatenbraut" in B-flat major gives way to "Das verlassene Mägdelein" in the relative G minor, forming a pair that moves from expectant optimism about a distant beloved to disappointed loneliness. The three-part "Tragödie" repeats and extends this narrative trajectory from the bright future contemplated by young lovers in E major to their demise in E minor, then adding a wry moral in C major. The interrelationship of keys between the three songs in the opus proves more loosely knit: major in the first number to relative minor in the second, which tonic stands as minor dominant to the final tonic of the last number (v–(III) (iii)–I). Parallel major-minor equivalence had become a commonplace by Schumann's time. Admittedly, however, the internal tonal scheme of op. 64 lies far from the straightforward i–V–I of op. 45.

The pair formed by "Soldatenbraut" and "Mägdelein" displays the range of Schumann's later style, into which all the composer's settings of Eduard Mörike (1804–1875) fall. The Swabian poet apparently came belatedly to Schumann's attention, even though Mörike published his first volume of *Gedichte* in 1838.[28] The two texts of op. 64 occur toward the end of Robert and Clara's *Gedichtabschriften*, entered in Robert's hand amid other poetry he set during the latter part of his career.[29] The first mention of Mörike in his household accounts, moreover, comes in June 1846.[30] Schumann employed his earlier quadratic style for "Die Soldatenbraut," where he adopts the topos of a pert march in recognition of a wife awaiting a husband in military service. Mörike's verse falls mostly in dactylic tetrameter (with upbeats) accommodated easily in common time, and within each phrase diatonic harmonies predominate (though the composer indulges the usual harmonic excursions moving from phrase to phrase). Its more adult content aside, this folkloric number could fit easily at the beginning of the *Liederalbum für die Jugend* (op. 79), save for its ternary form (which Schumann creates by repeating Mörike's first verse). "Das verlassene Mägdelein," on the other hand, features a much more chromatic palette, and in spite of its four-measure phrases gives little sense of rhythmic drive. This style participates in the general "Dresden" language that Schumann began to cultivate during his later years, in which the rhythmic ebb and flow attenuate the meter of a poem that already features some irregularity. While this approach fits the lament of the forlorn young lady well, the contrast with the first song of the Mörike pair is striking, a disparity that the composer used frequently in his later collections of songs for expressive purposes.

"Tragödie," by way of contrast, falls in quadratic style throughout, even though the multipartite structure of the text occasions a good deal of dramatic variety. Unlike Schumann's other selections from Heine's verse, this one did not appear in the *Buch der Lieder* of 1827. The composer seems to have encountered it instead in a *Taschenbuch für Damen. Auf das Jahr 1829*, where it bears a note from Heine: "The second [subsection] is a Rhenish folksong, and I have authored only the first and third [subsections] myself."[31] The poet used the preexisting material to his usual cynical ends: he casts the initial two-stanza section as a young man's fervent plea in first person for his beloved to elope. The intermediate "folksong" reports the lovers' fate in tercets: "They wandered hither and yon, / Neither luck nor stars shone on them, / They died, they perished." But the "age-old story" recurs. In the third section, the narrator describes a new couple exchanging sweet nothings under a linden tree growing above the grave of their predecessors: "The chattering lovers fall silent, / They weep and do not themselves know why." In Heine's world, experience teaches nothing about love.

Schumann initially imagined an orchestral setting of this song in November 1841, but he did not publish it in this form,[32] which may account for the operatic tinge of its writing. The opening number provides the most obvious example, with its relatively slow-moving harmonic rhythm (suitable for the cohesion of ensemble performance), an exceptionally wide vocal range featuring a number of ostentatious leaps, an emphatic appoggiatura on "*Va*-ter-haus," restless offbeats in the piano's right hand, and melodramatic accompanimental punctuations (see ex. 4.6). The middle number, recounting the dismal fate of the departed sweethearts, assumes the topos of a minimally accompanied dirge in parlando vocal style. Only the last number, a duet for soprano and tenor (which can be performed if necessary by solo voice), falls into the lyrical style expected of a lied, perhaps responding to the intimacy of the scene. As the conclusion of a collection of ballads, "Tragödie" traverses the whole range of Schumann's considerable talents in his first efflorescence as a composer of songs.

The question remains how either Schumann or Whistling could possibly have conceived the four volumes of *Romanzen und Balladen* as any kind of cycle. The opuses taken together do not display a unified scheme of keys or subject matter, however much individual volumes might cohere internally. The only thing that connects the various collections is their genre: all of the numbers fulfill in some way Goethe's dictum about the free combination of lyric, epic, and dramatic traits. We might recall David Ferris's observation that "the question of cyclic unity was of far less interest to [nineteenth-century critics, composers, publishers, and

Example 4.6.   Excerpt displaying range from "Tragödie, I."

consumers] than it is to modern-day scholars and that the distinction between a cycle and a collection may not have been as clear-cut as we believe it to be."[33] Schumann's "cycle" of *Romanzen und Balladen* offers a salient demonstration of Ferris's point.

A Ballad Published Individually

Belsatzar. Ballade von H. Heine. für eine tiefe Singstimme und Pianoforte . . . Op. 57
(composed 7 February 1840; published January 1846 by Siegel & Stoll, Leipzig)

If we are to believe the dates in *Liederbuch I*, *Belsatzar* represents the second text set by Schumann in the "year of song" (though his correspondence suggests that he may have worked previously on the Heine *Liederkreis* for op. 24; see the discussion of that cycle in Chapter 2). Heine's ballad appears toward the beginning of the *Buch der Lieder,* in the section entitled "Junge Leiden" and subtitled "Romanzen," which comes *after* the subsection of "Lieder" (thus raising further questions about the exact chronology of genesis). In any event, it would be altogether appropriate for Schumann to have composed op. 57 first among all his Heine songs. He wanted his lieder to gain him wider recognition, and a subgenre featuring more operatic style was most likely to be programmed on public concerts. If Leipzig orchestral concerts in the 1830s and '40s almost always included excerpted opera arias, then elaborate ballads were their equivalent in the realm of the lied. Schumann may have hoped that *Belsatzar,* like the orchestral version of "Tragödie," might find a public as well as private following. But whereas "Tragödie" does not maintain the theatrical style of its opening throughout, *Belsatzar* never abandons its dramatic tone, and this may account for the fact that the composer left the orchestral setting of "Tragödie" behind while having *Belsatzar* published as a separate work.

The isolated appearance of op. 57 also resulted from Schumann's growing fame as a composer in the mid-1840s, and the negotiations surrounding its publication provide a particularly apt conclusion to this chapter on the ballad. In 1845 an employee of C. F. Peters, Carl Siegel, decided to go into business for himself, and on 14 July he wrote to Schumann confidentially, asking for compositions to print, especially "one or two songs for solo voice and piano."[34] Schumann instead offered two works for pedal piano or organ (opp. 58 and 60).[35] But Siegel rejected these pieces on 22 July as too arcane and therefore unsuitable for his patrons, renewing his plea for items appropriate to "Liebhaber" (amateurs), particularly lieder.[36] After a long silence, the composer returned to Siegel on 9 October 1845 with *Belsatzar,* which Siegel accepted the next day[37] and even published in an arrangement for solo piano in 1849[38] (so popular had the song become—a development not unknown with such ballads as Schubert's "Erlkönig").

A superficial glance at the opening of *Belsatzar* will reveal what attracted Siegel and his contemporary audience to the piece immediately. It begins (see ex. 4.7) with a roiling ninth chord in a melodramatic minor mode articulated by an extroverted piano arpeggiation that we might expect more from one of Clara's songs (for instance, "Er ist gekommen") than from one of Robert's. This restless opening may also invoke the playing of an ancient kithara or harp for the story from Daniel 5 of the evil Babylonian king who denounces the Hebrew God, only to be slain by his courtiers for his blasphemy after Jehovah's reply appears in burning letters on the wall of the royal banquet hall. This opening becomes a ritornello demarking four main actions in Heine's verse (reprinted in its entirety at the beginning of Siegel's edition). The poet lays his scene in

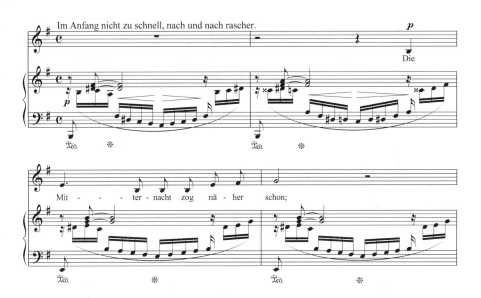

Example 4.7. Arpeggiated accompaniment at the beginning of *Belsatzar.*

third-person narrative describing the general rowdiness of the feast and Belshazzar's inebriation. Heine then focuses on the Babylonian king's blasphemy of the Hebrew God (the sole dialogue in the poem), the fiery handwriting on the wall, and finally the regicide. This last act is the goal and focus of both Heine's poem and Schumann's treatment, and it may provide yet another reason that the composer would call attention to the piece by publishing it under a separate opus number in 1846. During the period immediately preceding the 1848 revolution, defiance of the aristocratic order must have been much on the mind of the composer, his publisher, and their audience.

Because Heine's poem falls in sections of unequal length (eight, five, four, and four couplets), Schumann adopts a formal strategy that later became a favorite of composers such as Gustav Mahler. The four sections begin with an almost identical melodic phrase, but they then run their course according to the various necessities of their disparate dramatic action. This practice alludes to strophic setting without actually producing it (the first and last sections of the setting are more closely related: A and truncated A'). In this way the composer invokes the folkloric roots of the genre without limiting himself to the constricted choices offered by a truly strophic procedure. In *Kunstballaden* composers slowly took on the role that Goethe had initially assigned to the singer, "who can change mode at will, hurrying to the end [of his tale] or long delaying it." Schumann guides the performer in the presentation of *Belsatzar* at the end with precise instructions for the A' section: "In a slower tempo, recited softly and pointedly." This marking is particularly revealing, for the voice part is no less "lyrical" here than at op. 57's beginning. The composer had to alert the singer that the "moral" especially required a dramatic rendition, in spite of its relatively melodious vocal line.

Schumann always remained poised between the two schools of lieder, a position particularly evident in his *Romanzen und Balladen.* At one extreme composers provided the most meager framework over which singers could improvise, and at the other they preempted freedom of execution, determining by vocal line and piano accompaniment most of the crucial details of performance. Schumann's reticence to "paint too realistically" like the "moderns" certainly derived in some measure from his deference to the poets he set, but he was also tempted to try his hand at some of the techniques developed by musical predecessors such as Schubert and Loewe. *Belsatzar* appeared under a separate opus number that could elevate it to the status of a concert display piece and underline its political subtext. But the publisher also viewed the song as containing elements appropriate to a tradition of amateur performance in the home, which would ensure good sales of sheet music (recall Siegel's written admonition on 22 July 1845, cited above). *Belsatzar* exemplifies the middle way that Schumann sought in almost all of his lieder from his first period.

Lyrical Schemes:
Collections of Earlier
Lieder und Gesänge

Like the sets of romances and ballads originating in Schumann's initial efflorescence of song writing, his collections subsuming *Lieder und
Gesänge* composed during the same period (though often published later)
would seem poor candidates for the designation "work." We may perhaps imagine the composer forming coherent sets out of itinerant lyrical
numbers more easily than out of narrative poems, each of which tells its
own self-contained story. But the opuses containing earlier *Lieder und
Gesänge* included occasional later ones, and their diffuse key schemes
and subject matter would incline us to view them as simple miscellanies.
However, in an article on the third volume in Schumann's series of *Lieder
und Gesänge,* Nicholas Marston warns that the title "should not close
our minds to the [deep meaning] of this unsuspectedly cyclic composition."[1] Op. 77 receives consideration in the second part of this study, but
we may still take Marston's point that what seem mere catchalls can
sometimes present coherent sets even if they fall short of being actual cycles. In considering Schumann's lyrical collections below, we must examine whether the songs published together under one opus number betray
some planning on the part of the composer.

*Drei Gedichte von Emanuel Geibel für eine Singstimme mit Begleitung des
Pianoforte . . . op. 30* (composed 31 July–2 August 1840; published December 1840
by Bote & G. Bock)

Composition of the Geibel solo songs was surrounded by the creation
of the similarly titled *Drei Gedichte nach Emanuel Geibel,* part songs

that Schumann published as op. 29, also in December 1840.[2] Though
McCorkle lists the provenance of the exemplar for Geibel's verse as uncertain,[3] the composer almost certainly had access through a friend to an
advance copy of the poet's *Gedichte,* where "Der Hidalgo" and "Der
Page" lie on consecutive pages.[4] Schumann probably thought to capitalize on the publication of the new volume, since he wrote to an unknown
correspondent on 23 July 1840, "Could I of your kindness borrow the
Gedichte of Emmanuel [*sic*] Geibel for a short time. They have just appeared, I believe, from Duncker and Grünblock."[5] The north German
Geibel studied philology in Berlin, where he soon fell in with Chamisso
and Eichendorff and enjoyed an itinerant life, supported mostly by patrons. His poetry had enormous popular appeal, with thousands of settings and one hundred reprintings of the *Gedichte* by 1884.[6] Schumann
favored Geibel's verse not only in opp. 29 and 30 but also in the *Spanisches Liederspiel,* op. 74 (which drew its texts from *Volkslieder und
Romanzen der Spanier im Versmasse des Originals*)[7] and in the posthumous *Vom Pagen und der Königstochter,* op. 140. Of course, many of
Schumann's cycles revolve around the works of one poet. But op. 30 represents something slightly different: a collection of settings that do not
precisely form a cycle but serve to feature currently fashionable or recently published verse by a single author. This phenomenon became more
pronounced later in Schumann's career (see Chapter 7), and it usually
represented some attempt on the composer's part to remain au courant in
a literary sense.

The *Drei Gedichte von Geibel* gain coherence in more than just their
common author, however, and the underlying connections between the
individual numbers may guide our inquiry into Schumann's other collections featuring disparate poets. For one thing, the three selections all
present portraits of young men, a wanderer in "Der Knabe mit dem
Wunderhorn," a youthful suitor in "Der Page," and a noble young blood
in "Der Hidalgo." What is more, the personae occupy exotic climes with
an Iberian tinge. This may not be apparent at first, because aficionados of
the lied will have quite different associations with "Der Knabe mit dem
Wunderhorn."[8] But the youth and the page both carry guitars in their kit,
not the usual German lute, and the hidalgo parades explicitly through the
streets of Seville. We might speculate that the exotic settings and overtones of Latin courtliness have something to do with the dedicatee of
op. 30, Josephine Baroni-Cavacalbò, née Countess Castiglione. Obvi-

ously from the Italian nobility, she was the sister-in-law of Julie von Webenau (née Baroni-Cavacalbò), whom Schumann had met and befriended in Leipzig in 1835. When the composer spent time unsuccessfully trying to establish himself in Vienna four years later, Josephine pressed his case with her influential acquaintances, and she received the dedication for the *Drei Gedichte von Geibel* in consequence.

The first two songs in op. 30 form a contrasting pair linked by key, the first in B major with the internal section of its ternary form in E major, while the second, through-composed number in the same compound meter falls in E major with a substantial excursion to G major. But the two characters could not be more different, a fact that their portraits inevitably reflect. Schumann supplies "Der Knabe" quite naturally with a riding topos, replete with horn calls for a carefree "hunter" tarrying in villages just long enough to break the local maidens' hearts (the middle section of the ternary form). Quadratic convention would suggest that he extend the final two syllables in the last word of each line two beats. Instead, the composer often compresses these words ("Ge-*sel-le,*" "*hel-le,*" "*Mun-de,*" "*Stun-de,*" and so forth) into one beat, thus lending the declamation an uneven quality.

Cast in the same meter and a related key, the self-effacing "Page" delivers his lines in a parlando style that deemphasizes the highly regular tetrameter of his verse. In this song the accompaniment generally supports the voice with punctuating block chords and minimal ritornelli, lapsing into regular figuration just briefly for Geibel's fifth and sixth stanzas. And though Schumann's vocal part features regular phrases and some periodicity, repetition of melodic segments occurs irregularly. It were as if this song offered a humble arioso between "arias" sung by more assertive individuals. In "Der Page," Schumann hopes to capture the understated character of an enthralled young man who willingly serves his beloved even when somebody else wins her.

Just as understated meter characterizes the page in the second song of op. 30, an emphatically metrical bolero suits the bravura of "Der Hidalgo" (see ex. 5.1). This vigorous accompanimental pattern underpins a vocal line full of wide leaps, exuberant arpeggiations, and far more melismas than Schumann usually employed. Also cast in a clear-cut ternary form beginning and ending in D major, the internal episode falls in A major (replete with change of key signature), thus tying it distantly to the E

Example 5.1.   Bolero pattern and ornament in "Der Hidalgo."

major of the preceding song. The composer uses the inner two octaves to form the B section, counterbalancing its length by repeating a considerable amount of poetry from the outer two stanzas in the A sections. In this way he seems to conform the verse more to the expectations of the dance than the other way around, which seems entirely appropriate to a text containing so many musical references.

Op. 30 offers a glimpse of the techniques available to Schumann in the most coherent kind of lyrical collection, one in which a single poet and related subject matter combine to form a performable entity. Key relationships in such collections may evince underlying connections without offering progressions; contrasting styles of vocal writing and accompanimental texture in a rationalized pattern can provide a sense of dramatic motion as well as closure; and the underlying poetic conceit (here, portraiture of young men) can suggest consistency. But none of these devices compels performance of op. 30 as a single work, and indeed the record shows that even Clara Schumann did not promote the *Drei Gedichte von Geibel* in the concert hall as an inseparable entity (she gave her first public rendition of no. 3 in 1847, no. 1 in 1856, and no. 2 in 1877).[9] If the singer and the pianist choose to program the songs of op. 30 as a set, however, the result will satisfy.

Two Volumes of Lieder und Gesänge

Though Schumann's four volumes of *Lieder und Gesänge* (opp. 27, 51, 77, and 96) ultimately formed a loose set of twenty songs paralleling the four volumes of *Romanzen und Balladen* (see Chapter 4), the composer did not begin by projecting a finite series in either case. His negotiations with Friedrich Whistling initiating the publication of the song collections provide a most revealing portrait of a composer who was not averse to sharp business dealings. In this case Schumann used a letter from Carl Hagemann in Rostock on 16 February 1849 to leverage Whistling's compliance:[10]

> A request from a music dealer in Rostock, Hagemann, reminded me of you. He specifically wants primarily songs, and I already thought about which ones to give him. Then you occurred to me, who stand much closer to me, and, if I am not mistaken, wished for the same thing.
>
> I imagined to have them appear now in the manner of the *Balladen und Romanzen* in an indeterminate [number of] volumes,—among which would be space for later songs—, and want to include older ones scattered here and there in albums.
>
> The content of the first two volumes appears on the enclosed page.
>
> But now, I find it difficult to say, yet on account of my own circumstances I cannot forbear to—you must pay a bit more of an honorarium than earlier. My compositions—I may tell you in confidence—begin to excite the interest of publishers, and I receive more commissions than I can satisfy. If I stood alone in the world, I would not gladly ask for more from my old publishers. But I owe this to myself and mine. This between us.
>
> If you reckon on *twelve talers* for the printed bifolio of *4 pages,* then our business is concluded. You can have the manuscript soon; I don't need the honorarium right away, if only I can rely upon you to send it *when I need it later.* You must answer me straightaway, however. If you do not, I will assume that you will not go along with my suggestion—and I shall give the volumes to the man in Rostock.[11]

Whistling acceded immediately by return post: "In accordance with your wishes, I advise you prospectively that I will take your lieder, Op. 51 [*sic*], for publication, and that I am fully in agreement with the conditions put to me, the latter of which would raise hardly any question, since we indeed know one another too well not to speak with greatest frankness."[12] The publisher went on somewhat invidiously to warn Schumann about doing business with the Rostock book dealer. Whistling did a particularly large business in the composer's songs, in token of which the firm later began attaching a supplementary dust cover to its prints of individual opus numbers proudly listing the many Schumann lieder in its catalog.

Initially Schumann projected ten songs split between two volumes under a single opus number (51), but on 5 March he wrote to his publisher, enclosing a sample title page that allowed for multiple possibilities: "Here I am sending you the first volume [of songs]. On the title page I have placed 27 as the opus number, because this one remains unused in my *operibus*. But if this is not all right with you, then change it to Op. 51."[13] Of the ten songs ultimately published, seven were composed during 1840 and 1841. But the insertion of later songs should not by itself lead us to suspect the integrity of a given volume. By the very act of gathering lieder written at various times under a single cover, the composer had to make a conscious choice of which songs to market together.

Lieder und Gesänge für eine Singstimme mit Begleitung des Pianoforte . . . Heft I, Op. 27 ("Sag' an, o lieber Vogel mein" by Hebbel, composed 1847; "Rothes Röslein" by Burns, composed 15 May 1840; "Was soll ich sagen!" by Chamisso, composed 25 February 1840; "Jasminenstrauch" by Rückert, composed 4 March 1840; "Nur ein lächelnder Blick" by Zimmerman, composed 4 November 1840; published May 1849 by F. Whistling)

This sampler of five different poets exhibits several principles of loosely knit grouping. It begins with folkloric verse and progresses to more cosmopolitan sentiments. It features a core centering around A major and its dominant, held within the parentheses of C major in the first song and E-flat major in the last. And its central number ("Was soll ich sagen!") displays a more declamatory style that deflects the lighthearted trajectory of the first two songs in a more serious direction. The music therefore reinforces the sense of forward motion inherent in the sequence of the texts, should one choose to perform the opus as a set (a possibility rather than a necessity). The composer offers, in other words, an exemplar for programming lieder in disparate styles.

The first song in op. 27 takes its text from the 1842 *Gedichte* of Friedrich Hebbel (1813–1863), a poet who eventually settled in Vienna, where he wrote several plays produced at the Burgtheater. At one point during July 1847, Hebbel visited Schumann and entered into unproductive discussions about a libretto for *Genoveva* (the composer based his opera on dramatizations by Hebbel and Ludwig Tieck).[14] Schumann had a proclivity for setting folklike poetry from Hebbel's output: "Sag' an, o lieber Vogel mein" could just as well have found its way into *Lieder für die Jugend* (op. 79), which contains a setting of the poet's "Das Glück." The first three stanzas of "Sag' an" unfold in a highly diatonic framework, replete with horn fifths for the second half of each strophe. Declamation of the text is not quite so straightforward, however: the second line of text compresses in the initial stanzas so as to land the rhyme on the downbeat, and the third and fourth lines do not scan iambically. This give-and-take owes much to the fact that "Sag' an" presents a miniature ballad, with a question from the persona (speaking in quotation marks, lines 1 and 2) and an answer from the bird (lines 3 through 5). Hebbel's final stanza marks the intrusion of a third-person narrator, who receives a coda with a unique melody and a more chromatically inflected accompaniment. This folkloric vignette, with its character marking of "Einfach" ("simply"), thus assumes sophisticated undercurrents in Schumann's setting.

"Rothes Röslein" also possesses more underlying sophistication than its folkish surface at first suggests. Gerhard's translations of verse by Robert Burns particularly intrigued the composer during 1840 (see the discussion of *Myrthen*, vol. 3 in Chapter 1), and this setting exhibits several features of conventionally "Scottish" style, especially a "snap" accenting the first beat in many measures. This rhythmic tic, together with a disjunct melody tracing diatonic chords, lends the song a distinctly dancelike flavor. But Schumann apportions Gerhard's verse in anything but a simple manner, distributing the translation over a classic six-part rondo. The first stanza unfolds over the rondo theme, which runs immediately into the B episode ("Wie schön du bist") for the first couplet of the second stanza. The truncated return of the rondo theme then sets the second couplet ("Und lieben wird's"). The C episode occurs at the beginning of the third stanza ("Und würden trocken"), and the remaining six couplets (one and a half stanzas) unfold to ABA, fulfilling the formal convention. Lest we miss the last return of the rondo theme (significantly for the line "Bald kehr' ich wieder"), the composer abandons Gerhard's painstakingly crafted *Langzeilenvers* by placing "Bald" on an accented downbeat rather than the natural upbeat suggested by iambic meter. This sprightly emphasis highlights the fact that the composer has superimposed an instrumental form on the poetry by vivisecting quatrains at will.

If "Sag' an" and "Rothes Röslein" form a folkloric twosome, then one can imagine "Was soll ich sagen!" (Chamisso) and "Jasminenstrauch" (Rückert) as a pair—each too brief to stand by itself—marking the turn to more elevated realms. The two poems deal with age and renewal, the older suitor's anxious affection in the first finding hope in the second from the overnight blooming of jasmine in spring. Schumann may originally have envisaged both of these songs as part of *Myrthen*, for he sketched them both during the same period. But in the event no Chamisso found its way into op. 25, and the composer notes in the margin of his working autograph beside the Rückert: "Entirely too difficult to compose, the mysterious essence of nature in the poem should be addressed to some extent. Little more than an attempt."[15] The comment may concern the brevity of the setting as much as anything: it gains substance only upon following "Was soll ich."

The two numbers also mark the first appearance of through-composed form in op. 27, though as we have seen, this structural approach does not by itself denote sophistication. More important in this respect is the tentative mood of "Was soll ich sagen!," resulting largely from its wavering, chromatically inflected tonality, which plays ambiguously with C-sharp minor before finally attaining a clear E major cadence in measure 8. Other cadences carry us through chromatic twists and turns to B major and briefly even to G major before settling finally in E major (though even the cadential arrival on "sehr" toys with chromatic motion). Combined with a very slow tempo and a lack of periodicity that blunts the regularly iambic meter, this chromaticism lends an introspective, not to say somber, mood to the whole. "Jasminenstrauch," with its busy figuration and fairly reliable trochaic rhythm, then dispels the gloom of "Was soll ich." It too offers an internal digression from its A major tonic to F-sharp minor and an interrogative cadence on a held D-sharp diminished-minor seventh. This serves to set up the final couplet of Rückert's octave from *Liebesfrühling* (third bouquet), which ends with an accompanimental cascade of arpeggiations.

"Nur ein lächelnder Blick" intensifies the chromatic progress of the group as a whole, though in a genial, melodious way. It is firmly anchored in E-flat major, but the B section of each strophe modulates briefly to G-flat major, which alludes distantly to the preceding F-sharp minor interlude in "Jasminenstrauch" if we translate the keys enharmonically. The melody of "Nur ein lächelnder Blick" traces a rising chromatic scale (see ex. 5.2) in its first phrase to the apogee on the word "Auge" in the first stanza ("Munde" in the second), emphasizing those features of the

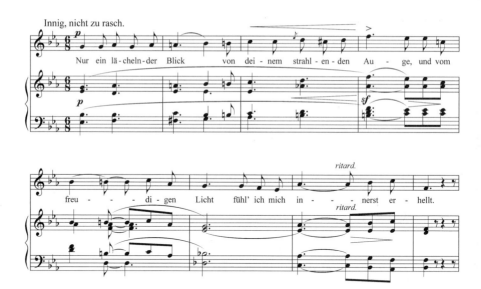

Example 5.2.   Opening phrase of "Nur ein lächelnder Blick," with rising chromatic melody.

beloved that most inspire the persona before gently descending. Schumann rounds each strophe by reiterating this comely arch at the end of both stanzas, bringing tonal closure in each case by appending a four-measure cadential progression for the voice and then a brief coda for the piano.

Schumann's source for the verse has long remained obscure. Even such eminent Germanists as Helmut Schanze and Krischan Schulte could not find a preexisting version,[16] and various scholars have offered several candidates as author. Schanze and Schulte speculate about Johann Georg Ritter von Zimmermann (1728–1795), whose dates leave much to be desired for a composer who strongly preferred the "moderns." Nauhaus attributes the poem to the much more suitably contemporaneous Balthasar Friedrich Wilhelm Zimmermann (1807–1878),[17] but his many given names lack the presence of a *G* entirely. A clue to the whereabouts of the poem (but not to the identity of its author) appears coincidentally in Schumann's collection of mottos, edited by Leander Hotaki. He discovers in one of the composer's volumes a motto culled from the poem "Geheimes Wirken," written by a Friedrich Gottlieb (sometimes Gottlob) Zimmermann (1782–1835), appearing in an 1833 edition of *Morgen-*

blatt für gebildete Stände.[18] Gottlieb Zimmermann's contributions to the fashionable literary and artistic daily often bear the signature "G. Zimmermann." But no such poem as "Nur ein lächelnder Blick" appeared in the volume during his lifetime, and because the Stuttgart newspaper tended to publish living authors almost exclusively, the contributions of "G. Zimmermann" understandably disappear after 1835. Magically, however, the signature "G. Zimmermann" reappears with a vengeance in the 1840 volume of the newspaper, now retitled *Morgenblatt für gebildete Leser.* His verse is featured three times in September of that year, and the 3 October 1840 issue contains the source of Schumann's text under the title "Blick und Wort" (see Table 5.1). Schumann wasted little time setting the poem (we can only speculate about the interval between the publication of the daily in Stuttgart and its arrival in Leipzig), for his household accounts give 4 November as the date of composition.[19] This squares well with Schumann's constant efforts to remain up-to-date, but who was the new poet? If reissuing the late Gottlieb Zimmermann's writings seems unlikely in the context of the *Morgenblatt,* then we are left with only one plausible candidate, the relatively unknown but still estimable Georg Zimmermann (1814–1881), sometimes published as G. Ludwig Zimmermann or under the pseudonym G. Wilhelm.[20] He attended the University of Heidelberg, then the University of Giessen, studying first law, then theology and German literature. He taught subsequently at gymnasia in Worms, then in Darmstadt (city of his birth), and he was the author of plays, short stories, poetry, and articles and monographs on German literature.[21] In his twenties when "Blick und Wort" appeared, he would have been just the right age for such romantic sentiments.

The relatively unremarkable conceit of the poem, however, piqued Schumann's interest less than its poetic form, which presented a considerable challenge for setting, a fact revealed by the title in his household accounts ("Distichon") and in the initial version appearing in a supplement to the *Neue Zeitschrift* ("Distichen"). A single "distich" consists of two lines, the first in hexameter and the second in pentameter, each with an internal caesura.[22] In the first published version of the song the composer observes poetic form scrupulously, providing for internal caesuras by means of a longer note (e.g., "Blick"—"Licht") and separating each distich with a two-measure interlude to emphasize the traditional pairing:

Table 5.1 Comparative versions of "Nur ein lächelnder Blick"

Source in *Morgenblatt*	Schumann's Setting
"Blick und Wort"	"Distichen"
Nur Ein lächelnder Blick von deinem strahlenden Auge!	Nur ein lächelnder Blick von deinem strahlenden Auge,
Und von freudigem Licht fühl' ich mich innerst erhellt.	und vom freudigem [*sic*] Licht fühl' ich mich innerst erhellt.
Also erheitert am nebligten Tag' ein freundlicher Strahl uns,	So erheitert am neblichten Tag, [*sic*] ein freundlicher Strahl uns,
Wenn den düsteren Flor plötzlich die Sonne durchbricht.	wenn den düsteren Flor plötzlich die Sonne durchbricht.
Nur ein liebliches Wort aus deinem rosigen Munde!	Nur ein lächelnder Blick vom [*sic*] deinem strahlenden Auge
Und mein ganzes Seyn fühl' ich belebend erquickt.	und vom freudigen Licht, fühl' ich mich innerst erhellt,
So durchduftet, wie Stark! Ein Tröpfchen Oel, von der Rose	innerst, innerst erhellt.
Würziger Blume gepreßt, Locken und Brust und Gewand.	
	Nur ein liebliches Wort aus deinem rosigen Munde,
G. Zimmermann	und mein ganzes Sein fühl' ich belebend erquickt.
	So durchduftet wie stark ein Tröpfchen Oel, von der Rose
	würz'ger Blume gepresst Locken und Brust und Gewand.
	Nur ein liebliches Wort aus deinem rosigen Munde
	und mein ganzes Sein fühl' ich belebend erquickt,
	belebend, belebend erquickt.
	G. Zimmermann

Morgenblatt für gebildete Leser 34 (1840): 947. *Sammlung von Musikstücken alter und neuer Zeit als Zulage zur Neuen Zeitschrift für Musik*, 12 (1840), 16–18.

Nur ein lächelnder Blick von deinem strahlenden Auge,
   Und vom freudigem [*sic*] Licht fühl' ich mich innerst erhellt.

So erheitert am neblichten Tag, [*sic*] ein freundlicher Strahl uns,
   Wenn den düsteren Flor plötzlich die Sonne durchbricht.

For republication in op. 27 Schumann removed these interludes and ran the two distichs in each stanza together. This creates a far more intricate and interesting metrical ebb and flow by displacing the beginning of the second couplet to the weaker half of the compound measure.[23] Here we find Schumann at his best, eliciting a graceful result by intensifying the effects of unusual verse. It supplies a charming conclusion to the "program" of diverse songs found in the first volume of Schumann's *Lieder und Gesänge*, op. 27.

Lieder und Gesänge für eine Singstimme mit Begleitung des Pianoforte . . . Heft II,
Op. 51 ("Sehnsucht" by Geibel, composed 8–9 August 1840; "Volksliedchen" by Rückert, composed spring [?] 1840; "Ich wand're nicht" by Christern, composed 30 December 1841; "Auf dem Rhein" by Immermann, composed 24 June 1846; "Liebeslied" by Goethe, composed 28 October 1849; published March 1850 by F. Whistling)

On the sample title page Schumann had dispatched with the engraver's copy for the first volume of *Lieder und Gesänge* in March 1849, the composer had projected a somewhat different lineup for the second volume. It began with "In der Fremde" by Eichendorff, continued with "Volksliedchen," placed "Was soll ich sagen!" by Chamisso at midpoint, and concluded with "Sehnsucht" and "Auf dem Rhein."[24] But Schumann inserted the Chamisso in volume one, and by the time he sent volume two to Whistling for engraving on 20 November 1849, "In der Fremde" had already found its way into the second version of the op. 39 *Liederkreis* (displacing "Der frohe Wandersmann").[25] Schumann had at least decided on the inclusion of the first three songs by 4 May 1849: he asked Whistling to secure their copyrights, because they had appeared in earlier anthologies.[26] The composer had slated the Immermann setting for op. 51 from the beginning, and a little more than three weeks before handing the set over for engraving, he set the Goethe text specifically to end the second volume of *Lieder und Gesänge*.

The hypothetical "program" represented in Op. 51 adopts a very different structure from the progressive trajectory we find in op. 27. The

Geibel and Goethe settings exhibit theatrical styles, though of two very different kinds. The inner three songs, on the other hand, assume a deliberate simplicity, almost folkloric in its frame of reference. The tonal relationships in the volume function differently from the content, with consecutive numbers often falling in pairs. "Sehnsucht" begins and ends in D minor (though large internal segments allude to F major or its dominant C), which leads naturally enough to the G major of "Volksliedchen" (with its middle section in D major, naturally). "Ich wand're nicht," in B-flat major, and "Auf dem Rhein," in F major, move toward the flat keys, though backward around the circle of fifths. "Liebeslied" would seem to be the odd number out, but we can view its A major as dominant to the D minor of "Sehnsucht." The key scheme of this opus avoids progression, moving at times in retrograde, just as the volume eschews a stylistic trajectory.

Only one thing runs as a unifying thread through op. 51: the deeply internalized, often concealed sentiments of the personae. If the classic lied revolves around what German writers often call "the lyrical first person" ("das lyrisches Ich"), then these texts are particularly introspective. In two out of three cases where the verse specifies gender, moreover, the speaker is female rather than male, most significantly in the Goethe song Schumann wrote to complete the volume just before it went to press. This suggests that the composer may have regarded op. 51 as proceeding from a woman's point of view.

Schumann's setting of "Sehnsucht" by Geibel comes from the same period in the midsummer of 1840 during which the composer initially turned his attentions to the poet's *Gedichte* for op. 30. But unlike in the songs in that pronouncedly masculine collection, the gender of the speaker here remains undisclosed. We learn only that the persona has a vision of distant lands that will remain unvisited owing to some unspecified constraint:

O hätt' ich Flügel durch's Blau der Luft,	Oh could I but wing though the azure sky,
Wie wollt' ich baden im Sommerduft,	How I would bathe in summer's perfume,
Doch umsonst! Und Stunde auf Stunde entflieht—	But in vain! As hour upon hour expires—
Vertraure die Jugend—begrabe das Lied—	Mourning my youth—interring my song—

O die Schranken so eng, und die Welt so weit,	Oh the bounds so narrow, and the world so wide,
Und so flüchtig die Zeit!.[27]	And so fleeting the time!

Geibel's last line serves as refrain for both stanzas, and they bid us to wonder what confines the persona, a question answered easily if we assume a woman restricted to hearth and home.

Schumann sets the text in a style quite different from those of the male speakers in op. 30. His instruction to perform "with passionate delivery" highlights the unusually melodramatic piano ritornello that frames the song (see ex. 5.3) as well as the relentlessly hammered, sixteenth-note block chords in the right hand supporting a voice part of uncommonly wide range. This accompaniment, together with the wide leaps in

Example 5.3.   Beginning of "Sehnsucht," featuring virtuosic accompanimental flourish.

the melody, is reminiscent of "Ich grolle nicht." The composer casts "Sehnsucht" in the topos of a vehement lament, a notion reinforced by minor mode and a semioperatic vocal line. Because of the contrasting sentiments at the beginning of each stanza—regret and tears in the first, paradisiacal vision of distant climes in the second—Schumann chooses a through-composed form that casts the initial lines of Geibel's second strophe ("Ich weiss ein Land") in C major (dominant of the relative major, F). He makes his way back to D minor chromatically just in time, sealing the tonic with a repeat of the virtuosic piano flourish.

"Volksliedchen" stands in great stylistic contrast to "Sehnsucht" and yet completes it in a remarkable way. Not only is the former prepared tonally by the latter (minor dominant moving to major tonic), but Rückert's message serves to ameliorate and illuminate the genderless malcontent in Geibel. Rückert's persona is definitely female, and she shares confinement (here explicitly to a domestic sphere) with her cousin in "Sehnsucht":

Wenn ich früh in den Garten geh	When I walk in the garden early
In meinem grünen Hut,	In my green hat,
Ist mein erster Gedanke,	My first thought is,
Was nun mein Liebster thut?	What's my darling doing now?
Am Himmel ist kein Stern,	In heaven there's no star,
Den ich dem Freund nicht gönnte.	That I'd begrudge my boyfriend.
Mein Herz gäb' ich ihn gern,	I'd gladly give him my heart,
Wenn ichs heraus thun könnte.	If I could take it out.

But unlike Geibel's tortured persona, Rückert's contents herself with waiting, and her stroll elicits a delicate processional from Schumann, who makes somewhat free with the text. He changes the verb "ist" in the first line of the second strophe to "steht," and he repeats the first strophe to create a ternary form, reiterating the last two lines yet again to emphasize thoughts of the absent lover[28] and appending a relatively long coda. The walking bass line, often marked by staccato articulation, lends a pert aspect to the speaker's reverie. She seems happy to wait at home for her friend.

Though "Ich wand're nicht" certainly comes from a male speaker, Karl Christern's poem articulates a point of view that the woman in "Volksliedchen" would have appreciated. Christern (b. 1812) composed songs, contributed articles to the *Neue Zeitschrift,* and also edited the *Hamburger Blätter für Musik.*[29] From time to time he enclosed his verse in letters, where "Ich wand're" probably originated (though the exemplar for this poem seems to have disappeared);[30] the composer devoted only this one setting to the poet. No tonal bond joins this song to its predecessor in op. 51, though the juxtaposition succeeds because the descending scalar patterns and detached articulation of "Volksliedchen" carry over into "Ich wand're nicht." The female speaker in the Rückert would also have approved of the decision by Christern's man to forgo roaming. His sweetheart will not be able to accompany him, there is nothing he could find in the wider world that he cannot find at home, and he can see the fabled azure heavens mourned by Geibel's unhappy persona mirrored in his sweetheart's eyes. Her smile, moreover, promises a good deal more than the "rapture of spring." How could any young woman fail to value these sentiments in an admirer?

For this anti-*Wanderlied* Schumann understandably avoids the stereotypical wayfarer's march, but he must then face the problem of how to relieve Christern's perfectly regular *Langzeilenvers*. The composer does this by beginning lines 1, 2, and 7 of each octave on the second eighth note of the measure (rather using a conventional pickup note in the previous measure to set the iambic pattern). We have seen this device at least once before, in Schumann's breathless treatment of Reinick's "Nichts Schöneres" in op. 36. In op. 51, no. 3 the effect is not so unsettling, because it does not pervade the strophic setting throughout. Christern's persona expresses complacency more than ardor; unlike the traveler in the *Sechs Gedichte* of Reinick, this speaker can get what he wants by staying home.

Karl Immermann's "Auf dem Rhein," by way of contrast, adopts a far more serious tone than "Ich wand're nicht" for a more introspective message. On the autograph draft of a proposed title page sent to Whistling on 5 March 1849 for the two volumes of songs that eventually became opp. 27 and 51, the composer placed the Immermann as the concluding number of the second group. He had composed this lone setting from the poet's *Gedichte* (1835) on 24 June 1846, during a summer vacation in Maxen, just south of Dresden. We may suppose that the Schumanns carried the volume of Immermann's verse with them, and indeed the household accounts show that Robert spent considerable time during this excursion entertaining the visiting poets Reinick and Geibel and reading various others poets, such as Mörike.[31] The composer's treatment of Immermann (1796–1840), a soldier in the Napoleonic wars and a playwright, author, and translator,[32] invokes the familiar topos of the chorale, with solemn block chords processing in a stately tempo ("rather slowly"). This seems entirely appropriate for a text that compares a secret "treasure" concealed in the depths of the ungendered persona's heart to the Rheingold guarded by the river's waves until the "Day of Judgment." The word for "treasure"—"Schatz"—has a double meaning, for it could refer to the poem's treasured memory or colloquially to a beloved individual, affection for whom will remain "forever and ever within." The sacred tones of chorale texture therefore suit contemplation of eternity, even though Schumann blurs the bounds of Immermann's three neatly analogous stanzas in a through-composed setting that still declaims the poet's *Langzeilenvers* meticulously.

"Auf dem Rhein" would have provided a somber, brief, and cryptic valediction to op. 51, and this may explain why Schumann felt compelled to supply the more impassioned "Liebeslied" to a text by Goethe just a few weeks before he sent the collection off for publication. This would be the composer's last involvement with the poet's *West-östlicher Divan*, and he approaches the verse quite differently from the earlier settings in *Myrthen*. Part II of this study deals more extensively with the style of Schumann's later songs, but it suffices to say here that four-square periodicity engendered by paired, repeated phrases recedes as a feature of the composer's vocal melody. And accompanimental cadences divide phrases less clearly by ending deceptively more often, promoting a sense of continuity and muting hypermetric regularity.

The irregularity of this setting treats Goethe's text almost like prose declaimed over accompaniment, something to which this particular poem lends itself. Included among a section of "Ciphers" in the *Divan,* the verse falls into four sestets with short lines of two feet in shifting metrical patterns. Schumann often combines couplets in his setting (as he does for the first stanza), but sometimes he separates lines ("Und sonsten keiner / Und keine Feindspur"), and he even makes so free as to drop most of a line from Goethe's third stanza:

Goethe's versification	*Schumann's reorganization*
Mein Leben will ich	Mein Leben
Nur zum Geschäfte	will ich nur
Von seiner Liebe	zum Geschäfte von seiner
Von heut an machen.	Liebe machen,
Ich denke seiner,	
Mir blutet's Herz.	ich denke seiner, mir blutet das Herz

This excerpt displays the text roughly as it falls in Schumann's melodic phrases, a treatment that selectively ignores both syntax and poetic structure at will. Instead, the composer emphasizes single words such as "Leben," "nur," "Liebe," and "Herz" by according them longer rhythmic values, while omitting or changing what he wishes. Schumann's method of setting text here originates more from the operatic theater of Wagner than from the folkloric roots of the lied, and it leads toward the declamation of poetry in songs by Wolf and Strauss. With its incessant, restless piano arpeggiations, which provide continuity for sporadic vocal interjections, "Liebeslied" returns to the realm of melodrama, not in the sense of the overstatement in "Sehnsucht" but in the strictly technical sense. Here we find verse "spoken" over an accompaniment that mainly imparts mood.

Though tonally distant from the first song in op. 51, "Liebeslied" still draws us back, then, within the ambit of the collection's opening number. The persona in Geibel's text longs for the outside world and despairs. Speakers in subsequent installments focus on their inner, often quite private existence. The woman in Goethe's "Cipher" would disclose feelings as buried as in Immermann's "Auf dem Rhein," but she finds herself helpless:

Kraft hab' ich keine	Power have I not
Als ihn zu lieben,	But to love him,
So recht im Stillen.	Though just in silence.
Was soll das werden!	How shall it end!
Will ihn umarmen	I would embrace him
Und kann es nicht.	And cannot.

We can regard op. 51 as expanding on a theme inaugurated in its first song; performing the set as a whole would yield a rewarding section on a concert program. But we can also justifiably detach these lieder from one another and recombine them in other satisfactory ways for presentation to the public.

Two Valedictory Collections

At the very end of his life, plagued by deteriorating relations with the Düsseldorf musical establishment and by severely declining health, Schumann was nonetheless actively courted by music publishers seeking his lieder as important and profitable items for their catalogs. When pressed, he dipped into his reserve of previously composed material, and for this reason two of his last volumes of songs derive in large part from his first mature period of lied composition. In late 1853, the composer planned what came to be opp. 127 and 142 as two volumes in a single group of songs, though he did not live to see publication of the second set, nor did either opus take the exact shape he wished. The history of their appearance illuminates the relationship between composer and publisher in the realm of the lied, and it also shows his widow acting as executor of her husband's musical legacy.

The history of opp. 127 and 142 traces its roots to August 1850, when Schumann offered "Mein Altes Ross," one of the songs in what would later become op. 127, to the publisher Johann André amid selections that would ultimately appear in opp. 77 and 125 (see Chapter 8).[33] André declined the offer, and the composer made other arrangements, setting aside the surplus lieder until a letter arrived on 3 October 1853 from Wilhelm Paul in Dresden specifically asking to publish songs or "some other composition from a genre such that wide dissemination might be expected."[34] While we do not possess Schumann's side of this exchange, we know from his index of correspondence that his initial reply to Paul of 8 October 1853 proposed two volumes of songs and that the composer enclosed the manuscript for the first set, probably consisting of three Heine settings left unused in *Dichterliebe* and one song on a Kerner text left unused in op. 35 (see Table 5.2).[35] The composer sent the second group the next day, and it appears to have included five songs, among them a fourth *Dichterliebe* relic, another Kerner remainder, and settings of Shakespeare, Moritz von Strachwitz, and most likely Lily Bernhard.[36]

Paul now had two volumes in hand, and on 11 October he asked

Table 5.2   Possible Contents of Schumann's Lieder, Op. 129 [*sic*], as Originally Projected*

Volume 1	Volume 2
1. "Trost im Gesang" (Kerner)	1. "Sängers Trost" (Kerner)
2. "Lehn' deine Wang'" (Heine)	2. "Mädchen-Schwermuth" (Bernhard) or "Ein Gedanke" (Ferrand)
3. "Dein Angesicht" (Heine)	3. "Es leuchtet meine Liebe" (Heine)
4. "Mein Wagen rollet langsam" (Heine)	4. "Mein altes Ross" (Strachwitz)
	5. "Schlusslied des Narren" (Shakespeare)

* We have little idea about the actual order within the various volumes, except from a later draft title page.

whether he might publish only the second group of songs for eight louis d'or, deprecating the humbleness of his firm in the face of Schumann's "genius." Paul also cited the difficulty of selling the three hundred copies required to recoup the fee requested for all nine items in light of the composer's extensive output of lieder to that date.[37] Schumann made a counteroffer on 14 October: both volumes of songs for twenty louis d'or—a quantity discount, apparently.[38] But by 17 October Paul had sent the first volume of songs back together with an honorarium of fifty taler (about nine louis d'or) for the second. Even then he made one editorial substitution, "Dein Angesicht" for "Mädchen-Schwermuth," because it too could be engraved to fill just two pages.[39] Schumann capitulated to Paul's desire for one volume and to the proposed substitution. But he must have lobbied for "Dein Angesicht" to appear first in the set, because in sending proofs on 11 November 1853, the publisher maintained, "As regards the order, I could not entirely follow your specifications, because otherwise the short song 'Dein Angesicht' would have to have gone unused, which is always unpleasant with short songs of two pages. I had to begin therefore with 'Sängers Trost'; the others remain according to your specifications."[40]

What could possibly have motivated Paul in his quest for a shorter number (though not "Mädchen-Schwermuth" or "Ein Gedanke") to follow the longer "Sängers Trost"? His desire for an additional setting of Heine may explain his rejection of the little-known Bernhard or Ferrand poetry. But that leaves the mystery of his insistence on placing the longer Kerner before the shorter Heine, requiring just "two pages." We find the answer by looking at the first edition print, where "Sängers Trost" runs from page 3 to page 5, both recto sides of a sheet. The two-page "Dein Angesicht" then falls open on pages 6 and 7, facing verso and recto, thus entailing no page turn. Thereafter, the remaining songs all carry forward the verso-recto openings, "Es leuchtet meine Liebe" from 8 to 11, "Mein altes Ross" from 12 to 15, and "Schlusslied" on 16 and 17. Schumann usually followed his own artistic instincts in assembling his volumes of songs, but in this instance he acknowledged his publisher's commercial and practical wisdom; he also recognized the exigencies of layout in other circumstances.[41] Eventually this set received opus number 127, because in the midst of negotiations with Paul, the composer reached agreement with Breitkopf on 5 November 1853 for the assignment of op. 129 to the Cello Concerto.[42]

In placing op. 142 some five years later (after her husband's death),

Clara simply executed Robert's original plan for two volumes of songs in the series. Regarded as a whole, the poetry in both sets displays a pervasive sense of valediction that served both Robert's premonitions of leave-taking during the end of 1853 and Clara's bereaved farewell in 1858. What appears at first an oddly fragmented history of two disparate miscellanies turns out to be another search for logic (albeit with varying motivations) on the part of composer, publisher, and widow. As we see in Part II, a few stragglers from 1840–41 still made their way into other volumes of songs composed predominantly during Schumann's late period.

Lieder und Gesänge . . . für eine Singstimme mit Begleitung des Pianoforte . . . ,
Op. 127 ("Sänger's Trost" by Kerner, composed 8 December 1840; "Dein Angesicht" by Heine, composed 24 May 1840; "Es leuchtet meine Liebe" by Heine, composed after 25 [?] May 1840; "Mein altes Ross" by Strachwitz, composed 1 August 1850; "Schlusslied des Narren" by Shakespeare (trans. Schlegel), composed 1 February 1840; published January 1854 by Wilhelm Paul)

Op. 127 proves that in collaboration with a publisher, Schumann could assemble an interesting and viable lieder "program" from remnants lying around his workshop. The final ordering proved to be fortunate, for "Sängers Trost" introduces a poet-persona sentimentally contemplating the melancholy subject of his own mortality, and "Dein Angesicht" engages a similar topic, but now with the persona regarding the dead visage of his beloved. "Es leuchtet meine Liebe" provides an ironic antidote to the previous two, an unhappy tale of love in which a suitor is figuratively murdered, his beloved frightened away. "Mein altes Ross" continues the theme of loss and decay, horse and rider regarding past adventures and failed romance. The appositely titled "Schlusslied" then provides a wry commentary about the futility of all human endeavor in the face of an indifferent creation. We find no true narrative progression in op. 127, just poems that play well against one another, constantly tempering melancholy with philosophical cynicism, as if recalling the ironic distance of Schumann's first Heine songs in op. 24 by revisiting early lieder at the end of the composer's creative life.

The songs' various keys also work together nicely, "Trost" ending in B-flat major (though beginning in G minor), dominant to the E-flat major of "Angesicht." "Es leuchtet" then returns to G minor, closing with a Picardy third that moves logically to the relative E minor of "altes Ross," which serves in its turn as minor dominant to "Schlusslied," in A minor.

By the very act of gathering songs, selecting some and rejecting others, then ordering them, Schumann and Paul made artistic choices that had the power to create more than a simple miscellany.

In light of the fate soon to befall its composer, "Sängers Trost" takes on even more melancholy connotations than it possessed when it was written in December 1840. Schumann might have considered it for the end of the Kerner *Liederreihe,* since it was one of the last songs composed for possible inclusion in the grouping. Because it mentions wandering obliquely and addresses the gloomy outcome the composer had determined for op. 35, it would have worked well enough. But ultimately he sought a less definitive ending for the loose narrative implied in the *Liederreihe,* one he ultimately found in the twin "Wer machte dich so krank?" and "Alte Laute." "Sängers Trost" performs several functions in op. 127, first identifying the persona as a both poet and a "singer" of the song, a role, we will remember, assigned by Schumann to composers in his reviews of lieder. To this somewhat personal identification in Kerner's verse must be added the fact that Clara must have held this as one of her favorite Kerner poems, since she entered it into the *Gedichtabschriften* herself.[43]

Perhaps because of its deep sentimentality and personal significance, Schumann takes great pains to set this verse simply. Over a conventionally arpeggiated accompaniment that persists from beginning to end, the composer creates a perfectly quadratic melody that encompasses each of the first three quatrains within the bounds of a period (4 + 4, with parallel initiation of antecedent and consequent phrases). To enliven this repetition, however, Schumann indulges a harmonic ambiguity to close each eight-measure unit, ending repeatedly on the dominant of B-flat major before pulling back chromatically to G minor at the last moment. The last stanza ("Blumen, Hein, und Aue") pays this "promissory note," however, by arriving conclusively in B-flat. This occasions a new melody for Kerner's last stanza and a chromatic excursion that reinforces the role of F major as dominant by way of a German augmented sixth chord. While the phrase structure of "Sängers Trost" seems perfectly conventional, then, its harmonic structure is considerably more complicated and open-ended.

"Dein Angesicht," in E-flat major following from the previous number's emphasis on B-flat, now takes up the topic of remembrance but from the reverse point of view. Schumann initially positioned this song as the fifth selection in a twenty-song *Dichterliebe,* but its removal from the final edition was altogether logical and fitting.[44] The original version would have seen the beloved dead and buried before she ever jilted her suitor (by deleting this song, in fact, the composer postponed mention of the beloved's death until "Ich hab' im Traum geweinet"). "Dein Angesicht" finds a good home in op. 127, introducing an ironic note to the collection. Schumann's setting seems perfectly ordinary at first, but at the end of the first stanza ("so schmerzenreich") things begin to go awry. First the composer syncopates the accompaniment for this phrase; then he modulates briefly to G major (connecting to the initial key of "Sängers Trost"), ending in G-flat major for Heine's last couplet ("erlöschen wird ..."). This requires a repeat of the first strophe (slightly varied), to which Schumann appends a postlude exiting chromatically. Just as the speaker's dream of his beloved introduces oddly discordant notes, so the pianist cannot decide in the end about the basic mode of the piece.

The subtly macabre uncertainty of "Dein Angesicht" proves a fitting preparation for "Es leuchtet meine Liebe," the centerpiece of op. 127. It is one of Schumann's greatest songs from 1840, a demonic pseudo-ballad that serves as an admonitory parable of amorous failure. The persona compares his beloved to a fairy tale about a nighttime tryst between a knight (presumably the oaf from the prologue to the "Lyrisches Intermezzo") and a maiden. Their wooing is interrupted by a passing giant (naturally),[45] who frightens the maiden away and thrashes her suitor. Heine supplies the fable's sarcastic tag: "And when I am buried, the fairy tale will end." This song might have been excised from op. 48 for two reasons. It would have foreshadowed the end of the narrative in ballad form, thus stealing the thunder from "Aus alten Märchen," and it would have dwarfed the surrounding songs (coming right after "Am leuchtenden Sommermorgen" and before "Ich hab' im Traum geweinet").

Schumann provides a relentlessly motoric accompaniment with an extended, compound *romanza* meter for "Es leuchtet" (see ex. 5.4). Minor mode accords well with the initial conceit, but when we arrive at the touching scene of the knight pressing his suit on bended knee before the maiden, the composer supplies a tonal excursus through several major keys (E-flat, A-flat). All this merely serves to prepare the main event: assault and romantic disaster ending in a vehement C minor (relative to the E-flat major of "Dein Angesicht"). At this point the accompaniment, already predominant, seizes the initiative from the singer by rounding back

Example 5.4.   Opening line of op. 127, no. 3, in *romanza* style.

to the opening phrases, while the voice part is relegated to monotone interjections that declaim the last, fateful lines ("Wenn ich begraben werde . . ."). And after the singer finishes, the pianist remains undeterred, pressing forward in a hammered series of rising and falling chromatic scales. The accompaniment eventually debouches in a series of chorale-like major-mode progressions, as if to say "Amen!"

Schumann originally thought to include "Mein altes Ross" in a proposed collection of eight songs offered to Johann André as "op. 92" in August 1850 that never came to press. Composed almost a decade after "Es leuchtet meine Liebe," the Strachwitz setting found a happier place in op. 127, falling in well with the strongly "characteristic" style of the earlier Heine. Instead of the compound meter of a *romanza* for the portrait of an old wayfarer remembering his youthful wandering, the composer selects a martial dirge. The minor mode, occasional drum cadences, and dotted rhythms invoke the same topos encountered earlier in "Der Soldat" (op. 40) and "Die beiden Grenadiere" (op. 49). The last stanza of the text may have occasioned this style:

Mein Kamerad,	My comrade,
Den geliebten Pfad,	The beloved path,
Den hat verweht der Schnee!	It's covered by the snow!
Und das Thor verbaut	And the gate blocked
Und verloren die Braut,	And the bride lost,
Und mein Herz so weh, so weh!	And my heart so full of woe, of woe!

The manner in which Schumann came by the poem may have suggested this topos, for it was sent to the composer by Paul Baumeister, a lieutenant in the Prussian infantry. Moritz Karl Wilhelm Anton Graf von Strachwitz (1822–1847) was Baumeister's cousin, and in a letter to Schumann of 30 July 1850, Baumeister apparently enclosed a copy of "Mein altes Ross" with a request for a setting. The composer obliged, perhaps moved by the poet's death at an early age.[46] Baumeister's position might have prompted the military references and also the form of this song, which has a rather grand internal "trio" in A major. The aspect of valediction entailed in an address to an "old mount" could have prompted the song's inclusion in op. 127.

The selection of "Schlusslied des Narren" from *Twelfth Night, or What You Will* to close op. 127 certainly seems to carry a personal note of farewell. Most of the studies devoted to Schumann's lieder list this isolated setting of a Shakespeare text as the first song set in 1840, and not without good reason.[47] The piece appears as the second entry in the first *Liederbuch*, where it bears the earliest recorded date of any song, 1 February 1840.[48] The dates in the *Liederbücher,* however, do not always offer a consistent point of reference: sometimes they represent the date of composition (which is to say sketching), sometimes the date of first realization. The Heine *Liederkreis*, op. 24, undated in the first *Liederbuch*, may well have come first, as I have suggested elsewhere on the basis of Schumann's correspondence. This seems more plausible than the notion that the composer began his *Liederjahr* by setting an English author. The conjecture that a visit from Mendelssohn on 31 January 1840 somehow suggested the choice of Shakespeare on the following day is slightly more believable.[49] Schumann admired the incidental music to *A Midsummer Night's Dream* deeply,[50] and we know that he had a thorough acquaintance with Shakespeare's plays and particularly with *Twelfth Night* from an early age.[51]

Whatever attracted Schumann to this text so early in 1840, it constitutes a perfect ending to op. 127. The composer treated Schlegel's translation freely, changing some words and setting just the first, third, and fifth verses.[52] He set them in a rollicking compound meter that uses fractious dotted figures to give a comic face to the clown's song. Sams goes so far as to link Schumann's prelude and postlude to Mendelssohn's music for the bumbling tradesmen in the closing area of his *Overture to a Midsummer Night's Dream* (see exx. 5.5a and 5.5b).[53] However that might be, the odd simplicity of this strophic setting acted as an ironic antidote to the melancholy of "Mein altes Ross," a parallel to the irony of "Es leuchtet meine Liebe" following "Sängers Trost" and "Dein Angesicht."

Examples 5.5a–b. Closing material from *A Midsummer Night's Dream* (a) and prelude to "Schlusslied des Narren" (b).

Shakespeare's text may also impart a final message from Schumann:

Die Welt steht schon eine hübsche Weil,	A great while ago the world begun,
Hop heisa, hop heisa, bei Regen und Wind;	With hey, ho, the wind and the rain,
Doch das Stück ist aus, und ich wünsch' euch viel Heil,	But the piece is done, and I wish you much luck,
Und daß es Euch künftig gefalle!	And that it might henceforth please you!

The German version does not render the original English exactly, but the parting comment to the audience in both song and play is clear enough. The poet, actor, composer, and singer alike bid farewell and hope they have given satisfaction. It is tempting to surmise that this collection of texts on the subject of valediction records the composer's presentiments of artistic leave-taking. If so, he closed, as he had begun, on an ironic note, with a piece that brought him full circle to the beginning of his mature years as a composer of songs.

Vier Gesänge für eine Singstimme mit Begleitung des Pianoforte . . . , Op. 142
("Trost im Gesang" by Kerner, composed 20–21 November 1840; "Lehn' deine Wang'" by Heine, composed 24 May 1840; "Mädchen-Schwermuth" by Bernhard, composed 16–17 November 1840; "Mein Wagen rollet langsam" by Heine, composed 29–30 May 1840; published January 1858 by J. Rieter-Biedermann)

Clara Schumann published these four songs after her husband's death as op. 142, but no record of her dealings with Rieter-Biedermann of Winterthur (who worked in concert with Hofmeister in Leipzig) survives. When Robert was confined to a mental hospital in Endenich, near Bonn, his wife became the sole support of their family, and she adopted a variety of tactics to cope. She toured as a piano virtuoso for the rest of her life, she taught, and she also sold a large number of her husband's musical autographs, which he had deliberately saved for just this purpose. The Prussian State Library eventually came into possession of the *Liederbücher* in this way, and after Clara's death her children continued to trade upon their patrimony well into the twentieth century.

Since Clara had been involved from the very beginning with Robert's composition of songs—copying out poems for setting, collaborating on a joint opus, acting as accompanist for private and public renditions—she was the perfect musical executor. In the case of op. 142, she fulfilled her husband's original plan for a second volume in "op. 129." Clara performed this task with sensitivity and taste, for she obviously took care to use op. 127 as a model for the ordering of content. Op. 142 begins with a substantial number once destined for the Kerner *Liederreihe*, it includes two songs omitted from the revised *Dichterliebe*, and it also introduces a little-known poet whose verse Schumann set as a personal favor. The key scheme for op. 142 is understandably diffuse, though not lacking connections entirely. "Trost im Gesang" opens in E-flat major, "Lehn' deine Wang'" follows in the not so distantly related G minor, but it ends inconclusively on a half-cadence. The E minor of "Mädchen-Schwermuth" then follows the previous number in a deceptive progression, resolved by a brief internal episode in G major. It would be hard to argue for a tonal connection between the third song and the final one, in B-flat major, but this key does stand in a dominant relationship to the opening song's E-flat major.

Narrative trajectory also proves a complicated issue in op. 142. Schumann's original intent in his larger scheme for a two-volume set carried a strong sense of taking leave. In Clara's ordering the first number suggests that one can take "comfort in song," and it falls into the general category of *Wanderlieder*. "Lehn' deine Wang'" expresses vehement passion, while the remaining songs address loss and mourning. The relationship of the four is not strong, but they generally progress from solace through passion to grief. It would not be unreasonable to suppose that Clara regarded this collection as an epitaph for her husband, and her dedication of the volume to the couple's old Leipzig friend Livia Frege reinforces the sense of valediction.

"Trost im Gesang" presents another one of Schumann's magnificent remnants. In his original "short cycle" of seven Kerner lieder, this number came second, between "Lust der Sturmnacht" and "Stirb, Lieb' und Freud'!" We may suppose that he removed it from the final version of the op. 35 *Liederreihe* for narrative and stylistic reasons. Had it retained its original position, it would have introduced the subject of wandering before the motivation for departure (which "Stirb, Lieb' und Freud'!" provides). And once "Stirb" took its place, Schumann required a jaunty wayfarer's song next. "Trost im Gesang" does not fit this bill, for it adopts the topos of an exalted march by intermixing duple meter and punctuated dotted figures with chorale texture (see ex. 5.6). For this reason the composer marked its beginning "soft throughout, but not slowly." Schumann apparently concluded that a solemn march did not belong at the beginning of op. 35, and a *Wanderlied* must have seemed equally inappropriate near the end of the collection.

"Trost im Gesang" begins op. 142 well precisely because it links a journey with the banishment of grief through singing (a combination of sentiments that may have assumed personal significance for Clara). Schumann pairs Kerner's original quatrains to create octaves, which he then sets in varied strophic form, though between the first two quatrains he introduces a long interlude that modulates to the dominant for the second half of the first double strophe. Schumann removed this interlude from the second double strophe and simply transposed the music for the second quatrain, then, to end his fourth quatrain in the correct tonal position. The dotted figures that add buoyancy to the duple meter also provide the composer with an opportunity to vary Kerner's iambic *Langzeilenvers* by placing the initial syllable of a line on a downbeat rather than an upbeat occasionally (compare "Nacht" with the voice's first entrance on "Der Wanderer"). The remaining syllables follow the

Example 5.6.   Combined march topos and chorale texture for "Trost im Gesang."

drum cadence in the accompaniment, as they do in Example 5.6. This makes for more natural declamation of words that fit poorly on an anacrusis. All in all, "Trost im Gesang" displays Schumann at the height of his powers, providing a wonderful portrait of a reverent wanderer finding assurance in music.

"Lehn' deine Wang'" originated as the sixth number in the first version of *Dichterliebe*. But the song may have seemed redundant when preceded by "Wenn ich in deine Augen seh'," since the two portray a similar kind of overreaction. In "Lehn' deine Wang'" the overstatement runs:

Lehn' deine Wang' an meine Wang',	Lean your cheek against my cheek,
Dann fließen die Thränen zusammen;	Then our tears will flow together;
Und an mein Herz drück' fest dein Herz,	And press your heart fast to my heart,
Dann schlagen zusammen die Flammen!	Then their flames will beat together!
Und wenn in die große Flamme fließt	And when into that great flame flows
Der Strom von unsern Thränen,	The stream of our tears,
Und wenn dich mein Arm gewaltig umschließt—	And when I embrace you tight in my arms—
Sterb' ich vor Liebessehnen!	I'll die of love's desire.

Whether we interpret "die" as an erotic metaphor or not, the vehemence of expression is clear from Heine's language: clichéd "streams of tears" "flow" alliteratively into "flames," and anaphora prevails overall. In his torso of a setting (which lasts all of forty-five seconds), Schumann engenders unrest by displacing the verse's iambs strategically: "Lehn'" and "Sterb'" fall on downbeats, though the remaining lines scan normally. He captures the passion of the outburst in a piano accompaniment that uses offbeat triplet chords in the right hand to create vehemence. The conclusion on an emphatic half-cadence then leaves the listener to wonder what will come next.

"Mädchen-Schwermuth," one of Schumann's most delicate songs, deals ironically with the forceful expectations created by the ending of "Lehn' deine Wang'." As mentioned earlier, the E minor of "Mädchen-Schwermuth" presents a deceptive progression from the latter song's half-cadence on a D major chord, just as Lily Bernhard's text speaks of depression, not of passion. Bernhard had been a childhood friend of Clara Schumann's, and inspired by the publication of Robert's *Myrthen*, Bernhard sent a poem to the couple in the fall of 1840. Schumann set her verse in mid-November and had Clara send the result to the poet.[54] The auto-biographical connotations of the last lines have much resonance in a posthumous volume of songs published by a composer's widow:

Gottes Augen seid ihr nimmer,	The eyes of God never appear
Sternlein in dem Himmelszelt!	As stars in the heavenly vault!
Ach, es strahlt kein Trostesschimmer	Ah, no gleam of comfort shines
In die freudenlose Welt!	Into the joyless world!

Though the verse is undistinguished, Robert's setting is a gem. For much of the song the voice floats almost motionless above a minimal accompaniment, often no more than three-note block chords in one hand. Only the penultimate couplet receives a consistent four-part texture, with "*Him*melszelt" emphasized by a departure from the voice's usual monotone and harmonies that dwell on the dominant. But flat affect returns for the last couplet, and the song closes as simply as it began. If the text speaks of mourning, the music is not so much gloomy as wistful.

Though "Mein Wagen rollet langsam" features a male rather than a female persona, it ends op. 142 in the same delicate and subdued tones introduced by "Mädchen-Schwermuth." The Heine song, like its immediate predecessor in *Dichterliebe*, "Es leuchtet meine Liebe," may have seemed conspicuous among its miniature neighbors. "Mein Wagen" features a lengthy postlude and falling arpeggiations in its accompaniment, and the composer might have considered these traits redundant after the falling arpeggiations and extended postlude in "Sommermorgen."

Schumann makes quite free with the three stanzas in "Mein Wagen," treating them as two sestets. The first manufactured sestet paints the scene, with its slowly rolling carriage and concluding thoughts of the beloved ("die Liebste mein"). It also modulates from B-flat to D-flat major. The second false sestet introduces mysterious phantoms who shadow the carriage from outside, mocking its occupant. The composer changes Heine's lines considerably here: "Three wraiths give greeting, nodding their heads" becomes "Three wraiths slip hurriedly by." And where they "caper and make faces" in the "Lyrisches Intermezzo," they "slip by and make faces" in op. 142, linking the ninth and twelfth lines of the poem. Schumann's second "strophe" also fails to attain the home key, landing instead in F major, which then transforms into a dominant prolongation of seventeen measures in the postlude.

The composer also indulges an uncanny contrast in polyrhythm between the two halves of each false strophe. In the first part the accompaniment features falling arpeggiations that alternate between eighth notes and sixteenth notes in a halting ostinato quite independent of the slowly moving vocal part. But this texture changes drastically to recitative-like punctuating chords that move "stepwise with the voice" at "Ich sitze" and "Sie huschen," respectively. It seems almost as if the persona were conducting a conversation with the phantoms outside his carriage. Are these the harbingers of death, and is this an odd funeral cortege in triple meter? Of course we cannot answer this hypothetical question. But it is tempting to imagine Clara thinking, in her placement of this song, about the spiritual boundary that separated her dead husband from the shadows of earthly existence.

Epilogue to the "Year of Song"

Because Schumann remained active as an editor and a critic during the years when his first spate of songs broke upon the public, reviews in the *Neue Zeitschrift für Musik* were prevented by conflict of interest. It remained for the competing *Allgemeine musikalische Zeitung* to comment on the composer's lieder, though belatedly. In January 1842 an anonymous critic devoted an extensive article to this new area in Schumann's output, addressing specifically the Heine *Liederkreis*, op. 24, *Myrthen*, op. 25, the Geibel *Gedichte*, opp. 29–30, the duets and Kerner *Lieder-reihe*, opp. 34 and 35, and the *Zwölf Gesänge aus Rückerts Liebes-frühling*, op. 37.[55] This review in two installments provides our best window on the contemporary reception of Schumann's songs, at least by critics.

The reviewer proceeds from a conservative point of view, as was typical in the *Zeitung*, and while he admitted in his lengthy preamble that Schumann evinced an exceptional talent, he deplored the composer's leadership in a revolutionary rather than evolutionary philosophy of musical composition. He comes to a prejudiced verdict, therefore, on Schumann's new vein of activity:

> We find generally in these songs that sensitivity lies at their foundation, the whole rules over individual parts and leaves behind an impression of totality, that the conception is faithful and true, the melody can be called noble, often beautiful, the harmony pure, seldom disturbing. On the other hand we still run often enough into blunders, which reveal themselves mostly in

unusual, harsh modulatory twists and mainly in a heavy, often swollen, altogether much too prominent accompaniment that smothers the melody.[56]

It becomes clear from the collections and individual songs censured or praised by the reviewer that his conception of the lied entailed cantabile melody predominating over a subordinated accompaniment with predictable figuration (the Schubertian model that Schumann hoped to move beyond). For this reason, the Heine *Liederkreis* generally does poorly in comparison with *Myrthen*. Of "Warte, warte, wilder Schiffsmann," for instance, the reviewer says, "Although the poem contains musical moments, we would not have recommended it for setting, on account of its many proselike passages. As the song now lies before us, we agree with its character, but not with the heavy accompaniment that overwhelms the melody."[57] The critic considers the ending of op. 24 "completely unsuccessful," largely on account of the ebb and flow of "Mit Myrthen und Rosen" (though the arpeggiated postlude receives accolades). On the other hand, a song such as *Myrthen*'s "Der Nussbaum," with a text by the local Julius Mosen, wins the tribute "incomparable" for its "tenderness and loveliness."[58] This verdict stemmed from a consistently arpeggiated accompaniment that draws little attention away from its lyrical melody.

The reviewer does not lay great store by the overall structure of a volume of songs or the meaning that might arise from their juxtaposition in a cycle: "[The last three songs in the Kerner *Liederreihe*] bear less the stamp of the artistic than the unusual. The consistency with which the concept has been carried out is often the only thing to praise. We do not find beauty in them, the main requisite in a work of art, because this does not result from the overall concept alone, but also from external manifestation."[59] In other words, the sum of a particular opus could never amount to more than the defects of its objectionable parts. The critic attributes the unevenness of the various collections to their rapid composition:

If we inquire into the reason why, amid so much excellence, so much is to be found that no period will view as classic (even if it has at heart an artistic idea), then we believe it is to be discovered in the choice of means and in the rapid execution of the ideas conceived. If we consider specifically the span of time in which such a multitude of lieder appeared among many other compositions, then we will probably find the explanation why many a song does not bear the stamp of perfection, even if this is no excuse. That talent, that a genuinely musical spirit expresses itself almost everywhere, offers the consumer no recompense for the lack of maturity.[60]

With the benefit of hindsight, it would be easy to find the critic's lack of vision amusing, for Schumann's early songs have indeed become classics, whereas those by most of his contemporaries have fallen into obscurity. But it would be far more enlightening to consider the different standards applied by a contemporary writer against those of our present aesthetic. The reviewer interested himself in immediate accessibility to the amateur performer of modest abilities, and to the critic songs were overwhelmingly compositions for voice. He does not complain about Schumann's lyrical gift but objects to the piano's assuming too prominent a role in the polyrhythm between text, melody, and accompaniment. This shift in balance between voice and piano had been ongoing for some time (at least since the beginning of the nineteenth century), but Schumann nudged it further down the road. He was in fact not revolutionary, and therefore many of his songs fulfilled the reviewer's criteria, but some did not. The critic, moreover, was not concerned only with Schumann's full accompanimental texture but equally with "peculiar" harmonic twists. Here the contemporary objections to Schumann's early piano music returned to haunt him.

The increased parity between voice and piano and the singularity of Schumann's harmonic progressions are just the features, however, that have made his songs "classics" to us. That is to say, they sustain repeated performance and rehearing because they do not reveal all their facets on first acquaintance. They benefit also from the relocation of the lied from the home to the concert hall, where skilled professional artists can reveal their multifaceted subtlety. This point raises questions of cause and effect, for we might argue that Schumann's songs, aided immensely after his death by Clara's public renditions, played a role in moving lieder into the professional arena, a progression completed by recordings in the twentieth century.

The second shift in assessment between Schumann's time and ours concerns the importance of evaluating individual lieder in the context of their opus number, particularly those labeled "Liederkreis" or even "Liederreihe." Such an exercise seems to have meant very little to the critic in the *Allgemeine musikalische Zeitung*, whereas we find it almost impossible to make aesthetic sense of op. 24's "Lieb' Liebchen" without the neighboring "Schöne Wiege." Juxtaposition of contrasting fragments was one of the primary devices Schumann had employed in his early sets of piano miniatures, and it remained so in his volumes of songs. Taken by themselves, some of his lieder would certainly seem less satisfactory than others and his output would appear highly uneven. Schumann catered to the tastes of his day when he occasionally excerpted some of his songs for music journals and anthologies. But he obviously took great care in designing whole opuses, even going so far as to calculate the effect of dividing longer cycles into multiple volumes for publication. The reviewer focuses closely on the properties of individual numbers, but the debate today about the meaning and significance of Schumann's songs is deeply involved in questions about the status of musical "works."

Finally, the continuing literary merit of the texts (as opposed to their suitability for musical treatment) naturally means more to us today than it did to the contemporary critic. Schumann took great pains to set the best poets of the recent generation, even though he indulged some poetry for its middle-brow popularity. The 1842 review of his songs, however, does not distinguish between settings of great and commonplace verse. This may be the least surprising aspect of the disparity between contemporary assessment of the 1840 songs and ours, for we apply a second layer of historical filtering. Schumann fares well today because he set a relatively large amount of what we regard as extraordinary verse. For this reason, modern listeners and performers tend to pay less attention to the composer's treatment of authors who have not withstood "the judgment of history," which may be our loss if we believe lieder to be more than the sum of their parts.

Whatever critics thought of his lieder, Schumann took some comfort in the fact that they were in great demand from publishers. This can only mean that these firms found a ready market for the songs among well-educated and talented amateurs. Where he had failed to find an audience for his early piano music, Schumann succeeded immediately in selling his vocal music, perhaps because what seemed abrupt and capricious changes of mood in sets of instrumental miniatures found poetic justification in collections of songs. Once established with the public, his reputation as one of the best lieder composers persisted, providing the impetus for a second burst of creative activity when the copious vein from 1840 finally played out.

P A R T

II

Schumann's Later Songs

The Advent of the "New Style" and the Later Cycles

Between 1842 and 1846 Schumann composed virtually no solo lieder (though he occasionally realized sketches from earlier years), and he did not return in force to the genre until 1849. Then we find a second efflorescence of song in 1849 and 1850, with more sporadic activity through the end of 1852. Two factors combined in prompting Schumann to begin composing songs again. One derived from the simple fact that most of the ample supply generated during his first mature period eventually appeared in print and needed to be replenished. The second came as a by-product of his relocation from Leipzig to Dresden at the end of 1844. The Schumanns' move had several motivations: disappointment over Robert's failure to be selected as Mendelssohn's replacement to direct the Gewandhaus concerts, his declining health, and his interest in writing opera.[1] During the first years in Dresden the composer suffered from nervous disorders that greatly slowed his output. By the end of 1847, though, he had regained a semblance of good health, sufficient to take over the Dresden Liedertafel (male voices) from the departing Ferdinand Hiller. To this he added a mixed Verein für Chorgesang, which he organized.[2] These two groups naturally elicited a large number of part songs, but their programs also featured solo lieder, and this spurred Schumann back into the field as a composer.

By the time he again focused serious attention on the lied, however, Schumann's style of vocal writing had undergone a marked change. We must count the proximity of Richard Wagner as the single biggest influence in this new development. Schumann already had a long, if not in-

volved, history with Wagner, who had served from time to time as a correspondent for the *Neue Zeitschrift* and had visited Leipzig (where he
grew up) during Schumann's residency. When they both lived in Dresden,
the two composers socialized regularly but at spaced intervals, perhaps
because they possessed such different dispositions. Schumann in person was taciturn, Wagner garrulous. Of a chance encounter in March
1846, Schumann wrote, "[Wagner] possesses an enormous gift of gab,
crammed full of overwhelming thoughts; one cannot listen to him for
long."[3] The opera director confirmed the temperamental disparity in his
autobiography: "We met from time to time for walks, and to the extent it was possible with this singularly laconic fellow, we exchanged
ideas about music."[4] Despite their different personalities, however, Schumann and Wagner obviously remained on good terms, even after Wagner
passed critical remarks on Schumann's libretto for *Genoveva*.[5]

Wagner's operas interested Schumann keenly. His first look at the score
of *Tannhäuser* prompted him to share reservations in a letter to Felix
Mendelssohn:

> Wagner has another opera ready here—certainly an ingenious fellow full of
> extravagant ideas and audacious beyond measure—*Rienzi* exudes aristoc-
> racy—but in truth he cannot think out and write down four beautiful mea-
> sures in good succession. Even in correct harmony—in four-voice part writ-
> ing—everything escapes him. What can come of it in the long run! And now
> the score lies before us in print—with its [parallel] fifths and octaves—and
> he would like to revise and cross out—too late.[6]

But after attending the premiere on 19 October 1845 and then hearing a
revised version performed in November, Schumann had quite a different
reaction: "Soon perhaps in person about *Tannhäuser;* I must take back
what I wrote you after reading the score; on stage everything presented itself quite differently. I was entirely taken by much of it."[7] He even examined the unpublished score of *Lohengrin* some years later, before it was
performed.[8] Schumann not only had the influence of Wagner's music
around him, he also came into direct contact with the opera composer's
readily shared writings.[9] In short, he encountered Wagner's various theo-
ries at their source and heard them on display in his works.

Two features of Wagner's theory and practice had direct relevance to
the German lied. Wagner felt that vocal music responded too little to the

underlying ideas motivating its text and too much to the "absolute musical" dictates of periodicity. These complementary shortcomings resulted in phrase repetition for its own sake rather than the sake of meaning and delimiting cadences that prevented the fluid unfolding of thought. The composer actually published these ideas later in *Oper und Drama*, but we must suppose that Schumann heard them at first hand during their formation. And they already had begun to affect transitional operas such as *Tannhäuser* and *Lohengrin* before they reached full fruition in the later "music dramas." What is more, Wagner's ally in promoting "music of the future," Franz Liszt, invoked the shortcomings of "absolute music" in June 1848 by charging in Schumann's presence that his Piano Quintet in E-flat Major (op. 44, 1842) was too "Leipsical" ("Leipzigerisch"). The composer was incensed, retorting almost a year later to a written query from Liszt about the *Faustszenen*:

> But, dear friend, wouldn't [my music] be "too Leipsical" for you? . . . Seriously—from you, who know so many of my compositions, I would have expected something more than the pronouncement of an indiscriminate verdict on the whole of an artistic life. If you examine my pieces more closely, you will immediately discover a rather wide variety of perspectives in them, for I have always endeavored to bring something different to light in each of my compositions, and not only in form.[10]

Schumann still felt a keen obligation to musical "progress," he wanted to remain in the vanguard, and he certainly wished to respond to the challenge presented by "music of the future."

The problem for the composition of songs lay in the fact that unlike Wagner's version of *Stabreim* crafted specifically to discourage periodicity, preexisting, end-rhymed verse for lieder inherently entailed "quadratic" regularity.[11] That is to say, authors generally designed "lyrics" to fit four-square melodic phrases. By definition, then, Schumann would need to alter the focus of the polyrhythm between verse, melody, and accompaniment to fulfill the aesthetic of the new style. Natural accentuation of syllables was still requisite, but even-measured phrases, regular harmonic rhythm, clear-cut cadences, and melodic repetition were not a foregone conclusion. A composer might use the old devices to achieve a deliberately simple effect, but he or she could abandon the quadratic style in more complicated settings. In the new style, dramatic emphasis of individual words and thoughts replaced the allure of tunefulness. Of course, Schumann had already explored the possibilities of dramatic technique in the lieder of his first maturity. His later vocal compositions simply shift emphasis away from quadratic setting in favor of what the new aesthetic regarded as more profound and natural expression.

Lieder für die Jugend . . . Op. 79 (nos. 1–26, 28 composed 21 April–13 May 1849; no. 27 composed 23 June 1849; published November 1849 by Breitkopf & Härtel)

Also known under the title *Liederalbum für die Jugend,* this large collection of songs modeled on the so-called *Klavieralbum für die Jugend* (op. 68)[12] ironically demonstrates Schumann's transition to his later style of song. The reason for this seeming paradox lies in its composer's deliberately progressive ordering of the album's contents, which in turn qualifies op. 79 as a loose cycle similar to *Myrthen.* Like its earlier predecessor, *Lieder für die Jugend* belongs to the genre of the *Liederstrauss,* a "bouquet of songs" with personal significance. But in the case of op. 79, the various flowers are arranged with greater formality and purpose than the bridal bouquet offered by op. 25.

Schumann initiated the plan for a children's song album in April 1849, according to his diary of planned projects; his household accounts record "3 children's songs" for the first time on 21 April 1849.[13] Thereafter, almost every day in April saw the composition of two or three additions to the collection until the Dresden uprising began on 3 May.[14] The violence alarmed the Schumanns, and they fled the city with some of their children on 5 May. Clara returned on 7 May just long enough to gather the remainder of the household, and eventually the Schumanns took up temporary residence in the nearby village of Kreischa until the unrest passed.[15] All the while Robert continued to work on the planned *Liederalbum,* finishing all but one last song by 13 May. The family returned to Dresden on 12 June, and Robert decided to add the "Lied Lynceus des Thürmers" on 23 June. By 27 June he was wrestling with exactly which selections to publish in the *Liederalbum* and their order (he ultimately omitted eight numbers written for the project).[16]

Some authors have regarded Schumann's involvement with various collections of pieces for children during the revolutionary period of 1848–49 as a flight from reality.[17] But the fact that the composer turned his attention to domestic music does not necessarily imply a lack of political awareness or conviction. We can have no doubt that the Schumanns held strong republican views, which they expressed explicitly if not publicly,[18] and German patriots had often seen the influence of culture in the home as crucial to establishing a constitutional state. In reviewing the nationalistically motivated *Des Knaben Wunderhorn,* for instance, even the august Goethe wrote, "There ought to be a law that this book be found, at least where sensible people dwell, on the sill under the mirror, or wherever else song- and cookbooks are wont to be placed, to be opened at moments of high or low spirits. Then one might always find something that resonated or stimulated, even if one had to turn a couple of pages at need."[19]

Schumann had long regarded the lied as one of the main pillars of German art, and his creation of an album for children carried with it a politically didactic intent. He featured poetry from patriotic authors and collections—Hoffmann von Fallersleben, Schiller, Goethe, *Des Knaben Wunderhorn*—to inculcate proper cultural values at home in the younger generation at their most impressionable.[20] The songs accomplish their task by example rather than by overt political statement, as Schumann hints in a letter to the reviewer Emanuel Klitzsch on 19 December 1849: "You would do well to express what I meant by [the collection], namely that I chose poems suited to the young, and in fact by the best poets." He goes on to reveal "how I made the effort to progress from the simple and easy to the more difficult. Mignon closes, directing her sight presciently toward a more active life of the soul."[21]

Schumann's grouping of the initial six songs confronts us with the political, didactic, and progressively cyclic nature of the *Liederalbum.* All of the texts come from anthologies by August Heinrich Hoffmann von Fallersleben (1798–1874), possibly the most politically charged poet of his day. He was appointed professor of German language and literature at Breslau in 1830, but his ironically titled *Unpolitische Lieder* (1840–41) led to a ban on their publisher, Campe, throughout Prussia and to a trial that resulted in von Fallersleben's dismissal.[22] After this he led an itinerant existence writing political poetry, among which was the future German national anthem, "Deutschland über Alles" (a paean to national unity above the rule of local princes). In December 1843 the poet compiled a collection of *Funfzig* [sic] *neue Kinderlieder* with Ernst Richter, and they solicited from Schumann a setting of one of the poems ("Soldatenlied"). Schumann drew both on von Fallersleben's *Gedichte* and on his two volumes of *Kinderlieder* (the second from 1845) for op. 79.[23] The composer's decision to begin with six of von Fallersleben's texts and include four more over the course of the *Liederalbum* possessed political implications in exposing children to the "best poets."

The first six songs in op. 79 also imply musical cyclicity, most obviously in their steady progression around the circle of fifths from A major ("Der Abendstern") to D major ("Schmetterling") to G major ("Frühlingsbotschaft" and "Frühlingsgruss") to C major ("Vom Schlaraffenland") to F major ("Sonntag"). Whatever the remaining tonal relationships in the *Liederalbum,* this initiation signals coherent progression, as does its succession of polyrhythmic interactions. Schumann begins mostly with so-called second-epoch settings,[24] which respect natural accentuation of words but in which the accompaniment gains almost no independence from the vocal melody. Thus in "Der Abendstern" (see ex. 6.1), the piano plays almost exclusively homorhythmic block chords, with the top note in the right hand mostly doubling the melody throughout. "Schmetterling" seems more complicated at first glance because of its prelude and interludes, but here the composer responds to von Fallersleben's dimeter by using the accompaniment to produce even phrases by means of call and response (the piano "lines out" a melody echoed by the voice). Again we find block chords, many reduced to three rather than four voices (a texture typical of the lied two generations earlier). "Schmetterling" falls technically in the style of "third-epoch" lieder (minimal preludes, interludes, and postludes), but just barely, as does "Frühlingsbotschaft." The accompaniment of the latter falls mostly in four-voice block chords, the top line of which often doubles the voice, though here a precise homorhythmic relationship between voice and piano yields to a brief interlude and postlude as well as to occasional punc-

Example 6.1.   "Second-epoch" style of setting in "Der Abendstern" (complete first verse).

tuating chords in place of exact doubling. Schumann's repetition of many lines of the poem simply reflects the need to regularize von Fallersleben's original verse in order to create a consistent tetrameter. "Frühlingsgruss" ("Frühlings Bewillkommen" in *Funzig neue Kinderlieder,* which served as literary source) returns to "second-epoch" style, the voice supported by block chords in a mostly homorhythmic accompaniment that doubles the vocal line without interludes.

This less "mature" style addresses the verse quadratically; that is to say, lines of text usually fit into even-measured phrases demarked by clear cadences. However, some of these initial songs hint at a more complicated polyrhythm: "Vom Schlaraffenland" ("From the Land of Milk and Honey") compresses von Fallersleben's tetrameter into phrases of one and a half measures, resulting in periods of three measures that lend the song an aspect of childish eagerness for sweets. Schumann offsets this irregularity with an overly pronounced periodicity in which the three melodic units setting the first sestet of each octave run almost exactly parallel. Touchingly, the composer suppresses the graphic second stanza of this song, with its roasted pigs running by with forks sticking out of them. Op. 79 was, after all, a *Liederstrauss* designed partly as a gift for the Schumanns' children, and Robert apparently wanted to avoid any disturbing indelicacies.

Schumann concludes this harmonically progressive unit of the cycle with the pious comforts of "Sonntag," and here he allows his setting a slightly more sophisticated polyrhythm. For one thing, he composes a four-measure prelude with content independent of the ensuing vocal line, and he repeats the prelude with rhythmic elaborations at the end of the song to create a sense of closure. The accompaniment also gains some independence in "Sonntag," for while we do find passages where the piano doubles the voice homorhythmically, some stretches feature arpeggiated patterns that create just a hint of counterpoint to the vocal line. The composer also takes more extensive liberties with the poetry, forming von Fallersleben's quatrains into double strophes that dovetail cleverly: the last musical phrase of each stanza replicates the opening phrase (the familiar conceit of "my end is my beginning"), which blurs the strophic form in the absence of an interlude.

The next eight numbers (really nine songs, because the "Zigeunerliedchen" divide in two) form a subgroup. Most of these songs present "characteristic" miniature portraits (the sad plight of a Gypsy boy, a shepherd boy, a tiny screech owl, the sandman, a ladybug, an orphan), with a secondary theme of play in spring (a Maying duet, an outdoor song). All of these songs move in the ambit of A minor, its relative C major, and the dominant or subdominant of C. In this section Schumann introduces new poetic sources: Geibel for the Gypsy songs, Uhland for the shepherd boy, two selections from *Des Knaben Wunderhorn,* a broadsheet from a folk-song collection, and Hermann Kletke for "The Sandman." Hoffmann von Fallersleben again plays an important role as the source of two numbers. The songs in this subsection, though mostly in quadratic style, sometimes complicate the polyrhythm between poetic meter and melodic declamation ever so slightly. And while Schumann still confines himself as a rule to simpler relationships between voice and doubling piano, the accompaniment can assume more independence.

The first of the two "Zigeunerliedchen" affords the piano this larger role in order to establish "characteristic" style. Thus we find minor mode, a dancelike melody that serves the voice and later as an accompanimental interlude, and slightly more chromaticism. This tale of a Gypsy boy turned soldier, then sentenced to die for stealing, seems particularly grim for a children's album, though the setting renders it delicately. Perhaps the composer included it because of its last verse, in which the lad, marched out for his execution, grabs a weapon to shoot back at his assailants (thus satisfying a child's longing to thwart adult authority). This subject matter also touches very gently on the political unrest and military response in Dresden during 1849. The second song in the pair assumes similarly plaintive tones in A minor, potentially connecting its content to the first song (though nowhere near as explicitly). It relates the story of a persona who washes his or her face with tears upon rising. The minor mode here is less chromatic than we find in the first song, and the piano part allies itself far more closely with the voice, lending the song a childish, singsong quality.

"Des Knaben Berglied" returns to the more cheerful realms of C major, though it is as folkloric in its own way as the preceding Gypsy songs. This unassuming text about a shepherd boy marks Schumann's only engagement with the verse of Ludwig Uhland (1787–1862) in the realm of the solo lied (he treated the poet's verse in part songs and later in more elaborate works for soloists, choir, and orchestra). Uhland was an extremely prominent Swabian author, born in Tübingen, educated in law, and particularly active in literary circles around Stuttgart and in political circles in Wüttemberg. He focused his activities as an author on patriotic subject matter, including *Vaterländische Gedichte* and the historical dramas *Ernst, Herzog von Schwaben,* and *Ludwig der Baier* (yet again we encounter a poet with strong political leanings in this collection).[25] Schumann relied on the poet's *Gedichte* as the source for "Des Knaben Berglied," and it inspired him to a slightly more elaborate setting, replete with horn calls in prelude and postlude, occasional independence for the piano when accompanying the voice, and a fairly wide vocal range that adopts the disjunct motion of stylized yodeling.

Lest we believe that the introduction of a duet in "Mailied" marks some sort of turning point in the sophistication of the settings in op. 79, we should note that the right hand of the piano accompaniment doubles the two voices almost without exception from the outset, that the interludes either presage or echo the singers' ensuing phrases, and that the harmonic language strays seldom and very little from the diatonic ambit of G major (dominant of C). The voices themselves proceed homorhythmically, for the most part in parallel thirds or sixths. Only the phrase structure essays a more complicated style, for though it begins with quadratic, paired repetition, it quickly becomes unpredictable so as to disguise the straightforward *Langzeilenvers* of what we believe served as Schumann's source. The composer attributes the verse to a broadsheet ("Fliegendes Blatt"), but Schulte and Schanze trace the original to Christian Adolf Overbeck (1755–1821), a prominent Lübeck attorney who dabbled in literature. Schumann probably did not obtain this poem, "An den Mai," directly from Overbeck's *Sammlung vermischter Gedichte* (1794). He seems to have encountered it instead in Karl von Hase's *Liederbuch des deutschen Volkes* (1843), bearing the attribution there "Aus den Liedern der Jugend" in a section of "Kinderlieder. Kinderwünsche."[26] The title of von Hase's anthology continues the political and patriotic subtext of earlier selections.

Schumann's choice of two related texts from *Des Knaben Wunderhorn* maintains the political subtext, since Achim von Arnim and Clemens Brentano's anthology carried avowed patriotic overtones from the time of its initial publication during the Napoleonic wars. The composer's actual selections convey no overt message, however, for both in this subsection of op. 79 relate animal stories, the first about a screech owl that can frighten children ("Käuzlein" offers reassurance) and the second about a ladybug (encouraging kindness). While "Käuzlein," in A minor, presents a very simple relationship between block chords moving in step with the vocal melody, "Marienwürmchen" offers a much more complicated picture. The verse as it appears in the first volume of the *Wunderhorn* anthology begins and ends with tercets surrounding two intermediate sestets.[27] Schumann first reworks the poem into three equal sestets, picking up on the return of the word "Marienwürmchen" at the head of every seventh line. But while this allows for a strophic setting, the length of a sestet means that the composer must repeat text to create even-measured phrases, and in the end he avoids even this. The sentiment may be childlike and the music may seem guilelessly repetitious at first, but the changing declamation, rhythmic variety, and distribution of text follow anything but a regular pattern. The overall effect has a great deal of refined charm, making this a favorite excerpt from op. 79 for professional singers.

The simple text possesses its own involved history. It actually came from the pen of Caroline Rudolphi (1754–1811), a governess who eventually established a school for children near Hamburg. Befriended by Klopstock, she published a volume of *Gedichte* in 1781, later an essay on the education of girls, and also individual poems in various periodicals and anthologies, including *Des Knaben Wunderhorn*. Arnim and Brentano labeled the derivation of "Marienwürmchen" as "oral," but the imposture surfaced later when Rudolphi's writings appeared posthumously in 1835.[28]

At the other end of the spectrum we find the two settings of Hoffmann von Fallersleben in this subgroup (nos. 11 and 14), both in "second-epoch" style, with the right hand of the piano doubling the voice, completely four-square phrasing, and absolutely minimal postludes. It seems likely that Schumann found both texts in *Funzig neue Kinderlieder,* "Hinaus in's Freie!" on the first page and "Die Waise" on page 56, both deriving from "folk tunes."[29] Of course the different stories in each warranted different affects. The composer accords "Hinaus in's Freie" a major-mode setting, with athletically ascending arpeggios for the voice at several points to communicate a love of spring conjoined with the childish delight in outside play. "Die Waise" (not directly juxtaposed in the volume) also speaks of spring's return, but this time as the source of melancholy in the absence of family. In fact, the text paints a rather grim picture, which ends with the orphan standing by the grave of his mother. For the sake of narrative progression, Schumann omits one of von Fallersleben's internal verses in order to make a direct connection between the absence of a mother's love and the concluding scene at her graveside. The composer treats this somber picture appropriately in A minor with a restrained vocal range.

Only one of the songs in this second subsection of *Lieder für die Jugend*, "Der Sandmann," affords a glimpse of a "fourth-epoch" (polyrhythmic) relationship between poetry, voice, and piano. Schumann seems to have found the poem in Georg Scherer's *Alte und neue Kinderlieder, Fabeln, Sprüche und Räthsel* (Leipzig, 1849), and though we hear little today about its author, Hermann Kletke (1813–1886), he played an important role in the Berlin literary milieu of his time. Beginning in 1838, he served on the staff of the *Vossische Zeitung*, becoming editor in 1849 and director from 1849 to 1880. Kletke not only published his own poetry but also took a particularly prominent role in collecting and printing traditional German fairy tales and anthologies of German poets. Like that of so many authors selected for op. 79, then, his work carried strong nationalistic connotations. The composer used Kletke's poem as a pretext for what is almost a piano miniature. The song consists largely of preludes and interludes punctuated with injections by a voice part restricted (with just a few prominent exceptions) to quite a narrow range (see ex. 6.2). By means of the dainty sixteenth-note figures in the piano, Schumann means to suggest the elf's tiny steps, and since the voice cannot participate in this kind of iconic instrumental writing, the vocal melody goes its own way. While this approach responds in part to the demand for regularization placed on the accompaniment by Kletke's ten-line stanzas, the voice plays a much less prominent role here than in any other song in op. 79 to this point. The singer predominates only at the end of each

Example 6.2.   Vocal entrance and interlude from "Der Sandmann."

stanza, where the accompaniment steps aside for a recitative-like passage that emphasizes Kletke's message about children feeling secure at night. This is a charming, scherzo-like gem.

In his correspondence with Breitkopf offering op. 79 on 20 May 1849, Schumann writes that "a couple of the songs (from the second—more difficult—half [of the collection]) are being sent today to Mrs. Frege; perhaps she will sing you one of these."[30] We do not know exactly where the composer placed the beginning of the collection's "second half," but a fair guess might fall on a subgroup including numbers fifteen through twenty-one, in which "fourth-epoch" settings become the rule rather than the exception. This section begins with a duet, "Das Glück," in D major, and then dwells mostly in the area of C with "Weihnachtlied" (G major), "Die wandelnde Glocke" (G minor), "Frühlingslied" (C major), "Frühlings Ankunft" (G major), "Die Schwalben" (C major), and finally "Kinderwacht" (F major).

"Das Glück" provides a good example of the more complex relationship between poetry, vocal melody, and piano that surfaces with increasing regularity in the second half of op. 79. We will recall that in "Mailied" (no. 9), the only two-voice song in the collection to this point, the voices proceeded homorhythmically in parallel thirds or sixths doubled by the piano's right hand. "Das Glück" initially divides lines of Hebbel's verse antiphonally (we encountered the poet earlier, in op. 27), with the accompaniment providing a contrapuntal layer. This setting effaces Hebbel's quatrains entirely and lends a faux-canonic impression. Eventually the voices begin to coincide, though mostly spaced by the interval of a measure, complicating the texture by means of stretto. Of course, at the end they finally proceed in parallel, but here the piano indulges just a bit more chromaticism by touching briefly on the secondary dominant key.

"Weihnachtlied," with text by Hans Christian Andersen from an edition of his collected works published in Leipzig in 1847,[31] receives an appropriately chorale-like setting from Schumann and includes an *ad libitum* multivoiced refrain for "Hallelujah, Kind Jesus!" While the song proceeds strophically, as we might expect, if we look more carefully at the text and its musical treatment, it reveals irregularities. Both verses of Andersen's original, entitled "Arme Kinder auf der Strasse," consist of sestets, making them difficult to set in conventional bar form. And though the voice proceeds homorhythmically with the accompaniment for the most part, the melody features few pairs of repeated phrases. Schumann means to lend an art song the outward appearance of a chorale.

"Die wandelnde Glocke" provides a good deal of whimsy and also a deceptive intrusion of sophisticated writing on Schumann's part. This marks the entrance of Goethe into *Lieder für die Jugend,* an event that proved significant not only for op. 79 but for the composer's later collections of songs as well. Schumann had not dealt with this touchstone of German authors in the realm of the solo lied since a handful of texts in *Myrthen* almost a decade earlier. Here Goethe provides a ballad (also a first for op. 79) about the bell summoning people to church. One child wanders into a meadow to play, "as if coming home from school," despite its mother's stern warning that the bell will fetch those who do not attend services. Sure enough, the bell comes waddling after the child with alarming speed, and in fear of being covered by it, the truant hurries to church and does so ever after, remembering the lesson. Schumann begins this setting strophically, but that lasts only three stanzas. When the avenging bell pursues the child, the composer lets his melody wander away from the key of G minor and also away from singsong melody into something more resembling parlando style. Goethe's moral about obedience receives its own unique melody. This more dramatic treatment, together with the accompaniment's imitation of a tolling bell, combines humor with musical cleverness.

Schumann took the texts for numbers eighteen and nineteen in op. 79 from Hoffmann von Fallersleben's *Gedichte* of 1843. Both concern spring, and both receive highly figured accompaniments that seldom double their respective voice parts. The composer set "Frühlingslied" as a duet, and he took considerable pains to recast von Fallersleben's verse in a form acceptable for musical treatment. The original poem alternates tercets with septains, but by means of repetition Schumann creates stanzas of twelve lines that he then employs strophically. The parallel motion of the two voices in thirds and sixths should not deceive us, for the vocal range is wide and features some substantial leaps. The composer also declaims the text with considerable rhythmic variety, rendering this a rather challenging duet to perform in comparison with earlier numbers in the collection. Similarly, "Frühlings Ankunft" appears deceptively simple at first glance. A strophic treatment of three quatrains in stereotypical *Langzeilenvers,* this song nonetheless offers no paired, repeated phrases.

And the accompaniment (see ex. 6.3), far from merely arpeggiating chords, provides a running counterpoint to the slower-moving vocal melody. Schumann achieves a lovely effect here, more akin in its relationship between piano and voice to a song such as "Zwielicht" in op. 39 (though in a happier mood) than to the simple arpeggiations in the immediately preceding "Frühlingslied."

According to Schumann's headings, the last two numbers in this segment of op. 79 derive from broadsheets (*fliegende Blätter*). The text for "Die Schwalben" comes in fact from the pen of Auguste von Pattberg (née Auguste von Kettner, 1769–1850), the daughter of a bureaucrat in the Palatinate. Her father was acquainted with a number of literary figures, including Schiller, and her poetry found its way into periodicals and anthologies, including the third volume of *Des Knaben Wunderhorn.* Schumann seems to have encountered "Die Schwalben" in von Hase's *Liederbuch des deutschen Volkes* (1843), where so many other texts for op. 79 originated.[32] The composer's setting of the irregular verse takes the form of a duet reverting to parallel thirds and sixths. But the accompaniment goes its own way, with a series of lively and sometimes intricate rhythmic figures, folkish drones, and offbeat accentuations that lend a great deal of spice to the strophic form. Only "Kinderwacht" returns to simple "third-epoch" style (accompaniment doubling the voice but with short interludes and a postlude), perhaps in deference to its pious sentiments. Schumann probably found this text in von Hase's *Liederbuch* as well, but we can trace it back to Melchior von Diepenbrock (1798–1853), who served in the Napoleonic wars, then entered the priesthood. He rose high in the Catholic hierarchy as canon, deacon, and archdeacon at the Regensburg cathedral before becoming prince bishop of Breslau in 1845 and cardinal in 1850.[33] He also served briefly in the Frankfurt Na-

Example 6.3.   Beginning of "Frühlings Ankunft."

tional Assembly of 1848, and thus "Kinderwacht" combines pious sentiments with the nationalistic associations so pervasive in op. 79's texts.

The final section of *Lieder für die Jugend* moves quite decisively into
the realm of great poets, with two contributions from Schiller, two from
Goethe, one from Mörike, one from Rückert, and only one folkloric selection (again from von Hase's *Liederbuch*). This subsection possesses
less tonal coherence than the others we have seen, but it tends toward
keys with flats. It begins in C major with "Des Sennen Abschied," moves
to A major ("Er ist's") but then to B-flat major, E-flat major, B-flat major,
and ends in the relative G minor. Though these poems still deal with subject matter concerning children, their settings can be very adult indeed,
and at the end Schuman appends one of the monuments to his later style.

Schumann's decision to take two poetic excerpts from Schiller's *Wilhelm Tell* in itself constituted a variety of political statement. The composer set verse by this famous author of the former generation very little
(he treated only one other Schiller text, "Der Handschuh," a tale spurn-
ing courtly manners; see Chapter 7). But the classic play about the Swiss
revolution against Austrian rule served as a republican touchstone in
nineteenth-century Germany. Both of the Schiller texts in op. 79, moreover, came by way of von Hase's *Liederbuch des deutschen Volkes,* lending a double imprimatur to their patriotic significance.[34] We might aptly
classify "Des Sennen Abshied" ("The Cowherd's Farewell") as a "dance
song" (*Tanzlied*), with its droning open fifths in the left hand, its orna-
mented and reel-like melody in the right hand, and a vocal melody that
runs quite independently of the accompaniment in its lack of periodic
phrases and irregular spacing of the text. Though Schumann provides
his own title (von Hase had supplied "Der Hirt"), he follows the basic
structure of Schiller's poem in adopting the ternary repetition of its first
stanza. The middle section especially receives special treatment, with
some text painting (for the cuckoo) and an unprepared modulation to E
major, which is abandoned just as abruptly.

If the *Ländler* establishes the basic topos for "Des Sennen Abschied,"
an irregular march creates the backdrop for "Des Buben Schützenlied,"
about the joys of hunting. This setting also eschews quadratic phrase
structure and predictability in favor of expressiveness, and while it invokes some measure of the folkloric in its repeated accompanimental
fanfares, these cannot disguise the sophistication of its declamation.
Schumann offers no repetition of a melodic phrase throughout the first

strophe, which combines two of Schiller's stanzas. Moreover, the composer sets the first two lines of the second stanza in three measures, and he then repeats these lines to create a strophe of equal musical length to the first. All this rearrangement of poetry serves to efface Schiller's clear *Langzeilenvers*—a drastic departure from what could have been guileless simplicity. Both Schiller settings are minor gems, with "Des Sennen Abschied" holding the best claim to individual performance outside the context of the collection for its sheer gracefulness.

When we arrive at "Er ist's," we are prepared for a more sophisticated polyrhythm. This song in A major breaks through the C major compass that dominates the middle of op. 79 and also foretells the move toward a wider chromatic vocal range. In the middle section of the ternary form ("Veilchen träumen schon . . ."), Schumann reacts to Mörike's irregular scansion with a recitative-like passage that also indulges a bit of mimesis in rolled chords for "the tones of the harp." And to create closure, the composer then repeats the last three lines to a variation on the opening melody. This number comes close to becoming a miniature aria.

The "Spinnelied" marks the last appearance of a part song in this collection, though Schumann marks the second and third voices "*ad libitum.*" The composer also found this text in von Hase's *Liederbuch,* in a section of "Berufslieder. Hausstand," where the anthologist attributes it to *Des Knaben Wunderhorn* (vol. 3).[35] Schumann made quite free with this text, using only five of its nine original stanzas. And while the stereotypical spinning figures lend a folklike element, the irregular spacing of the vocal entrances (the piano often completes the singers' phrases) belies any implied simplicity.

Schumann's setting of Rückert's "Schneeglöckchen," similarly in strophic form, spins out a delicate cantilena with no periodicity and divides its poet's admittedly irregular quatrains with wonderful peculiarity. Here we have another poem the composer discovered in von Hase's *Liederbuch,* in a section of "Zeit-, Natur- und Stimmungslieder."[36] And these notions of "time, nature, and affect" certainly find resonance in Schumann's highly evocative accompaniment. Its gently descending arpeggiations manage to intimate snowflakes ("Flöckchen") drifting down at the beginning of the poem and melting into trickles of water falling upon sylvan glades ("Hain"). These phenomena result in late-winter snowdrops, white flowers on the forest's floor that droop delicately from their stems, serving as harbingers of the awakening that will occupy the last two

songs in the *Liederalbum*. Rückert's presentiments of spring, also marking the arrival of more elevated verse, elicit the very embodiment of
graceful loveliness from the piano.

The final two texts in op. 79, while originating in different literary
sources by Goethe, nonetheless relate to one another in subject matter.
The first, sung by Lynceus on the ramparts of a castle in Act V of *Faust*,
heralds the second, as it were. The watchman gazes out over the land as
he paces in Schumann's setting to the strains of a slow march, not only
guarding the keep but beholding a highly satisfactory "eternal design."
This philosophical quip drew the composer's attention, for he repeats it
to create the beginning of a false second strophe. It directs us to the next
lied, sung by Mignon in *Wilhelm Meisters Lehrjahre*.

We should remind ourselves of the composer's letter to Klitzsch, claim-
ing that in op. 79's progress toward maturity, "Mignon closes, directing
her sight presciently toward a more active life of the soul." "Kennst du
das Land?" finds her on the threshold of adolescent uncertainty, a girl
dressed in men's clothing who identifies the young Wilhelm successively
as her beloved, her protector, and her father. Mignon's increasing sexual
and emotional unease reveals itself in progressively fantastic and disturbing images that combine growing agitation and resolve.

Schumann accords this poem (which also appeared later, in op. 98a)
one of his finest settings, but not in the clear-cut, neatly parsed quadratic
style of his 1840–41 lieder or even of the earlier, "less mature" songs in
op. 79. As a critic he would write of other approaches to this poem:

> To take the *Wilhelm Meister* songs, for example, if a hexameter follows a
> three-foot iambic line, is this not . . . a poetically regular heartbeat, the like
> of which has never existed on earth. It offends me, then, that the expressive
> "dahin" in "Kennst du das Land" is taken so lightly by most composers,
> like a sixteenth note. This should certainly not happen, . . . surely it should
> be more fervently and meaningfully accentuated than one finds in most of
> the well-known settings.[37]

Schumann's own strophic setting begins with a chromatically tentative,
arpeggiated prelude that leads to a declamation of Goethe's first line that
almost resembles recitative. This unfolds over three measures, though
Schumann knew well enough how to accommodate iambic pentameter in
quadratic style when he wished.[38] He provides the second line with a new

melody lasting just two measures, whereas the third and fourth lines of Goethe's sestets receive unrelated four- and three-measure phrases respectively. Schumann saves his masterstroke for the refrain: it elides with the previous phrase, which cadences inconclusively on a second-inversion tonic chord (see ex. 6.4). At the same time the music breaks into a triumphant major mode, repeating Mignon's imploring "Kennst du es wohl?" The composer highlights the word "dahin" (the middle of Goethe's fifth line) by placing it on a high pitch. And after we hear it once in major mode, the exclamation "Thence! Thence would I with thee, oh my beloved!" appears a second time at the end of the strophe in a dramatic return to minor mode. Summarized briefly, Schumann ignores the meter of Goethe's verse, treating it almost as prose and emphasizing the most

Example 6.4.   Preparation and beginning of the refrain from "Kennst du das Land?"

striking lines or individual words. He employs a range of Wagnerian devices, including irregular phrases, avoidance of periodicity, subversion of clear-cut cadences, and rapid alternation between lyrical and dramatic styles. Mignon's "maturity" elicited a new depth of expression from Schumann that was anything but "Leipsical."

Lieder für die Jugend does not offer the kind of narrative cycle that suggests indivisible, sequential performance in the manner of the Heine *Liederkreis, Frauenliebe und Leben, Dichterliebe,* or even the Eichendorff *Liederkreis.* But Schumann nonetheless arranged op. 79 cyclically according to didactic principles that have stylistic implications. By placing the songs roughly in order of growing sophistication, the composer not only imparts some thoughts about the different ages of children to whom various numbers and segments might appeal, he also comments on his own changing approach to the lied. He begins with quadratic style and uncomplicated polyrhythm and ends by abandoning expectations of rhythmic predictability and tunefulness in favor of dramatic expression. At the same time, he retains the option of invoking quadratic style for folklike material, for uncomplicated personae, or where antique subject matter might suggest it. Though some critics may still find his earlier songs preferable because of their tunefulness, Schumann means to tell us in a new style "directing [its] sight presciently toward a more active life of the soul" that he has the range to answer the "New German" challenge.

Lieder, Gesänge, und Requiem für Mignon aus Goethe's Wilhelm Meister für Gesang und Pianoforte . . . Op. 98. Erste Abtheilung, Op. 98.a. Die Lieder Mignon's, des Harfners, und Philinen's für eine Singstimme mit Begleitung des Pianoforte (nos. 1 and 3 composed 12 May 1849; nos. 5 and 9 composed 20–21 June 1849; nos. 2 and 7 composed 30 June–1 July 1849; nos. 4, 6, and 8 composed 6–7 July 1849; published October 1851 by Breitkopf & Härtel)

The coherent span of time in which Schumann composed the solo songs from *Wilhelm Meister* and their narrow, interrelated range of keys would by themselves suggest that this group of lieder forms a cycle. To this we must add the composer's initial correspondence offering op. 98 to Johann August André of Offenbach on 2 April 1850: "I have set all the lieder and *Gesänge* from Goethe's *W. Meister,* and also in addition the 'Requiem for Mignon' for solo voices, choir, and orchestra as finale. I would prefer to publish the songs and requiem as *one* opus. I would also consider it appropriate in the publication of the lieder and *Gesänge* if they were to come in the order they do in the novel."[39] André declined Schumann's offer, however, and though Friedrich Kistner expressed interest in op. 98, Schumann ultimately returned to Hermann Härtel: "A Leipzig publisher has heard [one] of my settings from Goethe's *W. Meister* and wishes to print them. Because you already have the first song in press, however, I consider myself obliged to inform you beforehand of the existence of the work; it was always my intention to offer you the work for publication."[40] The mixed medium for the two parts of op. 98 prevented its appearance under one cover, however, and so Härtel decided to print the two parts separately as op. 98a and op. 98b. Though op. 98 presents a coherent "work," we will consider only the solo songs here.

Schumann had set relatively few Goethe lieder before 1849—a youthful ballad and just a handful of selections in *Myrthen* in early 1840. The year 1849 saw three in *Lieder für die Jugend,* a selection for op. 51, and eight in op. 98a, the latter possibly in response to the centenary of Goethe's birth. Schumann discussed the subject in his May 1849 correspondence, and he also attended a series of conferences about a Goethe celebration in Dresden from 14 July to 21 August.[41] As his letter to André suggests, the composer took pains to square the order of his songs with the original novel, but with a twist. To create a successful cycle, he alternates Mignon's songs with those of the harper and then follows the correct sequence for each character. Philine's song appears not only for the sake of relief, but also to establish a regular alternation of male and female voices when op. 98a is performed as a unit. The cycle's scheme of closely related keys begins with G minor, moves to its relative major of B-flat (no. 2), back to G minor (no. 3), to E-flat major and its relative minor C (nos. 4 and 5), to A-flat major (no. 6), E-flat major (no. 7), and the relative C minor (no. 8), ending in the G major of "So lasst mich scheinen."

The songs in op. 98a often puzzle critics, for if "Kennst du das Land?" explores a new style, then the remaining numbers for Mignon and the harper test its outer limits. But Philine's song reminds us that Schumann could still invoke quadratic style when he chose, and so the highly irregular phrases and variable rhythms of the other selections require some explanation other than the composer's losing his touch. The late John Daverio hit the mark when he suggested quite directly that "the interplay between lyricism and drama reflects the tension between the inner world of the soul and the outer world of action so powerfully presented in Goethe's novel. No less than the literary operas of the late 1840s, Schumann's most emotionally charged song cycle is animated by a crucial theme of its literary source."[42] Mignon is an unhappy, orphaned waif confronting the uncertainties of adolescence, and the harper is an itinerant minstrel haunted by the sin of incest with his sister (the result of which, unbeknown to him, is none other than Mignon). Schumann sought to capture Goethe's characters in his tortured songs, and he must also have hoped to avoid repeating Schubert's quadratic approach in his powerful and well-known settings of these texts.

   Nowhere does Schumann's penchant for literary characterization shine so clearly as in the harper's first song in op. 98a (Mignon's opening number is examined as part of op. 79). In Goethe's collected poetry, this text receives the title "Der Sänger," but Schumann places it squarely in *Wilhelm Meister* by labeling it "Ballade des Harfners." If there were any further doubt that the composer wanted this song situated in its narrative context, he designates the character singing, Harfner, in boldface at the entry of the voice (a procedure followed for the other numbers in op. 98a as well). We know that he had finished reading *Wilhelm Meister* just two years before, in February 1847, and Schanze lists the novel in Goethe's complete works, not the collected poems, as the source of Schumann's texts.[43]

The "Harper's Ballad" marks the entry in the novel of the character, a deranged old man who often intimates personal details about himself obliquely. Here he appears in the common room of an inn to perform a reflexive ballad about a king inviting a wandering minstrel into his hall. Example 6.5 shows clearly enough the irregularly spaced, rolled chords with which the singer punctuates his story. It also displays uneven phrases that disguise Goethe's tetrameter almost completely, reinforcing Schumann's instruction "to be performed as free declamation." But no excerpt from this song can convey the strange, unpredictable way in which the accompaniment varies constantly, from rolled chords to block chords to arpeggiations to single bass notes answered by chords in the right hand. At one point the song modulates from B-flat major to D minor to G major and back again, and often the harmonies do not support the vocal line "correctly." Schumann leaves us with a brilliant impression of an erratic performance by a distracted yet powerful figure.

Mignon, by way of contrast with her father, is not deranged by guilt but confused and isolated. As a result, in Schumann's settings her musical

Example 6.5. "Harp" accompaniment in the "Harper's Ballad."

character exhibits more consistency of accompanimental pattern. And while her vocal lines are not simply quadratic, they do occasionally offer direct repetition of cells and slightly more predictable declamation. Daverio points out that "Nur wer die Sehnsucht kennt" begins with the same head motive on the same pitches as "Kennst du das Land?," as well as featuring the same opening motive in the accompaniment (the similarities are fleeting, however).[44] Though Schumann places strong first syllables on the unaccented third beat of the measure, he sets a couplet such as "Seh' ich an's Firmament / Nach jener Seite!" to a period with parallel antecedent and consequent phrases. This song also gains some regularity through its arpeggiated accompaniment, largely cast in steady triplets. The composer uses Goethe's repetition of the opening couplet in his single strophe as an excuse for a ternary form that repeats much of the opening music and its text. In contrast, he treats "Heiss' mich nicht reden" almost as prose "to be performed freely and passionately" (according to the initial instruction). At the thought that Mignon might someday reveal the secret past she has sworn to conceal ("Zur rechten Zeit vertreibt die Sonne Lauf / Die finst're Nacht, und sie muss sich erhellen"), the song almost breaks into lyricism. But this proves illusory, and even the accompaniment's steady eighth-note chords yield to the final truth that "only a god" may release her from her vow of silence. Schumann isolates this last phrase by halting forward motion, before rounding the song by conjoining its opening line of text with its final couplet.

"So lasst mich scheinen, bis ich werde," Mignon's farewell to life, may be the most touching song in the cycle, and it provides a fitting conclusion. Schumann begins in G major, but mode and key change often in this song. The chromatic phrases elide one into another through an enchained set of deceptive cadences that would have done Wagner proud in *Tristan und Isolde*. By these means Schumann manages to run Goethe's first three stanzas together almost without pause, effacing the breaks between quatrains in one continuous melody. Eventually periodicity asserts itself at the line "dann öffnet sich der frische Blick" ("then a new vista will reveal itself"), but it articulates neither poetic structure nor meter in the least. The composer sets Goethe's last quatrain apart, with a special chromatic detour into minor mode for the lines "but I felt deep pain enough; sorrow changed me all too early." The vocal line then bounds in large leaps for the last line of hope ("Make me young again forever"), to which the piano appends a long, fervent postlude that finally closes securely in G major. Schumann bent his musical powers to serve semantic rather than lyrical ends here, which is to say he became much more concerned with dramatic characterization than with cantilena.

After his introduction, the harper's remaining songs, like Mignon's, entail more of a balance between dramatic and lyrical writing, with the emphasis falling on the former. "Wer nie sein Brot mit Thränen ass" records Wilhelm's first glimpse of the old man in his poor garret. Schumann seems to respond almost literally to Goethe's description, "The old man was rhapsodizing, repeating stanzas, half singing, half reciting." Number four thus begins with a regular accompanimental figure, paired repeated motives (no longer than a measure), and relatively even phrases. But this placid regularity breaks down in the second stanza of the poem, disintegrating into an outraged exclamation at "Ihr führt in's Leben uns hinein," which the composer accompanies with arpeggiated flourishes. Though the opening melodic phrase returns to round the song ("Dann überlasst ihr ihn der Pein"), the harper never quite regains his composure, nor his accompaniment its predictability. Schumann treats Goethe's iambic tetrameter cavalierly, mostly by placing the poet's weak initial syllables on downbeats. "Wer sich der Einsamkeit ergiebt" explores this same mixed style, but with much less coherence, perhaps because the harper expresses himself here in a set of paradoxes: "And if I can at last be truly lonely, then I'll not be alone." His anguish accompanies him everywhere, and to underpin his pain ("mich Einsamen die Pein") Schumann provides an extraordinary harmonic progression using common tones, a minor E-flat chord, a doubly diminished seventh on A natural, an A major chord, and a doubly diminished seventh on C-sharp. The accompanimental patterns vary as well, and again the composer ignores the scansion of Goethe's *Langzeilenvers*. Distracted by guilt and sorrow, the harper produces music seemingly as deranged as he is.

The harper relates his mendicant future in "An die Thüren will ich schleichen." This number comes close to quadratic style, because for semantic reasons Schumann adopts the topos of the funeral march to set Goethe's trochaic tetrameter. But this is not the military dirge of "Der Soldat" in op. 40 or the implacable demise of romance in "Die alten bösen Lieder." The harper slinks quietly from door to door as the object of pity. His drum cadences are muted, his interludes irregular (sometimes one measure, sometimes two), and his voice always enters in the middle of the common-time measures rather than at the beginning. The heaviness of his fate has unbalanced his tread: the primacy of characterization has led Schumann to parody quadratic style, which intrudes here only to show how far the harper has fallen.

Lest there be any doubt that Schumann could still summon tunefulness, he inserts "Singet nicht in Trauertönen" in the cycle as the exception that proves the rule. He uses conventional melody to characterize the flighty actress, Philine, who suffers from no guilt but just wants to enjoy the night's recreations. Not only is her accompaniment carefree (a staccato patter almost from beginning to end; see ex. 6.6), but her two-measure phrases fall in regular series of predictable pairs. Even the unexceptional ternary form of her song poses no problems. In assigning this style to the one frivolous character in op. 98a, Schumann reemphasizes the message he sent in op. 79: in the new aesthetic, quadratic style characterizes either the childlike or the heedless. It is unsuitable for those with depth of soul. Philine's straightforward music provides the dramatic foil for Mignon's and the harper's complex style.

Schumann's *Wilhelm Meister Lieder* form a powerful and moving cycle when performed as a unit. Where op. 79 pointed the way to the stylistic development for which the composer began to strive in his songs af-

Example 6.6.   Entrance of the voice in Philine's song.

ter 1848, op. 98a exemplifies the new style in characterizations drawn so clearly and forcefully that they cannot be regarded as mere aberrations. They mark Schumann's conscious transposition of the lied from the home to the concert hall, from the hands of talented amateurs to the ministrations of professional singers who can realize their dramatic import. Johann André explained to the composer in his letter rejecting their publication:

> As you yourself will remember, I wished mainly for solo songs like your op. 42 [*Frauenliebe und Leben*], songs more for presentation in private circles or appropriate to such musical arenas. I must see that I bring to my press such items as might expect a market with a larger public. Indeed, I purchase all of your songs for myself, even those like your *Album [für die Jugend]*, op. 79, but lend many of them out, from which I see that there are only a few amateurs who will sacrifice for the sake of art in order to obtain a vigorously powerful enjoyment. A publisher is ill at ease when an artist often values works more highly [than warranted] by their eventual public recognition.[45]

Of course, the composer and the publisher had two different publics in mind. André's firm sold or lent songs to talented amateurs for their use at home, and this still constituted the larger market for outright sales in a mercantile environment that made no provision for royalties from performing rights. In Op. 98a Schumann had begun to write lieder that might reach the ears of the much larger concertgoing public through professional singers and pianists (ironically, too small in number to account for extensive sales of sheet music). Under the influence of his Dresden surroundings, he composed *Zukunftsmusik* in more than one sense of the word. We now live predominantly in the world of professional renditions, and Schumann's *Wilhelm Meister* cycle deserves better than it has received at the hands of performers and most critics. Accorded its due, op. 98a casts many of Schumann's other late songs in a new light.

Vier Husarenlieder von Nicolaus Lenau für eine Baryton-Stimme mit Begleitung des Pianoforte . . . Herrn Sänger Heinrich Behr zugeeignet . . . Op. 117 (composed 17–18 March 1851; published October 1852 by Bartholf Senff)

Why Schumann waited so long to set poetry by Nikolaus Lenau (the nom de plume of Nikolaus Franz Niembsch Edler von Stehlenau, 1802–1850) remains something of a mystery. The composer had a casual acquaintance with Lenau in Vienna during 1838, and he recorded "mottos" from the poet's verse in December.[46] But the Lenau poems entered into the *Gedichtabschriften* came much later, judging by the immediately surrounding verse.[47] A mistaken report of Lenau's demise prompted Schumann to action initially in 1850, with op. 90 serving as a memorial (discussed in Chapter 7). Perhaps the renewed interest led to a further engagement with the poet's works; perhaps the composer had a political motive for continuing with the "Hussarenlieder." In any event, the poems appear as a group in the second edition of Lenau's *Neuere Gedichte*[48] and thus constitute a ready-made cycle.

Writers have puzzled over the tone of the *Husarenlieder*, both Lenau's poetry and Schumann's settings. Albrecht Riethmüller regards them as part of a genre, "Soldier's Songs,"[49] which Schumann had explored earlier ("Der Soldat" in op. 40; "Die beiden Grenadiere" in op. 45). But whether Lenau meant his verse ironically, in using banal rhymes and clichéd images, remains an open question. Schumann, in any event, reads the poetry darkly, beginning with musical parody and arriving at a subtly chilling conclusion, a disquieting effect not unlike that produced by Mahler's counterfeit *volkstümlichkeit* in songs such as "Wo die schönen Trompeten blasen." In op. 117, we could guess, Schumann recalled unpleasant associations with the bloody military suppression of the Dresden uprising, which occasioned, in Clara's words, "horrible atrocities" by troops, including the fatal shooting of twenty-six students and the defenestration of rebels.[50] Whatever the cause, the poetry and music of the *Husarenlieder* do not sound heroic or patriotic overtones but confine themselves to personal traits, mostly swagger, however the poet and composer viewed them.

As Reithmüller observes, the hussar (a nineteenth-century mounted shock trooper) in Lenau's first poem articulates the passions that will occupy the remainder of the cycle: proverbial "wine, women, and song," together with a bloody saber.[51] With its two-foot lines and nonsense refrain, it poses something of a challenge for setting, and Schumann tends to smooth out irregularities by means of quadratic phrases. We could regard the composer's use of compound meter as a rollicking allusion to a carefree "riding" topos in B-flat major. But the vocal phrases are so short and the rudimentary chord progressions so heavy-footed as to seem facetious. With his braggadocio punctuated at intervals by trumpet calls, this fellow appears to be a simpleminded boor, a point lurking in sentiments such as "What's danger to him? / His wine, lively, lively! / Saber flash, saber drink! / Drink blood! Ta-da!" Again we find Schumann using quadratic style as an emblem of an uncomplicated, in this case puerile, character.

The B-flat major of the first song presents a fitting dramatic contrast to the second song, in the relative G minor, an ode to wine and sword cast as a varied strophic funeral march. The slow duple meter, minor mode, dotted rhythms, and low tessitura for the voice all invoke this topos, and in fact it bears a very distant melodic resemblance to "Der Soldat," op. 40, no. 3. Because the verse again features short two-foot lines in a series of eight short quatrains, Schumann merges pairs of couplets and then combines Lenau's stanzas to make four strophes. But there is something off-kilter about the march, for after each two-measure vocal phrase (see ex. 6.7), the piano interjects a one-measure interlude, creating a series of three-measure phrases. The hussar's drinking seems to have thrown him off balance, leaving the image of an inebriated soldier lurching unevenly toward battle with his bloodthirsty saber. The implacable dotted rhythms and strophic design (only the last stanza receives a little variation) assume a relentless quality, lending the imminent slaughter a viciously inevitable air.

Op. 117 divides in the middle, with the first and second songs in the relationship of exuberantly heedless major mode to grim relative minor (B-flat major–G minor). The same relationship translated around the circle of fifths (E-flat major–C minor) holds for the third and fourth songs. "Den grünen Zeigern" has just two short stanzas of six lines each, and this prompts Schumann to repeat Lenau's first stanza in a ternary form. Here too we find an arrogant, assertive march that accommodates six lines in quadratic style until the last couplet, which concludes in three

Example 6.7.   First vocal phrase of the first verse from no. 2 of the
Husarenlieder.

measures, necessitating the addition of an interlude to even the tally. The
composer varies the trick for the contrasting second stanza by inserting
two one-measure fanfares to herald the musical roar of the cannon. Schumann then rounds the song by repeating the first stanza, which confirms
that this song mostly concerns the incidental joys of campaigning: wine,
women, and song again.

By selecting quadratic style for the first three numbers, Schumann prepared a reversal in the last song of the cycle, "Da liegt der Feinde ge-
streckte Schaar" ("There lies the enemy host arrayed"). This song abandons any lyrical pretense in favor of dramatic characterization of the
gory detail that pervades Lenau's verse. For this reason the accompaniment changes unpredictably between soft, uneasy triplets in minor mode
and sudden outbreaks of major-mode fanfares ("Wie haut er so sharf"—
"How keenly he hacks"). Schumann sets Lenau's first two stanzas strophically, but he treats the last stanza as a coda, perhaps because of its particularly grotesque imagery. The dotted trumpet fanfares in compound
meter transform themselves into yet another riding topos, but with a macabre twist. The hussar wipes his bloody saber on his horse's mane, and

the last couplet then describes the spirited mount "galloping on with red hooves." After all the poetic and musical clichés in the previous three songs, this parting image assumes a ghastly seriousness. To intensify its impact, Schumann provides a lengthy postlude that intimates a final charge, which ends chillingly in a major-mode trumpet call.

The *Vier Husarenlieder* enjoyed a certain currency in the nineteenth century: the cycle stands as one of a handful presented as a whole as early as 1862 by Carl Haslinger at the Gesellschaft der Musikfreunde in Vienna.[52] If singers today accord them relatively few performances, this obscurity may not result from the quality of the songs; they are brutally effective in their laconic way. Rather, the subject matter as intensified by the setting is profoundly disturbing. But this short cycle offers one of the few vehicles Schumann designed specifically for baritone voice (he dedicated it to the Bremen singer Hermann Behr, whom he had befriended),[53] and it seems to rebuke militarism.

Gedichte der Königin Maria Stuart. Aus einer Sammlung Altenglischer Gedichte übersetzt von Gisbert Freiherrn Vincke . . . Op. 135 (composed 9–15 December 1852; published July 1855 by C.F.W. Siegel)

Op. 135 represents the last set of solo lieder Schumann composed and in fact the last work that he took a personal hand in publishing. The year 1852 marked a period of particularly bad health for the composer, and he was forced to abandon many of his duties as Düsseldorf's music director, which brought him into direct and painful conflict with the board that oversaw his activities.[54] He continued to write, but at nowhere near the pace of 1851 or 1853. During 1852 he worked mainly on correcting pieces written previously and on proofing works in press. *Vom Pagen und der Königs Tochter* (published posthumously as op. 140) constitutes the only substantial piece he wrote before the end of the year.

In December 1852 Schumann felt well enough again to return to his conducting duties, and Clara recorded in her diary for Christmas, "Robert gave me the gift of songs with texts by Mary Stuart, his first attempt at composition in a long time."[55] The poetry came from *Rose und Distel: Poesien aus England und Schottland,* assembled and translated by Gisbert Freiherr von Vincke (1813–1892),[56] and most authors have assumed that Robert personally chose it. But in fact Clara entered the texts in the *Gedichtabschriften,*[57] and it is quite possible that she selected them. Right about this time the biography of Mary Stuart was enjoying a considerable vogue, and we see her appearance in such novels as Sir Walter Scott's *The Abbot* and in such collections as *Songs of Mary Queen of Scots,* with texts by "Mrs. Crawford" and the British composer George A. Barker (1812–1876), published around 1853.[58] Clara may well have been attracted, moreover, to poetry ostensibly written by a female author, and Robert's presentation of the manuscript as a Christmas gift probably acknowledged his wife's partiality. These songs, Vincke's translations, and Schumann's settings are also part of a more general period sentimentality. We should remember that people in the mid-nineteenth century had a penchant for what we regard as morbid subjects and that sentimental predilections also find expression in Schumann's songs from earlier periods, such as the Kerner *Liederreihe,* op. 35.

The history of publication for op. 135, on the other hand, indirectly attaches a different autobiographical significance to the work. Schumann first offered the Mary Stuart songs in September 1853 to Henry Litolff in Braunschweig, but Litolff declined, then to Carl Luckhardt in Kassel on 7 October 1853 (also declined, apparently).[59] In January 1855, Carl Siegel wrote to the composer during his confinement in the mental asylum at Endenich about any pieces he wished to publish. Schumann mentioned op. 135, and though he signed the contract on 18 April 1855, his negotiations over financial details were settled under his wife's watchful eye.[60] Only through this somewhat oblique circumstance can we regard the texts of op. 135 as Robert's own presentiments of his impending demise.

If the Schumanns hoped to engage the sentimental fashion for the life of Mary Queen of Scots in op. 135, they confronted listeners with an unexpected irony. In a detailed study of Vincke's sources, Hans-Joachim Zimmermann has determined that most of the texts did not come from the pen of the unfortunate monarch at all. The "Abschied von Frankreich" was written by Anne-Gabriel Meusnier (1702–1780), "Nach der Geburt ihres Sohnes" was mistakenly attributed to Mary in a nineteenth-century travelogue by Fanny Lewald, and "Gebet" was probably written by the British song writer Henry Harington (1727–1816). Zimmermann argues for the authenticity of "An die Königin Elisabeth" on the grounds of its subject matter and imagery, but the actual text is transmitted in a lone copyist's manuscript. Only "Abschied von der Welt" actually exists in Mary's hand.[61] Schumann nevertheless took the poetry's authenticity on faith, and he used it to create a true cycle, as Joachim Draheim observes.[62] The first two and last two numbers fall in E minor, with the middle song in the minor dominant of A. In addition, the last four songs feature similar head motives (with the last three beginning on the same pitches).

In appealing to stylish sentimentality, the *Gedichte der Königin Maria Stuart* rely on recognizable topoi. Schumann adapted all of these, however, to his later, dramatic style rather than invoking the stereotypically "Scottish" traits of his earlier quadratic writing (see the discussion of ex. 1.2 in Chapter 1). We encounter the first topos immediately in the "Farewell to France." The piano's gently undulating sixteenth notes in the right hand, the slow, reiterative ebbing and flowing in the left hand, and the dynamic rise and fall offer a set of stylized, meandering wave or boat figurations over irregular harmonic motion (see ex. 6.8) In this way Schumann invokes all the stylistic features without reverting to the quintessential "gondola" song à la Mendelssohn or even Liszt. Additionally, the composer blunts the regularity of Vincke's iambic tetrameter by situating lines variously at the beginning or in the middle of his common-time measures or by running lines together. In these ways Schumann renders the text more as prose than as verse.

The two *preghiere* in the cycle do not seem nearly so odd in the frustration of their texts' scansion. "Nach der Geburt," with its iambic pentameter, and "Gebet," with its dactylic dimeter, would sound absurd if scanned in a singsong manner because of their solemnity. Both support their voice parts with simple block chords in a reference to chorale style. And while the four-square phrase structure of traditional hymn melodies is absent here, this does not prevent Schumann from using melodic material economically. "Nach der Geburt" employs one period twice in variation, the first time for the initial couplet, the second time for the next

Example 6.8.   Wave or boat topoi at the beginning of "Abschied von Frankreich."

three lines (thus setting the melody against the rhyme scheme for expressive purposes). "Gebet" receives an even more affective treatment that repeats the same phrase in ascending sequence four times, first setting two couplets but then single lines as the emotion builds. The structural tension in these two songs results largely (as it did in the *Wilhelm Meister* songs) from rapid alternation between or superimposition of lyrical and dramatic modes. Accompanied by chorale texture, "Nach der Geburt" and "Gebet" are not unlike Mahler's later "Urlicht," at once a recited prayer and a lied. The flexibility of Schumann's late style offered wider expressive possibilities.

Nowhere does the composer make better use of this new range of expression than in his setting of the two sonnets that probably come from Mary's pen. The sonnet is a form of poetry quite foreign to the normal world of nineteenth-century lieder. Its roots lie in the realm of Latin art poetry rather than in the tradition of German national song, and for this reason Schumann set very few.[63] To this we must add that Vincke, an ardent translator of Shakespeare,[64] cast both "An die Königin Elisabeth" and "Abschied von der Welt" in iambic pentameter, which poses yet further challenges for quadratic setting. For "An die Königin Elisabeth," Schumann chose to mirror the structure of the poem. He supplies a minimal accompaniment, mostly dotted punctuations that demark major sections. Otherwise, the voice declaims over chords. Supported by this scaffolding, the melody divides the sonnet's octave into its two quatrains, repeating almost exactly at "Und wenn mein Herz dies Blatt zum Boten wählt." The sestet passes without exact melodic repetition, though its first four lines mark an increase in the frequency of piano interjections. Schumann then shifts to the semantic level, emphasizing the apothegm contained in the last two lines by withdrawing dotted figuration in the accompaniment and minimizing it in the voice. In other words, he delivers the moral straight. Following her metaphor on life's voyage, Mary fears:

Vor euch nicht, Schwester! Doch des Schicksals Walten	Naught from you, my sister! But the rule of fate
Zerreißt das Segel oft, dem wir vertraut.	Oft rips apart the sail in which we trust.

The overall effect of this setting is all the more powerful for its economy of means. It renders indignant remonstrance against imperious fortune most eloquently.

"Abschied von der Welt" features this same economy of means but parses the sonnet's structure differently, using a topos subtly to shape both form and affect. If we were simply to diagram the repetition of material in "Abschied," it would fall in a conventional ternary form: AABA'. This fits naturally enough at first glance: the two quatrains in the octave each unfold over an A section. The sestet divides into its two tercets, the first cast in the C major of the B section, while the second repeats an abbreviated version of the A section. The procedure forgoes highlighting the last couplet ("And because I have been sorely punished here below, / Pray I partake of eternal peace") in the manner of the previous song, but it follows poetic structure even more faithfully. The regularity of the phrase structure (see ex. 6.9) throughout most of the song, however, betrays another level of compositional thought at work, for Schumann has adopted a minimalist version of the dirge topos. This is not the exaggerated funeral march of "Die alten bösen Lieder," the folkloric one of "Der Soldat," or even the irregular one of "Der leidige Frieden." Rather, the topos appears so highly stylized in "Abschied" that we might overlook it. But the relatively quadratic phrases, the occasional dotted rhythms, the generally low tessitura of the accompaniment, and the major-mode "trio" in the B section all rely on semiotic convention to

Example 6.9.   Beginning of funeral march in "Abschied von der Welt."

convey the import of Mary's farewell. In fact, the song might remind us of "Ich hab' im Traum geweinet" from *Dichterliebe*, partly because of the topos and partly because the voice sometimes goes unsupported by the piano. At the same time, the irregular declamation of individual phrases such as "mir zugemess'ner Zeit," with its elongation of the word "mir" ("me") betraying a royal ego, communicates a dramatic expressivity that an unreflectively conventional approach could never attain. One of Schumann's last solo songs is also one of his most precisely and delicately wrought.

Wide emotional range, from the subtlest understatement to the most demonstrative outcry, from the quadratic to the freely formed, characterizes Schumann's later style of song composition. He had not forgotten his earlier technique, but he chose to explore other realms more fully. His songs from 1840 and 1841 contain the seeds of the later dramatic style, to be sure, but they always adopt regular lyricism as their underlying premise. Carl Dahlhaus once maintained that "the operas Wagner wrote before 1850 can be seen as forerunners of his later music dramas in certain respects, but if Schumann had lived to Wagner's age, it is unlikely that he would have done anything more than repeat himself."[65] In fact, Schumann's later songs already challenged previous stylistic bounds. Only those who have the ears to hear his lieder after 1848, however, can appreciate their significance and power.

Poets in Review during the Later Years

Whereas a limited number of lieder volumes from Schumann's "first maturity" had served exclusively to underscore the work of admired poets (*Drei Gedichte von Emanuel Geibel*, op. 30, for example), an increasing number of the composer's solo collections after 1849 existed primarily as samplers of poets who had caught his eye. Some of these authors (von der Neun and Kulmann) came from the generation after Eichendorff, Heine, and Rückert, and one (Pfarrius) had just recently published an anthology that came to the composer's attention. Schumann's motivation in setting these minor writers often derived from a desire to introduce new faces, the kind of artistic generosity he practiced at the end of his life by heralding the young Brahms.[1] Other poets set during the later period, such as Schiller, Lenau, and Byron, had long been familiar to Schumann, but he had largely overlooked them in his previous output. In these cases he sought to redress the balance.

Most of the poets specifically honored in collections bearing their names appear to have struck the composer as fashionable for one reason or another. In making his selections, Schumann often catered to the sentimental currents of the time, which, though prevalent internationally (for instance, in Victorian or antebellum American middle-class circles), may have served as a special refuge for the German bourgeoisie dismayed by the failed "March revolution." In addition, the poetry on which Schumann dwelled in this later period reflects the tastes of a mature rather than young man. A focus on the consolations of nature, on the sacred, and even on mortality tended, understandably, to replace the emphasis on romance, courtship, and wandering in the earlier songs.[2]

In his correspondence Schumann sometimes designated the later opuses honoring poets as cycles, sometimes not. We can discern underlying themes, but not the strong narrative trajectories supplied by external frameworks that we find in the cycles discussed in Chapter 6. The ordering of the *Wilhelm Meister Lieder* has its roots in the plot of Goethe's novel; the progression from early to later childhood lends a sense of direction to the *Lieder für die Jugend;* Lenau constructed his "Hussarenlieder" to grow increasingly gory; and Vincke's grouping of the Mary Stuart songs organizes around the chronology of the doomed monarch's life. While the volumes discussed below lack strongly expressed sequential organization, we must still search for the rationale behind Schumann's selection and ordering of texts, a matter to which he always devoted much thought. Before we turn to these collections, however, we must consider the one ballad the composer published as an independent opus during this period, the origins of which lay in collections of part songs.

A Last Independent Solo Ballad

Der Handschuh. Ballade von F. v. Schiller für eine Singstimme mit Begleitung des Pianoforte . . . Op. 87 (composed originally for choir 18 March 1849; date of rearrangement unknown; published for solo voice November 1850 by F. Whistling)

The ballad seems almost to disappear from Schumann's later output until we look at his many volumes of romances and ballads for chorus, opp. 67, 75, 145, and 146, all composed in 1849 for the ensemble he led in Dresden. There are also the ballads for declamation to a piano accompaniment, op. 122, and a longer work for soloists and chorus after Uhland, *Des Sängers Fluch,* op. 139. These choral works exhibit a preference for established poets: we find Herder, Goethe, Uhland, Eichendorff, and Burns as the authors most frequently adopted for setting. Schiller, on the other hand, appears only three times in Schumann's output, and perhaps the composer meant the appearance of *Der Handschuh* as a freestanding opus to fill this lacuna.

Schiller's poem relates a story from Saintfoix's *Essais historiques,* with the scene set at the court of Francis I of France. A lady-in-waiting, Kunigunde, lets her glove fall into an arena during a bloody spectacle pitting lions, tigers, and leopards in savage battle. She bids her lover, Sir

Delorges, to retrieve the item before the whole court as proof of his devotion, which he does without hesitation. But having done so, he throws the glove in her face and leaves her forever. As is often true of ballads from Schiller's generation (as opposed to romances, which generally used more lyrical forms of verse), the author's "Erzählung" (for this is the subtitle of his poem) assumes an irregular form.[3] It begins with a sestet, then moves to a series of much longer stanzas, ranging from ten to sixteen lines in irregular meter.

Though Schumann was certainly capable of smoothing out the irregularities in Schiller's verse, he chose not to do so, which explains why op. 87's treatment might not have worked as well in a choral setting as it does for solo voice. The composer proceeds almost exclusively in recitative (see ex. 7.1), a preview of what his ballads declaimed to the accompaniment of the piano would look like and a marked contrast to the much more lyrical romances and ballads that he wrote during this same period as part songs. To give the ballad a sense of forward motion amid its highly idiosyncratic declamation, Schumann changes mode from D major to D minor at crucial points in the action. He sets the scene in major (opening stanza), the appearance of the various predators and their battle in the next three stanzas occurs basically in dramatic minor, the action of the falling glove returns to major, and the surrender of the item and the unchivalrous gesture transpire in minor (rounding occurs, however, in the reappearance of common time after the compound meter of the ballad's middle section). Of course, this characterization of keys involves a gross condensation and oversimplification. The composer inserts excursions to other, fairly closely related keys at will, and very occasionally he indulges extremely brief episodes of arioso. For instance, the taunting request by Lady Kunigunde for Sir Delorges to retrieve her glove

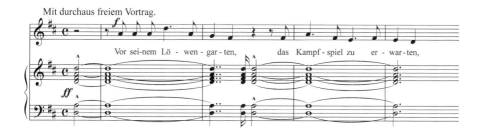

Example 7.1.   Excerpt from the beginning of *Der Handschuh.*

receives six measures of melodious treatment (see ex. 7.2). This highly inflected approach to the setting of text displays an aspect of the late style, to be sure, but it also reveals Schumann's recent preoccupation with opera. The episodes of arioso tend to characterize speakers, while the gory battle of the animals and the king's subtly imperious gestures (all described by the narrator) unfold in recitative. Comparison of this ballad, composed in 1849, with Schumann's other independently published ballad, *Belsatzar,* composed in 1840, shows just how much his residence in Dresden widened his perspective on setting texts for solo songs.

The two independent ballads have something in common, nevertheless, despite their widely spaced genesis and different approaches to the setting of text. Both look askance at noble prerogative and courtly life. The murder of King Belshazzar by his courtiers incorporates this trait explicitly as part of its story, but then Schumann composed it in 1840 and published it in 1846, during the Vormärz period. *Der Handschuh* falls later, just as the hopes of 1848 had begun to fail spectacularly in Dresden, and the song appeared in 1850, after the Prussian army had put down the Dresden insurrection violently. Some suggestion exists, in fact, that Schumann had difficulty locating a publisher for the piece, perhaps trying Johann André in Offenbach before placing it with Whistling in Leipzig.[4] The title page of the engraving manuscript reveals the length of this search in its several opus numbers (72, 77, 82 all crossed out before the final op. 87), as well as the indecision about the proper voice: "eine hohe Baritonstimme" eventually became "eine Singstimme."[5] Schiller's "Erzählung" relates the tale of amorous rebellion but also a breach in manners in the throwing of a glove in the face of a lady by a knight, the traditional gesture inviting a duel. We could read this loss of composure in the presence of the king allegorically as expressing disdain for courtly

Example 7.2.   Beginning of Kunigunde's arioso from *Der Handschuh.*

etiquette. This may explain the difficulty in securing a publisher and the removal of the male singing voice (which some might identify with the composer) in uneasy times. However much this interpretation pushes the limits, the publication of *Der Handschuh* as a freestanding opus invites some comparison with its more explicitly antiauthoritarian predecessor.

Lyrical Poetry in Review

Sechs Gesänge von Wielfried [sic] von der Neun für eine Singstimme mit Begleitung des Pianoforte . . . Opus 89 . . . (composed 10–13 and 18 May 1850; published August 1850 by Fr. Kistner)

Opus 89 records an act of artistic kindness on Schumann's part toward a theology student in Leipzig, Friedrich Wilhelm Traugott Schöpff (1826–1916), who published several volumes of poetry under the fanciful pseudonym Wilfried von der Neun (a reference to the nine muses). On 17 December 1849 Schöpff sent Schumann some verse with the wish "to see some small song of mine as the basis for a composition by you."[6] Schumann replied right after Christmas with thanks "for sending your mostly quite musical poems," asking that he might reserve them for a more opportune time (the composer was just then in the throes of preparing *Genoveva* for performance).[7] Schöpff persisted, forwarding to Schumann on 22 April 1850 a copy of his collection *Im Freien*. He hoped "there might be something here or there that might be worthy of your magic pen. For to see one or another of my poems elevated by the musical power of a celebrated genius would be the greatest praise for my lyrics and is one of my most ardent desires. Indeed, I cannot prevent this wish from transforming itself into a request."[8] The poet's second letter finally prompted the composer to action: he turned his attention to "Es stürmet am Abendhimmel" on 10 May 1850, to "Herbstbilder" 9 and 11 (nos. 3 and 4 in the published set) the next day, to "In's Freie" and "Röselein" on 12 and 13 May, and finally to "Heimliches Verschwinden" on 18 May.[9] What is more, Schumann invited Schöpff for two visits, one on 28 May and a second on 4 June, according to Jansen. The poet reported that "Schumann spoke amiably, completely without condescension, and I recall that I walked home proudly, which would not have been the case if he had been haughty or conceited."[10] The composer, moreover, placed the songs with a publisher almost immediately, writing to the firm of Friedrich Kistner on 6 June and correcting the proofs in July.[11] A reference to Schöpff in the *Haushaltbücher* on 26 August 1850 probably refers to the publication of the songs,[12] since the poet makes no further mention of a personal encounter with Schumann.

While Schöpff's adulation undoubtedly influenced Schumann, the composer had a great deal to do during this period, and in placing op. 89 so quickly, he must have seen some promise that lay beyond simple generosity or mere novelty in the verse of the unknown poet. Ulrich Mahlert speculates that in spite of the poetry's relative mediocrity, it touched on certain "post-March" themes that particularly affected Schumann after the foiled revolution in Dresden and its ultimate failure to effect political reform. According to Mahlert, this "retreat into the idyllic" entailed the use of natural imagery focusing on the departure of spring (as opposed to the expectant progression from winter to spring), on autumnal scenes, and on valediction.[13] The first four songs do indeed sound these themes: "Es stürmet am Abendhimmel" compares a stolen hope of love to a storm at sunset, "Heimliches Verschwinden" speaks of a lover who decamps without bidding farewell, and the two autumnal songs ("HerbstLied" and "Abschied vom Walde") address the waning seasons. "In's Freie" has less to do with ending than with the consolations of nature, and "Röselein, Röselein" provides something of a moral, that "all roses must have thorns" in payment for their beauty. These themes are at best loosely connected, as is the scheme of keys for op. 89: Schumann begins in C-sharp minor for the first song, moves to its submediant (A major) for the second, back to C-sharp minor becoming C-sharp major spelled enharmonically as D-flat in the third number, to *its* relative minor (B-flat) transformed into its parallel major in the fourth song, and the fifth song then remains in B-flat major. "Röselein," however, falls out of this more-or-less explicable progression, beginning in A minor and then changing to A major, which stands, if we force the issue, as submediant to the opening number's C-sharp minor and matches the key of the second song.

Schumann typically wrote his best songs to verse of high quality, and it should therefore come as no surprise that op. 89 does not stand as his most inspired group of lieder. "Es stürmet am Abendhimmel" elicited a conventional storm topos, replete with a continuous pattern of tremulous sixteenth notes in the right hand and chromatic rising and falling motives in the bass. The composer surely meant this melodramatically in response to the image of a storm, which serves Schöpff as a metaphor both for passion and for desolation. But Schumann's other melodramatic settings, whether in the earlier or later style, exhibit much more variety of texture, and despite the free declamation of the verse in "Es stürmet," the persistence of a single accompanimental pattern throughout (the right-hand sixteenth notes) blunts rather than enhances drama. This same violation of the composer's cardinal rule to avoid thoughtless patterning throughout a song also leads to monotony in "Heimliches Verschwinden," where the incessant arpeggiations again overcome the proselike declamation of the verse and continual variation of the melodic line. The constant accompanimental figuration stands at odds with the expressivity of the vocal part.

Schumann took a more creative approach to the next two settings, a pair of "Herbstbilder," numbers nine and eleven in Schöpff's published collection, *Im Freien*.[14] These songs have a tonal bond, C-sharp minor–D-flat major moving to its relative minor, B-flat. The returning dotted scalar motive for the left hand in "Herbst-Lied" (see ex. 7.3) proves a particularly effective mnemonic buttonhook joining the two sections of the song, despite the modal shift from minor to parallel major (C-sharp spelled enharmonically as D-flat) and concomitant change of piano figuration from sixteenth-note tremolo to arpeggiation. Logically enough, this shift accompanies "Dennoch spricht von naher Wonne / Greiser Wipfel Farbenpracht" ("But of coming rapture speak / the aged treetops' colored splendor"). Schumann rewrites Schöpff's lines, changing "naher Wonne" ("coming rapture") to "ferner Wonne" ("distant rapture"), then repeats the couplet and recalls its last line yet a third time. The shift of mode and figuration for this poem makes for a much more interesting setting, as do the composer's occasional interruptions of the sixteenth-note tremolos in the first section of the song for recitative-like interjec-

Example 7.3. Beginning of "Herbst-Lied," with recurring motive in left hand.

tions. The image of faint sunlight filtering through the variegated fir and linden forest seems to have caught Schumann's imagination. "Abschied vom Walde" introduces an entirely new accompanimental pattern: the bass moving mostly in half notes, syncopated quarter-note inner voices, and the upper voice moving on the beat in quarter-note counterpoint to the singer's melody. Here the complexity of rhythmically layered texture, with its right-hand counterpoint to the vocal melody, provides a musical interest that excuses the repeated figuration and lack of rhetorical pauses. The voice part in this song is particularly graceful.

"In's Freie" will strike several familiar chords. Schöpff's poem (entitled "Wann zu Singen") consists of three sestets in iambic tetrameter (Schumann omits the third sestet and repeats the opening stanza to create the ternary form of his song), and it invokes the standard elements of the *Wanderlied*. The persona assumes the stereotypical role of a sojourner-poet who flees narrow confines, taking his songs with him. The composer responds predictably with a semimarch, predominantly diatonic in outer sections, framed by fanfares taken over by the voice in a manner reminiscent of "Talismane" in *Myrthen*. The contrasting trio features a different accompanimental pattern, melody, and tonal ambitus (focused on subdominant and dominant areas with more chromaticism). If one does not listen too carefully, the "march proper" sounds quadratic enough, though the sestets pose something of a problem in this respect, because they fall in two tercets with different scansion for the cross-rhymed last lines of each:

> Mir íst's so éng all úeber áll!
> Es schláegt das Hérz mit láutem Scháll,
> Und wás da schállt, sind Líe-dér!
> Aus dúes'trer Máuern bángem Ríng
> Flieg' ích in's Wéite fróh und flínk:
> Da áthm' ích Wónne wíe-dér!

Schumann addresses the number of lines easily enough (he draws out some words, adds postludes, and so forth), but true to the later style, he does not distribute the tetrameter quite regularly within the framework of common time. Most puzzling of all, however, is the placement of "In's Freie" within the set. If the composer had placed it at the beginning of op. 89, we might detect a wanderer's cycle, beginning with a march, proceeding to the loss of the beloved ("Es stürmet," "Heimliches Verschwinden"), then hope and consolation taken from nature ("Herbst-Lied," "Abschied"). In such a scenario, "Röselein" would provide the parting apothegm. But for reasons known only to Schumann, the set does not invoke this narrative trajectory.

"Röselein" would have made a fitting conclusion to a wanderer's cycle, especially under Schöpff's original title of "Müssen denn Dornen sein?" ("Must There Be Thorns Then?"). In the event, this has become the best known of all the songs among the *Sechs Gesänge*, probably for its charm. Schöpff cast the poem as a miniature ballad in eight couplets, rather in the manner of Goethe's "Heidenröslein" (set by Schumann as a part song in 1849 for op. 67, no. 3). The first-person narrator's dialogue in op. 89, no. 6 begins for voice alone, before the piano enters quietly to pose the question. The composer then divides the text logically into three main sections, one for the dream of a thornless rose in A major, one for the awakening to the reality of thorned roses in C major, and then the reply of the brook about the inevitability of the price exacted by beauty or love. Here Schumann's text deviates markedly from the one Schöpff published in *Im Freien*, perhaps reflecting a manuscript version sent to the composer before it appeared in print or perhaps resulting from compositional license:

Printed version of "Röselein"	*Version in Schumann's setting*
Und das Bächlein lachte mein:	Und das Bächlein lachte mein:
"Laß du nur dein Träumen sein!"	"lass du nur dein Träumen sein!"
Sagt mir nun, ihr Röselein,	merk' dir's fein, merk' dir's fein,
Müssen denn Dornen sein?	Dornröslein müssen sein, müssen sein!

The printed version repeats the narrator's opening question; Schumann's continues the sage observation of the brook and answers the opening question. This provides a musical excuse for rounding, with a return to A major and a brief recapitulation of melodic fragments in the piano before the song closes with a coda for "Dornröslein müssen sein!" ("Thorned roses they must be!"). Singers perform this vignette often as an isolated number, and if op. 89 had been cast as a wanderer's cycle, "Röselein" would provide the customary ending. Taken as a group, however, the lieder in op. 89 are uneven in quality, the reason perhaps that Schumann did not stress their cyclicity. He dedicated them to Jenny Lind and sent her a copy, possibly hoping that her advocacy might bolster the collection.[15] The Schumanns had formed a personal acquaintance and collaborated with the singer in 1847 while giving series of concerts in Vienna, and during this brief partnership they discovered the value of attaching Lind's name to any enterprise. Her gracious consent to sing at one of the couple's joint recitals produced a large and enthusiastic audience.[16]

Sechs Gedichte von N. Lenau und Requiem, altkatholisches Gedicht, für eine Stingstimme mit Begleitung des Pianoforte . . . Op. 90 (composed 2–5 August 1850; published December 1850 by Fr. Kistner)

Like op. 89, op. 90 documents Schumann's personal acquaintance with a poet, though a more distant and retrospective one. Nikolaus Lenau had encountered Schumann during the composer's lengthy 1838–39 sojourn in Vienna. He first espied the author from afar in October at a café, then met him at a soirée during mid-December in the home of Salomon Sulzer, chief cantor for the Jewish congregation in the imperial city.[17] Like so many other German poets of the time, Lenau followed an itinerant path. Born in Hungary, he was a student in Vienna, Bratislava, and Stuttgart, where he became friends with Schwab, Kerner, and Uhland. He received his university degree from Heidelberg, thereafter traveling between Stuttgart and Vienna until he descended into chronic depression in 1844, which led to confinement in a series of mental asylums.[18] Lenau was already a well-known author, with two volumes of poetry and several plays to his credit when Schumann met him, and this immediately led the composer to read a selection of the poet's verse.[19]

Schumann's early personal acquaintance with Lenau did not translate, however, into an ongoing exchange, and the composer set none of his poetry during 1840 and 1841. But at some point in 1850 (we do not know precisely when or where), Schumann read that the author had died the previous year. In early August, as a memorial, he set six of Lenau's poems and appended a "Requiem" purportedly written in Latin by Heloise for Abelard, translated into German by Leberecht Dreves.[20] Schumann offered the set on 14 August to Kistner in Leipzig, and the firm requested a look at the manuscript. In the meantime the composer learned that Lenau had in fact just passed away, on 22 August, and Schumann then wrote to his prospective publisher of op. 90 on 27 August:

> Yesterday I learned . . . that I had actually sung his funeral song without knowing it. It would be fine with me now if you wanted the songs to appear

earlier than I wrote you, perhaps in the near future. Maybe the title page could be decorated with emblems of mourning—with a funeral bouquet and a star showing behind it. I would like the page in the middle, with the cross and the Latin text, to stand alone, as it does in the manuscript.

It would please me, if you could join hands in erecting a small monument to the unfortunate but very magnificent poet. And if I know you, you will certainly help to fit it out in a thoughtful way.[21]

In the event, Kistner provided an elaborate cover exactly along the lines Schumann suggested, framed by a crosier (on the left) and a crucifix (on the right), entwined at their bases with sprays of lilies. Black bunting at the top of the engraving threads through a laurel wreath encircling a star, and the wreath in turn upholds a black pall with "N. Lenau" emblazoned on it. As an added touch, another star shines dimly from beneath the pall. Lest we think this funereal symbolism excessive, similar covers appear throughout sheet music of the nineteenth century, and the engraving for op. 90 is tastefully restrained compared to more graphic deathbed scenes on popular sheet music from the same period.

Schumann's genuine sorrow ("[News of Lenau's death] . . . put us all in a melancholic mood," Clara confided to her diary)[22] combined with the quality of the poetry to elicit one of the composer's finest later efforts. If we can regard op. 90 as the "cycle" he mentions in his letter to Kistner, then its subject matter assigns it to the same genre as the loosely structured *Myrthen*. But instead of new beginnings, these songs group loosely around the themes of ending and valediction.[23] The tonal structure of op. 90, however, resides more strictly inside the boundaries set by the starting and concluding key of E-flat major. Within this framework, the second song ("Meine Rose") moves to the dominant of B-flat, with a striking intermediate modulation to its flatted submediant (G-flat) by means of a deceptive cadence. This internal detour engenders further consequences: "Kommen und Scheiden" (no. 3) begins in G-flat major but ends enharmonically in F-sharp major, which in turn serves as the dominant to "Die Sennin" in B major (or C-flat major, if one must), dying away oddly on its major mediant of D-sharp. In true Wagnerian fashion, Schumann then reminds us in "Einsamkeit" that the mediant of B major spells enharmonically as E-flat, which also exhibits in its parallel minor mode the same key signature as G-flat major. So back we go through the progression, the fifth song ending in E-flat major-minor, and the sixth ("Der schwere Abend") in E-flat minor. The "Requiem" (and with it the "cycle" as a whole) concludes in E-flat major. Op. 90 was the last group of songs composed in Dresden, and Schumann had learned well its artistic ways with keys. Movement by means of modulation from relative major to minor, then modal shift from minor to a parallel major, which in turn could serve as dominant, lie at the very heart of tonal structure in Wagner's operas.

The first song in the cycle, "Lied eines Schmiedes," does not immediately disclose that the listener is about to embark on so sophisticated a harmonic or stylistic journey. It is set with almost uniformly strophic regularity, and Schumann permits himself a rare mimetic gesture in this number. The heavily accented open fifths in the left hand alternating with block chords in the right seem at first to invoke the anvil strokes of the smith in the title (see ex. 7.4). But such musical "depiction" is rarely unambiguous: most of the poem describes a horse bearing its rider faithfully to good and pious fortune:

Trag' deinen Herrn	Bear your master
Stets treu dem Stern,	Always true to the star
Der seiner Bahn	That o'er his path
Hell glänzt voran!	Shines brightly on!
Trag' auf dem Ritt	Bear on the ride
Mit jedem Tritt	With every step
Den Reiter du	Your rider
Dem Himmel zu!	Toward heaven!

And so what appears at first to be the slow hammering of an anvil in the accompaniment can also assume the aspect of a loyal mount's steady gait. In these stanzas too we may find the impetus for the celestial symbolism Schumann placed on his cover, as well as for the simple formal treatment and apparently simplistic style.

Example 7.4.   First phrase from "Lied eines Schmiedes."

The folkloric simplicity of "Lied eines Schmiedes" becomes more complicated upon closer inspection, however. For while the artificially limited, diatonic vocabulary and basically even phrases appear straightforward enough, Schumann apportions the verse unusually. At first it seems as if he will combine couplets in Lenau's iambic dimeter into logical two-measure phrases, creating four-measure periods (instead of the usual eight we might find in simple duple meter). But in fact the composer uses the first three lines of each stanza for the first four-measure phrase, and he then repeats the last line twice, augmenting its note values to fashion a consequent unit. Schumann further complicates the picture by displacing the alternating bass in the left hand by a quarter note from the right hand, engendering confusion about whether the singer has entered on an upbeat or a downbeat. The polyrhythm of poetic meter, melody, and accompaniment synchronizes briefly in the second and fifth full measures of each strophe, but never permanently. To complicate this picture further, Schumann omits Lenau's third stanza as incompatible with the mimetic suggestion of the song's accompaniment:

Bergab, bergauf	Uphill, downhill
Mach flinken Lauf,	Make progress fleet,
Leicht wie die Luft	Light as the breeze
Durch Strom und Kluft!	Through stream and pass!

There is nothing "fleet" or "light as the breeze" about Schumann's left hand. And this omission conditioned by the semantic level of the poem reminds us that strophic setting is more challenging than we often imagine. Thus we become aware that the bucolic topos in "Lied eines Schmiedes" does not necessarily equate with naiveté.

"Meine Rose" and "Kommen und Scheiden" both follow in a very different style, more cosmopolitan according to the Dresden taste that predominated in vocal music from Schumann's later period. Both lieder set verse that entails peculiar challenges to a composer, and both organize around repeated motives rather than quadratic lyricism. "Meine Rose" offers Lenau's odd twist on the image of the dying flower, plucked and wilting but with the hope of being revived with water, just as a soul might respond to affection. Schumann would seem to cast doubt on such expectations with a falling motive first articulated in the right hand of the piano prelude against repeated block chords in the left hand. This motive carries over sporadically into the vocal melody, lending it a detached,

soporific air reinforced by random florid turns that derive more from opera than from the lied. The ternary form of the song seems to have been
prompted by the odd structure of Lenau's poem, a sestet followed by an
octave, which Schumann then rounds by repeating the opening sestet and
its music. The poet uses the octave to fashion his simile between restored
flower and restored beloved. Schumann's move to the flatted submediant
(G-flat major) for this sentiment recalls a similar modulation for the inner
section of "Widmung" ten years earlier. But the composer reaches the
distant key here not by common-tone movement but by deceptive cadence on the word "Bronnen." In both songs the technique is striking.
True to the later style, however, the means for accomplishing modulation
in "Meine Rose" is less abrupt, if equally arresting.

The move to G-flat major in the preceding number prepares for its use
as tonic in "Kommen und Scheiden," which unfolds more as arioso than
as aria. Lenau lays out this cryptic tale of a forest encounter over three
brief couplets in iambic pentameter. The persona describes his rapture at
repeatedly beholding a lovely woman in the first couplet, their undisclosed conversation in the second, and then his desolation at her departure in the third. Schumann proceeds logically enough, beginning all
three segments in parallel but moving in the last to a more chromatic palette and slower note values. Throughout the first two parts he punctuates
isolated phrases of Lenau's text with a repeated piano arpeggiation that
holds the vocal interjections together. But as the melody slows for the gesture of farewell in the last couplet, the accompanimental figure changes
and eventually disappears for the main point, "It was as if my last dream
of youth vanished." Then, as if in ironic comment, Schumann develops
his opening piano motive in a lengthy postlude that almost compensates
for the fact that he omitted one of Lenau's rhymes:

Lenau's second couplet	Schumann's version
Und was sie sprach, drang mir zum Herzen ein	Und was sie sprach, drang mir zum Herzen ein,
Süß, wie des Frühlings erstes Lied im Hain.	süss, wie des Frühlings erstes Lied.

Whatever the reason for the composer's omission (deliberate rewriting
seems likely), he did not neglect to respell the G-flat major of the setting's
opening enharmonically to F-sharp major, which then leads as dominant
to the next song, in B major.

"Die Sennin" ("The Milkmaid") presents us with one of Schumann's most haunting late songs, at once beautiful and poignant. The piano accompaniment does not amount to much at first glance, for it functions atmospherically, akin to the passage that Wagner later composed for the rainbow bridge at the end of *Das Rheingold*. In Schuman's song too we find ourselves in the mountains, with a vocal line that reflects an Alpine call in its frequently disjunct motion. A static bass alternates between tonic and dominant pitches before moving unexpectedly to the mediant. The repeated vocal phrases at the beginning result not only from a more quadratic structure, appropriate to the pastoral setting, but also from the echoing of the calls described in the second quatrain. For this reason Schumann logically sets Lenau's second stanza by repeating the music for the first. But from here on the song is cast in bar form, responding to the thought that all things pass away, including the maiden's call. The composer situates the third stanza in the dominant, while its continuous vocal line obscures the poem's clear tetrameter and rhyme scheme. The music for Lenau's fourth stanza quickly becomes immured in a static prolongation of the mediant chord (now major) that played such an important role at the opening. The hills' recollection of the departed *Sennin*'s tones now mingles with regret:

Und verlassen werden stehn,	And abandoned will stand,
Traurig stumm herübersehn	Sadly, mutely gazing at one another
Dort die grauen Felsenzinnen	The gray rock precipices there,
Und auf deine Lieder sinnen.	Reflecting on your songs.

For much of this stanza as well Schumann dispenses with quadratic phrase structure. He augments the note values in the vocal line as a token of mutability in all earthly things, and he supplies a dramatic chromatic ascent for the last couplet. But the disappearance of conventional periodicity and the operatic conclusion should not disturb us: they leave in their wake a delicate nostalgia for an earlier and less complicated time.

One of the more bizarre and intriguing settings of Schumann's late style appears in "Einsamkeit," not only for the way in which it confounds the separation of Lenau's first three stanzas but also for its constantly shifting mode. What at first appears a nonsensical progression of keys enables Schumann to slip from the initial E-flat minor to its submediant (C-flat major, here spelled enharmonically as B) and then back to an E-flat that mutates constantly between parallel major and minor modes. The limpid arpeggiations of the accompaniment reinforce the sense of waywardness engendered by this melancholy chromaticism. And a largely through-composed melody that effaces the division between stanzas (sometimes even between lines of text: "es weht der dich höret und versteht," for instance) also lends the impression of aimless suspension in a vacillating, depressed state. Such a combination of harmonic indecision and lack of melodic periodicity naturally erases almost all hints of the poetry's regular tetrameter and rhyme scheme (*abba*) for Lenau's first three stanzas. The musical uncertainty, however, serves to prepare the last stanza, which Schumann sets apart by a relatively long interlude and begins in a clear E-flat major. This brief stretch of harmonic firmness and quadratic phrasing highlights Lenau's moral:

Nicht verloren hier im Moose,	Not lost here among the moss,
Herz, dein heimlich Weinen geht,	Heart, is your secret weeping,
Deine Liebe Gott versteht,	Your love God comprehends
Deine tiefe, hoffnungslose.	As deep and hopeless.

Metric and harmonic certainty persists only through the second line, however; the last couplet returns, understandably, to chromatic waywardness in minor mode and to melodic asymmetry. When he chose, Schumann still had quadratic style at his disposal as a semantic tool. Here it highlights the one moment of consolation amid the poem's otherwise pervasive despair.

"Der schwere Abend" will elicit a flicker of recognition from listeners who perceive its kinship to one of Schumann's famous earlier songs, "Ich hab' im Traum geweinet." He has reversed the dialogue between the piano and voice, to be sure: in the song from *Dichterliebe,* the voice begins solo while the piano interjects its commentary. In "Sultry Evening" the piano begins and then the voice responds (see ex. 7.5). But the same dotted rhythms in triple meter pervade both E-flat minor songs, and both employ accompanimental block chords to punctuate the vocal line in a recitative-like texture. Indeed, the Heine and Lenau poems exhibit precisely the same number of quatrains scanning and rhyming in exactly the same patterns, with the result that one could interchange their texts. Schumann even accords both poems' three stanzas similar formal treatment: they unfold in three parallel but not identical strophes, with the contrasting final sections set apart by imposing interludes and modulating temporarily to major mode.[24] These similarities also serve, however,

Example 7.5. Beginning of "Der schwere Abend," featuring dialogue between piano and voice.

to emphasize the differences between the early and late styles. Where "Ich hab' im Traum" maintains more quadratic symmetry of phrase, "Der schwere Abend" sets succeeding lines in uneven groupings: a four-measure unit (including interlude) pits melodic duplets against the piano's triple meter, followed by a three-measure unit in normal meter, a four-measure phrase, and then another three-measure unit. The voice ends inconclusively in both songs as well: on a secondary dominant in "Ich hab'," on a deceptive cadence in "Schwere Abend," to underline the chilling import of the last lines, "Anguished, I wished / In my heart both of us dead."

The last lines in "Der schwere Abend" seem to have made for an unacceptably dismal ending even for this very melancholy grouping, and Clara relates, "The songs conclude with a Requiem by Heloise, which Robert sought out in order to close somewhat more gently."[25] Whether Schumann found the text in Leberecht Dreves's *Gedichte* (edited by Eichendorff, 1849) or in his *Lieder der Kirche* (1846), the composer set great store by this ending, separating it by reprinting the original Latin on the verso facing the song's initial page.[26] He heads the poem with the inscription "Requiem. Old Catholic Poem, attributed to Heloise, Abelard's beloved, as author," indicating that even he suspected the provenance of the verse. In order to create a consoling atmosphere for the ending of op. 90, Schumann casts the outer section of the ternary song in a bittersweet E-flat major that often devolves into C minor. And he employs a soporific arpeggiation marked "Im Harfenton" as the accompaniment throughout, in reference to the "angel's harps" in the third stanza of both the Latin and the German.[27]

The phrase structure of this "Requiem" sounds deceptively straightforward in the outer sections (the text of the first stanza repeats as the fourth stanza, even in the Latin original), while the two inner stanzas, circling around an unstable C minor, unfold more freely. But the text poses some unusual challenges in the outer segments, for both the Latin and German versions consist of sestets, with fewer feet in lines 4 and 5:

> Ruh' von schmerzenreichen Mühen,
> Aus und heißem Liebesglühen;
> Der nach seligem Verein
> Trug Verlangen,
> Ist gegangen,
> Zu des Heilands Wohnung ein.

Schumann's setting accords sole precedence to syntax at the expense of poetic form, distributing the first enjambed couplet over one four-measure phrase (shifted to begin in the second half of the common-time bar), casting the next enjambed couplet in a three-measure phrase, and then combining the last enjambed couplet into three and a half measures. This approach highlights the complexity (and odd punctuation) of Dreves's translation and, added to the harmonic ambiguity of the accompaniment, creates a much more involved polyrhythm than its surface betrays. Schumann's seemingly conventional memorial, with its somewhat trite sentiment, nonetheless summons all the lyrical subtlety of his late style.

Drei Gesänge aus Lord Byron's Hebräischen Gesängen für eine Singstimme mit Begleitung der Harfe oder des Pianoforte . . . Fräulein Constanze Jacobi zugeeignet . . . 95tes Werk (composed 5–6 December 1849; published June 1851 by Nicolaus Simrock)

In op. 95, Schumann returned to Byron's "Hebrew Melodies" after touching on them twice before, once in his youthful songs and once in *Myrthen*. His friendship and professional contacts with one of his former students, the singer Constanze Jacobi, most likely provided the impetus to revisit this part of Byron's oeuvre. The alto, most probably of Jewish descent (she married the Jewish actor Bogumil Dawison), had studied with the composer at the Leipzig Conservatory, and he engaged her relatively often as a soloist during his tenure as director of the Dresden

Singverein.[28] She also paid frequent visits to the Schumanns' home in Dresden, providing entertainment at soirées on a number of occasions (she sang at the premiere of op. 90, for instance). In October 1849, a bit before the composition of op. 95, she came for dinner and music making twice, with Robert noting in his household accounts, "Pretty singing."[29] After he had composed the songs in December, he records a trial run of the "Lieder with harp" on 23 December 1849, performed by Jacobi and Heinrich Richter, a Dresden composition student (whether Richter played harp or rendered the accompaniment at the piano we do not know).[30] The sketches of op. 95 reveal that Schumann originally conceived the pieces for voice and harp, since he added the notation "o.[der] das Pianoforte" as an afterthought to the autograph.[31] The December rehearsal may have served to test Schumann's writing.

Harp was not entirely uncommon in accompaniments during the first half of the nineteenth century, but we find it rarely enough in the German lied that its selection has two significant consequences for op. 95. For one thing, Schumann had some difficulty placing the *Drei Gesänge*. He offered them first on 13 January 1850, together with opp. 94 and 101, to Johann August André in Offenbach, who declined "because I do not know whether these particular compositions are suitable for my press."[32] The composer paused to reconsider, then suggested opp. 94, 95, and 108 to Peter Simrock in Bonn on 26 October: "I enclose the titles of some of my compositions, from among which you might select for your press. I do not wish the works published all at once, but over the course of the coming year, which will probably be preferable to you."[33] Simrock accepted, but Schumann did not send a copy of op. 95 for engraving until 16 January 1851 and then proceeded to read proof that spring.[34] The harp accompaniment has also meant that this set receives almost no attention from performers today. The writing in the first and third numbers, while feasible on a piano, sounds more idiomatic for harp, with the result that only the second number, "An den Mond," has even the slightest present-day currency.

Lack of exposure, however, does not mean that op. 95 is entirely unworthy of attention. On the contrary, it stands as one of Schumann's more interesting late sets. Literary critics usually connect Byron's "Hebrew Melodies" to other "ethnic" verse popular in Britain during this period (e.g., Moore's *Irish Melodies*), and in fact the texts originally appeared in songs published by John Braham and Isaac Nathan in 1815.[35]

The poems sometimes refer to specific events in the Old Testament, sometimes not, but all are meant to carry a Levantine flavor. Not surprisingly, many are laments of one kind or another, a nod perhaps to the travails of the Diaspora.

Schumann's settings of Körner's translations nominally belong to the same family as the composer's treatment of Burns. While op. 95 stands squarely in the late style, the reliance on strophic form and the use of an "ethnic" instrument (a reference to David in Byron's "The Harp the Monarch Minstrel Swept")[36] both suggest this conclusion. The set derives coherence not only from its common poet and subject matter but also from related keys, the first song in C minor, the second in its minor dominant, G, and then the third in G minor's relative major, B-flat.

Schumann set "Die Tochter Jeptha's" ("Jeptha's Daughter") "with affect," according to his performance instruction. In consequence it features minor mode, a relatively disjunct melody, and a number of expressive vocal leaps, including both major and augmented sevenths. Byron's text addresses duty more than sorrow—

> Since our Country, our God—Oh, my Sire!
> Demand that thy daughter expire;
> Since thy triumph was bought by thy vow—
> Strike the bosom that's bared for thee now![37]

—and Schumann deviates substantially from Körner's translation of the first verse to emphasize just this point:

Körner's translation of verse 1	Schumann's version
Da die Heimath,—o Vater,—da Gott Von der Tochter verlanget den Tod, Dein Gelübde den Feinden gab Schmerz, Hier—entblösst ist's—durchbohre mein Herz!	Da die Heimath, o Vater, da Gott von der Tochter verlanget den Tod, dein Gelübde vom Feind uns befreit, duchbohr' mich, ich stehe bereit.

The composer may have consulted an alternate translation for this verse,[38] or perhaps he himself fashioned a rendition more faithful to Byron's original. Whatever the case, the rhythm of the vocal melody for the first three quatrains adopts an almost militant anapestic pattern in common time (two eighth notes followed by a quarter), with only one dramatic pause on a held note to emphasize "Tod," "um!" and "Blut" in successive stanzas. For Byron's two final strophes Schumann basically doubles the note values of this pattern, creating a new melody for the fourth stanza. He returns to a variation on the original tune for the fifth with its concluding point, "And forget not I smiled as I died." The accompanimental level of the polyrhythm is considerably less complex for this setting, with chords in the "left" hand, arpeggios in the "right," probably reflecting the choice of harp as supporting instrument.

This same straightforward relationship between accompaniment and melody persists in "An den Mond," Schumann's version of Körner's "Der Mond" (which translates Byron's "Sun of the Sleepless"). The harp (or piano) supports the voice here with either gently rolled chords or "left-hand" chords under "right-hand" arpeggiations, an uncomplicated arrangement that may have addressed the ethnic quality of the song. This setting has other features that we might possibly consider ethnic, including strophic form and relatively quadratic phrases (4+4+3+4+3). Schumann's more conventional approach also aids him in solving several poetic issues. The strophic form divides Körner's (and Byron's) single octave into two manageable quatrains, and the melody's lyrical regularity tames the translation's (and original's) iambic pentameter. Here again, however, the composer is not content to leave Körner's translation alone, introducing such a large number of minor variations that we must wonder again whether Schumann consulted alternate translations or tinkered with his exemplar. For instance,

> So gleams the past, the light of other days,
> Which shines but warms not with its powerless rays;
> A night-beam Sorrow watcheth to behold!
> Distinct, but distant—clear—but, oh how cold!

becomes

Körner's version	*Schumann's version*
So glänzt Vergangenheit ihr fernes Licht,	So glänzt auch längst vergangner Tage Licht,
Es scheint, doch wärmt sein matter Schimmer nicht,	es scheint, doch wärmt sein schwaches Leuchten nicht,
Der wache Gram schaut eines Sterns Gestalt,	der Gram sieht wohl des Stern's Gestalt,
Sichtbar—doch ferne; hell—doch ach! wie Kalt!	sharf, aber fern, so klar, doch ach! wie kalt!

The removal of a poetic foot in the third line is somewhat perplexing, because the composer could easily have fit Körner's version into the measure allotted. Perhaps direct expression took precedence over fidelity to either original English or German translation.

In "Dem Helden" (Byron's "Thy Days Are Done") Schumann offers a bravura piece appropriate to the praise of a fallen warrior. The musical traits entailed in this militant elegy include dramatic alternation between block chords and flourishes in the harp, fanfarelike motives for the voice, predominantly major mode, and rhythms strongly accentuating the beat (see ex. 7.6). At first glance, this strophic setting seems to adopt a quadratic approach, and the composer does in fact deploy Byron's (and correspondingly Körner's) sestets logically enough over three four-measure groupings (the last of these has an extension of one measure). But even the brief excerpt in the musical example reveals that Schumann places the couplets irregularly within the confines of each four-measure grouping. Technically the melody unfolds in three and a half measures, each vocal phrase beginning on an upbeat to the second half of the first measure. This may be a counterintuitive approach to the scansion of the text, but it instills vitality in what could otherwise have been a rather heavy-footed declamation.

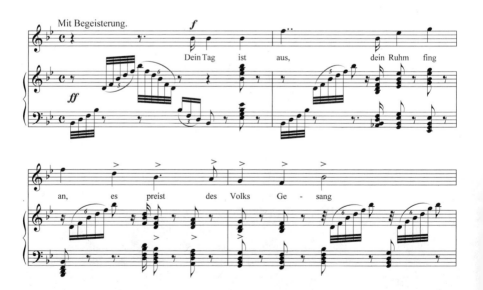

Example 7.6. Harp flourishes and vocal fanfare motives in "Dem Helden."

In this song too Schumann tampers with Körner's translation, arriving at a version slightly closer to the English original. Byron's last stanza, for instance, reads:

> Thy name, our charging hosts along,
> Shall be the battle word!
> Thy fall, the theme of choral song
> From virgin voices poured;
> To weep would do thy glory wrong;
> Thou shalt not be deplored!

Körner captures Byron's meter well enough, but Schumann arrives at a more finely nuanced and arguably more accurate rendition that corresponds better line by line:

Körner's translation	*Text in Schumann's setting*
Dein Name sey dem Heer Signal	Dein Name sei dem Heer Signal,
Begiebt's zum Kampfe sich;	rüstet's zum Kampfe sich;
Und Jungfraun klagen im Choral,	und Jungfraun künden's im Choral,
Dass unser Held erblich!	dass unser Held erblich!
Die Thrän' entweihete dein Mahl,	Es netze keine Thrän' dein Mahl,
Wir weinen nicht um dich!	wir klagen nicht um dich!

It almost seems as if Schumann wanted a more literal take, line for line.

Op. 95 may not count as Schumann's most compelling set of lieder, but it numbers among his most intriguing. Because its translations follow the scansion of their English originals for the most part and because the composer offers more literal translations, we might wonder whether Schumann ever considered a dual-language edition of his *Hebräische Gesänge,* in the manner of the German-Danish version of the Andersen lieder, op. 40. In any event, performance of op. 95 using Byron's verse does not lie outside the realm of possibility. Simply on account of the songs' novel sonority, they at least deserve consideration by vocalists who can secure a proficient harpist. What is more, the use of the harp in this context must raise the question of these pieces' musical "ethnicity." Does op. 95 record Schumann's representation of "Jewish" style in the same way that some of his Burns settings encode a "Scottish" topos? In spite of the fact that the composer occasionally confided anti-Semitic feelings to his diary,[39] his circle always included Jewish friends whom he valued highly and honored. It may be significant that the composer did not use Körner's historical supertitle, "Israelitische Gesänge" ("Israelite Melodies"), but the linguistically oriented label of Byron's originals, "Hebräische Gesänge" ("Hebrew Melodies"). For all these reasons—parallel texts, unusual instrumentation, ethnic association—the *Drei Gedichte* remain a fascinating chapter in Schumann's output of songs.

Sieben Lieder von Elisabeth Kulmann zur Erinnerung an die Dichterin für eine Singstimme mit Begleitung des Pianoforte . . . Op. 104 (composed 28 May–1 June 1851; published October 1851 by Fr. Kistner)

If the *Hebräische Gesänge* offer Schumann's most unusual foray into ethnic color, his group of solo songs on texts by Elisabeth Kulmann represents his oddest encounter with the genre of children's songs. Indeed, the history of the texts themselves verges on the bizarre. In 1835 (and then in seven subsequent, expanded editions until 1857), Karl Friedrich von Großheinrich published *The Collected Poetry of Elisabeth Kulmann* (1808–1825). She was the daughter of a poor Russian army lieutenant who died young, leaving a widow and a large family, most of whom perished in the Napoleonic wars. According to Großheinrich's biography of Elisabeth accompanying the fourth edition of her poetry (Leipzig, 1844), she wrote during her brief seventeen years over one thousand poems in Russian, German, and Italian, poetic fragments and fairy tales in Russian and German, and over 350 letters in German, French, Spanish, Portuguese, Latin, and classic and modern Greek.[40] In Großheinrich's account Elisabeth was a literary prodigy who died tragically young, adoring all the while her dedicated tutor, who just happened to be none other than Großheinrich himself. In the late 1980s and early 1990s, Olga Lossewa began to examine Kulmann's life and works more closely, in the context of Schumann's settings, by researching such basic materials as cemetery records and archival materials, including ostensible autographs. While she found ample evidence for the existence of Kulmann in the former, the handwriting in the surviving "autographs" and in copies made by Großheinrich was essentially identical, no matter the language in which the documents were written. This led Lossewa to suspect that the poetry published under the young lady's name had been heavily edited, completed, or simply fabricated by her former instructor.[41] Großheinrich may well have manufactured the touching story of genius nipped in the bud to effect the publication of his own verse (he would not have been the first eighteenth- or nineteenth-century poet to construct an elaborate ruse of this kind for "children's" or "folk" poetry).

Whatever the actual provenance of the verse published under Kulmann's name, Schumann believed Großheinrich's story. We do not know exactly how the poetry came to the composer's attention, though the short biographical paragraphs interleaved with his songs lead us to surmise that he had access to the combined 1844 biography and poetic anthology.[42] Whatever his source, Schumann's household accounts first note "poems by Elis. Kulmann" on 28 to 29 May 1851 and initial composition of songs from 30 May to 1 June, with an additional song composed on 11 June.[43] All this activity resulted in two collections, opp. 103 and 104, devoted exclusively to Kulmann settings, the former for two female voices and the latter for solo voice. Combined, the two sets comprise eleven songs; Schumann's household accounts list a total of twelve, suggesting that one is no longer extant.[44]

Ulrich Mahlert makes a case for considering op. 104 as a cycle, and he provides many good reasons. The first six numbers fall either in the key of G minor or in its relative major, B-flat. The last number appears in the relatively proximate E-flat major, though by the same token it is unprepared by the G minor final cadence of the penultimate song.[45] Mahlert also finds motivic threads connecting some numbers, but nothing so strong as the rounding in *Frauenliebe* or *Dichterliebe*. He refutes the largely pejorative assessment of previous commentators, who characterize op. 104 as artificially simplistic. Mahlert claims instead that op. 104 belongs to the genre of *Kinderlieder*, much like op. 79. He may overreach, however, in suggesting a progressive stylistic "maturation" over the course of op. 104 and in comparing the Kulmann solo settings to those Schumann provided for Mignon in op. 98a. The Kulmann lieder do exhibit aspects of the late style, but their accompaniments never attain the complexity accorded the *Wilhelm Meister* songs. This distinction resulted from the fact that a literary masterpiece by Goethe, with its subtlety of characterization and accompanying subtexts, demanded more artifice and emotional range, while the verse of a youngster entailed no such expectations, no matter how promising her talent.

Schumann's interest in Kulmann seems to have derived instead from the mid-nineteenth-century preoccupation with the death of children or young women.[46] Like the Lenau songs, the Kulmann lieder represent *memento mori*. If this strikes us today as maudlin, we must remember the relatively high infant and childhood mortality of the period, a fact well known to the Schumanns, who lost their fourth child, Emil, at the age of sixteen months in June 1847. The image of a deceased child, whether real or fictional, touched many nineteenth-century parents in the composer's audience. And it continued to do so as late as the early twentieth century, in Gustav Mahler's retrospective treatment of Rückert's verse on the death of children (to take just one example). Op. 104 presents us with nostalgic recollections à la op. 90 rather than chronological maturation in the manner of op. 79 or character development as in op. 98a. Großheinrich traded on a common sentimental predilection in publishing the poems (whether authentic or invented), and Schumann's rare printed commentary interspersed with his settings caters to the same fashion.

Schumann refers quite explicitly to the trope of a dying child in a preface unparalleled in the rest of his output of solo songs. It begins:

> These modest songs are dedicated to the memory of a girl who ceased to linger among us long ago, and whose name only a very few will recognize. And yet she may have been one of those wonderfully gifted beings who appear but rarely at infrequent intervals on earth. One encounters here the most sublime teachings of wisdom, and one must read for oneself how her life, spent in quiet obscurity, even in deepest poverty, attained the richest blessedness.

We find such sentiments in almost all songs on the death of children and young women from this period, often in just such explicit, prefatory elegies suggesting that the departed innocent was so beautiful (here, intellectually) and pure that she became almost divine (and therefore belonged in a higher plane of existence).

Each song features additional prefatory remarks to reinforce this beatification, the first two chosen to demonstrate Kulmann's devotion to mother and country. In "Mond, meiner Seele Liebling" we find her nursing her sick mother, using the imagery of a "sad" moon lamenting the absence of the ailing sun (the mother sleeps while her anxious daughter waits outside). The song begins as if strophically but finally essays something like bar form, with the first two quatrains set in parallel. But the last three stanzas entail new vocal lines and a departure from the original G minor, settling finally in G major. To reinforce the aura of simplicity, Schumann dispenses with a prelude, and while the right hand does not double the melody often, the minimal piano texture (usually bass notes alternating with chords in the right hand) rarely calls attention to itself.

The interaction between poetic meter and melodic accentuation proves more complex, for Schumann ignores the iambic pattern of the *Langzeilenvers* at will, sometimes placing the anacrusis on the beat (rather than on an eighth-note upbeat). The composer intimates simplicity of form and declamation but produces something more subtle, as Mahlert suggests.[47]

Schumann chose "Viel Glück zur Reise, Schwalben!" as a token of Kulmann's patriotism, and he links it to the previous picture of devotion (familial) by adapting the head motive of the piano postlude in "Mond" for the head motive of the vocal part in the second number.[48] The tag also helps to bridge the odd juxtaposition of keys, which finds the concluding G major in "Mond" progressing to the B-flat major of "Viel Glück" (though in the Dresden scheme of things, the underlying relationship of G major to B-flat major came by way of modal shift from G minor). The composer parses the poem's three stanzas logically enough in ternary form (ABA′), though the distribution of the *Langzeilenvers* is, not unexpectedly, rather more complicated. Some lines fit into the predictable two measures, but Schumann often uses the silent foot of each even-numbered line as an excuse to compress the pattern, placing "zum schönen warmen Süden," for instance, where a piano interlude would have filled the void in quadratic style. He elongates "frohem" and "kühnen" to arrive at an eight-measure setting for the quatrain nonetheless. If the declamation is less than straightforward, however, the accompaniment presents a very uncomplicated profile, something more reminiscent of Schubert's "Die Forelle" than of Schumann's later style.

The next two numbers, "Du nennst mich armes Mädchen" and "Der Zeisig," offer two contrasting depictions of childhood. Schumann casts the first, unhappy one logically enough in G minor, imagining that "[Elisabeth] was often reproached by uncomprehending children for her poverty; the following song is a reply to this." Though this poem also falls in *Langzeilenvers*, the composer effaces the meter and scansion almost entirely with a setting that begins more like recitative, which he supports with held chords. The song ends as arioso, but the through-composed melody blunts even this intimation of lyricism, as do the elision of lines and the indistinct division of quatrains. Only the repetition of the opening phrase at the very end suggests any kind of formal coherence in a setting designed to emphasize dramatic pathos. "Der Zeisig" ("The Finch"), "a song from earliest maidenhood, written perhaps in her eleventh year," reverts by way of contrast to the happy simplicity of a children's song in B-flat major. It comes as close as anything in op. 104 to quadratic setting, though closer inspection reveals a succession of three- rather than four-measure phrases. The relatively diatonic, effervescent accompaniment may remind us of something out of the early sections of op. 79 (say, "Marienwürmchen"), and even the brief diversion to E-flat major ("Komm', singen") barely clouds this impression. The song runs by so quickly and unassumingly that Schumann marks it *Da capo ad libitum.*

Having beatified Kulmann by detailing her devotions and her innocent sorrows and joys, Schumann turned finally to the central event in such narratives, the demise of one too beautiful and pure to tarry in sordid realms below. The first stage, in "Reich' mir die Hand, o Wolke," involves presentiments of departing earthly existence; the second, in "Die letzten Blumen starben," entails resignation to this inevitable fate; and the third, in "Gekämpft hat meine Barke," constitutes the actual farewell. "Reich' mir die Hand" takes the form of a stereotypical vision often found in deathbed scenes, the comforting thought of imminent encounters with those who have "gone before" and who stand ready to usher the dying safely into the hereafter. In this particular case the young woman beholds her deceased brothers awaiting her by "the open gates of heaven" in the first stanza, she sees her father among them in the second, and they reach out to her in the third. Such sentiments consoled the living as much as the mortally ill, since they provided assurances that the person dying would have company on her journey and would reunite with the previously "loved and lost." The poetry for this scenario is unremarkable, a predictable *Langzeilenvers* grouped in cross-rhymed quatrains. But Schumann chooses to ignore the demands of poetic structure in favor of melodramatic atmosphere, which he creates by using sixteenth-note tremolos in the right hand of the piano, by overriding the boundaries between stanzas, and by avoiding direct melodic repetition (the last phrase rounds, however, by repeating the opening phrase, mirroring the poetic refrain). Minor mode, a number of wide, expressive leaps in the vocal part, and a certain amount of chromaticism complete the affecting picture, and the simplicity of the piano texture (the paucity of contrapuntal lines in the inner voices and the relatively slow-moving left hand) reinforces the melodrama of the visualization.

The atmospherics of "Reich' mir die Hand" prepare its successor, "Die letzten Blumen starben," by way of dramatic contrast. The songs share the same key (G minor), are cast in the same verse form, and set out stereotyped images in three stanzas. "Die letzten Blumen" cannot help but remind us of "'Tis the Last Rose of Summer," with its conceit of withering flowers as a metaphor for the end of human life. Kulmann's (or Großheinrich's) "Then why should I not fade, / If roses themselves fade" invariably recalls Thomas Moore's "When true hearts lie withered, / And fond ones are flown, / Oh! who would inhabit / This bleak world alone?" Schumann responds with a setting that appears more conventional on its surface: an accompaniment of alternating bass notes and block chords supports a bar form. But the ambitus of the voice in the A section of the bar is severely limited, confined almost exclusively to a fourth (with the exception of one expressive leap at the end of the segment), reiterating many pitches in a declamatory monotone. The composer deploys the verse oddly over a fairly regular set of two-bar phrases that do not always preserve the integrity of the poetic line. The B section of the bar affords a diversion from G minor to E-flat major, at the same time expanding the range of the vocal melody considerably. Schumann clearly wanted to emphasize the sentiment just quoted, and he therefore devotes more expression to it, reinforcing it with a more regular phrase structure. But the simplicity of the accompaniment and the lack of true lyricism combine to lend an overall impression of flattened affect.

Following on the heels of "Die letzten Blumen," "Gekämpft hat meine Barke" provides the kind of release that Schumann had sought for the "Requiem" in op. 90. He may foreshadow the E-flat major in this concluding song just a bit in the B section of the preceding number, but it mainly stands in contrast to the pervasive B-flat major and G minor of all the other selections. In "Gekämpft" the departing maiden performs the stereotypical last act in the ritual of the dying child by consoling her mother, who remains behind:

O Mutterherz, dich drücke	O mother's heart, be not oppressed
Dein Schmerz nicht allzusehr!	By pain so oversore!
Nur wenig Augenblicke	Only a few moments
Trennt uns des Todes Meer.	Will death's sea divide us.
Dort angelangt, entweiche	Arriving there, depart
Ich nimmermehr dem Strand:	Shall I ne'er that shore:
Seh' ich nach dir, und reiche	I'll look for you, stretch out
Der Landenden die Hand.	My hand when you land o'er.

Because of its consoling function, "Gekämpft" is the most lyrical song in the Kulmann set, an "aria" that serves as swan song. The accompaniment again supports the voice here with an uncomplicated texture, though the entrance of the right hand on the offbeats of each bar produces a certain amount of animation (see ex. 7.7). The melodic line in the two outer sections in this ternary form tends toward arched phrases that may not produce bel canto exactly but come as close as Schumann does in any of his songs. He eschews these graceful melodic shapes only for the second quatrain, which conjoins the inevitability of death with the mother's pain. But discordant harmonies soon end, and after the melody for the last quatrain rounds the form, the composer permits the accompaniment an extended denouement that makes use of expressive appoggiaturas and retardations. "Gekämpft" counts as one of the loveliest songs from Schumann's late period and would be one of the most often performed, were it not for subject matter that suits it exclusively for the ending of op. 104.

The Kulmann lieder leave us today at a loss, for they feature conceits no longer considered appropriate to "classical" music. The astringency of modernism deals well with graphic depictions of violent death and with the anger occasioned by loss, but it addresses the overtly sentimental melancholy of grief and mourning unwillingly. Schumann's op. 104 pursued stereotypical narrative paths of its time, but these have become passé in high art. And so we have marginalized his Kulmann lieder—never the most prepossessing of his creations for solo voice, admittedly, but not a particularly lugubrious or maudlin exercise in the broader context of his own day.

Example 7.7.   Opening phrase of "Gekämpft hat meiner Barke."

Drei Gedichte aus den Waldliedern von S [recte G]. Pfarrius für eine Singstimme mit Begleitung des Pianoforte . . . 119tes Werk (composed 27 September 1851; published May 1853 by Adolph Nagel)

How exactly Schumann came upon the poetry of Gustav Pfarrius (1800–1884) remains something of a mystery. Pfarrius studied theology and philology at Halle and Bonn, settling finally as a *gymnasium* instructor, first in Saarbrücken and then after 1834 in Cologne. Up to 1850, when he published *Die Waldlieder,* from which Schumann culled the three poems in op. 119, Pfarrius was not especially prolific, with one collection and the epic poem *Karlmann* to his credit. But between 1850 and 1869 he published six anthologies of poetry and short stories, and he may have appeared as a new face to Schumann during the composer's Düsseldorf period.[49] If Schumann encountered the poet personally (entirely plausible, given Schumann's visits to nearby Cologne), he gives no indication in his household accounts. In fact, these abbreviated diaries record Pfarrius's name only once, on 27 September 1851, by way of mentioning the composition of "2 Lieder." These became the first and second numbers in op. 119, according to the autograph in the collection of the Paris Bibliothèque nationale, though Schumann entered only the texts for numbers one and three in his and Clara's copies of poetry meant for setting.[50] In the same section of that compendium the composer also noted "49," the page in *Die Waldlieder* on which the poetry for the second number in op. 119 appears, though he did not copy out its text.[51] To complicate matters further, we cannot tell for certain when Schumann composed the third number in the set, though most scholars assume that the September 1851 date in the autograph applies to "Der Bräutigam und die Birke" as well.[52]

The folkloric scenes in Pfarrius's verse apparently account for Schumann's attraction, and though the poems could assume a somber aspect (as "Warnung" demonstrates), the composer seemed more taken with the cheerful side of the *Waldlieder* evinced in op. 119's outer numbers. Schumann took his time publishing the set, laying it aside for almost a year after its composition before offering it in September 1852 to Adolph Nagel in Hanover. Schumann sent the manuscript for op. 119 in October, and Nagel promptly accepted,[53] perhaps on the basis of the intriguing variety entailed in its ordering of numbers. The engraving went badly at first, requiring a second set of galleys, for which Schumann pressed "on account of a surprise for Christmas."[54] In the event, the final proofs did not arrive until 10 January 1853, and publication was delayed until May.[55] The long gestation of the printing may also have resulted from a particularly elaborate cover engraving (festooned with floral sprays and fronds of greenery) that made reference to the forest hut in the first song and the birch tree in the third. Since the composer bestowed his Mary Stuart songs on Clara at Christmas 1852 (see Chapter 6), we might speculate that he intended this decorative "surprise" for the dedicatee of op. 119, Mathilde Hartmann, a Düsseldorf soprano intimate with Robert and Clara's family circle and godmother to Felix Schumann.

The *Drei Gedichte* taken together present no coherent narrative, nor do they constitute a cycle in any meaningful sense of the word. The set fits together tonally, however, to the extent that the composer casts the outer numbers in G major. The inner song rests in B minor, with a somewhat ambiguous ending on a second-inversion tonic that tends toward the relative major of D (the B in the voice drops out and the B grace note in the piano fades away, leaving only D and F-sharp). But the highly disparate style of the three songs precludes any strong progression.

"Die Hütte" begins this rustic collection with an appropriately jaunty march that finds Schumann in his most conventionally quadratic mode, at least at its outset. His setting of Pfarrius's first stanza features diatonic harmonic language and staccato support of the text by an unobtrusive accompaniment that offers minimal prelude, interludes, and postlude. Indeed, the piano largely doubles a vocal line (see ex. 7.8) that distributes Pfarrius's iambic tetrameter over fairly predictable four-bar phrases. The composer indulges only minimal displacement of the text toward the end of the quatrain with a two-measure extension created by repeating the last line. We cannot help but think of Schumann's setting for "Der frohe

Example 7.8. Entrance of the voice in "Die Hütte."

Wandersmann," initially published at the head of the Eichendorff *Lieder-kreis* before finding its way into op. 77 (discussed in Chapter 8).

Schumann invokes this conventional response to our first glimpse of the forest hut as the touchstone in a five-part rondo suggested by a refrain in Pfarrius's poem. His first stanza ("Im Wald, in grüner Runde") returns, varied but with parallel rhymes, in the fourth stanza ("Im Wald zur guten Stunde") and yet again more exactly in the seventh and last stanza. With the "rondo theme" in place, the composer then combines the second and third stanzas and the fifth and sixth stanzas to fill out the traditional five-part scheme (ABABA'). The "episodes" alternating with the rondo theme indulge harmonic excursions and feature less conventionally quadratic declamation of the verse, as we might expect. But the rondo scheme itself appears quite familiar, and the overall impression it leaves will strike listeners as unproblematic, folklorically straightforward, and unsophisticated.

"Warnung" adopts a different tone, one that would seem at first to summon Schumann's late style in response to its ominous text:

Es geht der Tag zur Neige,	Then comes the decline of day,
Der Licht und Freiheit bot,	Which offered light and freedom,
O schweige, Vöglein, schweige,	Be still, little bird, be still,
Du singst dich in den Tod.	Lest singing bring you death.
Die Winde nächtlich rauschen,	The nighttime winds rustle,
Die Blätter zittern bang,	The leaves tremble anxiously,
Den Feinden, die drin lauschen,	To the enemies who lurk within,
Verräth dich dein Gesang[.]	Your song betrays you.

First impressions can deceive, however, and a moment's reflection will summon another glint of reminiscence: "Warnung" resonates strongly with an earlier Schumann setting of foreboding, "Zwielicht," again from the Eichendorff *Liederkreis*. For the Pfarrius poem the composer employs only falling arpeggios in a minor-mode accompaniment that introduces syncopation to the pattern. But the earlier topos applies all the same as a response to an atmosphere of suspicion and dread. In this same vein, the phrase structure and overall form in "Warnung" are hardly unexpected: each line of the original text unfolds in the space of two measures (albeit offset unusually in each unit so as not to land on the first beat). Moreover, Schumann distributes Pfarrius's three stanzas over a perfectly comprehensible bar form. The singer's line, on the other hand, does reflect the affective idiosyncrasy of the composer's later practice. The vocal melody features no exact repetition within a given stanza and has a number of wide, expressive leaps, including a tense ending on the highest pitch at the close of each A section of the bar. The overall effect is unsettling, combining as it does the familiar and the exotic in counterpoint with one another.

In Schumann's last number for op. 119, "Der Bräutigam und die Birke," we discover one of the infrequent miniature ballads among his later collections. Pfarrius's poem unfolds as a dialogue in much the same manner as in Hebbel's "Sag' an, o lieber Vogel mein," which Schumann had set in 1847 and placed in the incongruously numbered op. 27. Hebbel's ballad introduced a narrator at its conclusion, but Pfarrius confines himself solely to the progressive interrogation of the birch tree by the bridegroom. The story recounted in the exchange is both lighthearted and just a bit touching. After the young man divulges his imminent wedding, he asks repeatedly what gifts the birch tree might offer. The obliging tree proffers leafy bouquets, a switch for the children, twigs to make a broom, a whip for the horse, and sap to make wine. At each offer the bridegroom asks for yet more, and finally the birch tree has nothing left but its very life, which the young man takes to provide heat for his cabin. Schumann sets the exchange quite differently from his earlier ballads, partly in consequence of the form taken by Pfarrius's verse. The poet devotes an initial and final quatrain to statements by the bridegroom, but the rest of the interchange, including all of the birch tree's utterances, takes place in couplets. Quite logically, then, the composer accords different musical styles to the two characters: the young man adopts an optimistic, assertive, and relatively diatonic march in G major as his topos, but the birch tree's answers take a more chromatic and rhythmically hesitant tone. As the interrogation proceeds, the birch tree's responses run further and further afield harmonically (see Table 7.1), though the bridegroom usually leads the conversation back to the home key. Only when he comes to the final throw does the young man venture away from G to the relative minor of E, which the unfortunate tree adopts ruefully in its reply, realizing that its time is at hand. The alternation provides a charming set of contrasts between four-square march and parlando supplications, and the song therefore cleverly links the folkloric tone of op. 119's first song and the more urbane style of the second by juxtaposing both in one number.

Drei Gedichte aus den Waldliedern von G. Pfarrius offers a brief, un-

Table 7.1   Progressive dialogue in "Der Bräutigam und die Birke"

Speaker	Content	Key Area
Bridgegroom	Introduces subject of wedding and gifts	G
Birch Tree	Offers green bouquet	D
Bridegroom	Accepts, asks for more	G
Birch Tree	Offers a switch	a
Bridegroom	Accepts, asks for more	G
Birch Tree	Offers a broom	e
Bridegroom	Accepts, asks for more	G
Birch Tree	Offers a whip	G
Bridegroom	Accepts, asks for more	G
Birch Tree	Offers sap for wine	C
Bridegroom	Accepts, asks for more	e
Birch Tree	Has nothing left to offer but its life	e
Bridegroom	Fells the tree for heat	G

assuming conclusion to the parade of poets discussed above. Still, it shows that even at the end of his life, Schumann interested himself occasionally in folkloric themes that fell more in the realm of cheerful than of bleak subjects. But for all the affinities between its components, op. 119 does not form a song cycle in any reasonable sense of the word. The set coheres only in respect to the authorship of one poet, its rural setting, and its tonal rounding. This is less than we find in a cycle, even less than in a *Liederreihe,* but more than we find in a miscellany, though as we have seen, and will see again in the next chapter, even Schumann's seemingly miscellaneous collections often have principles guiding the inclusion of various numbers.

8

Collections in the New Style

If we map the patterns applied to the anthologies examined in Chapters 4 and 5 onto the "miscellanies" of Schumann's later period, using the same assumptions and strategies with which we contemplated those collections, then we run the risk of presenting a seriously distorted view. The composer generally assembled his earlier miscellanies retrospectively from unused portions of the immense output he produced in 1840 and 1841 (with the occasional addition of later songs). However much he strove for some degree of logic and coherence in the four volumes of *Romanzen und Balladen* and the first two volumes of *Lieder und Gesänge,* their constituent pieces often originated in compositional activity spread over quite disparate stretches of time. Schumann might have achieved fortunate combinations in these collections, and he might have constructed satisfactory "programs" from compositionally unrelated bits. But as clever and imaginative as he could be, he was limited by the scattered origin of the components he assembled.

The collections considered in this chapter, opp. 77, 83, 96, 107, and 125, frequently present a different picture. With some notable exceptions, their compositional histories often fall into more coherent spans of time. Though they are anthologies in the sense that they collect various poets in one volume, small groups of songs or whole collections often arose over a period of weeks or even a few days. To the extent of the chronological proximity between numbers, we may search for stronger underlying musical and poetic interrelatedness. And this in turn tests one of the central tenets of this study: that Schumann regarded his published assemblies of lieder in some way as "works," albeit nowhere near as closely knit as multimovement instrumental genres might be.

Many of the volumes in this chapter collect the work of poets we have examined before, and one of the questions arising from the setting of different authors in one opus must concern how Schumann saw their poems as suitable for juxtaposition. By the same token, we might ask whether texts by the same poet composed during a relatively short period but appearing in different volumes could nevertheless reflect the composer's focus on that author (which often resulted in volumes devoted solely to his or her work, as we have just seen). Cross-sectioned in these different ways, the study of the late anthologies yields information about the changing attitude toward the lied at mid-century, its move from the home into the concert hall and from amateur performance to professional rendition.

Two More Volumes of Lieder und Gesänge

Lieder und Gesänge für eine Singstimme mit Begleitung des Pianoforte . . . Heft III, Op. 77 ("Der frohe Wandersmann" by Eichendorff, composed 22 June 1840; "Mein Garten" by Hoffmann von Fallersleben, composed 30 July 1850; "Geisternähe" by Halm, composed 18 July 1850; "Stiller Vorwurf" by Wolff, composed 11 June 1850; "Aufträge" by L'Égru, composed 11 April 1850; published March 1851 by F. Whistling)

Opus 77 had an oddly checkered genesis, which can serve as an exemplar, Nicholas Marston suggests, for the process by which Schumann arrived at such compilations.[1] Implored repeatedly by Johann André in Offenbach, beginning in the fall of 1849, to submit compositions, especially songs, for publication by his house, the composer dispatched a series of manuscripts for consideration, all of which were promptly rejected. These included the Four Fugues for Piano, op. 72, the ballad for choir and brass instruments, *Beim Abschied zu singen,* op. 84, the *Three Romances* for oboe and piano, op. 94, the Byron songs, op. 95, the *Minnespiel* by Rückert, op. 101, and the *Lieder, Gesänge und Requiem* from *Wilhelm Meister,* opp. 98a and 98b.[2] In his letters of refusal André constantly cited his desire for songs in the manner of op. 42 (*Frauenliebe und Leben*) or the recently published op. 79 (*Lieder für die Jugend*)—predominantly pieces in quadratic style. The publisher even went so far as to advance an honorarium of fifteen louis d'or as an enticement, and at his wits' end, Schumann finally dispatched on 11 August 1850 "a volume of eight songs, mostly of cheerful content," adding, "I find it appropriate to list the titles of the individual songs on the title page. With two-page songs one should take care not to have any page turns."[3] His index of correspondence records that he sent a letter "together with the 'bright songs.' Should [André] not want these, I would return his honorarium."[4] But nothing pleased the publisher, as his reply on 17 August reveals:

> My wish to have your works for my press was a sincere one. This you will recognize. I also exerted myself to indicate what songs would suit my press, for instance op. 42 and the new op. 89, dedicated to Jenny Lind.
>
> If you occasionally wish to give me such songs, I will gladly pay the same honorarium you have received for others, even something more.
>
> Presently I consider it best if you send me back by post the fifteen louis d'or, less the postage incurred.[5]

Schumann must have eaten his hat in frustration, but he dutifully returned the money.

We know from a manuscript title page preserved in the Paris Bibliothèque nationale[6] that the "colorful songs" included four of the songs that found their way ultimately into op. 77, as Table 8.1 (after Marston) demonstrates. We can see the tonal planning evident in the sequence of keys, which takes A as a tonic and explores the flatted supertonic, the dominant, and the subdominant. The four songs from this abandoned project that found their way into op. 77 already lay in close proximity and had strong tonal connections (especially if one removes "Husarenabzug" from between "Stiller Vorwurf" and "Aufträge"). With some minor rearranging, Marston demonstrates, the pairing of op. 77, nos. 2 and 3 and op. 77, nos. 4 and 5 exists here *in nuce*.[7]

When André rejected the proposed "op. 92," Schumann quickly began to make alternate plans for some of the songs on 24 August 1850, logically enough with the publisher of earlier anthologies, Friedrich Whistling.[8] The composer took some time to hit on the contents and ordering for this shorter volume, originally designated as op. 87. By October the firm of Whistling apparently had the manuscript in its hands,[9] though the press took its time in releasing the print to the public. Now positioned as the third volume of *Lieder und Gesänge* in the series already begun and renumbered op. 77, the collection began with "Der frohe Wandersmann," in D major, recently cast off from the Eichendorff *Liederkreis*.

Table 8.1   Annotated Contents of Schumann's Title Page for the "Bunte
Lieder, Op. 92" Proposed to André

Song Title (poet)	Key	Date of Composition	Ultimate Disposition
"Frühlingslied" (Braun)	A	24 July 1850	op. 125, no. 1
"Stiller Vorwurf" (Wolff)	a	11 June 1850	op. 77, no. 4
"Husarenabzug" (Candidus)	B♭	25 July 1850	op. 125, no. 5
"Aufträge" (L'Egru)	A	12 April 1850	op. 77, no. 5
"Mein altes Ross" (Strachwitz)	e	1 August 1850	op. 127, no. 4
"Frühlingslust" (Heyse)	D	13 July 1850	op. 125, no. 2
"Mein Garten" (Fallersleben)	a	30 July 1850	op. 77, no. 2
"Geisternähe" (Halm)	A	18 July 1850	op. 77, no. 3

Marston, "Schumann's *Lieder und Gesänge*," 83.

The volume continued with "Mein Garten" and "Geisternähe," the ending pair of the "Bunte Lieder," progressing from minor to major in A, and concluded with "Stiller Vorwurf" and "Aufträge," another minor-major juxtaposition in A.

The key and incongruity of style between "Wandersmann" and the remaining four numbers must lead us to question Schumann's motivation. One facile answer to the placement of "Wandersmann" might simply lie in the popularity of the poem (first song from *Leben eines Taugenichts*), on which the composer still wished to capitalize after he had detached it from op. 39 (see Chapter 3). But this initial number portends wayfaring so strongly that it bids us search for some common features of the wanderer's cycle, and these we can find in a loose way. After departure from the idealized homeland in op. 77, we encounter the loss of and search for love in "Mein Garten," nostalgic homesickness for sundered affection in "Geisternähe," resignation to dismissal in "Stiller Vorwurf," and one of the several classic endings in greetings borne to a distant beloved by nature in "Aufträge."[10] All of these features invoke the stereotypes of wayfaring cycles while falling far short of any implied narrative. But then, we observed in Chapter 3 that even wanderer's cycles often lack tightly knit plots.

Marston suggests that the stylistic incongruity between the 1840 Eichendorff setting and the remaining 1850 songs finds some mitigation in the strophic treatment and more sprightly rhythmic motion of "Aufträge," which establishes the concluding margin of a frame for op. 77 as a whole.[11] But he makes an even more telling case for the interconnection of internal harmonic idiosyncrasies among the numbers that a simple chart of their tonic keys cannot reveal. Though the first number in op. 77 features a tonic of D major, it migrates often to its dominant of A, at the end of the first stanza and most prominently at the beginning of the last stanza ("Den lieben Gott nur lass ich walten"), which takes its time modulating back to D only for the last line ("hat auch mein' Sach' auf's Best' bestellt"). In fact, to reestablish the tonic of D securely, Schumann repeated this line and then appended an eight-measure postlude. In other words, the pervasive A tonic of the remaining songs does not go unprepared in "Der frohe Wandersmann." By the same token, the pairing of "Mein Garten" and "Geisternähe," juxtaposed in the discarded set of "Bunte Lieder," strongly emphasizes the key of D in transition. "Mein Garten" closes inconclusively on an A major chord in second inversion that emphasizes the first-inversion B minor chord that opens "Geisternähe" (we do not arrive securely in A until the middle of last line of the first stanza, which ends nonetheless on a half-cadence).[12] Neither of the last two songs involves D nearly to this extent, but the voice in "Stiller Vorwurf" does end prominently on the pitch of D in the upper part of the vocal range, and the song concludes with a plagal cadence. "Aufträge" rests very firmly in A but ends literally up in the air, with a piano chord articulating C-sharp (leading tone to D) as its highest pitch. We cannot claim strong tonal rounding for op. 77 as whole, then, but the opening D major of "Frohe Wandersmann" aside, the remaining songs pair quite neatly into A minor-A major, with the initial member of each duo featuring a minimal accompaniment and declamatory vocal melody, while its partner follows in more lyrical style with a more highly figured and active accompaniment.

"Der frohe Wandersmann" appeared in some detail earlier (see Chapter 3, ex. 3.6), but the remaining four songs in op. 77 were new. Though we have encountered Hoffmann von Fallersleben earlier in the context of op. 79, "Mein Garten" originates in a different context from the poetry selected for his *Lieder für die Jugend,* which came from the poet's collections of folklike *Kinderlieder.* In op. 77 we find verse in an adult and more melancholic voice, from a section of poetry its author labels "Love and Passion" ("Lieben und Leiden"). Poems in this vein naturally elicit from Schumann a far more subtle response than children's songs. He assigns the lyrics a title (von Fallersleben gave them none), and he then supports his choice with common time marked "nicht schnell," a meter and tempo appropriate to a slow stroll around "My Garden." The regularity of the initial piano accompaniment reinforces this conceit, just as minor mode responds naturally enough to the persona's misfortune in love. To these relatively understandable selections, the composer adds what at first seems a straightforward declamation of von Fallersleben's trochaic tetrameter in normal four-measure phrases. We receive a hint early on, though, that Schumann does not want to treat the speaker's distraction so rationally: he changes the original wording of the poem's third line from "Lilien, Tausendschön und Rosen" to "Lilien, Tausendschönchen, Rosen." This line occasions a flurry of eighth notes, and it prepares a disintegration of the persona's "stroll." He or she pauses at the first line of the second stanza over a bit of recitative-like accompaniment, resumes for the second line, then pauses again at "nur das Glück"; that is, "the happiness of love" does not grow among the flowers. The composer emphasizes this thought with a modulation to F major for the word "nicht!" The stroll has given way to purposeless drifting, the placement of the text to pensive hesitation. Von Fallersleben writes that the heart can take comfort in the attempt to seek love, but Schumann's speaker remains unconsoled. And though the song regains A minor for its last phrases, the voice ends on a questioning note by rising stepwise to a high E rather than falling to the tonic of A.

The halting and uncertain conclusion of "Mein Garten" plays directly into "Geisternähe," both by tonal movement and release in mood. Where Hoffmann von Fallersleben's verse mourns failed romance, Friedrich Halm's poem, from a section of his *Gedichte* titled "Hochzeitlieder" ("Wedding Songs"), extends hope by means of thoughts about a distant beloved. Friedrich Halm was the pen name of Eligius Franz Joseph Freiherr von Münch-Bellinghausen (1806–1871), a Viennese poet born in Cracow who ultimately rose to high estate as the head curator of the imperial collections (libraries and natural sciences), intendant of the court theaters, and privy counselor. Schumann much enjoyed a performance of Halm's *Griseldis* at the Viennese Burgtheater in 1838 and tried unsuccessfully to solicit an opera libretto from him in April 1845.[13] "Geisternähe" is the only Halm poem set by the composer, and he accords it a highly lyrical treatment that hearkens back in certain respects to his earlier, quadratic style. He preserves the integrity of line in Halm's *Langzeilenvers* by proceeding in regular two-measure groupings, which unfold at first over a periodic melody. The first quatrain receives two parallel phrases, the second likewise. This tends to create a double strophe, and in the second half of the song Schumann borrows just enough melodic figures from the first half to suggest a varied strophic setting (for instance, m. 23 in the voice part—"Name ist's, der"—slightly resembles m. 7—"spielt um meine"). The second double strophe remains periodic until the last quatrain, when the composer breaks from the strictures of paired, repeated phrases to emphasize Halm's point, "Ich fühle deine Nähe!" The accompanimental figuration reinforces this impression of combined stanzas set strophically by switching from arpeggiation to block chords between pairs of quatrains. All this comforting regularity conveys the persona's confidence and hope, which Schumann then lends an ecstatic aura through expressive leaps in the vocal part. "Geisternähe" may be too predictable to represent one of Schumann's most inspired efforts from his late period, but it certainly forms a lovely contrast to the tentative dejection of the preceding Hoffmann von Fallersleben setting.

As Marston observes, the last two songs in op. 77 form another pair, with "Stiller Vorwurf" as the more declamatory, irregular, and melancholic antecedent. Schumann probably encountered the text for this song in *Liederbuch des deutschen Volkes,* edited by Karl von Hase and published in Leipzig during 1843.[14] There it appears as a "folk song" with no attribution, and the composer accordingly labels it as originating in a "broadsheet" ("Fliegendes Blatt") for his edition of op. 77. In fact the poem comes from the pen of Oskar Ludwig Bernhard Wolff (1799–1851), a Jewish author who converted to Christianity when he assumed a post at a Weimar grammar school. He subsequently held an irregular chair in modern literature at the University of Jena, his alma mater, but his early promise as an author did not gain him lasting fame, and Schumann did not knowingly set any of his poetry.[15] The significant point here lies in the fact that the composer believed "Stiller Vorwurf" to have folkloric origins. In the probable source for the poem, it appears not only in a section of "Liebeslieder" but also under the title "Volkslied, nach der Weise eines Walzers" ("Folk Song in the Manner of a Waltz").[16] Thus Schumann's decision to set Wolff's clichéd dactylic dimeter in common time and in the style of ultra-inflected recitative represents a deliberate subversion of the verse's fundamental nature. It would not be quite fair to say that the verse for "Stiller Vorwurf" would fit the tune of "Zu Lauterbach hab' ich mein Strumpf verloren" exactly, but it is close. Yet Schumann's halting harmonic language—the piano punctuating an irregularly placed vocal line with chromatic chords—diametrically opposes the idea of a "broadsheet," that is, verse published as a popular contrafact. We must guess that, as so often happens in the composer's later style, he reacted more to the semantic than to the metrical level of the poem. He observes line endings as it suits him, sometimes emphasizing what seem to be perverse enjambments, sometimes according privilege to syntax. Schumann gives the performance indication "more and more passionately," but he contradicts even this by casting the song in ternary form, though ending the A′ section with an interrogative phrase rising to a D (another brief reference to that important note in the context of op. 77). It is as if the persona does not believe in the poem's message of ultimate forgiveness, a disquieting thought emphasized by the pervasive disjunction in the song's polyrhythm at every level.

The unease engendered by "Stiller Vorwurf" prepares the vivacious effervescence of Christian L'Egru's "Aufträge" most effectively, and this setting is worthwhile, however inconsequential the verse and minor the poet. We know virtually nothing about L'Egru, whose only published volume of poetry, *Das Gewächshaus. Eine Sammlung selbstgezogener Blumen* (Magdeburg, 1851), contains neither of the poems set by Schumann.[17] But Schanze and Schulte venture the highly plausible guess that the poet enclosed the verse as part of a letter to the composer on 6 April 1850: "I take the liberty of sending you, my good sir, the enclosed song texts. It would make me very happy, if you were to consider them worthy of ennobling them with your music."[18] The actual verse enclosed with the letter has disappeared, but Schumann records the composition of "Aufträge" six days later, on 12 April, in his household accounts.[19] This chronology evinces yet again the composer's generosity toward new authors, together with his strong desire to remain au courant.

The text of "Aufträge," as we can piece it together from Schumann's song, also appears to document yet again his occasional predilection for dealing with problematic verse that he could elevate by means of his setting. In the absence of a source for the poem, Schulte and Schanze posit six parallel sestets in trochaic tetrameter with the rhyme scheme *aabcbc*. This seems reasonable enough, except for the fact that each second stanza ends with a slightly varied four-line refrain (in my italics):

Nicht so schnelle, nicht so schnelle!
wart' ein wenig, kleine Welle!
will dir einen Auftrag geben
an die Liebste mein.
Wirst du ihr vorüber schweben,
grüsse sie mir fein!

sag', ich wäre mitgekommen,
auf dir selbst herabgeschwommen:
für den Gruss einen Kuss
kühn mir zu erbitten,
doch der Zeit Dringlichkeit,
hätt' es nicht gelitten.

We might begin to suspect a different arrangement: groups of twelve lines or possibly octaves with a quatrain serving as refrain. However this might be, Schumann sets the text strophically in groups of twelve, which outlines L'Egru's successive messengers (wave, dove, moon) very clearly and also emphasizes by dramatic repetition the apothegm that ends every group of twelve, especially the last: "You are to blame, impatience, you would not have suffered [me to beg a kiss]." This thought (and all its preceding cousins) is emphasized by a cadenza-like progression that lingers on "would have" ("hätt'") and stops on the first syllable of "ge*lit*-ten." Against the regularity of strophic form, however, the composer distributes the tetrameter with delightful caprice within the confines of the compound duple meter (see ex. 8.1). This avoids singsong melodic patterns, as does the lyrical rise and fall of a melody sprinkled with large leaps that stress urgency.

The accompaniment is equally urgent. In adopting strophic form, Schumann sets for himself the classic task of "grasping the essence of the poem in one focal point." He accomplishes this in the piano by employing a constant stream of thirty-second notes in the right hand, often supported by staccato eighth notes in the left, which communicate haste at the very least. In the first stanza we can also hear the flowing right hand as consisting of stereotypical wave figures and in the second of quickly beating wings. This kind of suggestion, however, becomes less plausible in the third stanza, where the sluggish moon looks in on the beloved. But restless accompaniment still reflects the persona's impatience, which pervades the whole song and provides the underlying impetus for incessant

Example 8.1.   Beginning of "Aufträge."

movement throughout. L'Egru's poem may not represent the acme of German verse, but Schumann's setting elevates it to another plane.

Lieder und Gesänge für eine Singstimme mit Begleitung des Pianoforte . . . Heft IV, Op. 96 ("Nachtlied" by Goethe, composed 12 July 1850; "Schneeglöckchen" by an anonymous poet, composed 12 July 1850; "Ihre Stimme" by August Graf von Platen-Hallermünde, composed 14 July 1850; "Gesungen" and "Himmel und Erde" by Wilfried von der Neun, composed 27 July 1850; published September 1851 by F. Whistling)

Schumann offered the last in the four-volume set of *Lieder und Gesänge* to Friedrich Whistling on 27 June 1851 as a group of "colorful songs,"[20] which the publisher released in short order. Even more than the songs in the previous volume of the series, the individual numbers in this set originated in close chronological proximity—over the span of just a few weeks during July 1850—and in sequential order, leading us to suspect some plan surrounding their grouping. What joins them together, however, does not readily surface at first glance, so various are the individual textures, poets, and moods of the different numbers. Closer examination, however, discloses a central theme of transience. The composer frames op. 96 with thoughts of mortality, at one end in Goethe's metaphorical "Wanderers Nachtlied" and at the other end in von der Neun's more explicit "Himmel und Erde." Internally the collection explores other, less somber forms of transience: a passing season represented by the emergence of an early flower in "Schneeglöckchen," temporary separation in "Ihre Stimme," and fleeting strife and anger in "Gesungen!" We should not be surprised, then, to find the C major of "Nachtlied" echoing through the quizzical ending of "Schneeglöckchen" (nominally cast in A-flat major but concluding on a C major chord) and through the final Picardy cadence of "Gesungen!" (otherwise cast in C minor). Once we notice these underlying links, the more obvious connection with the remaining songs in A-flat, "Ihre Stimme" and "Himmel und Erde," falls easily into place. Collections are not cycles, of course, but Schumann did seem to have had some overall scheme in mind when he combined these highly disparate authors, texts, and settings to form this volume of songs.

Leon Plantinga calls Goethe's "Wanderers Nachtlied" "probably the most praised poem in the German language," citing its "artful enjambments whereby syntax is continuous between lines, and the congruence between sound and sense ('Ruh,' for example, is a long dark sound forcing a pause, a 'rest')."

Ueber allen Gipfeln	Over all the peaks
Ist Ruh',	Lies quiet,
In allen Wipfeln	In all the treetops
Spürest du	You apprehend
Kaum ein Hauch;	Scarcely a breath;
Die Vögelein schweigen im Walde.	The birds fall silent in the forest.
Warte nur, balde	Just wait, soon
Ruhest du auch.	You too will rest.

He continues, "Yet by its very delicacy of diction and meaning, its metrical irregularity and brevity, the poem creates serious problems for the composer."[21] Plantinga speaks in the context of Schubert's setting, which he praises for conforming the verse into 4/4 measures while still preserving its natural word accent.

Schumann's extraordinary setting follows a far different path, highlighting his departure from his predecessor (whose version he must have known) and even from his own earlier style. He adopts a chorale texture throughout, and instead of fitting Goethe's verse into a metrical framework, he effaces meter almost entirely and with it our sense of passing time. Schumann repairs the syntactic disjunctions of the first two couplets and therefore underlines their final rhymes ("Ruh'," "du"), at the same time concealing the cross-rhyme between "Gipfeln" and "Wipfeln." Then, reversing tactics for the second half of the poem, he preserves line endings, thus emphasizing Goethe's "artful enjambments," and he even introduces new breaks between "Warte nur" and "balde" to highlight the latter word. Yet nothing arrives "soon" in this treatment, which suspends us in an ethereal, sacred realm beyond all earthly longing. The composer permits only one element of progressive tension: a wayward internal harmonic excursion through the mediant and submediant keys, setting in motion a protracted series of secondary dominants (E minor–A minor–D major–G major) fraught with chromatic passing chords. This leads us back in the last few measures to a first inversion tonic by way of a doubly diminished, leading-tone seventh chord and an astonishing final upward leap of a minor seventh in the voice stressing "auch!" (see ex. 8.2). The repetition of Goethe's last line must remind us of Schubert's ending. But unlike the earlier master, Schumann does not indulge regular accompanimental figuration at any point in his song. In this way he manages to capture at once the consolation of nature, by means of imperturbable rhythmic languor; apprehensions of mortality,

Example 8.2. Closing measures of "Nachtlied."

by means of passing chromatic unease; and inevitable resignation to solemn repose at the last, by means of plagal motion under the final vocal note.

If repose forms the underlying tenor of "Nachtlied," "Schneeglöckchen," the account of flowers emerging at the end of winter and then passing away, adopts a more animated approach to transience. Schumann composed this song on the same day as "Nachtlied," and he must have imagined the two lieder as a contrasting pair. Whereas the first has practically no figuration (the few moving passages are melodic), the second has no measure without some sort of patterning, at least until the very end of the song. Whereas contemplative solitude emanates from "Nachtlied," dramatic uneasiness marks "Schneeglöckchen," which increasingly assumes the form of a miniature scene, with restlessly changing meter and modulation to far-flung keys. Whereas "Nachtlied" never abandons the internalized vantage point of its persona, "Schneeglöckchen" vacillates between third-person narrative and dialogue in sudden, unpredictable shifts of mood. And whereas the first member of the pair features a text by Germany's most eminent writer, Schumann apparently had no clue about the author of the companion piece. (Schanze and Schulte do not even offer their customary educated guess about the source for this verse.)[22]

Despite all these contrasts, we must regard "Schneeglöckchen" as the companion piece to "Nachtlied." For one thing, there is the matter of the transition Schumann fashioned between the two songs: the Goethe setting ends on a C major chord in root position with close spacing, and its successor begins with a dotted half C octave in the right hand that prepares a common tone modulation to the tonic A-flat major. Moreover, the extensive central section of "Schneeglöckchen" (devoted to the hasty and dramatic exit of winter's reign) modulates to A major, referring to the importance of A minor-major in the central section of "Nachtlied." And then there is the eccentric conclusion of the flower's tale, which lapses into chorale texture and modulates unexpectedly at its end to F minor (the relative of A-flat major), concluding with a half-cadence on a C major chord. In the snowdrop's last plaintive queries—"Whence do I come? Whither do I go? Where is my homeland?"—we hear the tonal echoes of "Just wait, soon you too will rest." The connection between the two songs essays an unusual irony.

"Ihre Stimme" expresses the most conventional sentiments and follows the most conventional course of the songs in op. 96. A simple love song, it represents the only poem Schumann set by August Graf von Platen (1796–1835), who led a somewhat malcontented life. Perhaps from some misbegotten sense of duty, von Platen chose a military career (even though his parents encouraged his writing), and he became a lieutenant in a Bavarian infantry regiment in time to participate in the 1815 campaign against France. In 1818 he received permission to study at the university in Würzburg, and in the course of his travels he became friends with Jean Paul, Rückert, Jacob Grimm, and Goethe. In the autumn of 1824 he went absent without leave for an Italian sojourn (he received three months' detention as punishment), and after study in Erlangen he departed to Italy for six years, in 1826. He returned briefly after the death of his father in 1832 but then left Germany for good, dying in Syracuse in 1835. He wrote a number of dramas, often on historical subjects, and he became particularly well known for his collections of *Ghaselen,* verse modeled on oriental literature, published in 1821 and 1824.[23]

Schumann fashioned his own title, "Ihre Stimme," for von Platen's poem, taken from a section of "Lieder und Romanzen" in his *Gesammelte Werke in Einem Band* (Stuttgart, 1839), labeled simply "1819" there.[24] The composer supplies a stereotypically arpeggiated accompaniment throughout, and his rhythmically irregular declamation of the text effaces von Platen's *Langzeilenvers* entirely, as we have come to expect in the late style. In place of quadratic predictability Schumann offers emphasis on particularly important or evocative words, such as "Zauberwesen" ("magic being") in the third line of the poem's first stanza, "abgethan" ("over and done") in the second stanza, and "Glut" ("glow") and "deine Stimme" ("your voice") in the fourth stanza. The irregular placement of poetic stress within the common-time meter, however, does not by any means exclude lyricism, which is particularly pronounced in the outer parallel stanzas of the three-part song form (ABA'). The middle section, encompassing von Platen's inner two stanzas, takes a more chromatic turn away from the tonic key, following the standard form, and its vocal line becomes slightly more declamatory. This plays well to the author's point that the persona forgets many insignificant utterances but needs only to hear the beloved's tones from afar to recall her every word (a sentiment that leads us right to the dominant preparation for A-flat major, "recalling" us, as it were, to the home key). "Ihre Stimme" may not count among Schumann's great songs, but it is solidly and thoughtfully constructed.

The remaining two songs in op. 96 feature texts from the pen of Wilfried von der Neun, the pseudonym of Friedrich Schöpff, whose volume of Schumann settings (op. 89) is discussed in the previous chapter. Schöpff pressed the composer to set his verse, and Schumann kindly granted the aspiring poet's request and spent some time with him. The author apparently had no inkling, however, that the composer would treat two more of his poems. When he received copies of the op. 96 songs in October 1851, he tendered his gratitude but added, "I was surprised that you set the terribly unmusical 'Gesungen' . . . , [although it] certainly pleased me uncommonly."[25]

We can see at a glance what Schöpff naively considered "unmusical" about "Gesungen!": instead of falling into the conventional tetrameter of the lied, the verse features pentameter that alternates two dactylic and three trochaic feet per line. But this created no problem at all for an old hand like Schumann, especially writing in the freer new style (though he could have treated the verse quadratically as well). Logically enough, the composer chooses a storm-and-stress accompaniment, with its minor mode, dramatically accented outer voices, and an affective sixteenth-note figuration for an inner voice filling out chords. To create further unease he places the beginning of each vocal line in the second half of the common-time measures, and he takes pains to reinforce this accentual peccadillo with phrases of varying length. The first line of both quatrains in the strophic setting occupies two and a half measures, the second fills three measures, and the final couplet unfolds continuously over six and a half measures. This distribution responds beautifully to the contrast between the parataxis of Schöpff's initial couplet and the enjambment of his second couplet. Schumann's migration from minor mode for the first couplet to major mode for the second speaks to the poet's central conceit, that in the midst of stormy surroundings one can always find peace. And demonstrating yet again Ulrich Mahlert's notion that postrevolutionary sentiments attracted the composer to Schöpff's otherwise unremarkable verse,[26] the poem draws an explicit parallel between the comfort found in an otherwise hostile natural world (stanza 1) and the consolation of art amid political strife (stanza 2):

Seht ihr im Lande der Zwietracht Fackel lodern?	Do you see in the land the torches of discord flaming?
Hört ihr den Frevel das Recht zum Kampfe fodern?	Do you hear wickedness challenging justice to battle?
Drum mit der Herzensgewalt friedvoller Lieder	Then will the strength of the heart's peaceful songs
Zaubert das wilde Geschrei des Wahnsinns nieder!	Enchant the wild cries of madness away!

"Himmel und Erde," the other Schöpff poem in op. 96, set on the same day as "Gesungen!," presented no such "unmusical" problems, falling as it does in a perfectly common iambic tetrameter. And in fact Schumann's treatment of its two outer stanzas features a relatively regular, four-square phrasing in A-flat major supported by a minimal accompaniment of repeated triplet block chords. We could not call the melody periodic. The vocal line does not offer paired repetition, but it certainly has a graceful lyricism that even includes an ornamental turn for the cadential preparation of the first stanza's conclusion and an expressive, almost bel canto extension for the apothegm ("Da ich dein, o Himmel, werde!") at the end of the third stanza. Even phrasing persists for the second stanza of Schöpff's poem as well, but Schumann calls our attention away from this feature toward a strikingly deceptive modulation. We expect to land in the conventional dominant key of E-flat for this central section of a three-part song form, but instead the composer moves quite suddenly to C-flat major (spelled enharmonically as the more approachable B major and prepared by a secondary C-sharp [D-flat] dominant moving to the dominant F-sharp [G-flat]). This particularly redolent excursion speaks musically to Schöpff's notion of May's flowers "blending" with the blue sky and autumnal colors intermingling with the rosy light of dawn. Thus Schumann transforms ordinary verse into something worthy of his last volume in the series of *Lieder und Gesänge*.

Pensive Collections and a "Cheerful" Ending

Drei Gesänge für eine Singstimme mit Begleitung des Pianoforte . . . Op. 83
("Resignation" by "J.B.," composed 30 March 1850; "Die Blume der Ergebung" by Rückert, composed 1 April 1850; "Der Einsiedler" by Eichendorff, composed 3 April 1850; published June 1850 by J. Schuberth)

The genesis of op. 83 remains the most cryptic of all Schumann's collections. The composer set the poetry within a very brief span: "Resignation" on Holy Saturday and "Die Blume der Ergebung" and "Der Einsiedler" on the Monday and Wednesday following Easter, respectively. Schumann seems to have designed the collection as a set, then, partially inspired by a return to famous poets (Rückert and Eichendorff) after the holidays. We do not have any of the correspondence he sent to Schuberth about the set (there was little), and Schuberth's reply is unenlightening.[27] We must suppose that the composer gave the collection to Schuberth because of his other projects with the publisher around this time (including the Second Piano Trio, op. 80, and the Twelve Pieces for Piano, op. 85). Extant documents give us only one other bit of concrete information: the autograph realization of the songs in full score bears on its title page "*für eine ~~Singstimme~~ Sopranstimme ~~oder Tenorstimme~~*."[28] Schumann rarely designated a specific voice for his songs, and the assignment to soprano does not appear in the published version.

We could not call the collection closely knit in musical terms, but real connections do exist between the numbers. At first the succession of keys seems puzzling. What can we make of a sequence that runs D-flat major–A major–D minor? "Resignation" turns out to indulge one of those harmonic excursions that form the hallmark of Schumann's late style. In the midst of the song the composer switches to the parallel D-flat minor, spelled for ease of execution as C-sharp minor. But C-sharp doesn't remain the tonic for long; the song migrates instead to E major (the strong cadence falls on "zehn!"). However brief this interlude, it has real harmonic force, suggesting that the A-flat/G-sharp serves as the leading tone to A major in "Die Blume." Schumann makes the dominant relationship between the A major of "Die Blume" and the D minor of "Der Einsiedler" more obvious by ending the former on a tonic chord in an upper register. The D octaves unisono that open the third song then follow as a very audible consequence. Schumann makes the progression from the beginning to the end of the collection more pronounced by stylistic means. He casts "Resignation" in the kind of free-form arioso that permeates his later style, the Rückert features a much more quadratic phrase structure and "Liedform" (a clear ABA'), and "Der Einsiedler," for reasons that will become apparent below, not only favors quadratic phrases but takes strophic form. Schumann seems to regress through the stylistic options available to him in deference to setting authors he had treated extensively in his earlier career.

Some writers list Julius Buddeus as the poet for "Resignation" because

of the initials J.B. on the autograph title page of the composing manuscript for op. 83, on its fair copy, and then on its printed title page.[29] But
the old complete edition simply gives "unknown poet." To complicate
matters, the only other references to a "Buddeus" appear in op. 125, no.
3 ("Die Meerfee," of which more below), and in Schumann's household
accounts.[30] The latter almost certainly refer to the owner of an art gallery
in Düsseldorf during the Schumanns' residency. But no published volume
of poetry by Julius Buddeus (b. 1812) survives, if indeed there ever was
one or if he wrote poetry at all.[31] In short, we have no literary source for
"Resignation" and no clear idea about its author. We can only say that
the poetry appears to fall, sometimes uncomfortably, into six quatrains in
Langzeilenvers:

> Liebén von gánzer Sée-lé
> Liebén herzínniglích [´]
> Dass nímmer ích's verhéh-lé
> Heiss líeben múß ich dich [´]

Schumann pointedly ignores this metric scheme, choosing instead a
kind a declamation that lies between the relatively flat melodic line of recitative and the ambitus of more regular aria. The voice rises and falls
through a wide range but without predictable periodicity, emphasizing
individual words (such as "Heiss" in the last line of the first quatrain).
The composer reinforces this arioso-like writing by instructing the performers to present the song "not fast, freely performed." The accompaniment also bolsters the freedom with which the text is declaimed by employing irregular interludes to punctuate the song's outer sections (which
do not parallel each other in melodic or harmonic content). Only for the
fourth quatrain (the inner section of the song in C-sharp minor-E major)
does the pianist indulge a steady sixteenth-note arpeggiation (sporadic
elsewhere) that portends something resembling quadratic style without
melodic periodicity. In short, "Resignation" is one of the more puzzling
lieder from the composer's late period.

Schumann probably meant the declamatory unpredictability of "Resignation" to serve as a foil to the sheer lyrical regularity of "Die Blume
der Ergebung." The parallel subject matter of the poems—abject love—
binds them together, as does their shared verse form. Their treatment,
however, places them at the opposite ends of Schumann's expressive spec-

trum, perhaps revealing what Rufus Hallmark asserts to be the composer's special regard for Friedrich Rückert.[32] This text does not originate, however, in the section of the poet's output most frequently mined by Schumann, "Liebesfrühling," but from "Bausteine zu einem Pantheon," toward the beginning of the edition of the *Gesammelte Gedichte* owned by the composer.[33]

Those who prefer Schumann's quadratic settings will consider "Die Blume" one of the gems from 1850, though it still bears the hallmarks of the later style. The four-measure prelude prepares phrases that tend to run in parallel groupings of two measures (see ex. 8.3). And if the middle section of the ternary form plays fast and loose with the verse by running lines of the third and fourth quatrains together, the central part of a three-part song form always constitutes a fluid diversion that takes liberties with key and melodic structure. The return of the opening section, bringing closure (this stems from the repeat of the last stanza in Rückert's poem itself), and the almost incessant presence of arpeggiated sixteenth notes in the accompaniment collude with the predominant regularity of the phrase structure to create a reliable consistency. "Die Blume der Ergebung" scarcely hearkens back to 1840, however: it displays a more pervasively chromatic language, partly as a response to the expectation of the persona, to be sure, but also as a result of recent trends in German music. This song has something for Schumann aficionados of all stripes.

"Der Einsiedler" ("The Hermit") elicits an appropriately solemn response from Schumann in the form of a chorale setting in strophic form, a topos well suited to Eichendorff's persona as well as to the explicit mention in the first verse of a sailor chanting a vesper hymn to God. This song too puts on a fairly regular face, with relatively even phrases, though not

Example 8.3.   Beginning of the vocal line from "Die Blume der Ergebung."

quite the same amount of parallelism found in "Die Blume." Eichendorff does not cast his verse in quatrains but in sestets—

O Trost der Welt, Du stille Nacht!	O earthly solace, thou stilly night!
Der Tag hat mich so müd gemacht,	The day has made me so weary.
Das weite Meer schon dunkelt,	The distant sea already darkens,
Laß' ausruh'n mich von Lust und	Grant me respite from want and
Noth,	need,
Bis daß das ew'ge Morgenroth	Until the eternal rosy dawn
Den stillen Wald durchfunkelt.	The silent wood illumines.

—and the composer simply follows along by producing twelve-measure strophes, as if he has reverted to an earlier style of setting in which the accompaniment shadows the voice and interludes are held to a minimum. This creates exactly the archaic, religious atmosphere Schumann desires, of course, but he inserts some treasurably eccentric touches to highlight his portrait. Though the top line of the accompaniment essentially doubles the voice, there are occasional rhythmic disparities that create tension. And though the song falls basically in D minor, each verse cadences hopefully in F major, as does the song as a whole. It is hard not to connect this simple but effective treatment to that of "Nachtlied," op. 96, no. 1, set later that year, using the same minimal accompaniment formed primarily from block chords to convey a sober message from another classic poet.

Sechs Gesänge für eine Singstimme mit Begleitung des Pianoforte. Fräulein Sophia Schloß zugeeignet . . . Op. 107 (composition: see below; published August 1852 by C. Luckhardt)

Op. 107 reverted to a practice from Schumann's earlier output: that of publishing song collections in multiple volumes. In this case the two gatherings trace parallel trajectories, the individual numbers always moving from lament to consolation. The first volume casts this as a progression from E minor to B minor, then to its relative D major, with all the songs circling around amorous themes, whether tragically failed or coyly successful. The second, moving from B minor to A minor and then C major, repeats the focus on disappointed love for the first two songs, with the last number suggesting a more general solace that seems to apply to op. 107 as a whole. Holding the opus together is a kind of rhyme between the rhythmic motifs of the last song in each volume, both of which experiment with triplet patterns against duple ones. And finally, the B minor in the second number of volume one, "Die Fensterscheibe," and its feminine persona return in the first number of volume two, "Die Spinnerin." In other words, op. 107 coheres loosely as an opus, if we do not push the connections very far. Schumann must have considered the contents and their sequence carefully, for an early version of the title page includes a second setting of a Mörike text, "Jung Volkers Lied," while omitting "Im Wald." In the end the "Jung Volkers Lied" proved out of keeping with the more serious tone of the remaining numbers and found its way into op. 125, a group of "cheerful songs." "Im Wald" helped create the parallel sequence for each volume of op. 107.

Precisely how Schumann settled on Carl Luckhardt in Kassel as the publisher for the *Sechs Gesänge* remains unknown, though he had done regular business with the firm since December 1850, probably at the request of its proprietor. In any event, Schumann offered op. 113 (*Märchenbilder für Klavier und Viola*) and op. 107, specified for "alto voice," to Luckhardt on 3 March 1852, with the honorarium to be paid upon the receipt of the manuscript.[34] Though the print ultimately omitted the specification, a designation for mezzo-soprano or alto voice appears on a draft of the title page for the set as well, no doubt in conjunction with the ultimate dedication to Sophia Schloss, an alto soloist at the Gewandhaus who moved to Düsseldorf in 1850.[35] Clara Schumann and Schloss performed "Der Gärtner" (no. 3 of the collection) at a Düsseldorf concert for the Schumanns' benefit on 13 March 1851, and this number was first published by itself in a *Düsseldorfer Lieder-Album* during July of the same year.[36] To Robert's initial offer of the whole collection, including the previously published song, Luckhardt replied:

> Your offer in respect to manuscripts gave me quite particular enjoyment, and I am ready to accept these for engraving with greatest pleasure on the conditions you have set. Only, I must request most affably to delay payment of the honorarium until the end of May, because I have no disposable funds at the moment on account of the approaching Eastertide as well as on account of rather tepid business. But if it were especially to your liking to leave some other manuscripts for me later, then, and to pass these along to another publisher, I would gladly agree to this too.[37]

Schumann, however, stayed with Luckhardt, sending the manuscripts for opp. 107 and 113 on 24 April 1852 and agreeing to wait for the honoraria until May.[38]

Heft I: "Herzeleid" (Ulrich, 21 January 1851), "Die Fensterscheibe" (Ulrich, 21 January 1851), "Der Gärtner" (Mörike, 22 January 1851)

Schumann composed the songs in volume one within the span of two days, and it stands to reason that the numbers relate rather closely to one another. In token of this, the volume opens with two poems by Titus Ulrich (1813–1891), the son of a Silesian farmer, who gained a doctorate in philosophy in Berlin and went on in later life to serve for twenty-seven years as the dramaturge of the Royal Theater (he worked as a critic between his university days and his theatrical activity). Robert and Clara met Ulrich on a tour to Berlin in February 1847, recording two mornings spent with this "dear man, full of lucidity and shrewdness."[39] Robert later encountered the poems featured in op. 107 as entries in the *Deutscher Musen-Almanach für das Jahr 1851,* and his acquaintance with the author likely prompted the idea of setting them.[40] The first poem, "Herzeleid," paraphrases the lament of Queen Gertrude for Ophelia from *Hamlet,* Act IV, scene vii, "There is a willow grows askant the brook." The subject matter proceeds from Ulrich's lifelong engagement with Shakespeare, and his verse also reflects this in its unusual alternation of iambic pentameter (the meter of Gertrude's lament) with iambic tetrameter. The falling arpeggiated sixteenth notes that pervade the accompaniment to "Herzeleid" may remind us of a Schumannian lament topos, encountered in such earlier songs as "Hör' ich ein Liedchen klingen" or its major-mode counterpoint in *Dichterliebe,* "Am leuchtenden Sommermorgen" ("Herzeleid" modulates quickly to a C major). But the chains of limpidly descending thirds at the opening (see ex. 8.4) hint at something beyond the harmonic language of 1840, shading over into a sequence recalling nothing so much as Brahms's Intermezzo, op. 119, no. 1. Schumann treats the two stanzas strophically and confines the vocal line to a relatively narrow ambit, demarking the ends of

Example 8.4.   Chains of descending minor thirds in "Herzeleid."

poetic lines with melancholic appoggiaturas. The composer's response to Ulrich's poem is at once understated, delicate, and profoundly affective, debouching finally in a postlude of arpeggios dying away from the singer's plaintive repetition of "Ophelia" on the fifth degree of the scale.

"Die Fensterscheibe" offers a partner for "Herzeleid," appearing on the following two pages of the *Deutscher Musen-Almanach* and set the same day as its predecessor. The second number also proceeds from the standpoint of a female persona, now in the dominant B minor to the previous song's E minor. It too presents us with a kind of lament, this time for disappointed love. Again Schumann proceeds very delicately, with a minimally intrusive accompaniment for the tragic vignette of a woman beholding her unfaithful lover passing by. She catches his attention inadvertently by breaking the pane of glass she is cleaning, which wins a passing glance. Ulrich then draws an invidious comparison between the audible breaking of the glass and the muted breaking of her heart, which transpires unnoticed. This last event prompts the form of the song: strophic for its first three stanzas, but then wandering away into a coda for the last quatrain and its apothegm, "But you didn't look at all as my heart softly broke." The composer treats the tetrameter quadratically, and he deals with the silent foot for the last line of each stanza by inserting a one-measure interlude. He modulates to the parallel major in response to its essential event (the man walking by as blood runs down the persona's hand). The penultimate stanza, in which the passerby turns to look, breaks the pattern slightly, ending on a half-cadence, which then leads to the more irregular coda setting the final quatrain. Again we find a delicate setting that makes its point with utmost simplicity.

Schumann must have designed "Der Gärtner," composed the next day, as the counterpoise to "Die Fensterscheibe." The Mörike poem reverses perspective, with its male persona admiring a passing female (a princess riding by) in the relative major to the preceding song's B minor. The most winning feature of this scenario is its triplet accompanimental figures, which feature a prancing variation on a riding topos marked "tenderly and lightly." The song begins with arioso interrupted frequently by the piano interludes that create the topos, and this style of through-composed setting persists for the first three stanzas of the text. Not until Schumann reaches the central action of Mörike's poem does he make the transition to something more lyrical: when, in the third stanza, a feather floats out of the princess's hat into her admirer's hand, the voice part breaks into an aria featuring paired, repeated phrases that offer "a thousand flowers" in return for the single token. Schumann repeats this final sentiment to make his point, and the long postlude then finds the princess and pony trotting away. These lighthearted gestures avert the gloominess of the preceding two songs in the first volume.

Heft II: "Die Spinnerin" (Heyse, 8 January 1852), "Im Wald" (Müller, before 10 September 1851), "Abendlied" (Kinkel, 23 January 1851)

The second volume of op. 107 has a more varied chronology than volume one, though we could claim that the last number, "Abendlied," was always intended as some sort of general conclusion, composed as it was right after the numbers in volume one. However that might be and despite the separation of the opus into two parts that purchasers could acquire separately, Schumann made some attempt to bridge the divide between volumes by casting "Die Spinnerin" in the B minor of "Die Fensterscheibe" and relative minor of "Der Gärtner." The parallel content and trajectory of the second volume from despondency to consolation has been noted, with the exception that "Im Wald" and "Abendlied" do not engage amorous themes.

"Die Spinnerin" constitutes the first treatment Schumann accorded the poetry of Paul Heyse (1830–1914), an author of the new generation best known for his dramas, novels, and novellas. He came from an intellectual background (his father was a university professor in Berlin), and he went on to greater fame by becoming the first German belletrist to win the Nobel Prize for literature, in 1910 (which prompted his elevation to the nobility that same year). We may know him best in Wolf's later settings of the *Italienisches Liederbuch* (though poetry formed a very small part of Heyse's output), but he seems to have gained Schumann's interest as a rising literary talent very early. Heyse spent 1850 to 1852 (the year Schumann set "Die Spinnerin") in nearby Bonn, where he received his doctorate at the university for a dissertation on Provençal poetry.[41]

The original source for "Die Spinnerin" remains unknown, but given his geographic proximity to the author, Schumann could have obtained the verse from the poet himself. This may account for the considerable variants between the versions of the poem in op. 107 and in Heyse's *Gesammelte Werke* (1871–1910), where it appears under the heading "Mädchenlieder."[42] The main deviations arise in the first and third stanzas:

Heyse's "Mädchenlieder"	*Schumann's "Die Spinnerin"*
1.	1.
Auf die Nacht in der Spinnstuben	Auf dem Dorf' in den Spinnstuben
Da singen die Mädchen,	sind lustig die Mädchen.
Da lachen die Dorfbuben,	Hat Jedes seinen Herzbuben,
Wie flink geht die Rädchen!	wie flink geht das Rädchen!
3.	3.
Kein Mensch, der mir gut ist,	Kein' Seel' die mir gut ist,
Will nach mir fragen.	kommt mit mir zu plaudern;
Wie bang mir zumut ist,	gar schwül mir zu Muth ist
Wem soll ich klagen?	und die Hände zaudern.

Another possible source may be some local journal in which Schumann encountered Heyse's verse.

Whatever its exact origin, this melancholy tale of a young woman at the spinning wheel with no bridegroom toward whom to direct her domestic labors elicits a stereotypical response from Schumann. A spinning song requires the incessant sixteenth-note topos in minor mode that runs continually throughout the piano's right hand. This is quite unlike the accompanimental plasticity of the last number in the previous volume of op. 107, though something of a twin in consistency to the funereal topos for "Herzeleid." The composer further intensifies Heyse's rustic and antique frame of reference with a lyrical, relatively four-square melody and an alternating bass in the left hand that tends to dwell on a B pedal. A time-honored bar form completes the archaic portrait of romantic desolation. Schumann uses Heyse's first two quatrains as parallel *Stollen*, while the last two quatrains together—their new melody has just a hint of rounding at "Und die Thränen . . ."—combine to form a classic *Abgesang*. Here again we find the simplest tools engraving a picture of great precision and delicacy.

Schumann set Wolfgang Müller von Königswinter (a pseudonym of Peter Wilhelm Carl Müller, 1816–1873) only once, in a treatment of an untitled poem for which we can find only one printed source, the *Deutscher Musen-Almanach für das Jahr 1852*.[43] Since the composer fashioned this song sometime before 10 September 1851 (when he gave the poet's wife an album leaf citing the lied),[44] he must have obtained the verse from the author himself. Müller was a contributor to the *Neue Zeitschrift* when Schumann edited the journal, but he occupied himself primarily in his early career as a physician (educated in Bonn, Dresden, and Berlin). In

1842 he assumed his father's practice in Düsseldorf, where he eventually treated Schumann when the composer moved there. Müller also played a political role in the failed 1848 Frankfurt National Assembly, and in 1853 he moved to Cologne, forswearing the practice of medicine for literature and scientific research.

Schumann appears to have given the title "Im Wald" to Müller's poem, which at first appears somewhat irregular (sestets with an uneven refrain: "Und bin ich so allein / Voll Pein!"). But the first two lines of the poem unfold in iambic dimeter (which easily combines into groupings of four feet), and the two-line refrain similarly fuses into a line of tetrameter, fragments of which the composer then repeats. Müller's verse offers us the standard conceit of a *Wanderlied*, one in which the solitary traveler is beset by his loneliness. This is not the confident wayfarer of "Der frohe Wandersmann" or of Kerner's "Wanderlied" (op. 35, no. 3) and "Wanderung" (op. 35, no. 7); it prompts Schumann to respond by casting the topos of the wayfarer's march in minor mode. We find all the usual traits: compound duple meter, dotted rhythms, and relatively even phrasing (which tends to run slightly out of step with common time because many anacruses to the first accented syllable of each line occur in the middle of the measure). While minor mode predominates, the central section of each stanza in this almost perfectly strophic setting modulates to C major, as we might expect with an A minor tonic. This helps to mediate between the B minor-D major of "Die Spinnerin" and the strongly defined C major of "Abendlied." "Im Wald" again serves up an elegant yet unpretentious miniature in a group of finely wrought settings.

"Abendlied" then finishes the second volume and the opus with a gem of most exquisite cut. The author of its verse, Johann Gottfried Kinkel (1815–1882), moved in Rhenish circles as a native of Oberkassel near Bonn, where he pursued an education at the university in theology (his father was a minister) and philosophy. In 1838 he moved to Düsseldorf, where he became a private instructor in theology, and there he met Rhenish poets such as Geibel, Freiligrath, and Peter Müller, who encouraged his literary ambitions. Kinkel also participated in the 1848 revolution, with the rather dire consequence of being sentenced to life imprisonment. In 1850 he escaped to England, however, and taught German and art history in London, later making his way to Switzerland.[45] We know from Schumann's copybook of poetry that the composer found "Ein geistlich Abendlied" in Kinkel's second edition of *Gedichte*, published in

1850,[46] and it seems possible that the author's fellow traveler in republican sentiments, Müller, recommended the verse.

From Kinkel's original four octaves in *Langzeilenvers*, Schumann chose just two, which emphasize the ethereal and hopeful in preference to the more concrete and specific inner stanzas:

Es ruht die Welt im Schweigen,	The world rests in silence,
Ihr Tosen ist vorbei,	Its tumult is past,
Stumm ihrer Freude Reigen	Its joyful reels mute
Und stumm ihr Schmerzenschrei.	And mute its painful cries.
Hat Rosen sie geschenket,	If it gave you roses,
Hat Dornen sie gebracht—	If it brought you thorns—
Wirf ab, Herz, was dich kränket	Cast away, heart, what ails you
Und was dir bange macht!	And what affrights you.
Und hast du heut gefehlet,	And if you failed today,
O schaue nicht zurück;	O look not back;
Empfinde dich beseelet	Feel yourself inspired
Von freier Gnade Glück.	By free grace's fortune.
Auch des Verirrten denket	Even the wayward are minded
Der Hirt auf hoher Wacht—	By the Shepherd from his high watch—
Wirf ab, Herz, was dich kränket	Cast away, heart, what ails you
Und was dir bange macht!	And what affrights you.

Having chosen to set the outer stanzas, with their description of dusk falling to the gentle tread of an angel's feet and the appearance of the evening sky replete with stars and a poetically figurative moon ("the golden wagon"), the composer crafted a setting of gossamer beauty from accompanimental threads of continually enchained triplet chords (see ex. 8.5). Delicately voiced *una corda* ("Verschiebung"), the piano triplets work gently at odds with the duple rhythms of the voice, and though the effect

Example 8.5.   Entry of the voice part in "Abendlied."

is polyrhythmic in the fullest sense of the word, it does not disturb the listener. Rather, the technique creates the sensation of floating calmly above all earthly care. Schumann reinforces this serenity with a heavy emphasis on the subdominant tonal region of F major (which also entails briefer excursions to D minor). The plagal realm invokes sacred overtones that respond directly to the sound of the angel's tread in the first stanza as well as obliquely to Kinkel's omitted third stanza. This ravishing song, one of Schumann's most deeply moving altogether (the setting, though not the verse, is on a par even with "Mondnacht"), by itself would be worth the price of op. 107's second volume.

For all of the last number's beauty, the *Sechs Gesänge* do not rely on any one of their members for aesthetic justification. Each setting displays Schumann at his mature best in a lyrical foil to the more dramatic later groupings such as the *Wilhelm Meister Lieder* and the Lenau *Lieder*. The latter, as "cycles" with greater poets, demand and support the more dramatic technique the composer developed in his later years. But he had not by any means lost his touch for the deft, fine-spun tracery of the character pieces that marked his first decade of composition for the piano. All the virtues of those miniatures reveal themselves in op. 107 again, making it a highly worthwhile experience for performers and audience alike.

Fünf heitere Gesänge für eine Singstimme mit Begleitung des Pianoforte . . . Opus 125 ("Frühlingslied" by Braun, composed 23–24 July 1850; "Frühlingslust" by Heyse, composed 13 July 1850; "Die Meerfee" by Buddeus, composed before 13 June 1850; "Jung Volkers Lied" by Mörike, composed 22 January 1851; "Husarenabzug" by Candidus, composed 24–25 July 1850; published March 1853 by Heinrichshofen'sche Musikalien-Handlung)

If we should doubt the deliberation that Schumann invested in grouping songs together for publication, then the title for this final miscellany of late solo *Gesänge* provides enlightenment. The history of op. 77 reveals that the composer initially tried to place three of the numbers (1, 2, and 5) with Johann André as part of a collection of eight "Bunte Lieder" in August 1850. When André demurred and four of the songs found their way into the third volume of *Lieder und Gesänge*, Schumann laid aside the remaining songs for a more propitious moment. But he never abandoned the notion of deliberately publishing a brighter group amid his darker mature collections. Gathering some of the numbers left unpublished in op. 77 together with two subsequent numbers that had not fit other volumes, he offered the collection first to the firm of Bote & Bock on 11 October 1852.[47] The Berlin publisher declined after some delay, and Schumann then responded to an 1850 request for material from Theodor Heinrichshofen,[48] who had grand ambitions for his family business. To the composer's offer of 1 November 1852, Heinrichshofen replied with delight on 3 November:

> As a result of your friendly letter, with which, my dear sir, you have surprised me in the most pleasant way, I implore you most devotedly to send me directly by post the manuscript of your songs, in order to get the honorarium of ten louis d'or immediately on its way. Later, however, and still before the end of the year, [you will] receive the desired free copies most finely outfitted.[49]

The composer dispatched the manuscript on 6 November[50] and thus realized his long-standing intention of publishing some "cheerful songs."

Schumann received the honorarium promptly, but the production of the volume took longer than originally planned and occasioned some problems. Heinrichshofen printed the songs in the order in which they appear in the list of contents above, but the title page enumerated the individual items in quite a different sequence: "Meerfee," "Husarenabzug," "Jung Volkers Lied," "Frühlingslied," and "Frühlingslust." Neither Schumann's *Briefverzeichnis* nor his received correspondence make any further mention of Heinrichshofen, leaving no evidence one way or the other that Schumann read proof.

The sequence of keys in op. 125 suggests that the order of the printed music should probably take precedence over the title page. Because of their lighthearted mood, the songs assume a relatively diatonic language, and the first four group clearly around A major, the key of "Frühlingslied." "Frühlingslust" begins on the pitch of A, though it falls mostly in D major, "Meerfee" returns to A major (with a brief diversion to F major), and "Jung Volkers" ends in E major, dominant of A. "Husarenabzug," in B-flat major, was always the odd song out, even among the proposed "Bunte Lieder, op. 92" (see Table 8.1). Why Schumann did not transpose the last number down a half-step will always remain a puzzle, unless it had something to do with the voice range or less brilliance in the piano at the lower pitch. However that may be, the numbering on the title page—1. "Meerfee" (A), 2. "Husarenabzug" (B-flat), 3. "Jung

Volkers" (E), 4. "Frühlingslied" (A), and 5. "Frühlingslust" (D)—makes a bit less sense. If op. 125 is taken as the plausible grouping suggested by the title "Five Cheerful Songs," "Husarenabzug" stands as a tonally detached but rousing coda.

"Frühlingslied" combines Schumann's penchant for novelty with loyalty to an old *Neue Zeitschrift* contributor. The verse for this song appeared in the *Deutscher Musenalmanach für das Jahr 1850,* a complimentary copy of which the composer had received at the end of January 1850 because it contained one of his little-known settings of a poem by its editor, Christian Schad.[51] It took Schumann some time to address the rest of the yearbook's contents. But when he did, in the summer of 1850, he found a poem by Frédéric Ferdinand Braun (1812–1854), an Alsatian teacher who moved to Paris as a private German tutor and served as correspondent there for the *Neue Zeitschrift.* Braun published volumes of both prose and poetry, but the *Musenalmanach* seems to be the only source for this poem.

If we view this "Frühlingslied" as an undistinguished piece of verse, then we judge it against standards to which it had no pretensions. It appears in the 1850 almanac under the title "Für ein Kind," and its sestets actually belie a rather simple scheme in which two lines of iambic dimeter alternate with a line of iambic tetrameter to create a rhyme scheme of *aabccb* and so forth:

> Das Kóernlein spríngt,
> Der Vógel síngt,
> Der Frúehling íst gekóm-mén;
> Es rínnt der Quéll
> Der Bách fließt hell—
> Das Físchlein íst geschwóm-mén.

Schumann uses this arrangement of lines and the poem's unprepossessing vocabulary to have fun, while observing the poetry's disposition strictly. In the perfectly strophic setting, the composer inserts an mimetic interlude suggesting birdsong between lines 1 and 2, a two-measure interlude between the first and second tercet, and a one-measure break between lines 4 and 5. A longer passage for the piano then sets off the last line. The piano often takes up motives heard in the voice at a later time, and likewise the vocal melody appropriates motives from the accompaniment in a free give-and-take. The effect is lighthearted and unassuming without resorting to the singsong cliché of simple quadratic declamation. This may account for Schumann's alternate title, "Frühlingslied," rather than "Für ein Kind." The composer accords the poem a sprightly treatment in the new style that avoids childish repetition, focusing instead on the youthful optimism of the season.

The more distinguished verse in Heyse's "Frühlingslust" receives a slightly less playful setting, but one that is equally accessible. Unlike the unknown source for "Die Spinnerin" in op. 107, a poem from *Der Jungbrunne, Neue Märchen von einem Fahrenden Schüler* served Schumann as the basis for op. 125, no. 2. The composer distributes Heyse's three stanzas over a ternary form, with no interlude between the first two strophes. And although the melody of the first A section has something singsong about it, the accompaniment indulges a running pattern of slightly more chromatic sixteenth notes that complicates the initially quadratic nature of the vocal part. The chromaticism is in no way extreme or tortured: it constantly emphasizes the dominant (A) by means of its secondary dominant (E), which also serves to connect "Frühlingslust" to the key of the previous "Frühlingslied." One of Schumann's more charming touches comes in his postlude. After having separated the two couplets of Heyse's last strophe by means of a measure's interlude ("Im Tempo"), the composer extends the meaning of the last couplet ("The merry songs fly / up into the treetops") by means of an octave leap to A (second highest pitch in the accompaniment). The "merry songs" then make an almost stepwise descent back to earth, expiring gracefully on hitting a unison tonic D in both hands. This number exhibits a blithe aspect of Schumann's art.

Playfulness returns with "Die Meerfee," a text laconically ascribed by Schumann to "Buddeus." As we have seen in the discussion of op. 83, the only person by this name to appear in the composer's household accounts is Julius Buddeus, an art dealer in Düsseldorf of the Schumanns' acquaintance.[52] This yields absolutely no literary background for the poem, which probably originated as a set of four quatrains in trochaic *Langzeilenvers* about a procession of fairies filling a boy's dreams of a ship surrounded by enticing *fata morgana*. The mirage disappears as sea foam with the dream, not unlike the conclusion in "Aus alten Märchen winkt es." But Schumann outfits the vision here with a much less demented and frenetic aspect. He employs a delicate march in A major marked "Nicht zu schnell" and, like "Abendlied" in op. 107, "Mit Verschiebung" (*una corda*), a nod to the diffident steps of the mythical creatures.

"Meerfee" is not a children's song, however: Schumann composed it as a birthday offering for one of his favorite Leipzig singers, Livia Frege. Her birthday fell on 13 June, and the first performance of "Meerfee" took place in Leipzig on that date during the Schumanns' summer visit to the city (thus the dating of this song "before 13 June 1850," from the dedicatory autograph given to the soprano). The composer treats the little-known poet's conventionally simple verse in quite an unusual way, first by introducing most couplets in the middle of a measure (thus relieving the four-square trochaic meter), then by distributing them over the span of three and a half measures, and finally by avoiding almost completely paired, repeated melodic phrases (the only exception involves "und auf leichtem Perlenwagen . . ."). The melody is through-composed, and very occasionally it features a little touch of arpeggiated coloratura (probably the reason for the periodicity that marks "und auf leichtem Perlenwagen . . .": the repetition makes the roulades easier to negotiate). For the last stanza Schumann returns to full voicing ("Ohne Verschiebung") with a tiny harmonic excursion toward F major (never really established). The key dissolves just as quickly back into A major at the phrase "But the foaming waves carry the vision away," a delightful bit of text illustration.

To offset this varied and complex polyrhythm between vocal melody and verse in "Meerfee," Schumann's mincing accompanimental march much resembles the one we encountered in his setting of Mörike's "Der Gärtner," with its lovely princess on parade. It may puzzle us to think that the composer would lavish the same dainty intricacy on a poem by an insignificant author (Buddeus) as on verse by one of the great German writers. The explanation probably lies in the Schumanns' high regard for Livia Frege, whose voice seems to have fit this particular type of writing well. We know, for instance, that Robert had Frege audition "the second, more difficult half" of *Lieder für die Jugend,* op. 79, for Härtel's consideration.[53] The care with which he fashioned "Die Meerfee" reveals his continuing esteem for the Leipzig soprano.

Mörike plays a limited role in op. 125 by way of his "Jung Volkers Lied." The poet's title has a double entendre: this "young folk's song" contains a cautionary tale in humorous form. It concerns a young woman who had no use for men and who joked, "I'd rather be the wind's bride than to enter into marriage." Of course, the "wind" comes along and makes her pregnant with a child named "Jung Volker," at least in Schumann's version. But this play on words appears only in the composer's text, less explicit than Mörke's original last stanza (translated literally):

Da kam der Wind, da nahm der Wind	The wind then came, the wind then took
Als Buhle sie gefangen:	And captured her as lover:
Von dem hat sie ein lustig Kind	From him she a merry child
In ihren Shoos empfangen.	In her womb conceived.

Schumann alters the last couplet to read: "From him she conceived a merry child, Jung Volker's who I am." We will never know whether the composer rewrote the poem out of a sense of delicacy or because he thought it wittier (and perhaps the change responds to both considerations).

"Jung Volkers Leid" is the most declamatory of all the songs in op. 125. The vocal line does not lack rise and fall, but we could hardly call it tuneful. And Schumann disperses the verse irregularly, sometimes separating lines of one couplet from one another, sometimes running them together. He spaces both lines, couplets, and stanzas by means of the same repeated accompanimental figure that initiates the prelude. As a result, the listener can never quite make out where the division between line, couplet, and strophe falls; thus the composer treats the text almost as if it were prose. The dotted figures in the accompaniment, as much as the held chords disintegrating into sixteenth-note runs and arpeggios (representing the wind?), lend the treatment vigor. It becomes clear that Schumann wants to focus on declamation of the text more than on musical charm.

The setting of Candidus's "Husarenabzug" would seem at first to start where Mörike's "Jung Volkers Lied" left off, with the lines of its couplets detached from one another by accompanimental interludes. But the effect in this last song of the opus is quite different. The lines space more regularly, the interludes imitate drum cadences and trumpet calls (echoed in the vocal line), and the strophic setting always ends with a refrain over what we might construe as a galloping topos (see ex. 8.6). In short, "Husarenabzug" receives a folklike treatment that accords well with one

Example 8.6.   Closing refrain from the first strophe of "Husarenabzug."

aspect of its author's background. Carl August Candidus (1817–1872) was the son of an Alsatian minister, and Carl himself became a clergyman in the Reformed Church, first a curate in Altweiler (1842), next a vicar in Nancy (1846), and finally a pastor in Odessa (1858).[54] Though Candidus often treated theological themes in his writings, he also evinced an early interest in traditional Alsatian literature, contributing to the journal *Erwinia.* Schumann encountered his poem in Schad's *Deutscher Musenalmanach für das Jahr 1850,* the same volume where the composer discovered the Alsatian Braun's "Frühlingslied," the first number in op. 125.[55]

"Husarenabzug" has a somewhat more elaborate poetic structure than its opening counterpart in op. 125, and that may account in part for Schumann's deployment of the verse in his setting. Candidus cast this poem in three septains that divide further into a quatrain and then a concluding tercet with two extended lines, the last of which features enjambment to the very short final phrase:

Platz für die schönen Husaren! Milchmädchen bei Seite!
Drückt euch an's Brückengeländer! Es zieh'n in die Weite
Lustige Knaben.

The composer therefore treats the opening quatrain in each strophe as a device to build excitement by means of the mimetic interludes separating individual lines. It seems as if the aural report of the approaching riders precedes them. When they appear, the accompanimental figures repeat more regularly (the mounted troops arrive before us), culminating in a refrain that Schumann fashioned from the last sentence of Candidus's septain (see ex. 8.6). The composer then closes with military trumpet calls in the piano that make for a most satisfying conclusion of op. 125 as a whole. Though the poem relates the story of a soldier departing from his beloved, it assures the listener in the end that the young man will return, bravely unscathed.

Schumann had fun with the songs in op. 125: they are often playful and never dreary (though they can have serious messages). After the many fashionably sentimental themes he entertained in his later years, it is refreshing to hear him enjoy himself in a delicate way. But we would never consider these songs in the least bit comical, as the critic for the *Neue Berliner Musikzeitung*, Gustav Engel, put it subtly at the time: "The 'five cheerful songs' are not really in the actual sense of the word cheerful—with the pronounced exception of Husarenabzug—but only 'not melancholy.' The construction is full of character and graceful."[56]

Epilogue:
Reception of the Late Style

At the beginning of his public career as a composer of lieder, Robert Schumann entered the field unknown, a well-respected music critic and editor who had authored a series of more or less eccentric pieces for piano. He had cultivated relations with the flourishing industry of music in Leipzig (where he wielded no small amount of influence as a critic), but his compositions had earned him no widespread acclaim. His 1840 songs, together with his symphonies, chamber works, and the secular oratorio *Das Paradies und die Peri,* enhanced his standing tremendously, such that during the last eight or nine years of his life he became a composer of enormous stature. Publishers sought his works relentlessly, and for the most part he could print what and when he wished in a style of his choosing. But as we have seen from his correspondence with publishers, his new solo vocal style occasioned sporadic resistance, and this ambivalence carried over into the reception of his songs in the German critical press. It is worth our while here to explore this ambivalence briefly, for it has marked the reception of his lieder down to the present day.

In one camp fell supporters, who either under their signature or anonymously penned the overwhelming majority of reviews about Schumann's later songs. We find a good example of this, though directed at a less problematic opus, in Emanuel Klitzsch's article on the *Lieder für die Jugend,*[1] for which Schumann supplied a good deal of background information in a letter to the critic.[2] Klitzsch (1812–1889) was personally acquainted with the composer, studied law in Leipzig, and later served as city cantor and music director in Zwickau.[3] He begins by distancing himself from the polemics that had been permeating the *Neue Zeitschrift*, diatribes originating with ardent Wagnerians who lauded the opera composer's music at the expense of Schumann's. Klitzsch excuses himself from the debate by remarking that "it would be a sin against the holy spirit of composition to cloud the discussion of so childlike and pure a work through polemic."[4] He proceeds to repeat almost verbatim the rationalization for the album that Schumann had supplied him. The collection progressed from "easy and simple" numbers to more "difficult" ones, an intensification that "concerned not the mere external [and] technical, but mainly the content," all of which derived from "the best of our [German] poets."[5] Klitzsch finds most admirable the way in which Schumann fleshed out his overall scheme and portrayed childhood without "indulging useless frivolity and depiction lacking a substantial core: in this *Album* the spotlight falls especially on the important point, on that which penetrates the soul and should fulfill it—on *melody*. Indeed it is, moreover, the truthfulness and freshness of the same that lends an appropriate accessibility from every aspect, but without injuring a higher artistic conception."[6] Of course, the songs in op. 79 tended by their nature toward quadratic melody, and so Klitzsch could easily look with favor on the accessibility of the vocal writing. He admits immediately, however, that in doing so he touches upon a polemic he had wished to avoid, the nature of which will become clear below.

Faced with so many numbers, Kltizsch chooses to group the songs in op. 79 according to themes (songs about nature, songs dealing with the exotic, such as "Zigeunerliedchen," and songs encouraging piety), but he singles out the final number, Mignon's song, for special attention. Schumann had found a fitting way to portray the character from *Wilhelm Meister* in music, "her desire for the misty distance beyond which she hopes to find the satisfaction for her desire, that painful, ecstatic longing for the expression of that desire. Thus in this song the twisting through dissonances that follow one upon another, thus the dreamlike, entangled introduction beside the repeated closing ritornello."[7] In short, motivated by semantic content and pursuing lofty artistic goals attained through complete technical mastery, Schumann could do no wrong. This held equally true of the *Lieder für die Jugend* in an anonymous review from the *Neue Berliner Musikzeitung*, which praises the collection's "*simplicity* of musical treatment, that nevertheless does not exclude novelty and originality of invention."[8]

Klitzsch and some of his fellow travelers took an almost hagiographic approach to Schumann's later songs. The critic begins his appraisal of Schumann's third volume of *Lieder und Gesänge,* op. 77, effusively: "From among the countless myriad of lieder that the critical telescope seeks and surveys in the firmament of song during propitious hours, these shine forth especially on account of their gentle, calmly beaming brilliance, while others pass by suddenly like sparkling comets, but disappear again as quickly, others appear all at once as dark spots of cloud, and yet others burst like mere shooting stars into nothingness."[9] In this brief review (two paragraphs), Klitzsch finds something to praise in each song, citing "Aufträge" (no. 5 in the collection) as possessing "particular charm and loveliness, but also deeper meaning in its easy playfulness." The writer perceives no disparity in style among the various songs (written at disparate times in the composer's career), perhaps because he regards them individually. Only later, in his review of the last volume of *Lieder und Gesänge* (op. 96), does Klitzsch note briefly the advent of the later style: "One must already be somewhat more deeply acquainted with our master, if [the collection's] content is to be grasped in its entirety, because the musical expression, concealed here and there by the idiosyncratic form, does not manifest itself immediately, but presupposes a certain receptivity to these kinds of conceptions."[10] The writer especially praises Schumann's setting of Goethe's "Nachtlied" for "the same solemn peacefulness that wafts to us from the poem." We find similar sentiments in an anonymous review from the *Neue Berliner Musikzeitung* about op. 83 (with settings of Rückert and Eichendorff), which draws a comment about "the idiosyncratic impression [left by] Schumann's muse, in the rich harmonic unfolding of the accompaniment, as well as in the certainly more declamatory than melodious-lyrical behavior of the voice part."[11] The composer's later songs were just a bit less accessible than his admirers had come to expect.

By early 1854, in one last review of op. 119 (the end of articles on Schumann in the *Neue Zeitschrift* because of the disastrous decline in his health), Klitzsch takes a decidedly defensive and apologetic stance in the face of invidious comparisons drawn by Wagner's admirers to Schumann's detriment: "The composer has realized how to extract the unique element in each of these three poems [by Pfarrius], and if he assumes less of a lyrical than declamatory posture in the second, 'Warnung,' which does not seem to be suited to the poem, it is nonetheless incredible that the author of 'In Appreciation of R. Wagner' (No. 19, vol. 39 of this *Journal,* footnote on p. 200) can misconstrue Schumann in these very songs and call [him] 'in the tragic sense of the word mannered.'" [12] Klitzsch goes on to characterize the harmonic language of the songs as "clear and simple, indeed easy and accessible overall"; he appreciates the "harmless jest" of the last song and maintains that "failure to recognize all of this betrays narrow-mindedness 'in the tragic sense of the word,' since this kind of judgment is only one step away from blasphemy."

But there were others not engaged in polemics who found the *Drei Gedichte aus den Waldliedern von G. Pfarrius* less than appealing, not so much because they lacked originality or inventiveness, according to the anonymous writer in the *Neue Berliner Musikzeitung,* but because they posed difficulties for singers and performers. In this we can perceive the gradual migration of the lied from the realm of talented amateurs to that of professional singers. The Berlin critic, however, leaves no doubt about his disappointment in the last song of op. 119: "It should be a cheerful song, but turn it this way or that as one will, it makes a rather dry and pedantic impression." [13] In the same review, however, the writer praises op. 127, though he did not know it consisted largely of songs from 1840.

As a rule, the composer fared better in the Berlin journal. Gustav Engel approved of the *Fünf heitere Gesänge,* op. 125, "the setting of which [poetry] is full of character and charming. Schumann follows the text with assurance and with an ease that leaves the unity of the whole undamaged, for instance at the words in no. 2, 'Du schwanker, loser Falter, du hilfst dir nimmer heraus.'" [14] The composer's reputation among his proponents remained undimmed, however much they might like or dislike this or that particular song.

The defensiveness of Schumann's admirers formed one side of a larger debate over the "Weimar" (Liszt, Wagner) as opposed to the "Leipzig" (Mendelssohn, Schumann, Brahms) school, encouraged to some extent by all parties. This controversy began mostly in the pages of the *Neue Zeitschrift,* and it persisted until the end of the nineteenth century, with aftereffects in the twentieth. It pitted "absolute music" (Wagner's dismissive term for the work of Schumann, Joachim, Brahms, and many others), composed mostly on the basis of abstract musical patterning, against operatic music and tone poems. Lieder sorted themselves oddly into this dispute, for though they derived their artistic impetus from verse, the texts preceded their musical settings. Diatribes hurled from one side or another may often seem arbitrary in their characterizations of this piece or that, lacking deeper examination of the works in question or representing simply the product of faction. Klitzsch's outrage about a characterization of Schumann in an anonymous article about Wagner resulted from just such a "narrow-minded" ("einseitig") pronouncement:

> In every little love song one seeks to insert something extraordinary, a bit of modern consciousness—this conveys the words, and lyrics become piquant. Thus the full flow of musical sentiment becomes inhibited, one sees oneself obliged to clothe harmless texts in a costume that easily assimilates isolated melancholy [*schmerzlich*] accents, one assumes a reserved tone, a moderate demeanor. It cannot be denied, either, that [this practice] truly reflects our situation as it currently is. Our sentiment has lost its innocence, we live continuously in a thousand situations that all lay legitimate claim to us and interpose themselves between us and our sentiment. The modern lieder style of Schumann and Franz bespeak these exigencies. They shade their melodic motives by means of progressions that constantly throw new light on [those motives], sometimes calling them into question, sometimes strengthening them.[15]

In a footnote the author cites the example of Schumann's opp. 119 and 125, the artificial mannerisms of which he then compares invidiously to the natural feeling expressed in Wagner's setting of text in his operas. And at just this point the editor, ostensibly Franz Brendel, registers a protest in a footnote about the extremity of the article's characterization of Schumann's later work.

The objections to the excessive sophistication of Schumann's later song style seem fair from one point of view and not entirely inaccurate, though they take an oddly antiquated stance. Preexisting poetry for the lied in its lyrical regularity seemed to dictate a much less dramatically prepossessing approach, one that would largely restrict composers to quadratic style. Nowhere does this become clearer than in Theodor Uhlig's review of Schumann's op. 98, the *Lieder, Gesänge und Requiem für Mignon aus Goethe's Wilhelm Meister*. Uhlig, by this time an unabashed disciple of Wagner's, has only praise for op. 98b, the "Requiem" for choir, soloists, and orchestra (the latter reviewed in piano reduction), "which extensive text leaves much freedom for artistic display." But this commendation occupies a scant paragraph. Uhlig viewed the article as a vehicle to carry on "a thorough discussion of the most recent Schumann style," which "excludes harmonic clarity and calm far too much and imprints on the simplest creation a certain disagreeable coloring."[16] The *Lieder und Gesänge* in op. 98a bring this unpleasantness to the fore:

> The texts of these, the songs of Mignon, of the harper, and of Philine, are familiar to all. The more pronouncedly the content of these texts necessitates a response from the composer and the more pregnant their rhythmic form, the more musically satisfying is the impression left by Schumann's settings:—here are to be mentioned the *cheerful* song of Philine, "Singet nicht in Trauertönen!" and the strophic song, "Kennst du das Land?" Also where epic moments establish themselves decisively, as in the harper's ballad, "Was hör' ich draußen vor dem Thor, was auf der Brücke schallen?" the composer is torn away forcefully from his propensity for brooding and accomplishes something beneficial. The remaining six songs, however, which further his subjective proclivities all too readily, can be designated as disagreeable with little distinction between them in the main, although they surpass without any doubt the songs just discussed in originality and depth of conception. One might address the matter squarely with the following assertion: Schumann's most recent musical manner taken as a whole is original but disagreeable. Where he strives to evade [this manner] out of particular artistic motives, he not only appears less original but also less vigorous than in the settings from his best period.[17]

Lyrical texts require straightforwardly lyrical settings in Uhlig's scheme of things (therefore his praise of Schumann's earlier songs and of Philine's and Mignon's songs in op. 98a); epic texts might admit of a more dramatic treatment. But lyrical texts must never receive overly dramatic setting. Wagner, ironically, escaped this reproach by writing his own verse: one could never claim that he had violated his own poetic style. Schumann transgressed, moreover, not from a lack of technique but by applying his artistic mastery too willfully to the verse at hand, from the imposition of what Uhlig (following Wagner) characterized as "absolute music." Here musical technique trumped the content and structure of the verse, bending the poetry to musical needs rather than having music respond to poetic needs. Nowhere in this review does Uhlig show anything but the deepest respect for Schumann's musical talent or ability; he merely regrets its application.[18]

Uhlig's review of the lieder in Schumann's op. 98a constitutes the most negative assessment of the composer's late songs and one of the most polemic. But less partisan reviewers still expressed reservations, and perhaps we can find no better example than Julius Schäffer's review of the composer's *Sechs Gesänge*, op. 107, in the *Neue Zeitschrift*.[19] Everything about this review seems calculated to exude balanced objectivity, perhaps because of the preceding year's partisan attack by Uhlig. Schäffer's review appeared as the lead article near the beginning of the 1852–53 artistic season, it includes seven musical examples, and it discusses each song in some detail, reprinting long segments of poetry. Schäffer begins his article with praise for "Herzeleid" in prose reminiscent of Schumann's own poetic criticism: "A recitative-like melody soars over a muted, drawn out figure pervaded by mildly plaintive tones"[20] (the first two measures of ex. 8.4 reproduce the citation in the *Neue Zeitschrift*). The critic maintains that the vocal part and supporting accompanimental harmony in the second song remind him strongly of the composer's *Frauenliebe und Leben*, sometimes note for note. But he adds, "Only the closing is completely distinctive:

and will not fail to cause bad blood among Schumann's opponents (his admirers tolerate everything, as you know)."[21] This last aside begins to distance Schäffer from the composer, and while the author particularly admirers the graceful accompaniment in "Der Gärtner," he begins to highlight a series of disturbing cross-relationships between voice and accompaniment in the second volume of songs. About "Die Spinnerin," with its spinning motive in the piano, the critic writes, "The melody proceeds just like a finger that had come too close to the spinning wheel—as if it bumped against the accompaniment at all the corners and ends. . . . The song will elicit the dread of many 'singers.'"[22] Schäffer believes that Schumann could have varied the refrain of the strophic setting of "Im Wald" to increase expressivity, and returns in his comments on "Abendlied" to focus on the difficulty of placing the quarter-note triplets in the piano against the singer's regular quarter and eighth notes. "Schumann has long since ceased to trouble himself with such details, just as little as with the collision between G and G-sharp in the following passage," and here the critic reproduces in a musical example the cross-relationship that occurs at "Rings in die *Tie*-fe senket."[23] The emphasized syllable (mine) falls on the offending G-sharp in the voice against the G natural in the top voice of the accompaniment, held over from a chord struck at the beginning of the measure. Schäffer has amateur singers in mind when he highlights such "difficulties," and he proceeds from a very conservative view on the treatment of dissonances that cause modern listeners no problems at all. But while his objections have disapproving overtones, he grounds them in concrete citations that maintain his objective stance.

Schäffer intends his objectivity to render the concluding point of his essay more credible:

> In general, what strikes the eye primarily in all of these songs is the thoroughly defined, individual physiognomy in every particular, and Schumann certainly understands almost like no other how to grasp this individuality in all of its features and hidden depths. Does he succeed in representing the object in all its pure, unclouded individuality? The reviewer must reply negatively to this question. Instead of immersing himself in the object and forgetting the rules of his special musical sensibilities in light of [the texts'] inner necessities, Schumann proceeds quite in reverse. He immerses the object in himself and forgets the inner necessities of the object in light of the customary rules of his own musical feeling. In this way [the object] receives a Schumannian physiognomy that always points from the object to the artist—and *this* physiognomy is either an excess or a dearth, depending on the nature of the object represented.[24]

In other words, Schumann obviously created polyrhythmic lieder that bore his distinctive stamp. This is equally true of Schumann's earlier songs, but their quadratic style makes it much less apparent.

While none of Schumann's supporters or detractors characterize his songs inaccurately, a whole politico-cultural agenda lay submerged beneath their aesthetic debate.[25] We have seen particularly in Schumann's late cycles and collections how he selected poetry by authors of liberal (in the European sense of the word) republican stripe. Adherents of Wagner, following *his* example, adopted a much more radical stance impatient with the liberal dictum "Wissen macht frei. Wir können warten." ("Knowledge liberates. We can wait.") They wanted art that would prompt much quicker and more drastic change, and Wagner would provide this art in the form of operas that questioned the rule of law (*Der Ring des Nibelungen*), flouted bourgeois mores (*Tristan und Isolde*), and advocated a mystic irrationalism (*Parsifal*). The rejection of constitutional law found its artistic counterpart in the rejection of musical "rules" (*Die Meistersinger*), and Wagner implied the alliance of both to pharisaical niggling. His pernicious "Das Judenthum in der Musik" endorsed a virulent anti-Semitism that also mixed into this equation. Privately Schumann may have held anti-Semitic views, but he never aired them in public, and his publication in 1851 of "Hebrew Songs," dedicated to Constanze Jacobi, may have served as a reply from a composer who valued his friendship with Felix Mendelssohn deeply. But to Wagner and his adherents, Mendelssohn was not essentially German, and thus Schumann's defense of his friend, set against his promotion of politically tinged German poetry, entangled his late songs in a controversy that entailed more than just music.

When a younger generation of Wagnerians such as Wolf and Strauss addressed the lied, however, they played fast and loose with its poetic structure in a manner pioneered by Schumann. Their dramatic declamation of lyrical verse, their increasingly abstruse vocal lines, their subordination of melody to accompaniment, and their liberties with dissonance followed trails Schumann had blazed. In the 1850s it seemed to disciples of Wagner that only large dramatic works could point the way to the future, but the future of "progressive" music, especially in the twentieth century, lay increasingly in the realm of idiosyncratic miniatures such as those Schumann composed.

The "judgment of history" seems most satisfying to us because it reflects our values. From the remove of a century and a half, Wagner's and Schumann's musical styles appear more to run in parallel than to diverge. This brings us full circle to the latter's critical writings from the 1830s, in which he viewed the art song as the ultimate vehicle for the display of German poetry and its virtues. Wagner's ideas about opera seem to mirror, *mutatis mutandis*, Schumann's pronouncements more than two decades earlier: "To drive foreign singing from the field and to conserve our love of the people—that is, to revive again the music that expresses natural, profound and clear feelings artistically—requires above all the care and protection of our good German lied."[26] Hans Sachs articulates just such sentiments in his moral to *Die Meistersinger*.

At the same time, Schumann's later songs now appear to proceed from and have much in common with his earlier ones; taken together, they form a continuum. Some scholars wonder why we always seem to apologize for the composer's later songs. It may be that a century's worth of prejudice against them after his death has required another fifty years to reinstate them. When we examine them closely, we find greater and lesser numbers among them, just as we do with his songs from 1840. But the late songs form an integral part of Schumann's output, a logical progression from his earlier work amid the artistic, cultural, and even political milieu in which the composer found himself. And in this respect, the body of his songs as a whole positions him not only as one of the most significant and finest composers of German lieder altogether but also as the link between Beethoven and Schubert on the one hand and Brahms, Wolf, Strauss, and Mahler on the other.

Abbreviations

Notes

Editions of Music Consulted
and Selected Bibliography

Index of Song Titles
and Text Incipits

General Index

Abbreviations

AGA	*Robert Schumann's Werke.* Ed. Clara Schumann. 32 vols. Leipzig: Breitkopf & Härtel, [1879–1893].
Briefe NF	*Robert Schumanns Briefe. Neue Folge.* Ed. F. Gustav Jansen. 2d ed. Leipzig: Breitkopf & Härtel, 1904.
BV	*Briefverzeichnis,* an index Schumann made of the correspondence he sent and received, now housed in the Robert-Schumann-Haus, Zwickau, 4871 VII C, 10 A3.
Corr.	Correspondence received and collected by Schumann, housed in the Biblioteka Jagiellońska, Uniwersytet Jagielleński, Krakow, cited by volume and letter number.
Erler	*Robert Schumanns Leben. Aus seinen Briefen geschildert von Hermann Erler.* 2d ed. 2 vols. Berlin: Erler & Reis, 1887.
GS	Robert Schumann. *Gesammelte Schriften über Musik und Musiker.* Ed. Martin Kreisig. 2 vols. Leipzig: Breitkopf & Härtel, 1914.
LB	*Liederbücher* I–III, autograph drafts of songs bound in three volumes, Music Division, Staatsbibliothek zu Berlin, Preußischer Kulturbesitz, Mus. ms. autogr. 16.
TB I	*Robert Schumann: Tagebücher. Band I, 1827–1838.* Ed. Georg Eismann. Leipzig: VEB Deutscher Verlag für Musik, 1971.
TB II	*Robert Schumann: Tagebücher. Band II, 1836–1854.* Ed. Gerd Nauhaus. Leipzig: VEB Deutscher Verlag für Musik, 1987.
TB III	*Robert Schumann: Tagebücher. Band III, Haushaltbücher, 1837–18[56].* Ed. Gerd Nauhaus. 2 parts. Leipzig: VEB Deutscher Verlag für Musik, 1982.

Verzeichnis   Margit L. McCorkle, *Thematisch-Bibliographisches Verzeichnis.* In *Robert Schumann, Neue Ausgabe sämtlicher Werke*. Series VIII, vol. 6. Mainz: Schott, 2003.

Vorlagen   *Literarische Vorlagen der ein- und mehrstimmigen Lieder, Gesänge und Deklamationen*. In *Robert Schumann: Neue Ausgabe sämtlicher Werke*. Series VIII, vol. 2. Ed. Helmut Schanze and Krischan Schulte. Mainz: Schott, 2002.

Notes

Introduction. Schumann's Criticism and Early Lieder

1. "Lied und Gesang," *GS* 1: 268–274. All translations are mine unless otherwise noted.
2. *GS* 2: 147.
3. Ibid., 336.
4. Ibid., 123.
5. Ibid., 1: 270.
6. Ibid., 2: 85.
7. Ibid., 1: 496.
8. Ibid., 494.
9. Walther Dürr, *Das deutsche Sololied im 19. Jahrhundert: Untersuchung zur Sprache und Musik* (Wilhelmshaven, 1984), 15.
10. *GS* 1: 271–272.
11. Robert Schumann, *Selbstbiographische Notizen Faksimile,* ed. Martin Schoppe [Zwickau, n.d.], 3ᵛ.
12. For an account of Schumann's early literary aspirations, see Martin Schoppe, "Schumann's frühe Texte und Schriften," Schumann Forschungen, vol. 2, ed. Bernhard Appel (Mainz: Schott, 1987), 7–15. See the *Verzeichnis,* 726–31, for the list of songs and fragments from this period.
13. John Daverio, *Robert Schumann: Herald of a "New Poetic Age,"* (New York, 1997), 29–31.
14. *TB I,* 94.
15. Ibid., 112.
16. Ibid., 119.
17. *Verzeichnis,* 730. We might surmise that the label "op. 2" came around the time of the *ABEGG Variations,* op. 1.
18. Ibid.
19. *Vorlagen,* 45–46; English text from George Gordon Noël Byron, *The Poetical*

Works of Lord Byron, ed. Robert F. Glecker, rev. Cambridge ed. (Boston, 1975), 218.

20. *TB I,* 114.
21. Dürr, *Sololied,* 21.
22. *Vorlagen,* 237–238.
23. *Briefe NF,* 6. More extensive discussion of Schumann's Kerner settings appears in Hans-Udo Kreuels, *Schumanns Kerner Lieder. Interpretation und Analyse sämtlicher Lieder Robert Schumanns nach Gedichten von Justinius Kerner mit besonderer Berücksichtigung der Liederreihe op. 35* (Frankfurt, 2003).
24. *Schumann's Eichendorff Liederkreis and the Genre of the Romantic Cycle* (New York, 2000), 141–142.
25. Schubert composed a second setting in 1815, but it did not appear during Schumann's lifetime.
26. The first mention of Schubert lieder (as opposed to works for the piano) occurs in Schumann's diary on 5 December 1828, in the context of an evening at the Carus home; *TB I,* 152. But this does not preclude some prior acquaintance.
27. *Verzeichnis,* 730.
28. *Selbstbiographische Notizen,* 4ʳ.
29. *Verzeichnis,* 726.

1. Songs of Marriage

1. Barbara Turchin, "Schumann's Conversion to Vocal Music: A Reconsideration," *Musical Quarterly* 67 (1981): 392.
2. Now housed at the Robert-Schumann-Haus in Zwickau, 4871/VIII,4—5977 A3. See Helma Kaldewey, "Die *Gedichtabschriften* Robert und Clara Schumanns," in *Robert Schumann und die Dichter: Ein Musiker als Leser. Katalog zur Ausstellung des Heinrich-Heine-Instituts,* ed. Bernhard R. Appel and Inge Hermstrüwer (Düsseldorf, 1991), 88–99. For more on the couple's attempt to establish Robert's career, see David Ferris, "Public Performance and Private Understanding: Clara Wieck's Concerts in Berlin," *Journal of the American Musicological Society* 56 (2003): 351–408.
3. *TB III,* 670.
4. Turchin, "Schumann's Conversion," 404.
5. Jon Finson, "Preface," *Robert Schumann. Symphonie Nr. 4 d-moll op. 120. Erstfassung 1841* (Wiesbaden, 2003), ix.
6. Turchin, "Schumann's Conversion," 404.
7. John Daverio, *Robert Schumann: Herald of a "New Poetic Age"* (New York, 1997), 194–196.
8. Heinrich W. Schwab, *Sangbarkeit, Popularität und Kunstlied. Studien zu Lied und Liedästhetik der mittleren Goethezeit 1770–1814* (Regensburg, 1975), 145.
9. *Briefe NF,* 428–429.
10. *LB I,* 15–45, 49–56, 59–62, 91–93, 108–110, 119–26, 129–130.

11. Daverio, *New Poetic Age,* 195.

12. Eva Weissweiler, ed., *The Complete Correspondence of Clara and Robert Schumann,* trans. Hildegard Fritsch and Ronald L. Crawford (New York, 1994–2002), 3: 118.

13. See the correspondence about *Liederhefte* in conjunction with *Myrthen* in *Verzeichnis,* 105–106.

14. See Kurt Hofmann, *Die Erstdrucke der Werke von Robert Schumann* (Tutzing, 1979).

15. Weissweiler, *Correspondence.*

16. *Vorlagen,* 144.

17. *TB I,* 379; *Briefe NF,* 44–45.

18. For a lengthier analysis of this song, see Konrad Küster, "Schumanns neuer Zugang zum Kunstlied: Das 'Liederjahr' 1840 in kompositorischer Hinsicht," *Musikforschung* 51 (1998): 4–8.

19. See Otto Paul and Ingeborg Glier, *Deutsche Metrik* (Munich, 1970), §107.

20. *Vorlagen,* 433.

21. Ibid., 34.

22. *TB III,* 176.

23. See Kazuko Ozawa, "Robert Burns, die Jakobitismus und die *Gerstenmehlbrode,*" in *Schumanniana Nova. Festschrift Gerd Nauhaus zum 60. Geburtstag,* ed. Bernhard Appel, Ute Bär, and Matthias Wendt (Sinzig, 2002), 539–568; also Kenneth Stuart Whitton, "Robert Schumann und seine britischen Dichter," in *Schumann und seine Dichter,* Schumann Forschungen, vol. 4, ed. Matthias Wendt (Mainz, 1993), 71–76.

24. For a catalog, see R. Larry Todd, "Mendelssohn's Ossianic Manner, with a New Source—*On Lena's Gloomy Heath,*" in *Mendelssohn and Schumann: Essays on Their Music and Its Context* (Durham, 1984), 137–160.

25. English text from George Gordon Noël Byron, *The Poetical Works of Lord Byron,* ed. Robert F. Glecker, rev. Cambridge ed. (Boston, 1975), 218.

26. *Vorlagen,* 97.

27. See Rufus Hallmark, "Schumann's Behandlung seiner Liedertexte. Vorläufige Bericht zu einer neuen Ausgabe und zu einer Neubewertung von Schumanns Liedern" in *Schumanns Werke—Text und Interpretation,* Schumann Forschungen, vol. 2, ed. Bernhard Appel (Mainz, 1987), 29–42; and Hallmark, "Textkritische und aufführungspraktische Probleme in Schumann's Liedern," in *Schumann und seine Dichter,* ed. Wendt, 110–121.

28. For a detailed account of the compositional process in these songs, see Kazuko Ozawa, *Quellenstudien zu Robert Schumanns Liedern nach Adelbert von Chamisso,* Europäische Hochschulschriften, ser. 36, vol. 18 (Frankfurt, 1989), 45–46, 65–74, 293–450.

29. See Ruth Solie, "Whose Life? The Gendered Self in Schumann's *Frauenliebe* Songs," in *Music and Text: Critical Inquiries,* ed. Steven P. Scher (Cambridge, 1992), 219–240.

30. "*Frauenliebe und Leben* Now and Then," *19th Century Music* 25 (2001): 28.

31. Ibid., 29. Matthias Walz makes some of these same points in "*Frauenliebe*

und Leben op. 42—Biedermeierdichtung, Zykluskonstruktion und musikalische Lyrik," in *Schumann Studien 5,* ed. Gerd Nauhaus (Cologne, 1996), 97–115.

32. Muxfeldt, *"Frauenliebe,"* 27–28.
33. Weissweiler, *Correspondence,* 2: 116.
34. Muxfeldt, *"Frauenliebe,"* 40.
35. Ibid., 39.
36. Ibid., 47.
37. Karol Berger, *"Diegesis* and *Mimesis:* The Poetic Modes and the Matter of Artistic Presentation," *Journal of Musicology* 12 (1994): 429–430.
38. Stephen Walsh, *The Lieder of Schumann* (London, 1971), 52.
39. *TB II,* 134.
40. Weissweiler, *Correspondence,* 2: 246.
41. *TB II,* 186.
42. *Verzeichnis,* 980.
43. *TB II,* 139.
44. Ibid., 168.
45. *Briefe NF,* 431–432.
46. For a list, see Rufus Hallmark, "Schumann und Rückert," in *Schumann in Düsseldorf: Werke—Texte—Interpretation,* Schumann Forschungen, vol. 3, ed. Bernhard Appel (Mainz, 1993), 91–118.
47. Rufus Hallmark, "The Rückert Lieder of Robert and Clara Schumann," *19th Century Music* 14 (1990): 13–16.
48. I have adapted this translation from ibid., 12.

2. Irony and the Heine Cycles

1. See for instance Eric Sams, *The Songs of Robert Schumann* (Bloomington, 1993), 36–37.
2. *Robert Schumann: Liederkreis von Heine op. 24* (Munich, 1996), 6.
3. *TB I,* 129.
4. Hans-Joachim Bracht, "Schumanns 'Papillons' und die Ästhetik der Frühromantik," *Archiv für Musikwissenschaft* 50 (1993): 71–84.
5. Beate Julia Perrey, *Schumann's Dichterliebe and Early Romantic Poetics: Fragmentation of Desire* (Cambridge, 2002), 35.
6. Quoted in Lilian Furst, *Fictions of Romantic Irony* (Cambridge, Mass., 1984), 26.
7. For a summary of the various issues, see Charles S. Brauner, "Irony in the Heine Lieder of Schubert and Schumann," *Musical Quarterly* 57 (1981): 261–281. For an overview in Schumann's songs, see Thomas Synofzik, *Heinrich Heine—Robert Schumann: Musik und Ironie* (Cologne, 2006).
8. *Verzeichnis,* 99.
9. The songs in *Liederbuch I* do not appear in their order of composition; ibid., 789–792.
10. *Vorlagen,* 175, 179–184.

11. Westphal, *Liederkreis von H. Heine,* 11.

12. See *Verzeichnis,* 100.

13. Westphal, *Liederkreis von H. Heine,* 12. For discussion of the various rhetorical devices employed in op. 24, see Yvonne Grolik, *Musikalisch-rhetorische Figuren in Liedern Robert Schumanns* (Frankfurt, 2002).

14. "Spricht der Dichter oder der Tondichter? Die multiple *persona* und Robert Schumanns *Liederkreis* op. 24," in *Schumann und seine Dichter,* Schumann Forschungen, vol. 4, ed. Matthias Wendt (Mainz, 1993), 22–24.

15. Westphal, *Liederkreis von H. Heine,* 16.

16. Ibid., 17.

17. Ibid., 19.

18. For just a sampling of the many studies, see Arthur Komar, *Robert Schumann: Dichterliebe,* in Norton Critical Scores (New York, 1971); Rufus Hallmark, *The Genesis of Dichterliebe: A Source Study* (Ann Arbor, 1979), and "The Sketches for *Dichterliebe,*" *19th Century Music* 1 (1977): 110–136; David Neumeyer, "Organic Structure and the Song Cycle: Another Look at Schumann's *Dichterliebe,*" *Music Theory Spectrum* 4 (1982): 92–105; Edward Cone, "Poet's Love or Composer's Love?" in *Music and Text: Critical Inquiries,* ed. Stephen P. Scher (Cambridge, 1992), 177–192; Perrey, *Schumann's Dichterliebe.* Just lately Berthold Hoeckner reviewed all these writers and added more in "Paths through *Dichterliebe,*" *19th Century Music* 30 (2006): 65–80.

19. Hallmark, *Genesis,* 21.

20. For more on the similarities between the two cycles and Schumann's possible motives for fashioning *Dichterliebe,* see Hallmark, "Warum zweimal 'Dichterliebe'? Opus 24 und Opus 48," in *"Das Letzte Wort der Kunst": Heinrich Heine und Robert Schumann: zum 150. Todesjahr,* ed. Joseph A. Kruse (Stuttgart, forthcoming).

21. Details of the correspondence appear in *Verzeichnis,* 207.

22. See Perrey, *Schumann's Dichterliebe,* 120–121, for details of the work's final stages.

23. Most recently Gerd Nauhaus in "'Dichterliebe'—und Kein Ende," *"Das Letzte Wort der Kunst,"* 193–206.

24. Schumann's initial sketch actually cast the ending in C-sharp major; see Hallmark, *Genesis,* 109–111.

25. For an assessment of the various claims put forward for tonal organicism in *Dichterliebe,* see David Ferris, *Schumann's Eichendorff* Liederkreis *and the Genre of the Romantic Cycle* (New York, 2000), 25–58.

26. *Schumann's* Dichterliebe, 26–32, 121–3. For a critique of Ferris's and Perrey's views, see Hoeckner, "Paths through *Dichterliebe,*" 67–70.

27. For details on the alteration of "Liebe Bronne" to "Liebe Wonne," see *Vorlagen,* 186.

28. Hallmark, *Genesis,* 48–49.

29. Ibid., 57–58.

30. Ibid., 74–79.

3. Cycles of Wandering

1. "The Nineteenth-century *Wanderlieder* Cycle," *Journal of Musicology* 5 (1987): 511–512.
2. Ibid., 499.
3. Extensive details of op. 35's chronology appear in Hans Joachim Köhler, "Schumann's Kerner-Lieder, op. 35: Die Datierungen und ihre Aussage zum Problem 'Liederreihe' oder 'Zyklus'," in *Schumann und seine Dichter*, Schumann Forschungen, vol. 4, ed. Matthias Wendt (Mainz, 1993), 87–96. More detailed analyses of individual songs appear in Hans-Udo Kreuels, *Schumanns Kerner Lieder. Interpretation und Analyse sämtlicher Lieder Robert Schumanns nach Gedichten von Justinius Kerner mit besonderer Berücksichtigung der Liederreihe op. 35* (Frankfurt, 2003).
4. Represented by seventeen selections; see Helma Kaldewey, "Die *Gedichtabschriften* Robert und Clara Schumanns," in *Robert Schumann und die Dichter: Ein Musiker als Leser. Katalog zur Ausstellung des Heinrich-Heine-Instituts,* ed. Bernhard R. Appel and Inge Hermstrüwer (Düsseldorf, 1991), 89–90.
5. "Interpretation von Kerner-Lieder in ausgewählten Beispielen," in Wendt, ed., *Schumann und seine Dichter,* 55.
6. "*Wanderlieder* Cycle," 515.
7. "'Liederreihe' oder 'Zyklus'," 96.
8. Originally "Wann" in the exemplar Schumann consulted; see *Vorlagen,* 241.
9. Kerner's title reads "Frühlingskur"; ibid., 244.
10. For a melodic similarity between part of this passage and a song by Ferdinand Kufferath recently published by Schumann, see Bernhard R. Appel, "Kompositionen Robert Schumanns in den Musikbeilagen der *Neuen Zeitschrift für Musik,*" in *Schumann Studien 5,* ed. Gerd Nauhaus (Cologne, 1996), 75–76.
11. "'Liederreihe' oder 'Zyklus'," 89.
12. *Vorlagen,* 249.
13. Although *Liederbuch I* records no date for "Alte Laute," we can reasonably assume that Schumann conceived it at the same time as or right after "Wer machte dich," on 11 December 1840.
14. *Verzeichnis,* 148.
15. See *Vorlagen,* 330–331. Schumann used the initial 1837 volume as the source for op. 36.
16. *Verzeichnis,* 152–153.
17. Eva Weissweiler, ed., *The Complete Correspondence of Clara and Robert Schumann,* trans. Hildegard Fritsch and Ronald L. Crawford (New York, 1994–2002), 3: 201–202.
18. Kaldewey, "Die *Gedichtabschriften,*" 93–94.
19. In chronological order, the lengthier studies devoted specifically to op. 39 include Herwig Knaus, *Musiksprache und Werkstruktur in Robert Schumanns "Liederkreis,"* Schriften zur Musik, ed. Walter Kolneder (Munich, 1974); Patrick McCreless, "Song Order in the Song Cycle: Schumann's *Liederkreis,*

op. 39," *Music Analysis* 5 (1986): 5–28; Turchin, "The Nineteenth-Century *Wanderlieder* Cycle"; Karen Hindenlang, "Eichendorff's 'Auf einer Burg' and Schumann's *Liederkreis,* Opus 39," *Journal of Musicology* 8 (1990): 569–587; Peter Andraschke, "Schumann und Eichendorff. Zur Rezeption von Schumann's Liederkreis op. 39," in Wendt, ed., *Schumann und seine Dichter,* 159–172; Finson, "The Intentional Tourist: Romantic Irony in the Eichendorff *Liederkreis* of Robert Schumann," in *Schumann and His World,* ed. R. Larry Todd (Princeton, 1994), 156–170; Reinhold Brinkmann, *Schumann und Eichendorff: Studien zum Liederkreis Opus 39,* in Musik-konzepte, die Reihe über Komponisten, vol. 35, ed. Heinz-Klaus Metzger and Rainer Riehn (Landshut, 1997); David Ferris, *Schumann's Eichendorff* Liederkreis *and the Genre of the Romantic Cycle* (Oxford, 2000); David L. Mosley, *Gesture, Sign, and Song: An Interdisciplinary Approach to Schumann's* Liederkreis *Opus 39* (New York, 1990); Christiane Tewinkel, *Vom Rauschen Singen: Robert Schumann's* Liederkreis *op. 39 nach Gedichten von Joseph von Eichendorff,* Epistemata: Würzburger Wissenschaftliche Schriften, Reihe Literaturwissenschaft, vol. 482 (Würzburg, 2003).

20. See history in *Verzeichnis,* 172–173. Schumann and Whistling's correspondence about the new edition appears respectively in letters dated 27 February 1849, *BV,* no. 1422, copy in the Robert Schumann Haus, Zwickau 4602-A2c, and 28 February 1849 in *Corr.* 20, no. 3606.

21. *Verzeichnis,* 169.

22. *Erzählungen,* in *Sämtliche Werke des Freiherrn Joseph von Eichendorff, Historisch-Kritische Ausgabe,* ed. Hermann Kunisch and Helmut Koopman, vol. 5, part 1, ed. Karl Konrad Polheim, (Tübingen, 1998), 86.

23. For a good discussion of organization in Schumann's cycles generally and in op. 39 particularly, see Ferris, *Eichendorff* Liederkreis, chaps. 2–3, 7–8.

24. *Schumann und Eichendorff,* 75.

25. See Finson, "The Intentional Tourist."

26. For the legend's background, see Annegret Fauser, "Rheinsirenen: Loreley and Other Rhine Maidens," in *Music and the Sirens,* ed. Linda Phyllis Austern and Inna Naroditskaya (Bloomington, 2006), 250–276.

27. *Eichendorff* Liedekreis, 157–158.

28. Hindenlang, "Eichendorff's 'Auf einer Burg'."

29. See, for instance, Knaus, *Musiksprache,* 14.

30. *Verzeichnis,* 169.

31. Knaus, *Musiksprache,* 73.

32. *Schumann und Eichendorff,* 50.

33. For further discussion of disorientation in this poem, see David Ferris, "'Was will dieses Grau'n bedeuten?': Schumann's 'Zwielicht' and Daverio's 'Incomprehensibility Topos,'" *Journal of Musicology* 22 (2005), 131–153.

34. *Musiksprache und Werkstruktur,* 87.

35. "The Nineteenth-Century *Wanderlieder* Cycle," 499.

36. *TB III,* 339–341.

37. Wolfgang Boetticher, ed., *Briefe und Gedichte aus dem Album Robert und Clara Schumanns* (Leipzig, 1979), 50.

4. Romances, Ballads, and the Via Media

1. Translated from the quotation in Christian Freitag, *Ballade*, Themen—Texte—Interpretationen, vol. 6, ed. K. D. Hein-Mooren (Bamberg, 1986), 36.

2. *Verzeichnis,* 790.

3. Ozawa regards Chamisso's *Gedichte* (Leipzig, 1834) as the most likely source of Schumann's texts; see *Quellenstudien zu Robert Schumanns Liedern nach Adelbert von Chamisso,* Europäische Hochschulschriften, ser. 36, vol. 18 (Frankfurt, 1989), 47–49, and *Vorlagen,* 57.

4. Ozawa says simply that all three songs "treat the theme of marriage in various ways"; *Quellen Studien,* 54.

5. "Painting too realistically," Schumann called this; *GS* I, 270.

6. Kristina Muxfeldt, "*Frauenliebe und Leben* Now and Then," *19th Century Music* 25 (2001): 28.

7. For a discussion of this kind of text, see Finson, "Between *Lied* and *Ballade*: Schumann's Op. 40 and the Tradition of Genre," in *Schumanniana Nova: Festschrift Gerd Nauhaus zum 60.Geburtstag,* ed. Bernhard Appel et al. (Sinzig, 2002), 250–265.

8. Adelbert von Chamisso, *Sämtliche Werke in zwei Bänden,* ed. Werner Feudel and Christel Laufer (Munich, 1982), 1: 705.

9. Ozawa, *Quellenstudien,* 57.

10. *Robert Schumann: Herald of a 'New Poetic Age'* (New York, 1997), 194.

11. The German original appears in Ozawa, *Quellenstudien,* 63.

12. Ibid., 64.

13. See Freitag, *Ballad,* 24–35.

14. See, for instance, Dietrich Fischer-Dieskau, *Robert Schumann, Wort und Musik* (Stuttgart, 1981), 93.

15. Ibid., 94.

16. *Nineteenth-Century Music,* trans. J. Bradford Robinson (Berkeley, 1989), 70.

17. See Ozawa, *Quellenstudien,* 59–61, for the details surrounding the Danish underlay. Schumann most probably used this ploy to secure a publisher and a wider audience.

18. *Das Märchen meines Lebens—Briefe—Tagebücher,* trans. Thyra Dohrenburg (Munich, 1961), 314. See also David Ferris's recent article, "Public Performance and Private Understanding: Clara Wieck's Concerts in Berlin," *Journal of the American Musicological Society* 56 (2003), 351–408. A more detailed account of the Schumanns' dealings with Andersen appears in Anna Harwell Celenza, *Hans Christian Andersen and Music: The Nightingale Revealed* (Aldershot, 2005), 101–106.

19. *Verzeichnis,* 196.

20. A more detailed discussion of this song appears in Jurgen Thym, "Text-Music Relationships in Schumann's 'Frühlingsfahrt,'" *Theory and Practice 5* (1980): 7–25.

21. Volker Kalisch, "Heines Geist aus Schumanns Händen," in *"Neue Bahnen."*

Robert Schumann und seine musikalischen Zeitgenossen, Schumann Forschungen, vol. 7, ed. Bernhard Appel (Mainz, 2002), 165. For an extended
exploration of political undercurrents in this ballad, see Susan Youens,
"*Maskenfreiheit* and Schumann's Napoleon-Ballad," *Journal of Musicology*
22 (2005): 5–46.

22. *Vorlagen,* 102.

23. Ibid., 405–406.

24. Ibid., 289. See also Schulte, "*. . . was Ihres Zaubergriffels würdig ware!" Die
Textbasis für Robert Schumanns Lieder für Solostimmen,* Schumann
Forschungen, vol. 10 (Mainz, 2005), 109.

25. Only "Aus den östlichen Rosen" from *Myrthen* intervenes; see *Verzeichnis,*
792.

26. Ibid., 277.

27. Ibid.

28. *Vorlagen,* 297.

29. Helma Kaldewey, "Die *Gedichtabschriften* Robert und Clara Schumanns,"
in *Robert Schumann und die Dichter: Ein Musiker als Leser. Katalog zur
Ausstellung des Heinrich-Heine-Instituts,* ed. Bernhard Appel and Inge
Hermstrüwer (Düsseldorf, 1991), 97.

30. *TB III,* 283.

31. *Vorlagen,* 175–176.

32. The sketching occurred on 27 October; *TB II,* 192. Bernhard Appel has published the orchestral version, *Tragödie (Heinrich Heine) for Solo Voices and
Orchestra* (London, 1994).

33. *Schumann's Eichendorff* Liederkreis *and the Genre of the Romantic Cycle*
(New York, 2000), 85.

34. *Corr.,* 18, no. 3111.

35. *BV,* no. 1099.

36. *Corr.,* 18, no. 3118.

37. See *BV,* no. 1122 and *Corr.,* 18, no. 3147 for this exchange.

38. *Verzeichnis,* 253.

5. *Lyrical Schemes:* Collections of Earlier Lieder und Gesänge

1. "Schumann's *Lieder und Gesänge,* 3tes Heft, op. 77: remarks on sources
and structure," in *Robert Schumann: Philologische, analytische, sozial- und
rezeptionsgeschichtliche Aspekte,* Saarbrücker Studien zur Musikwissenschaft, Neue Folge, vol. 8, ed. Wolf Frobenius et al. (Saarbrücken, 1998), 89.

2. *Verzeichnis,* 123–126.

3. Ibid., 127.

4. *Vorlagen,* 110–111.

5. *Verzeichnis,* 127–128.

6. On the affinity between composer and poet, see Ernst Herttrich, "Schumann
und Geibel," in *Schumann und seine Dichter,* Schumann Forschungen, vol.
4, ed. Matthias Wendt (Mainz, 1993), 122–131.

7. Herttrich speculates that Schumann's interest in Geibel's translations of

Spanish may have resulted from their personal encounters in 1846; ibid., 129, 131. Clara also set the poet's verse in her op. 13.

8. Dietrich Fischer-Dieskau, for instance, simply assumes that the title invokes Arnim and Brentano's famous collection; *Robert Schuman, Wort und Musik* (Stuttgart, 1981), 97.

9. *Verzeichnis,* 128.

10. *Corr.,* no. 3585.

11. Ein Anerbieten eines Musikalienhändlers in Rostock, Hagemann, erinnerte mich an Sie. Der will nämlich vorzüglich Lieder, und ich dachte ihm schon welche zu geben. Da fielen Sie mir ein, der Sie mir näher stehen und, wenn ich nicht irre, dergleichen wünschten.

Ich gedachte nun nach Art der *Balladen* u. *Romanzen* ein Opus in zwanglosen Heften erscheinen zu lassen,—unter bliebe Raum für spätere Lieder—, und will auch die Älteren, hier u. da in Albums zerstreuten mit aufnehmen.

Der Einhalt der beiden ersten Hefte steht auf dem Beiblatt. Nun aber, was mir schwer wird zu sagen, was ich aber doch meiner eigenen Verhältnisse halber nicht unterlaßen kann—Sie müssen mir schon etwas mehr Honorar zahlen, als früher. Meine Compositionen—ich darf es Ihnen wohl im Vertrauen sagen—fangen an bei den *Verleger* Interesse zu erregen, und ich bekomme mehr Aufträge, als ich befriedigen kann. Stünde ich allein in der Welt, so würde ich meine älteren Verleger nicht gerne steigern. Aber so bin ich mir und den meinigen dies schuldig. Dies unter uns.

Rechnen Sie also *zwölf Thaler* für den Druckbogen von *4 Seiten,* so ist das Geschäft für die Lieder abegmacht. Das Manuscript können Sie bald haben; das Honorar brauche ich nicht gleich, wenn ich nicht nur darauf verlassen kann, daß Sie mir es schicken, *wenn ich es später brauche.* Sie müssen mir aber umgehend antworten. Thun Sie es nicht, so nehme ich an, Sie gehen nicht auf meinen Vorschlag ein—und ich gebe die Hefte dann dem Mann in Rostock. Letter dated 27 February 1849, *BV,* no. 1422; copy in the Robert-Schumann-Haus, Zwickau, 4602-A2c.

12. "Ihrem Wunsche gemäß, zeige ich Ihnen angehend an, daß ich mit großem Vergnügen Ihre Lieder Op. 51 in Verlag nehmen werde, und mit den mir gestellten Bedingungen vollkommen einverstanden bin, welches Letztere fast keine Frage bedurft hätte, da wir uns ja genau genug kennen, um nicht mit größter Offenheit zu reden." *Corr.* 20, no. 3606.

13. For a facsimile of the autograph draft title page and the text of the letter, see Kazuko Ozawa, "Anmerkungen zu Schumans Liedern in den Beilagen der *Neuen Zeitschrift für Musik,*" in *Schumann Studien 5,* ed. Gerd Nauhaus (Cologne, 1996), 90–92.

14. *TB II,* 421, 554n.753; *Briefe NF,* 272.

15. "Gar zu schwierig zu componiren, soll das geheime Naturwesen im Gedicht einigermaßen getroffen werden. Kaum mehr als Versuch"; *LB I,* 56.

16. *Vorlagen,* 442.

17. *TB III,* 931.

18. *Robert Schumanns Mottosammlung: Übertragung, Kommentar, Einführung*, Rombach Wissenschaften—Reihe Litterae, vol. 39, ed. Gerhard Neumann and Günter Schnitzler (Freiburg, 1998), 500, 560.

19. *TB III*, 165.

20. This pseudonym led Fischer-Dieskau to confuse the name with Balthasar Friedrich Wilhelm Zimmermann; see Krischan Schulte, ". . . *was Ihres Zaubergriffels würdig ware!": Die Textbasis für Robert Schumanns Lieder für Solostimmen*, Schumann Forschungen, vol. 10 (Mainz, 2005), 31.

21. For brief biographical sketches, see Jan-Christoph Hauschild, "Zimmermann Georg," in *Literatur Lexikon Autoren und Werke deutscher Sprache*, ed. Walther Killy (Munich, 1992), 12: 496–497, and Wilhelm Kosch, *Deutsches Literatur-Lexikon*, 2d ed. (Bern, 1958), 4: 3529.

22. Otto Paul and Ingeborg Glier, *Deutsche Metrik*, 8th ed. (Munich, 1970), §140.

23. For a complete list of differences between the two versions, see Ozawa, "Anmerkungen," 92–94. She notes that many of the changes in the op. 27 version revert back to the autograph fair copy in *LB III*, 26–27.

24. Ozawa, "Anmerkungen," 91.

25. *Verzeichnis*, 227. The new title page for op. 39, also published by Whistling, coincidentally accompanied the engraver's copy for op. 51; ibid., 168–169.

26. Ibid., 227.

27. Schumann changes "Vertraure" to the less intense "betraure" and repeats the last line of text to make it parallel the length of the others.

28. *Vorlagen*, 362. The poem originates in *Liebesfrühling*, third bouquet.

29. Ibid., 71.

30. Ibid.

31. *TB III*, 282–283.

32. *Vorlagen*, 230.

33. For the history of Schumann's dealings with the publisher, see Renate Federhofer-Königs, "Die Beziehungen von Robert Schumann zur Familie André," in *Gutenberg-Jahrbuch 1988*, ed. Hans-Joachim Koppitz (Mainz, 1988), 190–205.

34. *Corr.*, 26/2, no. 88.

35. *BV*, no. 2332.

36. Schumann's enclosed title page suggests another number, "Ein Gedanke" by Eduard Ferrand; see *Verzeichnis*, 540. We shall see that Paul's correspondence seems to imply that Schumann actually sent the Bernhard instead.

37. *Corr.*, 26/2, no. 94.

38. *BV*, no. 2336.

39. *Corr.*, 26/2, no. 100.

40. Ibid., no. 116.

41. See, for instance, his dictum to André about the placement of two-page numbers in Federhofer-Königs, "Die Beziehungen," 203.

42. *Verzeichnis*, 545.

43. Helma Kaldewey, "Die *Gedichtabschriften* Robert und Clara Schumanns,"

in *Robert Schumann und die Dichter: Ein Musiker als Leser. Katalog zur Ausstellung des Heinrich-Heine-Instituts,* ed. Bernhard Appel and Inge Hermstrüwer (Düsseldorf, 1991), 90.

44. For an account of establishing the final form of op. 48, see Beate Julia Perrey, *Schumann's* Dichterliebe *and Early Romantic Poetics: Fragmentation of;Desire* (Cambridge, 2002), 121. Another version appears in Berthold Hocckner, "Paths through *Dichterliebe,*" *19th Century Music* 30 (2006): 65–80.

45. The composer substituted "Ritter" for "Riese" in his published version.

46. He received Baumeister's thanks on 17 August for the song; *Vorlagen,* 415.

47. See, for instance, Eric Sams, *The Songs of Robert Schumann* (Bloomington, 1993), 33.

48. *LB I,* 13–14.

49. Joachim Draheim, "Schumann und Shakespeare," *Neue Zeitschrift für Musik* 142 (1981), 243.

50. *GS* 1: 155–156.

51. *TB I,* 235.

52. *Vorlagen,* 410.

53. *Songs of Schumann,* 34.

54. See Colma von der Heyde, "Eine Jugendfreundshaft Clara Schumanns," *Neue Musik-Zeitung* 27 (1906): 411–416; *Vorlagen,* 25.

55. "Robert Schumanns Gesangkompositionen," *Allgemeine musikalische Zeitung* 44 (1842): cols. 30–33, 58–63.

56. Ibid., 32.

57. Ibid., 33.

58. Ibid., 58.

59. Ibid., 61.

60. Ibid., 62–63.

6. The Advent of the "New Style" and the Later Cycles

1. The best account of this period and its various currents appears in John Daverio, *Robert Schumann: Herald of a "New Poetic Age"* (New York, 1997), 294–301.

2. It still exists today; ibid., 397–399.

3. 17 March 1846, *TB II,* 398; translation after Daverio, *A New Poetic Age,* 296. *TB III* gives 16 March as the date of this encounter; 416.

4. *My Life,* trans. Andrew Gray, ed. Mary Whittall (Cambridge, 1983), 319.

5. *TB III,* 467n.658.

6. *Briefe NF,* 252.

7. Ibid., 254.

8. *TB III,* 460.

9. Ibid., 463.

10. *Briefe NF,* 305.

11. The term comes from Ulrich Mahlert's *Fortschritt und Kunstlied: Späte Lieder Robert Schumanns im Licht der Liedaesthetischen Diskussion ab 1848,* Freiburger Schriften zur Musikwissenschaft, vol. 13 (Munich, 1983), 115–

139. Mahlert provides an excellent summary of the changes in Schumann's style, its possible roots, and also its reception.

12. Originally published under the title *40* [sic] *Clavierstücke für die Jugend* by J. Schuberth in December 1848.

13. For information on the *Projektenbuch*, see *Verzeichnis*, 343; *TB III*, 489.

14. Ibid., 489–490.

15. For an account of Schumann's feelings about the revolution, see Daverio, *A New Poetic Age*, 422–425.

16. *TB III*, 495.

17. See, for instance Eric Sams, *The Songs of Robert Schumann* (Bloomington, 1993), 197–198.

18. See Daverio, *A New Poetic Age*, 421–422.

19. A reprinting of Goethe's review appears in Hoffmann von Fallersleben, "Zur Geschichte des Wunderhorns," *Weimarisches Jahrbuch für deutsche Sprache, Literatur und Kunst* 2 (1855): 263–265.

20. For discussion of children's collections during this period, see Roe-Min Kok, "Romantic Childhood, Bourgeois Commercialism and the Music of Robert Schumann," unpublished doctoral dissertation, Harvard University, 2003. For the special political connotations of texts in op. 79, see Ulrich Mahlert, "Pädagogik und Politik. Zu Schumanns *Lieder-Album für die Jugend,* op. 79," in *Robert Schumann: Philologische, analytische, sozial- und rezeptionsgeschichtliche Aspekte*, Saarbrücker Studien zur Musikwissenschaft, Neue Folge, vol. 8, Wolf Frobenius et al., eds. (Saarbrücken, 1998), 154–162. More on the choice of texts appears in Peter Jost, "Zur Textwahl in Schumanns Liederalbum für die Jugend op. 79," in *Schumann Studien 8* (Zwickau, forthcoming).

21. *Briefe NF,* 324.

22. *Vorlagen*, 214–215. See Krischan Schulte's elucidation in *". . . was Ihres Zaubergriffels würdig ware!" Die Textbasis für Robert Schumanns Lieder für Solostimmen*, Schumann Forschungen, vol. 10 (Mainz, 2005), 74–77.

23. *Vorlagen*, 216.

24. Again, I adopt Nägeli's terminology as amplified by Walter Dürr, *Das deutsche Sololied im 19. Jahrhundert: Untersuchung zur Sprache und Musik* (Wilhelmshaven, 1984), 14–16.

25. *Vorlagen*, 424–425.

26. See ibid., 316–318, for the complete history.

27. Ibid., 376.

28. Ibid., 374.

29. Ibid., 225–226. Schulte and Schanze take their text for the latter from von Fallersleben's *Gedichte*.

30. *Erler* 2: 86. Virginia Livia Frege studied voice with Wilhelmine Schröder-Devriant, then married a physician in Leipzig. She sang a solo role in *Das Paradies und die Peri*.

31. *Vorlagen*, 21.

32. For Pattberg's biography and the source for this poem, see ibid., 320–321.

33. Ibid., 75–76.

34. Ibid., 384.
35. Ibid., 7.
36. Ibid., 364.
37. *GS* I: 272.
38. For a consideration of how composers fit pentameter into quadratic musical phrases, see Rufus Hallmark and Ann Clark Fehn, "Text Declamation in Schubert's Setting of Pentameter Poetry," *Zeitschrift für Literaturwissenschaft und Linguistik* 9 (1979): 80–111.
39. *Verzeichnis*, 423–424.
40. Ibid.
41. See the letter to Liszt on 31 May 1849 quoted at the beginning of this chapter, n. 10; see also *TB III*, 498–501.
42. *A New Poetic Age*, 429.
43. *TB III*, 344; *Vorlagen*, 137.
44. *A New Poetic Age*, 430–431.
45. Renate Federhofer-Königs, "Die Beziehungen von Robert Schumann zur Familie André," in *Gutenberg-Jahrbuch 1988,* ed. Hans-Joachim Koppitz (Mainz, 1988), 202.
46. *TB II*, 74, 83.
47. *Vorlagen*, 280. See also Helma Kaldewey, "Die *Gedichtabschriften* Robert und Clara Schumanns," in *Robert Schumann und die Dichter: Ein Musiker als Leser. Katalog zur Ausstellung des Heinrich-Heine-Instituts*, ed. Bernhard Appel and Inge Hermstrüwer (Düsseldorf, 1991), 91–93.
48. *Vorlagen*, 285–288.
49. "Lenaus *Husarenlieder* als Klavierlied Schumanns (op. 117)," in *Schumann und seine Dichter*, Schumann Forschungen, vol. 4, ed. Matthias Wendt (Mainz, 1993), 45–46.
50. Daverio, *A New Poetic Age*, 424.
51. "Lenaus *Husarenlieder*," 47.
52. *Verzeichnis*, 498.
53. *TB III*, 520, 564.
54. See *TB III*, 604–610, and attendant footnotes.
55. Berthold Litzmann, *Clara Schumann: Ein Künstlerleben nach Tagebüchern und Briefen* (Leipzig, 1910), 3: 269.
56. For an extensive discussion of Vincke, his anthology, and how it came to Schumann's attention, see Hans-Joachim Zimmermann, "Die Gedichte der Königin Maria Stuart: Gisbert Vincke, Robert Schumann, und eine sentimentale Tradition," *Archiv für das Studium der neueren Sprachen und Literaturen* 214 (1977): 298–301.
57. Kaldewey, "Die *Gedichtabschriften*," 99.
58. Walter Scott, *The Abbot*, ed. Christopher Johnson, in *The Edinburgh Edition of the Waverley Novels*, ed. David Hewitt (Edinburgh, 2000); Baltimore: Miller & Beacham, n.d.. Barker's short biography appears in James D. Brown, ed., *Biographical Dictionary of Musicians: With a Bibliography of English Writings on Music* (London, 1886), 50.
59. *Verzeichnis*, 561; *BV*, no. 2329.

60. *Verzeichnis,* 561–562.
61. "Die Gedichte der Königin Maria Stuart," 307–322.
62. "Bedeutung und Eigenart der Maria-Stuart-Lieder, op. 135, von Robert Schumann," ibid., 325–327.
63. For more on the sonnet in German lieder, see Jurgen Thym and Ann C. Fehn, "Sonnet Structure and the German Lied: Shackles or Spurs?" *Journal of the American Liszt Society* 32 (1991): 3–15.
64. *Vorlagen,* 419.
65. "Neo-Romanticism," *19th Century Music* 3 (1979): 105.

7. Poets in Review during the Later Years

1. Ulrich Mahlert speaks to this point in "Rückzug in die Idylle: Robert Schumanns *Sechs Gesänge von Wilfried von der Neun* op. 89," in *Schumanns Werke—Text und Interpretation,* Schumann Forschungen, vol. 2, ed. Bernhard Appel (Mainz, 1987), 224.
2. Ibid., 225.
3. For a discussion of the distinction between ballads and romances around the turn of the nineteenth century, see "Die Ballade" in Walther Dürr's *Das deutsche Sololied im 19. Jahrhundert: Untersuchung zur Sprache und Musik* (Wilhelmshaven, 1984), 181–182.
4. See Renate Federhofer-Königs, "Die Beziehungen von Robert Schumann zur Familie André," in *Gutenberg-Jahrbuch 1988,* ed. Hans-Joachim Koppitz (Mainz, 1988), 199.
5. *Verzeichnis,* 385–386.
6. *Corr.,* 21, no. 3787; reprinted in *Vorlagen,* 308.
7. *Briefe NF,* 324.
8. *Corr.,* 21, no. 3899; reprinted in and translation adapted from *Vorlagen,* 309.
9. *TB III,* 526–527.
10. *Briefe NF,* 525n.401.
11. *Verzeichnis,* 391.
12. *TB III,* 535.
13. Mahlert, "Rückzug in die Idylle," 226–227.
14. *Vorlagen,* 512–513.
15. Dedication copy sent 4 August 1850; *BV,* no. 1673.
16. See Berthold Litzmann, *Clara Schumann: Ein Künstlerleben nach Tagebüchern und Briefen* (Leipzig, 1910), 2: 146–148.
17. *TB II,* 74, 84.
18. *Vorlagen,* 279.
19. *TB II,* 78, 83.
20. For details surrounding the identification of the source for "Requiem," see *Vorlagen,* 76–77.
21. *Erler* 2: 125–126
22. Litzmann, *Clara Schumann,* 2: 221.
23. For a cursory but insightful overview of the contents of the opus, see Klaus

Velten, "Robert Schumann's Lenau-Vertonungen, op. 90," in *Robert Schumann: Philologische, analytische, sozial- und rezeptionsgeschichtliche Aspekte,* Saarbrücker Studien zur Musikwissenschaft, Neue Folge, vol. 8, ed. Wolf Frobenius et al. (Saarbrücken, 1998), 90–96.

24. For a longer and more explicit discussion of the similarities between the two songs, see Beate Julia Perrey, *Schumann's* Dichterliebe *and Early Romantic Poetics: Fragmentation of Desire* (Cambridge, 2002), 148–162.

25. Litzmann, *Clara Schumann,* 2: 221.

26. See *Vorlagen,* 76–79, for a complete discussion.

27. For an extended discussion of this feature in Schumann's setting, see Daniel Beller-McKenna, "Distance and Disembodiment: Harps, Horns, and the Requiem Idea in Schumann and Brahms," *Journal of Musicology* 22 (2005): 52–56.

28. For details about her life and her dealings with the Schumanns, see Joseph A. Kruse, Bernhard R. Appel, and Inge Hermstrüwer, *Das Stammbuch der Constanze Dawison geb. Jacobi,* KulturStiftung der Länder—Patrimonia, vol. 34 (Düsseldorf, 1991).

29. *TB III,* 506.

30. Ibid., 512.

31. Gesellschaft der Musikfreunde, A-290. My thanks to Otto Biba for allowing me to inspect this source.

32. Federhofer-Königs, "Die Beziehungen," 201.

33. *Verzeichnis,* 411.

34. *BV,* no. 1766; *Erler* 2: 139.

35. See George Gordon Noël Byron, *The Poetical Works of Lord Byron,* ed. Robert F. Glecker, rev. Cambridge ed. (Boston, 1975), 216, 1010.

36. A text that some commentators tie logically enough to Moore's earlier and more famous "The Harp That Once thro' Tara's Halls"; ibid.

37. All quotation of English originals from ibid.

38. Surely not the 1820 translation by Franz Theremin, but possibly one published in 1839 by Schumann's longtime friend Adolf Böttger, mentioned in *Vorlagen,* 46.

39. See *TB I,* 413, or *TB II,* 122–123.

40. See Olga Lossewa, "Neues über Elisabeth Kulmann," *Schumann und seine Dichter,* Schumann Forschungen, vol. 4, ed. Mathias Wendt (Mainz, 1993), 78.

41. Ibid., 81–82.

42. A copy of the 1851 edition now housed at the Schumann-Haus in Zwickau was presented by Großheinrich in gratitude to the composer after he had published his songs; *Vorlagen,* 263.

43. *TB III,* 562–564.

44. *Verzeichnis,* 443.

45. ". . . *die Spuren einer himmlischen Erscheinung zurücklassend.* Zu Schumanns Liedern nach Gedichten von Elisabeth Kulmann," *Schumann in Düsseldorf: Werke—Texte—Interpretation,* Schumann Forschungen, vol. 3, ed. Bernhard Appel (Mainz, 1993), 119–140.

46. For the many examples of this phenomenon in popular song, see Jon W. Finson, *The Voices That Are Gone: Themes in Nineteenth-Century American Popular Song* (New York, 1994), 84–93. For Schumann's specific predilections, see also Roe-Min Kok, "Falling Asleep: Schumann, Lessing, and Death," in *Studien zur* Wertforschung, vol. 48, ed. Andreas Dorschel (Vienna, forthcoming).

47. "... *die Spuren*," 129.

48. Ibid., 131.

49. My information about Pfarrius originates in *Vorlagen*, 323.

50. Helma Kaldewey, "Die *Gedichtabschriften* Robert und Clara Schumanns," in *Robert Schumann und die Dichter: Ein Musiker als Leser. Katalog zur Ausstellung des Heinrich-Heine-Instituts,* ed. Bernhard R. Appel and Inge Hermstrüwer (Düsseldorf, 1991), 92.

51. *Vorlagen*, 323.

52. *Verzeichnis*, 504.

53. Ibid.

54. See D. A. Wells, "Letters of Mendelssohn, Schumann, and Berlioz in Belfast," *Music & Letters* 60 (1979), 182–183.

55. *Verzeichnis*, 504–505.

8. Collections in the New Style

1. "Schumann's *Lieder und Gesänge,* 3tes Heft, op. 77: remarks on sources and structure," in *Robert Schumann: Philologische, analytische, sozial- und rezeptionsgeschichtliche Aspekte,* Saarbrücker Studien zur Musikwissenschaft, Neue Folge, vol. 8, ed. Wolf Frobenius et al. (Saarbrücken, 1998), 76–89.

2. For this vexed history, see Renate Federhofer-Königs, "Die Beziehungen von Robert Schumann zur Familie André," in *Gutenberg-Jahrbuch 1988,* ed. Hans-Joachim Koppitz (Mainz, 1988), 198–202.

3. Ibid., 203.

4. *BV,* no. 1679a.

5. Federhofer-Königs, "Die Beziehungen," 203.

6. Ms. 340.

7. "Schumann's *Lieder und Gesänge,*" 84.

8. *Verzeichnis,* 333. For the initial correspondence concerning this series, see Chapter 5.

9. Ibid., 333–334.

10. Marston offers a slightly different but not at all antithetical assessment in "Schumann's *Lieder und Gesänge.*"

11. Ibid., 80.

12. Marston shows that in its first version, this juncture portended yet a different tonal progression, to B minor; ibid., 83–84.

13. *TB II,* 75–76, *BV,* no. 1064.

14. *Vorlagen,* 436.

15. Ibid., 435.

16. Ibid., 437.
17. Ibid., 275.
18. *Corr.*, 21, no. 3896; translation adapted from ibid.
19. *TB III*, 524.
20. *BV*, no. 1856; see *Verzeichnis*, 414.
21. *Romantic Music: A History of Musical Style in Nineteenth-Century Europe* (New York, 1984), 121.
22. *Vorlagen*, 5.
23. This biography is taken from *Vorlagen*, 327–328.
24. Ibid., 329.
25. *Corr.*, 24, no. 4307, as quoted in ibid., 310.
26. See "Rückzug in die Idylle: Robert Schumanns *Sechs Gesänge von Wilfried von der Neun* op. 89," in *Schumanns Werke—Text und Interpretation*, Schumann Forschungen, vol. 2, ed. Bernhard Appel (Mainz, 1987), 224.
27. See *Verzeichnis*, 371; *Corr.*, 21, no. 3897.
28. *Verzeichnis*, 372.
29. Ibid., 371–372.
30. *TB III*, 545, 614.
31. *Vorlagen*, 30.
32. "The Rückert Lieder of Robert and Clara Schumann," *19th Century Music* 14 (1990): 3–30.
33. *Vorlagen*, 364.
34. *BV*, no. 1964.
35. *Verzeichnis*, 456.
36. Ibid., 455.
37. "Ganz besonders erfreute mich Ihre Offerte in Betreff der Manuscripte und bin ich mit dem größten Vergnügen bereit, dieselben zum Stich zu übernehmen, unter den von Ihnen angesetzten Bedingungen, nur müßte ich sie freundlichst ersuchen, die Auszahlung der Honorare bis Ende Mai anzusetzen, da ich leider durch die herannahende Ostermesse sowie durch ziemlich lauen Geschäftsgang für den Augenblick nicht Gelder disponibel habe, sofern es Ihnen aber besonders angenehm wäre, mir dann später einige andere Manuscripte zu überlassen und diese einem anderen Verleger zu übertragen, so würde ich auch hiermit gern einverstanden sein"; *Corr.*, 24, no. 4432.
38. *BV*, no. 1972.
39. *TB II*, 416.
40. *Vorlagen*, 430.
41. *Vorlagen*, 211–212.
42. Ibid., 212.
43. Ibid., 306.
44. *Verzeichnis*, 456.
45. *Vorlagen*, 256.
46. Ibid.
47. *Verzeichnis*, 531.
48. See *BV*, no. 1670, dated 27 July 1850.

49. "Ihrem gefälligen Schreiben zufolge, mit dem Sie, geehrter Herr! mich aufs Angenehmste überrascht haben, ersuche ich ergebenst, das Manuscript Ihrer Gesänge mir direct mit Post überschicken zu wollen, um sofort das Honorar von zehn Louis dor auf eben dem Wege, später aber und noch bevor das Jahr zu Ende geht, die verlangten Freiexemplare in bester Ausstattung zu empfangen"; *Corr.*, 25, no. 4560.
50. *BV*, no. 2126.
51. *Corr.*, 21, no. 3817.
52. See Krischan Schulte, *". . . was Ihres Zaubergriffels würdig ware!" Die Textbasis für Robert Schumanns Lieder für Solostimmen,* Schumann Forschungen, vol. 10 (Mainz, 2005), 31.
53. Letter to Härtel dated 20 May 1849, in *Erler* 2: 86.
54. *Vorlagen*, 51.
55. Ibid.
56. "Robert Schumann, Schön Hedwig. Ballade von F. Hebbel für Deklamation mit Begleitung des Pianof. Op. 206. [*sic*] Leipzig, B. Kuff [*sic*]. Fünf heitere Gesänge für eine Singstimme mit Begleitung des Pianof. Op. 125 Magdeburg. Heinrichshofen," *Neue Berliner Musikzeitung* 7 (1853): 250–251.

Epilogue: Reception of the Late Style

1. "Robert Schumann, Op. 79. Liederalbum für die Jugend.—Leipzig, Breitkopf & Härtel. Preis 3 Thlr.," *Neue Zeitschift für Musik* 13 (1850): 57–59.
2. See Chapter 6.
3. See *TB III,* 530.
4. "Liederalbum für die Jugend," 57.
5. Ibid.
6. Ibid., 58.
7. Ibid., 59
8. "Liederschau," *Neue Berliner Musikzeitung* 5 (1851): 132.
9. "Lieder und Gesänge," *Neue Zeitschift für Musik* 34 (1851): 245.
10. Klitzsch, "Lieder und Gesänge," *Neue Zeitschift für Musik* 36 (1852): 167–168.
11. "Liederschau," 132.
12. Klitzsch, "Lieder und Gesänge," *Neue Zeitschrift für Musik* 40 (1854): 58.
13. "Liederschau," *Neue Berliner Musikzeitung* 9 (1855): 210.
14. "Robert Schumann, Schön Hedwig. Ballade von F. Hebbel für Deklamation mit Begleitung des Pianos. Op. 206. [*sic*] Leipzig, B. Kuff [*sic*]. Fünf heitere Gesänge für eine Singstimme mit Begleitung des Pianos. Op. 125 Magdeburg. Heinrichshofen," *Neue Berliner Musikzeitung* 7 (1853): 251.
15. "Zur Würdigung Richard Wagners," *Neue Zeitschrift für Musik* 39 (1853): 200.
16. "Robert Schumann, Op. 98. Lieder, Gesänge und ein Requiem für Mignon aus Goethe's Wilhelm Meister für Gesang und Pianoforte . . . ," *Neue Zeitschrift für Musik* 35 (1851): 219.

17. Ibid., 220.
18. More on this controversy appears in Jurgen Thym's "Schumann in Brendel's *Neue Zeitshcrift fürMusik* from 1845 to 1856," in *Mendelssohn and Schumann: Essays on Their Music and Its Context,* eds. Jon Finson and R. Larry Todd (Durham, 1984), 21–36. Thym gives a much more negative impression of the objections to Schumann's later style, however.
19. "Robert Schumann, Op. 107. Sechs Gesänge für eine Singstimme . . . ," *Neue Zeitschrift für Musik* 14 (1852): 141–143.
20. Ibid., 141.
21. Ibid.
22. Ibid., 142.
23. Ibid., 143.
24. Ibid.
25. Ulrich Mahlert explores many of the political demands placed on the German lied in his *Fortschritt und Kunstlied: Späte Lieder Robert Schumanns im Licht der Liedaesthetischen Diskussion ab 1848,* Freiburger Schriften zur Musikwissenschaft, vol. 13 (Munich, 1983).
26. *GS* 2: 271–272.

Editions of Music Consulted
and Selected Bibliography

Editions of Schumann's Music Consulted

"Der Fischer." Ed. Martin Kreisig. *Zeitschrift für Musik* 100, 1 (1933), Noten-beilage Nr. 1.

"Ein Gedanke." Ed. Robert Hernried. *Musical Quarterly* 27 (1942): 57–58.

Robert Schumann's Werke. Ed. Clara Schumann. 32 vols. Leipzig: Breitkopf & Härtel, [1879–1893].

Sechs frühe Lieder für Gesang und Klavier. Ed. Karl Geiringer. Vienna: Universal-Edition, 1933.

Tragödie (Heinrich Heine) for Solo Voices and Orchestra. Ed. Bernhard R. Appel. London: Eulenberg, 1994.

Selected Bibliography

Andersen, Hans Christian. *Correspondence.* Ed. Frederick Crawford. London: Dean and Son, n.d.

———. *Das Märchen meines Lebens—Briefe—Tagebücher.* Trans. Thyra Dohrenburg. Munich: Winkler Verlag, 1961.

Appel, Bernhard, ed. *"Neue Bahnen." Robert Schumann und seine musikalischen Zeitgenossen.* Schumann Forschungen, vol. 7. Mainz: Schott, 2002.

———. *Schumann in Düsseldorf: Werke—Texte—Interpretation.* Schumann Forschungen, vol. 3. Mainz: Schott, 1993.

———. *Schumanns Werke—Text und Interpretation.* Schumann Forschungen, vol. 2. Mainz: Schott, 1987.

———, Ute Bär, and Matthias Wendt, eds. *Schumanniana Nova. Festschrift Gerd Nauhaus zum 60. Geburtstag.* Sinzig: Studio-Verlag, 2002.

——— and Inge Hermstrüwer, eds. *Robert Schumann und die Dichter: Ein Musiker als Leser. Katalog zur Ausstellung des Heinrich-Heine-Instituts.* Düsseldorf: Droste Verlag, 1991.

Beller-McKenna, Daniel. "Distance and Disembodiment: Harps, Horns, and the Requiem Idea in Schumann and Brahms." *Journal of Musicology* 22 (2005): 47–89.

Berger, Karol. "*Diegesis* and *Mimesis:* The Poetic Modes and the Matter of Artistic Presentation." *Journal of Musicology* 12 (1994): 407–433.

Best, Walther. *Die Romanzen Robert Schumanns.* Europäische Hochschulschriften, Reihe 36, vol. 35. Frankfurt: Peter Lang, 1988.

Boetticher, Wolfgang, ed. *Briefe und Gedichte aus dem Album Robert und Clara Schumanns.* Leipzig: VEB Deutscher Verlag für Musik, 1979.

Bracht, Hans-Joachim. "Schumanns 'Papillons' und die Ästhetik der Frühromantik." *Archiv für Musikwissenschaft* 50 (1993): 71–84.

Brauner, Charles S. "Irony in the Heine Lieder of Schubert and Schumann." *Musical Quarterly* 57 (1981): 261–281.

Brinkmann, Reinhold. *Schumann und Eichendorff: Studien zum Liederkreis Opus 39.* Musikkonzepte, die Reihe über Komponisten, vol. 35. Ed. Heinz-Klaus Metzger and Rainer Riehn. Landshut: Bosch-Druck, 1997.

Brown, James D., ed. *Biographical Dictionary of Musicians: With a Bibliography of English Writings on Music.* London: Alexander Gardner, 1886.

Burger, Heinz Otto. *Schwäbische Romantik: Studie zur Charakteristik des Uhlandkreises.* Tübinger Germanistische Arbeiten, vol. 6. Ed. Hermann Schneider. Stuttgart: Verlag W. Kohlhammer, 1928.

Byron, George Gordon Noël. *The Poetical Works of Lord Byron.* Ed. Robert F. Glecker. Rev. Cambridge ed. Boston: Houghton Mifflin, 1975.

Celenza, Anna Harwell. *Hans Christian Andersen and Music: The Nightingale Revealed.* Aldershot: Ashgate, 2005.

Chamisso, Adelbert von. *Sämtliche Werke in Zwei Bänden.* Ed. Werner Feudel and Christel Laufer. Munich: Carl Hauser Verlag, 1982.

Cone, Edward. "Poet's Love or Composer's Love?" In *Music and Text: Critical Inquiries.* Ed. Stephen P. Scher. Cambridge: Cambridge University Press, 1992, 177–192.

Dahlhaus, Carl. "Neo-Romanticism." *19th Century Music* 3 (1979): 97–105.

———. *Nineteenth-Century Music.* Trans. J. Bradford Robinson. Berkeley: University of California Press, 1989.

Daverio, John. *Robert Schumann: Herald of a "New Poetic Age."* New York: Oxford University Press, 1997.

———. "Schumann's Ossianic Manner." *19th Century Music* 21 (1998): 247–273.

Draheim, Joachim. "Bedeutung und Eigenart der Maria-Stuart-Lieder. op. 135, von Robert Schumann." *Archiv für das Studium der neueren Sprachen und Literaturen* 214 (1977): 325–327.

———. "Schumann und Shakespeare." *Neue Zeitschrift für Musik* 142 (1981): 237–247.

Dürr, Walther. *Das deutsche Sololied im 19. Jahrhundert: Untersuchung zur Sprache und Musik.* Wilhelmshaven: Heinrichshofen, 1984.

Eichendorff, Joseph von. *Erzählungen. Sämtliche Werke . . . Historisch-Kritische*

Ausgabe. Ed. Herman Kunisch and Helmut Koopman. Vol. 5, part 1, ed. Karl Konrad Pohlheim. Tübingen: Max Niemeyer Verlag, 1998.

Engel, Gustav. "Robert Schumann, Schön Hedwig. Ballade von F. Hebbel für Deklamation mit Begleitung des Pianos. Op. 206. [*sic*] Leipzig, B. Kuff. Fünf heitere Gesänge für eine Singstimme mit Begleitung des Pianos. Op. 125 Magdeburg. Heinrichshofen." *Neue Berliner Musikzeitung* 7 (1853): 250–251.

Fauser, Annegret. "Rheinsirenen: Loreley and Other Rhine Maidens." In *Music and the Sirens.* Ed. Linda Phyllis Austern and Inna Naroditskaya. Bloomington: Indiana University Press, 2006, 250–276.

Federhofer-Königs, Renate. "Die Beziehungen von Robert Schumann zur Familie André." In *Gutenberg-Jahrbuch 1988.* Ed. Hans-Joachim Koppitz. Mainz: Gutenberg-Gesellschaft, 1988, 190–205.

Ferris, David. "Public Performance and Private Understanding: Clara Wieck's Concerts in Berlin." *Journal of the American Musicological Society* 56 (2003): 351–408.

———. *Schumann's Eichendorff* Liederkreis *and the Genre of the Romantic Cycle.* New York: Oxford University Press, 2000.

———. "'Was will dieses Grau'n bedauten?': Schumann's 'Zwielicht' and Daverio's 'Incomprehensibility Topos.'" *Journal of Musicology* 22 (2005): 131–153.

Finson, Jon W. "The Intentional Tourist: Romantic Irony in the Eichendorff *Liederkreis* of Robert Schumann." In *Schumann and His World.* Ed. R. Larry Todd. Princeton, N.J.: Princeton University Press, 1994, 156–170.

———. "Les mélodies nationalistes de Schumann: *Sechs Gedichte aus dem Liederbuch eines Malers von Reinick,* op. 36." *Ostinato rigore* 22 (2004): 91–106.

———."Schumann's Mature Style and the 'Album of Songs for the Young.'" *Journal of Musicology* 8 (1990): 227–250.

———. *The Voices That Are Gone: Themes in Nineteenth-Century American Popular Song.* New York: Oxford University Press, 1994.

———, ed. *Robert Schumann. Symphonie Nr. 4 d-moll op. 120. Fassung von 1841.* Wiesbaden: Breitkopf & Härtel, 2003.

——— and R. Larry Todd, eds. *Mendelssohn and Schumann: Essays on Their Music and Its Context.* Durham, N.C.: Duke University Press, 1984.

Fischer-Dieskau, Dietrich. *Robert Schuman, Wort und Musik.* Stuttgart: Deutsche Verlags-Anstalt, 1981.

Frobenius, Wolf, Ingeborg Maaß, Markus Waldura, and Tobias Widmaier, eds. *Robert Schumann: Philologische, analytische, sozial- und rezeptionsgeschichtliche Aspekte.* Saarbrücker Studien zur Musikwissenschaft, Neue Folge, vol. 8. Saarbrücken: Saarbrücker Druckerei und Verlag, 1998.

Freitag, Christian. *Ballade.* Themen, Text, Interpretationen, vol. 6. Ed. K. D. Hein-Mooren. Bamberg: C. C. Buchners Verlag, 1986.

Furst, Lilian. *Fictions of Romantic Irony.* Cambridge, Mass.: Harvard University Press, 1984.

Gerstmeier, August. *Die Lieder Schumanns: zur Musik des frühen 19. Jahrhunderts.* Münchner Veröffentlichung zur Musikgeschichte, vol. 34. Tutzing: H. Schneider, 1982.

Grolik, Yvonne. *Musikalisch-rhetorische Figuren in Liedern Robert Schumanns.* Frankfurt: Haag und Herchen, 2002.

Hallmark, Rufus. *The Genesis of Dichterliebe: A Source Study.* Ann Arbor, Mich.: UMI Press, 1979.

———. "The Rückert Lieder of Robert and Clara Schumann." *19th Century Music* 14 (1990): 3–30.

———. "The Sketches for *Dichterliebe.*" *19th Century Music* 1 (1977): 110–136.

———, ed. *German Lieder in the Nineteenth Century.* New York: Schirmer, 1996.

——— and Ann Clark Fehn. "Text Declamation in Schubert's Setting of Pentameter Poetry." *Zeitschrift für Literaturwissenschaft und Linguistik* 9 (1979): 80–111.

Heyde, Colma von der. "Eine Jugendfreundshaft Clara Schumanns." *Neue Musik-Zeitung* 27 (1906): 411–416.

Hindenlang, Karen. "Eichendorff's 'Auf einer Burg' and Schumann's *Liederkreis,* Opus 39." *Journal of Musicology* 8 (1990): 569–587.

Hoeckner, Berthold. "Paths through *Dichterliebe.*" *19th Century Music* 30 (2006): 65–80.

Hofmann, Kurt. *Die Erstdrucke der Werke von Robert Schumann.* Tutzing: Hans Schneider, 1979.

Hotaki, Leander. *Robert Schumanns Mottosammlung: Übertragung, Kommentar, Einführung.* Rombach Wissenschaften—Reihe Litterae, vol. 59. Ed. Gerhard Neumann and Günter Schnitzler. Freiburg: Rombach Verlag, 1998.

Jost, Peter. "Zur Textwahl in Schumanns Liederalbum für die Jugend op. 79." In *Schumann Studien 8.* Zwickau: Robert-Schumann-Gesellschaft, forthcoming.

Killy, Walther. *Literatur Lexikon Autoren und Werke deutscher Sprache.* 13 vols. Munich: Bertelsmann Lexikon Verlag, 1992.

Klitzsch, Em[anuel]. "Lieder und Gesänge." *Neue Zeitschift für Musik* 34 (1851): 245.

———. "Lieder und Gesänge." *Neue Zeitschift für Musik* 36 (1852): 167–168.

———. "Lieder und Gesänge." *Neue Zeitschift für Musik* 40 (1854): 58–59.

———. "Robert Schumann, Op. 79. Liederalbum für die Jugend.—Leipzig, Breitkopf & Härtel. Preis 3 Thlr." *Neue Zeitschift für Musik* 13 (1850): 57–59.

Knaus, Herwig. *Musiksprache und Werkstruktur in Robert Schumanns "Liederkreis."* Schriften zur Musik. Ed. Walter Kolneder. Munich: Musikverlag Emil Katzbichler, 1974.

Kok, Roe-Min. "Falling Asleep: Schumann, Lessing, and Death." In *Studien zur Wertforschung,* vol. 48. Ed. Andreas Dorschel. Vienna: Universal-Edition, forthcoming.

————. "Romantic Childhood, Bourgeois Commercialism and the Music of Robert Schumann." Doctoral dissertation, Harvard University, 2003.

Komar, Arthur. *Robert Schumann: Dichterliebe*. Norton Critical Scores. New York: W. W. Norton, 1971.

Kosch, Wilhelm. *Deutsches Literatur-Lexikon, Biographisches und Bibliographisches Handbuch*. 2d ed. Bern: A. Francke, 1958.

Kreuels, Hans-Udo. *Schumanns Kerner Lieder. Interpretation und Analyse sämtlicher Lieder Robert Schumanns nach Gedichten von Justinius Kerner mit besonderer Berücksichtigung der Liederreihe op. 35*. Frankfurt: Peter Lang, 2003.

Kruse, Joseph A., ed. *"Das Letzte Wort der Kunst": Heinrich Heine und Robert Schumann zum 150. Todesjahr*. Stuttgart: Metlzer Verlag and Bärenreiter, forthcoming.

————, Bernhard R. Appel, and Inge Hermstrüwer. *Das Stammbuch der Constanze Dawison geb. Jacobi*. KulturStiftung der Länder—Patrimonia, vol. 34. Düsseldorf: KulturStiftung der Länder and the Heinrich Heine Institut, 1991.

Küster, Konrad. "Schumanns neuer Zugang zum Kunstlied: Das 'Liederjahr' 1840 in kompositorischer Hinsicht." *Musikforschung* 51 (1998): 1–14.

Laufhütte, Hartmut. *Die Deutsche Kunstballade: Grundlegung einer Gattungsgeschichte*. Heidelberg: Carl Winter Universitätsverlag, 1979.

"Liederschau." *Neue Berliner Musikzeitung* 5 (1851): 132.

"Liederschau." *Neue Berliner Musikzeitung* 9 (1855): 209–210.

Litzmann, Berthold. *Clara Schumann: Ein Künstlerleben nach Tagebüchern und Briefen*. 3 vols. Leipzig: Breitkopf & Härtel, 1910.

Loos, Helmut. *Robert Schumann: Interpretationen seiner Werke*. 2 vols. Laaber: Laaber Verlag, 2005.

Mahlert, Ulrich. *Fortschritt und Kunstlied: Späte Lieder Robert Schumanns im Licht der Liedaesthetischen Diskussion ab 1848*. Freiburger Schriften zur Musikwissenschaft, vol. 13. Munich: Emil Katzbichler, 1983.

McCorkle, Margit L. *Thematisch-Bibliographisches Verzeichnis*. In *Robert Schumann, Neue Ausgabe sämtlicher Werke*, ser. 8, vol. 6. Mainz: Schott, 2003.

McCreless, Patrick. "Song Order in the Song Cycle: Schumann's *Liederkreis*, op. 39." *Music Analysis* 5 (1986): 5–28.

Mosley, David L. *Gesture, Sign, and Song: An Interdisciplinary Approach to Schumann's* Liederkreis *Opus 39*. New York: Peter Lang, 1990.

Muxfeldt, Kristina. "*Frauenliebe und Leben* Now and Then." *19th Century Music* 25 (2001): 27–48.

Nauhaus, Gerd, ed. *Schumann Studien 5*. Cologne: Studio-Verlag, 1996.

Neumeyer, David. "Organic Structure and the Song Cycle: Another Look at Schumann's *Dichterliebe*." *Music Theory Spectrum* 4 (1982): 92–105.

Ozawa, Kazuko. *Quellenstudien zu Robert Schumanns Liedern nach Adelbert von Chamisso*. Europäische Hochschulschriften, ser. 36, vol. 18. Frankfurt: Peter Lang, 1989.

Paul, Otto, and Ingeborg Glier. *Deutsche Metrik*. 8th ed. Munich: Max Hueber Verlag, 1970.

Perrey, Beate Julia. *Schumann's* Dichterliebe *and Early Romantic Poetics: Fragmentation of Desire.* Cambridge: Cambridge University Press, 2002.

Plantinga, Leon. *Romantic Music: A History of Musical Style in Nineteenth-Century Europe.* New York: W. W. Norton, 1984.

"Robert Schumanns Gesangkompositionen." *Allgemeine musikalische Zeitung* 44 (1842): 30–33, 58–63.

Sams, Eric. *The Songs of Robert Schumann.* Bloomington: Indiana University Press, 1993.

Schäffer, Julius. "Robert Schumann, Op. 107. Sechs Gesänge für eine Singstimme mit Begleitung des Pianoforte. Zwei Hefte.—Cassel, bei C. Luckhardt. Heft I. 12½ Ngr. Heft II. 15 Ngr." *Neue Zeitschrift für Musik* 14 (1852): 141–143.

Schanze, Helmut, and Krischan Schulte, eds. *Literarische Vorlagen der ein- und mehrstimmigen Lieder, Gesänge und Deklamationen.* In *Robert Schumann: Neue Ausgabe sämtlicher Werke,* ser. 8, vol. 2. Mainz: Schott, 2002.

Scher, Steven Paul, ed. *Music and Text: Critical Inquiries.* Cambridge: Cambridge University Press, 1992.

Schulte, Krischan. *". . . was Ihres Zaubergriffels würdig ware!" Die Textbasis für Robert Schumanns Lieder für Solostimmen.* Schumann Forschungen, vol. 10. Mainz: Schott, 2005.

Schumann, Robert. *Briefe. Neue Folge.* Ed. F. Gustav Jansen. 2d ed. Leipzig: Breitkopf & Härtel, 1904.

——. *Gesammelte Schriften über Musik und Musiker.* Ed. Martin Kreisig. 2 vols. Leipzig: Breitkopf & Härtel, 1914.

——. *Robert Schumanns Leben. Aus seinen Briefen geschildert von Hermann Erler.* 2d ed. 2 vols. Berlin: Erler & Reis, 1887.

——. *Selbsbiographische Notizen Faksimile.* Ed. Martin Schoppe. [Zwickau]: Robert-Schumann-Gesellschaft, [n.d.].

——. *Tagebücher. Band I, 1827–1838.* Ed. Georg Eismann. Leipzig: VEB Deutscher Verlag für Musik, 1971.

——. *Tagebücher. Band III, Haushaltbücher, 1837–18[56].* Ed. Gerd Nauhaus. 2 parts. Leipzig: VEB Deutscher Verlag für Musik, 1982.

—— and Clara Schumann. *Tagebücher. Band II, 1836–1854.* Ed. Gerd Nauhaus. Leipzig: VEB Deutscher Verlag für Musik, 1987.

Schwab, Heinrich W. *Sangbarkeit, Popularität und Kunstlied. Studien zu Lied und Liedästhetik der mittleren Goethezeit 1770–1814.* Studien zur Musikgeschichte des 19. Jahrhunderts, vol. 3. Regensburg: Gustav Bosse Verlag, 1975.

Scott, Walter. *The Abbot.* Ed. Christopher Johnson. In *The Edinburgh Edition of the Waverley Novels.* Ed. David Hewitt. Edinburgh: Edinburgh University Press, 2000.

Synofzik, Thomas. *Heinrich Heine—Robert Schumann: Musik und Ironie.* Cologne: Verlag Dohr, 2006.

Tadday, Ulrich. *Schumann Handbuch.* Stuttgart: Metzler/Bärenreiter, 2006.

Tewinkel, Christiane. *Vom Rauschen Singen: Robert Schumanns Liederkreis op. 39 nach Gedichten von Joseph von Eichendorff.* Epistemata: Würzburger Wissenschaftliche Schriften, Reihe Literaturwissenschaft, vol. 482. Würzburg: Königshausen & Neumann, 2003.

Thym, Jurgen. "Text-Music Relationships in Schumann's 'Frühlingsfahrt.'" *Theory and Practice* 5 (1980): 7–25.

———, and Ann C. Fehn. "Sonnet Structure and the German Lied: Shackles or Spurs?" *Journal of the American Liszt Society* 32 (1991): 3–15.

Turchin, Barbara. "The Nineteenth-Century *Wanderlieder* Cycle." *Journal of Musicology* 5 (1987): 498–525.

———. "Schumann's Conversion to Vocal Music: A Reconsideration." *Musical Quarterly* 67 (1981): 392–404.

———. "Schumann's Song Cycles: The Cycle within the Song." *19th Century Music* 8 (1985): 231–243.

U[hlig], T[heodor]. "Robert Schumann, Op. 98. Lieder, Gesänge und ein Requiem für Mignon aus Goethe's Wilhelm Meister für Gesang und Pianoforte.—Leipzig, bei Breitkopf und Härtel.—Op. 98 a. Die Lieder Mignon's, des Harfner's und Philinen's für eine Singstimme mit Begleitung des Pianoforte. Preis 1 Thlr. 10 Ngr.—Op. 98 b. Requiem für Mignon für Chor, Solostimmen und Orchester. Clavierauszug. Pr. 1 Thlr. 5 Ngr." *Neue Zeitschrift für Musik* 35 (1851): 219–221.

Wagner, Richard. *My Life.* Trans. Andrew Gray. Ed. Mary Whittall. Cambridge: Cambridge University Press, 1983.

Walsh, Stephen. *The Lieder of Schumann.* London: Cassell, 1971.

Weissweiler, Eva, ed. *The Complete Correspondence of Clara and Robert Schumann.* Trans. Hildegard Fritsch and Ronald L. Crawford. 3 vols. New York: Peter Lang, 1994–2002.

Wells, D. A. "Letters of Mendelssohn, Schumann, and Berlioz in Belfast." *Music & Letters* 60 (1979): 180–185.

Wendt, Matthias, ed. *Schumann und seine Dichter.* Schumann Forschungen, vol. 4. Mainz: Schott, 1993.

Westphal, Christiane. *Robert Schumann:* Liederkreis von Heine op. 24. Munich: Emil Katzbichler, 1996.

Youens, Susan. "*Maskenfreiheit* and Schumann's Napoleon-Ballad." *Journal of Musicology* 22 (2005): 5–46.

Zimmermann, G[eorg]. "Blick und Wort." *Morgenblatt für gebildete Leser* 34 (1840): 947.

Zimmermann, Hans-Joachim. "Die Gedichte der Königin Maria Stuart: Gisbert Vincke, Robert Schumann, und eine sentimentale Tradition." *Archiv für das Studium der neueren Sprachen und Literaturen* 214 (1977): 294–324.

"Zur Würdigung Richard Wagners." 9 installments. *Neue Zeitschrift für Musik* 38-39 (1853).

Index of Song Titles and Text Incipits

Song titles (where they exist) appear in roman type, text incipits in *italics*.
Boldface page numbers indicate the initiation of the primary discussion of a given song (which may continue on the following pages).

General Index

Boldface page numbers indicate the initiation of the primary discussion of a poet or translator.

Carus, Ernst August, 9
Carus, Karl Erdmann, 9
Celenza, Anna Harwell, 282
Chamisso, Adelbert von, **36**, 37, 39, 41,
    80, 94, 95, 102, 121, 127, 131
  Gedichte (1834), 95, 98, 100
  Lieder und Lyrisch-Epische Gedichte
    "Frauen-Liebe und Leben," 35
  translations of Hans Christian Andersen,
    100
  translations of Pierre Jean de Béranger,
    97
Chopin, Frédéric, 31
Christern, Karl, **134**
Collin, Matthäus von
  "Der Zwerg," 95
Cologne cathedral, 64, 70
Cone, Edward, 279
Congress of Vienna, 51
Copies of Poems for Composition. See
    Gedichtabschriften
courtship song. *See Werbelied*
Cranz, A., 95
Crawford, Mrs.
  Songs of Mary, Queen of Scots, 186

Dahlhaus, Carl, 102
  Schumann's late style, 190
Daverio, John, xv, 98, 176, 178, 286
Dawison, Bogumil, 208
Dawison, Constanze Jacobi. *See* Jacobi,
    Constanze
Des Knaben Wunderhorn, 73, 121, 161,
    164, 165, 172
Dessauer, Joseph, 71
*Deutscher Musen-Almanach für das Jahr
    1850*, 255, 259
*Deutscher Musen-Almanach für das Jahr
    1851*, 247, 248
*Deutscher Musen-Almanach für das Jahr
    1852*, 250
Dickens, Charles
  David Copperfield, 72
Diepenbrock, Melchior von, **170**
distich, 129
Dorn, Heinrich, 16
Draheim, Joachim, 186, 286
Dreves, Leberecht, 200, **207**
  Gedichte (1849), 207
  Lieder der Kirche (1846), 207
Duncker & Grünblock, 121
Dürr, Walther, xiv, 6, 287, 289
Düsseldorfer Lieder-Album, 246

Eichendorff, Joseph Freiherr von, 4, 80,
    103, 104, 111, 121, 131, 191,
    192, 223, 242, 263
  Ahnung und Gegenwart, 87, 89
  Aus dem Leben eines Taugenichts, 71,
    84, 229
  "Der Einsiedler," 244–245
  editor of Leberecht Dreves's *Gedichte*,
    207
  Frühling und Liebe, 91
  tribute to Schumann, 92
Ekert. *See* Schumann, Robert: pseudonym
Engel, Gustav, 260, 264

Fanshawe, Catherine, 29
  "Riddle," 30
Fauser, Annegret, 281
Federhofer-Königs, Renate, 285, 291
Fehn, Ann Clark, 288, 289
Ferrand, Eduard, 139
Ferris, David, 13, 87, 115, 276, 281, 282
Finson, Dorothy, v, xvi
Fischer-Dieskau, Dietrich, 282, 284, 285
Francis I, king of France, 192
Frankfurt National Assembly of 1848, 171,
    251
Franz, Robert, 265
  Gesänge, op. 1, 3
Frege, Livia, 29, 102, 146, 168, 257
Frege, Richard, 29
Freiligrath, Ferdinand, 31, 251
Fröhlich, Abraham Emanuel, **109**
Furst, Lilian, 278

Garcia, Pauline, 21
Gedichtabschriften, 19, 73, 84, 113, 141,
    182, 185
Geibel, Emanuel, **121**, 132, 135, 137, 150,
    164, 191, 251
  Gedichte (1840), 121, 132
  *Volkslieder und Romanzen der Spanier
    im Versmasse des Originals*, 121
Geiringer, Karl, 9
Gerhard, Wilhelm, 25, **29**, 32, 126
Gesellschaft der Musikfreunde, Vienna,
    185
Gewandhaus, Leipzig, 157, 246
Glier, Ingeborg, xv, 277, 285
Goethe, Johann Wolfgang von, 6, 9, 12,
    14, 15, 23, 36, 73, 131, 161, 171,
    179, 192, 215, 239, 263
  ballad definition, 93, 115, 118
  centenary birth celebration, 176